RICHARD HARRI

Sex, Death & the Movies

By the same author

Did You Miss Me?
Sean Connery
Julie Christie
Anthony Hopkins: In Darkness and Light
Fifty Fingers (Poetry)
Best Irish Short Stories Vol. 2 (Anthology, ed. David Marcus)

RICHARD HARRIS

Sex, Death & the Movies

An Intimate Biography

by

MICHAEL FEENEY CALLAN

ROBSON BOOKS

First published in Great Britain in 2003 by Robson Books, 64 Brewery Road, London, N7 9NT

A member of the Chrysalis Group plc

British Library Cataloguing in Publication Data
A catalogue record for this book is available from the British Library.

ISBN 1 86105 766 0

Typeset by SX Composing DTP, Rayleigh, Essex
Printed and bound in Great Britain by
Creative Print & Design (Wales), Ebbw Vale

To Ree
a kiss on a lavender hillside in Provence

CONTENTS

ACKNOWLEDGEMENTS

In my first introduction for the original version of this book twelve years ago, I stated the axiom that book-writing, like living, is pleasure and pain. In my in-between years working in film and art, I have come to believe that the better exposition might be that book-writing is pleasure and self-education. When I first attempted to write about Richard Harris, I thought I comprehensively understood him, in so far as any unrelated biographer can know his subject. But in the course of writing about him, and in the aftermath months and years, the leap in learning, unsolicited but welcome, changed many perspectives. No biography, of course, is 'definitive'. By its very definition it is a living thing, with its own organic momentum. I learned, working with Harris, that time truly is the deceiver and the recent truth may not endure. Richard Harris, beyond most, presented a bulging, gift-wrapped, apparently conclusive image of himself to the world, in every medium available to him. In my years of knowing him, I took most of it at face value. When I first went on the interview trail to compose his biography and interviewed the gracious participants, I encountered many, like me, who 'went with the flow' and reported their memories in the vivid primary colours he so loved. Time and tide brought the changes, to them as to me. In the intervening years, working in other areas of film, I found new shared friends, people who had known and worked with Dick, and experienced a profound refocusing, and many fresh tales which illuminated shadow areas I'd only guessed at before. In this regard, conversations with people such as the actor James Coburn and the director Lindsay Anderson proved inspirational. In revising the book, then, I revisited notebooks, tapes and correspondence, focused harder, and changed my views on key areas of Harris's life, and his choices. This new book owes as much to new friends as to the generous original participants.

In no particular order, I would like to thank James Coburn, Rod Taylor, George Peppard, Frank Sinatra, Jilly Rizzo, Cyril Cusack, Franco Nero, John Phillip Law, Ray McAnally, Lindsay Anderson, Jack Donnelly, Maurice Gibb, Godfrey Quigley, Ronald Fraser, Joe Lynch, John B Keane, Fred Zinnemann, George Roy Hill, James Booth, Kevan Barker, Ian Bannen, Gavin Lambert, Michael O'Herlihy, Anthony Shaffer, Dan O'Herlihy, Roger Moore, Donal McCann, Frank Windsor, Jimmy Webb (and his assistant Laura), Don Taylor, Hazel McCourt, Sandy Howard, Beth Voiku, Innes Lloyd, Philip Hinchcliffe, Jim Sheridan, Manuel Di Lucia, Peter Duffell, Trevor Danker, Aliki Michael, Sean Simon, Joe O'Donovan, Eve Bennett, Jeff Bricmont, Cathy Fitzpatrick at HBO, Jim Griffiths, Joe Walsh, Karen Hodge, Trina Stalley, Earl Connolly, Gordon Jackson, Noel Purcell, Liam Flynn, Terence Baker, Jack Donnelly, John McEntee, Mick Doyle, Gerry Hannan, Jim Roche, Len Dineen, Kevin Dineen, Sheamus Smith, Dermot Foley, Willie Rocke, Noel Harris, Willie Allen, Crichton Healy and Charlie St George. Also the staff of the London Academy of Music and Dramatic Art (LAMDA), the Irish Heraldic Institute, the Margaret Herrick Library at the Academy of Motion Picture Arts and Sciences, in Los Angeles, Peter Todd and Tony Widdows at the British Film Institute, Sylvie Welib at the Theatre Royal, Stratford East, Peter Doggett at the *Record Collector* (who helped compile the detailed discography) and the helpful library and support staff at the *Irish Times* (a big hug, Irene), the *Irish Independent*, the *Limerick Leader* and the *Guardian*.

A special fond thank-you to the ever-patient loyal bearers of the midnight torch. To Andrew Fitzpatrick, Hugh Trayor, Blathnaid Trayor, John McColgan, Moya Doherty, Della Kilroy, Sue Kinsella, Alma and Olivier Capt, Patricia Mooney, Ciara Gibbons, Cathy Boyle, Antony and Jay Worrall Thompson, Ian and Bernie Condy, David Strassman, Lise McLaughlin Strassman, Susan Dickson, Shay Hennessy, Dr John Kelly, Dermot Byrne, Tommy and Jane Bracken, Jeannette and Jim Kearney, Dr Eamonn Callan, Corinne Callan, Arthur and Fran McGuinness, Don Bluth, Gary Goldman, Frederic Albert Levy, Tony Crawley, Catherine Barry, Ivan Waterman,

Eugene Phelan, Caroline Dunne, Carolann Manahan, Helen McGivern, Wendy Hopkins, Robert Redford and Michael Callan. And never forgetting those titan, much-missed (and ever-present) supporters, Francis Feighan, Carl Wilson, Bobby Farrell, Jim Carroll, the artists Mandy Hackman-Scott, Mick Harper and Geoff Stevenson and, beloved eternal, Margaret Callan.

I am in debt to Joanne Brooks for her wise and caring editing and also to copy-editor Andrew Armitage for his sharp eye and painstaking work. I also wish to express special gratitude to Jeremy Robson, for his belief and clarity of vision, to Lia O'Sullivan for diligent research and copy-typing, to Ellis Levine for legal guidance and to Brian and Melinda Wilson, who show me how to do it every day with or without the warmth of the sun. Also to Pablo and Jacqueline, *merci & gracias*.

Finally, *each evening from December to December* . . . inexpressible love and thanks to Corey and Paris, my guardians.

God Bless the Pirate

Richard Harris died on 25 October 2002 in University College Hospital, London, with both his ex-wives and his three sons by his bedside. It was the week that research clinicians at the hospital announced the significant potential breakthrough of the drug to cure rheumatoid arthritis. In London to prepare the premiere of the latest Harry Potter movie, young buck producer David Heyman and director Chris Columbus spoke comfortingly to Harris during his final days and expressed to the media their confidence in his recovery and emphatic desire to have him in the next of the Potters, due to start filming the following March. His brother Noel said he was sedated and comfortable. His ex-wife Ann Turkel said he was at peace. On that Friday evening, at seven o'clock, he passed away in his sleep.

For those who knew him, there was doubtless a certain joyous devilment in the timing. Late Friday, for Sunday journalism, is the flashpoint. The weight of a story is best judged by the Friday litmus. If it's lightweight, the Sundays can justifiably skip over it. If it's important, the machinery is cranked to red alert. For Harris, all the stops came out. As his only 'authorised' biographer, I was, not surprisingly, summoned from a dinner party at ten, with the obit commanded for midday Saturday. The parade was well attended. Director Jim Sheridan was called upon; lost cousins, ex-partners and every variety of hack who knew him during a lunchtime of yore had their say. Limerick, the city that bred him, immediately bridled at the news that he was to be cremated wearing his honorary Munster rugby jersey, but his ashes would be scattered off Paradise Island in the Bahamas, his home since the middle seventies. Limerick councillors bemoaned the omission. Wives stayed mum. Sons stopped answering calls. Harris's face was everywhere through the media – and University College Hospital's arthritis breakthrough had vanished into thin air.

This was popular culture and the way of the media in the twenty-first century. Richard Harris would have been thrilled by it, not just for the collective curtsy to his vanity, but for the peacock display of bad taste in poor priorities, hypocritical squabbling and crocodile tears. Ten years before, at a benefit lecture at Trinity College in Dublin, I had watched him tell his audience that the great ailment of contemporary society was 'the plague of good taste'. In his deeply felt view, a profound moral bankruptcy lay at the heart of contemporary Western society and the globalised world. He was personally useless at political activism because he lacked, above anything, patience and tact, but he felt compelled to stand up for the great unplayed card of democracy, the liberation of individualism. 'Convention I detest,' he would seethe. 'Because what it means is inertia – the mediocre middle-aged, middle-class meritocracy keeping the money with the shopkeepers.' This, of course, could easily have been the traditionally indulged eccentricity of the artist at work. But, in Harris's case, it wasn't. It *was* political and, in as far as he could muster it and manhandle his demons, strategic. He wanted change. Not for himself, but for the world. He wanted a different world, with different, kinder values. And he was original in that his modus was guileless. He didn't take to the podium or headline charities (apart from the scholarship fund established in memory of his late brother); he didn't run for office or occupy the op-eds; he didn't produce 'message' movies. When he had the forum of the tabloids or the broadsheets, he didn't even preach much, either. He just bawled. From the age of twelve he bawled and brawled and went on doing so till his fading days. 'It was Charles Lindbergh who flew across the world,' he liked to say. 'Not a committee of gentlemen. It was a pirate. God bless the pirate.'

The eulogies marking the passing of any distinguished figure concentrate the good. But Harris's distinctly individual lifestyle and the self-authored rules of his game demand a better, truer objectivity. I knew him for more than ten years before I squared up to writing this book. 'Knew', of course, is a relative word. When I first met him, in Cashel, County Tipperary, in 1975 or so, he was a young buck. He was still, in the shadow of *Camelot*, a quasi-pop-star recording artist (aged 45), a recently published poet and, he claimed, a soon-to-be novelist. Ann Turkel was only recently in his life and he had, apparently, the balls of a bull. His movie of the moment was called *The Last Castle* (it was later renamed *Echoes of a Summer*), and he gave me the screenplay like a warrior presenting the gift of a scalp. I was in my twenties, an impressionable Dublin apprentice at the feet of an Irish cultural colossus. I believed every word from his lips, and, when he told me he was interested in the screenplay I was writing and must send it to John McMichael, his business manager in London, immediately, I unplugged the phone and worked like a Trojan. I had no way of knowing that Limbridge, his production company, was a hand-to-mouth organisation (as most actor-driven production companies are); nor, more importantly, that he was buried in a mire of studio squabbles and bad-faith business crises that would effectively put paid to even modest Hollywood viability by the end of the seventies.

The upside of encountering him at this virile time was experiencing full force the magic of his energy. His 'minder' in County Tipperary was Jackie Donnelly, who had once been married to the late Harmay, Harris's older sister. Jackie was then manager of the baronial Cashel Palace Hotel and general deputy sheriff. In Jackie's confidential asides to me, here was Dickie at his even-keel best: 'What he really only does is hill-walk with Ann, dine in the town, take the odd Guinness at the bar and spend the afternoons lying on the bed reading westerns.' This was more fanciful prescription than practical description from the exhausted Jackie. In fact, Harris was like a spinning top. After filming *The Last Castle* in Canada, he would go to South Africa for a movie, thence the Bahamas, then Ireland. He told me he might buy a medieval castle in Ireland, to write in. He had his novel, *Flanny at 1:10*, to complete – 'very Dylan Thomas, a brain-teaser' – and the radical revision of *Hamlet* to revisit. There was a new record album on the cards and a book of poems to edit . . .

None of this came to much and I lost touch with him for ten years, during which his movie career hit the deck with landmark stinkers such as *Game for Vultures*, with Joan Collins, and Roy Boulting's *The Last Word*, which failed to find a distributor. In the early eighties my own career took me from scriptwriting on *The Professionals* television series at LWT to joining the production partnership designed to revitalise Ireland's national Ardmore Studios, and when I again encountered him, after the long hiatus, he seemed another man entirely – contained, retracted, almost torpid. He had, he told me, miraculously recovered himself from financial and career ruin by acquiring the stage touring rights of Lerner and Loewe's *Camelot*, and had bagged almost $8 million personally from touring the show for half a decade. After years of anguished romances – with two wives and uncounted showbiz girlfriends – he had calmed himself in 'a sensible relationship with an erudite New York socialite whom I see whenever I'm in the Big Apple, and leave it at that'. The Bahamas had become his great safe haven. Residing in the financier Huntington Hartford's old estate at the tip of Paradise Island, five miles from Sean Connery's bungalow on the private, more elegant Lyford Cay across the bridge at the opposite end of Nassau, he had been apparently softened by the seduction of seclusion. When I met him circa 1988 he was skipping, butterfly-fashion, from one occasional B-movie to the next, bemoaning only the paucity of high art in modern film, oblivious to the reality that his star had faded. Repeatedly, when I asked visiting producers at Ardmore about his viability, I heard him described as a has-been. The obvious was stated: that it had been 25 years since his Oscar nomination for *This Sporting Life* and 15 since he'd released a pop record. Harris seemed indifferent. At the time, I was working on a screenplay commission for Home Box Office, who had recently produced the filmed version of his touring *Camelot* with not a little anguish. One line producer told me Harris had been troublesome 'to the point of self-destructive mania', and, in the producer's view, had rendered himself all but unemployable. When I mentioned this to Harris he was calm and accepting: 'Sure, I don't need them. I made King Arthur. I did it. Not them. And it's the past. Who cares?'

Beneath the bravura stoicism, however, was the unchanged heart. As I spent more time with him in 1988 and 1989, the agitation of inactivity surfaced. I saw, still, a man capable of composure and compassion but, it struck me, one whose middle-age insights had sharpened raging artistic and existential instincts. Once, twenty or more years before, he'd told me, sex and death and the movies were his deep motivational interests. Whatever for sex, death and the movies now absorbed him again. In his hotel room he lectured me with a fanatic's attention to detail about the thirty or so medications and vitamin supplements he took every day to control his hyper-glycaemia. With meticulous discipline he avoided alcohol (he hadn't drunk since 1982, but returned to it, moderately, in the early nineties). He kept his diet sugar-free and salt-free and tried to walk a few miles every day. 'My brother Dermot died before his time,' he lamented. 'He was in his fifties and as strong as an ox, but this fucking business did him in.' Dermot, who was younger than he was by five years, oversaw Limbridge and had died of a heart attack during the marathon run of *Camelot*. 'The trick is to keep moving. Don't let 'em get you, and don't let 'em beat you down.'

But he was down, and it was the movies – the beloved alternative universe that shielded him from the world – that had him on his knees. By 1989 he was appearing in TV movies, Hollywood's retirement pastures. HTV's corny Gaelic-French *Maigret* and the Hallmark-style *King of the Wind* was the best he could do, and he made no bones about the fact that he loathed the productions. In truth, though he would never openly admit it, the years of boozy excess, and the victims downed, and the grudges left in their wake, had come back to haunt him. Many people from his irregular and inconsistent 'inner circle' did truly love him. Sandford Howard, the powerhouse producer behind the *Man Called Horse* series that, for a flash, rehabilitated the jaded western in the seventies, spoke with unbridled warmth – tinged with unmissable sadness – about his lusty old partner: 'Richard forgets things. He forgets how good our partnership was and how much we achieved. He even forgets how fine a performer he is.' Harris, for his part, remembered Howard letting him down – for a variety of inconsequential agitations, like ordering him to recut the title song of a movie because it was off-key and serving him up 'a pulp script' for the last of the *Horse* trilogy. Other ex-partners and producers were less convivial, chafing still from buckshot incidents of neglect and abuse. Lindsay Anderson, the director who launched Harris to international stardom in *This Sporting Life*, spoke with circumspect wariness about the man he had once, literally, adored who had gone on to spurn him in great, ambitious collaborative projects. Vanessa Redgrave hung up the phone when I called, on her former lover Franco Nero's recommendation, to discuss Harris. 'Fuck 'em all,' Harris announced grandly when I reported my early research for this book. 'If they're so up their own arses that they cannot comprehend the demons and the muses' – which seemed to me an Esperanto for his self-confessedly bad behaviour – 'then it's their loss. It diminishes their so-called art, because it reduces it simply to ego. And there's no surprise in that, is there, because ego more than anything drives this business. Movies and movie people lie all the time. They say it's art and they demand the accolades, but they really mean it's business and they want the money.'

All his life, startling, visionary honesty seemed to come to Harris in equal measure with self-delusion – a condition largely unaltered in the late eighties. What I personally found compelling about him, and what propelled the book into motion at that time, was the sense of crisis pathology: of an actor nearing sixty, physically spent but spiritually soaring, attempting to reorientate against the vicissitudes of fashion and the detritus of bad behaviour in his past. 'I will die soon,' he would say to me, with the resonance of a monarch addressing his legacy, 'and I don't want to die in the fucking *Cassandra Crossing* [a pop melodrama of sub-*Towering Inferno* genre]. I want to do *King Lear* before I go. I want to do Pirandello.'

And he did do Pirandello. Miraculously, it seemed to me, between the wasteful, drifting days of 1988, when all he truly wanted to do was watch international rugby videos and – maybe – record with the heavy-metal band Kiss ('I told Phil Coulter to fuck off, I don't want to be pop any more'), and the movie-renaissance summer of 1991, he managed, with the support of last-chance agent Terry Baker, to shuffle a regional production of Pirandello's arcane *Henry IV* successfully on to the West End stage. 'I surprised you, didn't I?' he told me defiantly. 'I surprised everyone. Because I move fast. I have always moved fast. And the consequence is that people are interpreting my shadow when I've already moved on. That's why the press misrepresent me. They see the shadow, just the shadow.'

This book came into being during the great creative surge of 1988–90, when Pirandello unfurled and, by fluke, Harris rose like the phoenix from the shrivelling flames of *King of the Wind* to take lead casting in Jim Sheridan's Oscar-nominated *The Field*. Its endorsement was, of course, deeply flattering to me, but it is worth revisiting it – and the circumstances of the rows that ensued during the making of the book – the better to understand Harris's particular nature and motivations.

When I first approached him, he was leery of an authorised book, initially claiming that he was too drunk most of his life to tell the tale accurately; thence that his contractual commitment to Random House, who had published his sole book of poetry, *I, in the Membership of my Days*, restricted him. I accepted his word, and told him I would press on with a critical analysis of his work in bio-filmographical format, which seemed to please him, as he liked talking about his work and unquestionably felt artistically neglected. But then the tack changed. The speed of his manoeuvre, and its combative aftermath, still amuses me.

Generosity was always key to his style. There are any number of small stories that speak volumes, but I best recall incidents like the time stalwart fans from his teenage playground of Kilkee, in the west of Ireland, shuffled up to Dublin for the very first time, plastic carrier bags chock-full of videos-to-be-signed in hand, to try to hunt him down. They found him at the Berkeley Court Hotel (it was always easy to find his hideouts: he liked to call himself 'the showcase fugitive'), and stood sentinel for hours by the door, held at bay by the

Regency uniforms of the doormen. Finally they encountered their idol, and the younger of the duo – a farmer of twenty – mumbled in a thick bucolic burr that he'd seen everything Harris ever did, and listened to every song he'd recorded. Harris was genuinely touched – as much by the tattered clothes and grizzled faces as by the declaration of devotion. 'Have you had lunch?' he asked the men, and when they said they hadn't, that the train journey to Dublin had taken them half a day, he dragged them into the ornate, fragrant lobby and into one of Dublin's most expensive restaurants. Inside, when the farmers admitted they'd never even heard of minestrone soup, Harris screamed the house down summoning the maître d'. 'Feed these fellas some of your best minestrone. Get them the menu. What's the best of the day? Do you have quail or venison? . . .' I made up the foursome at this bizarre lunch, humbled as much by Harris's genuine benevolence as by the passion of the fans. I learned that it was a drop in the ocean, that Harris's was a giving heart – with a twist.

The authorisation for this book came with the fervour of the minestrone. In hindsight, and with the experience of many years writing other biographies of living subjects, I have come to believe that the alleged blessing 'authorised' is as much a command to whitewash as a marketing slug; but at the time such endorsement seemed honourable, or at least desirable. I had given up on Harris's official support – and then the worm turned. Frank Sinatra was in town the day I was lunching with Harris and reporting progress on my researches. Naturally, Sinatra gravitated towards the presidential suite of the best hotel in town, which happened to be the one Harris was occupying at the Berkeley Court (which was then being co-managed by Jackie Donnelly). Harris immediately vacated the suite for his old friend, who was playing Ireland for the first time in a 55-year career. As I sat with Harris, I observed his obsessive fascination with the media blitz launched on the hotel. Liza Minelli and Sinatra's lifelong fixer Jilly Rizzo were travelling with the Chairman of the Board, and Harris entered into respectful conversation with them, thoughtfully introducing me, and later inviting me to his front-row attendance at Sinatra's sell-out at Lansdowne Road stadium, and later, backstage, to meet Sinatra. In the middle of this two-day din, out of the blue, Harris summoned a Sinatra-chasing journalist from a national newspaper and offered her an exclusive story. The story, it turned out, was me. After thirty years avoiding the confessional, Harris told the reporter, he had finally found an author he could entrust with the telling of his life story. I was that author, this was the partnership. This 'breakthrough' story made it into the evening papers, nudging Sinatra for column inches.

It took months for the contextual truth to reveal itself. And for those months I walked on air, believing I'd landed the role of the Boswell. Great promises were made. Lost revelatory diaries would be found for me. Tapes of personal reminiscences would be made. I would come to Nassau and walk the beaches of Paradise Island with him. I would read the almost-complete novel that would shame James Joyce and review the new book of poems to be called *Fragments of a Broken Photograph*.

None of this, of course, ever came to be. There were no finished books, or tapes, or diaries. Harris's first position had been the true one: that he was, more or less, drunk for twenty years and bore a speckled memory; that the best he could contribute were the flashes, the anecdotes and the intellectual post-rationalisations.

The great lesson of the Sinatra incident – about Harris's appetite for competition and the scurrilous imperative of the headlining performer – wasn't fully absorbed until phase two, when the by-product of Harris's deepening friendship came, unremitting, upon me. Working for perfection, I was travelling, interviewing, researching weekly, supported by two or three assiduous part-time assistants. This thoroughness was too much for Harris. Or precisely perfect for him. The thoroughness turned up all kinds of witnesses, fair and foul, to his life story and gave him the inspiration for another headline. I transgressed, it appeared, by interviewing the first woman he made love to, without consulting him. In fact, the approach from the eloquent and generous lady involved was unsolicited, and I *had* tried to contact Harris to tell him all about her, and my productive time with her. Harris's media-grab this time was the leading national radio show in Ireland, *The Pat Kenny Show*. Without forenotice, I suddenly found myself debating the integrity of this book 'live' on the air, and fending off exquisite rhetoric presented with passion by a theatrical dab hand and Oscar-nominated heavyweight.

I, of course, should have known better. The songwriter Jimmy Webb, who wrote Harris's major pop hit 'MacArthur Park', had warned me of perfidy. In the late sixties, Harris had borrowed him from a Johnny Rivers contract and taken the best of his songs to build two hit albums. A handshake deal was made: if Webb could win Harris a number-one hit song, Webb would be awarded with Harris's Phantom V Rolls-Royce, a car formerly owned by Princess Margaret, which still bore a royal seal. 'MacArthur Park' did reach number one in the international charts, but Harris refused to turn over the Rolls. 'Instead he offered me a catalogue to choose one from,' Webb told me. 'But that wasn't the point. I wanted the one I wanted, and that was the good-faith deal.'

Nothing much changed when Harris and I fell out, other than a comforting sense, for me, of secured integrity. I had already spent hundreds of hours with him, and charted the main events of his life. I had breakfasted with him, supped with him, walked with him, gone to the theatre with him and taken him for drives. I sat with him arguing the values of open activism in issues like the support of republicanism in the IRA cause, and helped him buy the research books – like Peig Sayers's classic Irish diary – for upcoming movies like *The Field*. I knew, better than most, the knowable Dickie Harris and that was what I wrote – mostly – in my account of his life, published just before the release of *The Field* in 1990.

The Field changed everything for Harris. It is tempting to consider the alternative life that might have befallen him in the nineties had the domino effect caused by the death of his old rival, the brilliant Irish actor Ray McAnally, not happened in the summer of 1989. McAnally had been cast in Sheridan's movie-in-planning and, even in the early preparatory stages, hopes were high for a movie of major award status. The pedigree of *The Field* elevated it. It was adapted from the triumphant stage play by John B Keane, and Sheridan had developed a visual script that embraced the Connacht landscape and nimbly introduced American elements for the mass market. Sheridan's reputation, moulded on the multi-awarded *My Left Foot*, which also starred McAnally, guaranteed wide distribution (something missing from all Harris's eighties movies) and the likelihood of a hit of some measure. Even before McAnally died, suddenly of a heart attack, Harris told me he wanted the role of Bull McCabe in *The Field*. 'It's a mighty part,' he said. 'Keane is like the Shakespeare of Ireland, because he writes in the dialect and understands that we Irish are different from the Brits. Bull McCabe is the best stage role since Hamlet.'

Sheridan cast Harris in a walk-on, as the priest in the movie, but rejigged with the offer of Bull when McAnally died. Everything about Harris's mood and attitude changed the day Sheridan cast him. When it happened, the Pirandello was in the works, but not yet tied down; but after the *Field* casting he assumed Herculean energies. On the day he told me of his break, I quoted a line from Alexander Pope to him – 'All chance, direction, which thou canst not see' – and he jumped off the chair and clicked his fingers, a man of thirty again, not sixty. 'That's it!' he said with relish. 'That's exactly fucking it. Art. That's all it has ever been for me. When I was a kid lying in bed with TB, watching the world slip away from me, I would curse my bad fortune and scribble little drawings and stories. And then, like a light bulb, the meaning of it came to me. That this was meant to be. That I was meant to be confined, to burn the badness off me and let me concentrate my energies, to focus me. I went to bed for a year and when I got up I wasn't a kid without aim in life. I was a kid with a direction. I said, I don't want fucking reality if reality is lying dead in a bed. I want to create a world, a better world. Creation is art. That is why I was put here.'

The conclusion of my book on Harris – finally published without the word 'authorised' in the subtitle (perhaps 'de-authorised' would have been more apt!) – coincided with his filming of *The Field* in what seemed a happy confluence. I felt vindicated: that I had spotted the neglected talent he believed himself to be and constructed painstakingly a vivid and accurate account of his life while he, in tandem, proved himself all over by masterfully rising to his first major work in ten years and, in the process, brought home a second Oscar nomination.

But at the same time, objectively, I felt frustration and want. In full accountability, I had pulled punches, many punches. My failing was the failing of many who loved him, who partnered him professionally or married him. I yielded too much. I conceded. I omitted. I stalled. The reason was simple, and, really, unseen in the process of being with him. One conceded, because of the bigness of generosity in him, because of his colossal lack of self-consciousness, because he was lovable.

When he died, the haemhorrage of eulogies for Dickie naturally centred on the work accomplishments. He had virtually no education, yet he took Hollywood and worked brilliantly with erudite adepts such as Anderson, Michelangelo Antonioni and John Huston. He was the catalytic cut 'n' thrust of Britain's Angry Young Man challenge to Hollywood's Ike-era inertia. He stole King Arthur from Richard Burton. He gave purpose to the post-John Wayne western. He won the classic theatre stage, beat The Beatles in the record charts, rebuilt his skills as an elderly actor spanning the lexicon from Bull McCabe to Harry Potter's Albus Dumbledore.

But the best of him was only amorphously in the eulogies. Yes, he was a Beat-like bum who feasted on cocaine, LSD and every variety of hooch the world offered. Yes, he knocked over double-decker buses and had his driver's licence rescinded by a judge 'for life'. Yes, he bedded as many groupies as any rock star and maintained his passion for women till his dying days. But he also had the gift of detachment, the artist's inherent skills of subtraction and abstraction, of being able to stand back – once sober – and extrapolate from the hysteria the whys and why-nots.

He was never a candidate for serious counselling or psycho-analysis. Instead, in my view, he missed a vocation, for he could, assuredly – and, granted, in later life – have made his way as an analyst, or a substance-abuse/sex counsellor. No other person I have encountered willingly faced – embraced – the demons, and came through so lacking in self-pity and so comprehensively balanced. The Ireland he grew up in was, effectively, a theocracy whose institutional abuses matched the tyrannies of ancient British rule.

Drink inured him – and he drank to forget, but remembered exactly why he drank. 'I love the taste of it,' he would tell the press. 'I drink because I love it.' But in mellow moments, in reflection, he would admit, 'I grew up in a mythical kingdom – Ireland – that was knocked six ways by institutional bigotry and oppression. I grew up with the threat of death and damnation on my shoulder, and you build insulators against that because you have to.' Drink was an insulator, as was an abandonment to sex that was pagan and joyous, never obsessive or blind. 'I love women,' he once told me, 'because they are creators. Their role in life is to love and nourish and give birth. It's anthropological. Men are just hunter-gatherers. They're pathetic, when you think about it.'

There was always the boyish glint of mischief in such pro-nouncements; and, indeed, if there is a clinical psychological categorisation of 'adult-child' that is what he was, and remained till the end. But, personally, I found his capacity for blue-chip candour, for the honesty that stretched to self-contradiction and bare-faced denial (that great facilitator of human endurance), edifying and uplifting. I cherish countless memories of sagelike wisdom to match Hogwarts' Dumbledore. More than anything, there was his proficiency at putting drink and sex in perspective. Once, as I walked with him in Ballsbridge in Dublin, he was accosted by a blabbering admirer who wanted an autograph but had nothing to write on, neither pen nor pencil. The man was obviously inebriated, finally rude, but something was shuffled up and a signature on a bus ticket was delivered. I may have made some remark about the audacity of the drunk, but all Harris said was, 'Poor fella'. Another time, I was intent on interviewing him about his strange, quasi-sexual relation-ship with the critic and filmmaker Lindsay Anderson. I wanted to connect the invention of the character of Frank Machin, the rugby player in *This Sporting Life*, with his long-in-development radicalised *Hamlet*, but Harris was more interested in the elegant, middle-aged women in pearls taking tea at the next table in the hotel. At some moment of critical academic analysis he suddenly splurted, in stentorian tones, 'Would you like to ride the arse off her?' – which elicited a flushed collective rise from the women, and from me.

Seeing my discomfort, he roared a laugh and slapped my leg. 'Jaysus, it's only fun, isn't it? It's what they expect of me. It makes their day.'

One might invoke bullying sexism and all the clichés, but you had to live it to see it for what it was. In context of the ridiculous environment we were in, in a super-luxury hotel, sipping overpriced drinks amid the scandalously wealthy, it seemed an ironic levelling gesture, an act of civil retrenchment not unrelated to the uncomfortable ground-breaking of social historians such as Camile Paglia, who remind us that institutional civilisation is the balance pole that keeps us from barbarity; that we are, at heart, animals with the capacity for unspeakable brutality and callousness, for limitless rape and violence. I would challenge him about his cavalier sexuality and he would chide me: 'It's only sex, for God's sake, it isn't rocket science' – which was the provocation to push me further, inevitably into the minutiae of his value system, which, always, took us circularly back to Aristotelean principles of drama, or Shakespeare, or the Russian writers, or the interpretations in great drama of the human condition. 'You don't just play a Hollywood pin-up or King Arthur off the cuff,' he would say. 'You go to Shakespeare, to the eternal verities. Human beings are marvellous and mighty. Human behaviour is extraordinary. Finally, not just in every performance, but in facing each day as you get out of bed, you decide: Is the human spirit basically good, or is it bad? I choose to believe it is good. And I approach it all from that point of view. You can play a better villain, when you know that life is benevolent. You can face anything when you know God cares.'

It was no surprise to anyone who knew him that both Richard Harris's ex-wives – Ann Turkel and the former Elizabeth Rees-Williams – were at his bedside the night he died. Both, reportedly, wanted a share of his ashes and a place in the legacy. Both loved him, despite the roller coaster of his raucousness and betrayals, and he loved both of them. A moment sticks in my mind of his *truth*, of the deeper humanity that gets lost in the scandal records and the phony testimonials. We were together – again in a hotel room (where he spent most of his life) – discussing our Irishness and the specific nationalism of island people. The then *tanaiste* (Irish foreign minister), Brian Linehan, was in hospital, suffering the liver failure that would eventually cost him his life. Harris didn't know him, but admired Charlie Haughey, his boss and the prime minister, and decided to send flowers and a message of goodwill. The talk shifted to Catholicism, and his love of the Jesuit disciplines of his secondary schooling. I opined that we, as Irish people at a turbulent time in our growth and emergence in the globalised community, had a harder time than most in letting go of the past. Heritage, I felt, was important; but heritage with perspective. We belong in a pluralist world, where we can embrace past and future, our separate ethnicity and our inevitable fusion. Harris agreed. 'But in the end,' he said, 'a country is just a clump of dirt. It's *who* we love that matters. I was blessed. I loved two women who were goddesses. I would die for them still today. I gave them all I could give them, and in return I got love. What more can a man ask for?'

I remember that sudden softness catching my blind side and I remembered it again when I readdressed this book, and re-evaluated his life. He had a huge heart and was deeply loved by those – like Ann and Elizabeth, and sons Damian, Jared and Jamie and his two grandchildren – who intimately shared his world. But I let him down in some ways by letting him off easily, by succumbing too often in my earlier text to his affections, and to his bullying. Unquestionably, he was a decent man. But he was also an adventurer supreme who, once freed from the TB bed of his youth, took no prisoners in pursuing a life of sensory exploration. Along the way, the bullish arrogance of his probing energies became, by way of the seduction of art, a spiritual quest. My memories of him today are of a man looking frantically for answers, an artist who had chosen the most dubious and contentious of art forms in which to pursue his goals. Physically he was huge – well past six foot tall and extremely broad-shouldered – and he lingers in memory as a bull at the corrida, storming the corners and charging the capes, determined not just to survive, but to *see* the game.

I believe he satisfied himself in the acquisition of a peaceful vision and I see that accomplishment in his transcendent calm portraying

Dumbledore, and in the loving mutual regard shared at the end with his grandchildren.

But along the way he fought like fury. He started in the rugby scrum pack in Limerick in the depressed forties and bare-knuckled his way into London theatreland. Thereafter, he fucked and flayed his way into the history books and into a life of meaning. In revisiting Dickie Harris's story, I trust I'm serving him well – in recapturing the ups and downs of his turbulent existence and the triumph of the resolution of his personal truth.

I once asked him about his awards and their significance in his life. The question seemed tantamount to insult. 'Awards? I've no idea where they are. The Palme d'Or [given for *This Sporting Life*], I seem to remember on a shelf in someone's apartment – my son Damian maybe? I don't care about those things. An actor acts, that's all there is to it. He draws from truth, from the truth he knows. The rest is nothing.'

Here, then, is the truth I know, gleaned from years of acquaintanceship and the best of his own memories.

Michael Feeney Callan
Dublin, January 2003

PART I

PRINCE DICK

'Keep switching the lights on and off in all the rooms until you find the one where you belong. But for God's sake shake the shackles from your feet and find your pride and dignity. The world owes no one anything and all we owe it is a death . . .'

Richard Harris, *Profile* magazine, 1968

'So much confusion to remain so pure.'

Salvador Dali, *Diary of a Genius*

CHAPTER 1

The Mouse-catcher

'Richard who?'

'Richard Harris, the actor.'

'Oh, Dickie, that *barnac*. One of our own, he is. There's a story goes: you're not a true Limerickman unless you've got a decent Dickie Harris story.'

Round the bars they gather – farm folk, factory folk, bucolic yuppies pink-nosed from the western winds – as they have done since unrecorded time, to whittle down the gossip, lay bare the heart of home truths and hail the local hero. Politics is their main staple, wry and derisive in the traditional Munster way; heroic Harris a close-runner. They remember him fondly over their Guinnesses, even those too young ever to have known him, and claims to blood ties through marriage are dizzyingly frequent. (Two claims to cousinhood in the very first week of research for this book proved insubstantial.) By and large he is, heroically, a *barnac*, a wry honorary Kilkee title derived from the word 'barnacle', which celebrates his lifelong fidelity to the locality and all things Limerick-Irish, as distinct from plain Irish. He stands in memory monumentally higher than that Johnny Carson clone Terry Wogan, a 'blow-in' who blew out at a tender age, or Frank McCourt, or The Cranberries, or anyone else of the Limerick cut. Harris, for so many Limerickmen, personifies a proud and magisterial Limerick – this regardless of the fact that Limerick residency occupied just 25 years of his life, and the rest of his days were spent bickering in one way or another with the city, its institutions and his friends there.

'I don't want to go back,' Harris once told the *Limerick Tribune*'s notorious myth-popping journalist, Gerry Hannan, 'because they hate me there.' Reassured that the absolute opposite was the case, he whacked his thigh and chirruped, 'OK, they don't hate me. They just don't know what to make of me, that's the trouble. They never knew what to make of me.' Len Dineen, whose father Kevin founded the Limerick College Players, where Harris humbly started, tells of the actor's unending equivocality about his home town. When Harris's brother and manager, Dermot, died in 1986 Richard returned to Limerick for the first time in many years. At Mount St Lawrence's churchyard on the city's outskirts, home of the unkempt Harris family graves, Harris complained to Dineen about the poor funeral turn-out. The absence of his boyhood Crescent and Garryowen rugby cronies in particular irritated him.

'You're losing the run of yourself, man,' Len Dineen told him. 'Look around you. All the old faces are here. They all respect and admire you. It's *you* who forgets them, not the other way around.'

The confused, volcanic feelings, most will tell you, owe their origins to a row almost twenty years before. In 1970, at the crest of a roller-coaster career, Harris brought his directorial debut movie, *Bloomfield*, to Limerick for a charity premiere in aid of the Limerick Handicapped Children. The best charity shows at that time averaged £500 to £,1000 takings; the week after the event, Harris proudly announced that *Bloomfield* yielded more than £3,500. But Limerick still wasn't satisfied. Within a month he was raging worldwide, to anyone who would listen, 'I will never in my life, ever, appear in Ireland again. The local newspaper wouldn't cover it, didn't even mention my world premiere – simply because I hadn't got down on my knees and knelt at the institutional shrine. My sin was simple: I refused to give the newspaper's proprietor the four free seats she required. In my book, for charity, nobody gets free seats! That is the mind-set of Limerick. It's either go the way of the pack, or no way at all. And I am not, and will never be, a pack animal.'

Twenty years later, as he discussed his dislocation with Hannan, the anguish of love–hate, of the lack of resolution and the urge for resolution disturbed him still. He would visit more often, he told Hannan, and maybe lecture or fundraise there – if only anyone bothered to ask him. 'There is no understanding and no forgiveness. Ireland is changing all the time. It is merging with Europe and reversing itself from cowed emigration to proud immigration. The theocratic bullying is over. The people are becoming Europeans. There is education. Money. Freedom. But Limerick still wants to dwell in the nineteen hundreds, like a feudal place. It's stubborn, that's its problem. It can't welcome me, it can't understand me – because it *won't give in.*'

Understanding Richard Harris, the art and the obstinacy, the wisdom and the wildness, begins with a heritage exercise beyond Limerick, complicated by mixed blood, unlikely marriages and five generations of drifters. The Harris family is of Protestant lineage, Welsh-descended, its name adapted from the ancient Welsh Ris, or Rhys. Harris's great-great-great-grandfather, the farmer John Harris of Llanadog, claimed ancestry from a celebrated peer of the realm and married well-heeled Anne Stephens in November 1774 in the wooden chapel on the River Tywi, expanding instantly his sphere of wealth and influence. The Stephenses were Normans, ardent followers of Vallance, the earl of Pembroke. Through intermarriage with the Vallances and the Marshalls, the succeeding earls of Pembroke, they – and the Harrises after them – assumed the heraldic rights to the boar's head crest and the motto 'I Will Defend'. Its defiant spirit chased down the generations. Limerick publican Charlie St George, an ally of Harris's for nearly half a century and in whose premises Harris often speculated on origins and destinies, researched the Harris family of his own accord and found 'an unusual clan, distinguished, you would have to say, by ambition'. Harris himself, once dismissive of genealogy and anthropology, developed a profound curiosity about his ancestry in late life. 'What I primarily learned was that [the family] wasn't bums. Over centuries there was some sense of the lure of faraway pastures. They say so much of behaviour is genetic. I believe it. I believe my future was cast five hundred years ago.'

The Irish Harris dynasty began when John Harris moved his farming interests to Waterford in the 1790s, bringing with him his sons, Richard, Tom and Henry. Richard and Henry married local Protestant sisters, but Richard's marriage quickly failed. Serving the Yeomanry, he ditched his wife, moved to Clonmel and married the well-heeled Eleanor Haymon, daughter of a prominent lawyer and granddaughter of the town's mayor.

Recklessness accompanied restlessness. As the Haymon-Harrises nested comfortably in the Midlands, other branches of the populous family splintered and drifted. Some cousins ended up prospecting in South Africa, others went to America. The Haymon-Harrises quickly caught the bug and Richard and Eleanor's second son drifted to St Louis in his teens and vanished from record. The next son, Richard Jr, made for London and drowned in the Thames in 1838.

Richard and Eleanor's tenth child, James, born in Wexford, where the family had settled to a life of pasture farming in 1824, was the one who pitched for Limerick. Breaking with tradition, he married Anne Meehan, a Catholic, and marked his conversion by building an oratory called Littleark, which stood for a century. Together James and Anne had six children, among them Richard, grandfather of the actor. It was James who established the Harris Flour Mills business on which Richard Harris's father built his wealth, and it was he who first became 'famous', if only for his business acumen, his munificence and what Charlie St George called 'his aristocratic, which is not to say arrogant, demeanour'. Richard Harris Sr, the mills' founder, was the first of the dynasty known to the actor: 'And what I knew of him was mostly coloured with the hues of legend. Because he brought employment and wealth to the area, and because of his celebrated flamboyance, he was the stuff of kings. Some part of him, or his reputation, filtered into me when I created my versions of regal nobility. He was a ghost in my life, an old man I never knew, but Old Richard became King Arthur by some form of osmosis.'

Kevin Dineen, a baker by profession and inheritance, lived 'a life of rivalry, across the street and across the divide from the Harrises' but stood in awe of Old Richard's empire. Later, he became friendly with Ivan, the actor's father: 'Bit by bit they developed [the mills] into a booming concern that was one of the key businesses in town. It became more than a flour-and-meal mill. It expanded as a huge bakery in Henry Street. And there wasn't only the bakery. Harris Mills had their own Shannonside silos and a fleet of the Harris cargo boats that plied the Shannon. The boats docked and loaded at the mills daily, then ran their cargoes down the coastline. As a business, [the family] drew the envy of the town. But people liked them. They were amongst the wealthiest folk, but they were renowned for charm and warmth. They weren't snobs. In the local lingo, they never lost the country cut.'

In the 1920s, Harris Mills fought heavy competition. Three other major mills in the southwest vied for the business: Russell's, Clynn's of Kilrush and Roche's. Roche's was the fiercest competitor, based just a few doors away from the main Harris manufacturing complex at Williams Street. Jim Roche, grandson of the founder, recalled two generations of friendly sparring. His grandfather was on the best of terms with Richard, his father in turn with Ivan, who gradually took full control of the business in the teens of the century. 'In the heyday the Harrises were probably the biggest producers,' Jim Roche remembered. 'But we shared the market, which was concentrated on supplying all of Clare and North Kerry. Harris's boats served the towns down as far as Tarbert and Kilrush, and we were always a step behind. But there was plenty of room for us both. The Harrises concentrated on flour and we concentrated on the meal. It was respectful, symbiotic competition.'

When grandfather Richard retired in his eighties, his sons Ivan and Billy split the inheritance, with Ivan taking control of the mill and the bakery and Billy the residential assets. The sum total passed on, according to Charlie St George, 'was an exceptional booty, really a prince's inheritance'. But it was also, in Ivan's case, a commitment to a murderous workload. Ivan put his heart into it, but by the late twenties the bite of the postwar depression and the overload of competition had taken its toll. The bakery was first to show the pressure cracks. 'There was a feeling that Ivan had overextended,' said Roche. 'That the markets were becoming more specialised, and he was still trying to spread himself like butter over everything. It was the twentieth century, and he was trying to run it like it was still the nineteenth. He didn't delegate well, and he got tired.' Workaholic though he was, Ivan distracted himself by concentrating on his hobbies – hockey and tennis – and widening his social scene. On the sports circuit he met Mildred Harty, a local beauty from the wrong side of the tracks. 'In today's world it would mean nothing,' a family friend of the Hartys recalled, 'but in the twenties, in provincial Ireland, concerns like whether or not your family had money meant everything. The Harrises were money people. The Hartys weren't. Milly's folks didn't have tenpence. It surprised many people when Ivan took up with Milly.' But the disapproval was short-lived, because, out of the blue, old Mrs Harty inherited a small fortune from an aunt. 'Everything changed overnight,' the family friend remembered. 'Mammy Harty spared nothing on Milly and her sister. She was suddenly the new Rockefeller in the neighbourhood and she made it clear that she intended to get the best for her daughters. The shoe went on the other foot. Now it was Ivan Harris who had the begging bowl, and Milly the bank account. After that, the gossips just shut up and let them get on with it.'

Ivan married Milly, and their privileged life began in a large estate house off the North Circular Road. They had four children in quick succession but the arrival of the fifth, Richard St John, on 1 October 1930, coincided with a significant downturn in their fortunes. In the winter, six weeks after Richard's birth, the bakery closed and the long, agonising decline of the mill began. Throughout, said Jim Roche, Ivan retained a great calm dignity. 'He was a private, unflappable man who gave off a kind of air of composure despite everything.' Another mill worker of the era contends, 'He was decent, but he was weak. The truth was, he wasn't a brilliant businessman and he enjoyed his pastime activities a bit too much. That was his downfall. The mill in Williams Street and the wholesale shop at Henry Street went on doing fair business for quite a while. But he should have drafted in Billy, or found proper management skills. He could have fought harder.' Grandfather Richard lived to see the first decline of his empire but died when Richard St John, later to be a multimillionaire actor, was two. His grandson remembered 'being aware of great wealth and luxury and all anyone could ever want in a home. There were maids and butlers and gardeners and big cars in the drive. And then, in a snap instant, the world changed. One day was luxury, the next morning my mother was on her knees scrubbing floors and pegging out the Monday washing. I was too young to understand anything, but I knew we'd lost a lot.'

The family moved to Overdale, a six-bedroom 'return' house (two floors and a stepped-back annexe) in a terrace on the Ennis Road, a mile from the mill. This was Richard Harris's first true home, the weedy, mystical place where his incipient creativity flowered. This was the 'greenhouse' of his early poetry, where the fantasies of Beau Geste, Wells Fargo and Tarzan took him away from the background kitchen talk of job lay-offs and bank liens. His recollections, from the start, were summery-bright, obstinate, tunnelled: 'My first memory is of walking down Post Office Lane, pushing a baby in a pram. My mother said, "Dickie, whatever you do don't take your hands off that pram", and I looked in and saw Noel [his younger brother] and asked her, "Will I ever be that small again?" and she told me no.' The poignancy of the moment rooted in his brain and bloomed, aged nine, in his first – and surprisingly adult – poem called "My Young Brother", scribbled in a blue-lined copybook that lived under his bed.

The young Harris wasn't, however, conventionally literary. It was Ivan who read for the house, favouring potboilers like Mickey Spillane, and the avalanche of lurid-covered paperbacks that peeped out of drawers everywhere, beefing up his son's fantasies. 'I didn't know it, of course, but I was dyslexic,' Harris remembered. 'It took me years – well into my thirties – before I understood my reading difficulties as a disability. Right from the start, at school, all through the early years in theatre and films, I plodded through text trying to figure why it took so long for the words to connect with images in my head. I always *got it*, but it took forever, and as a kid you don't live like that, you don't give yourself five minutes, you just *live* the moment.'

'Living the moment' summed up the childhood Dickie Harris. 'There's a real disconnection between my memories and the recollections of my brothers,' he said. 'At family gatherings, right into the nineties, I would say to my brothers Ivan or Noel that I recalled such-and-such – and they would say, Never! It never happened like that. I often thought we lived under the same roof in different universes, but I think it was really just my response to my surroundings. I loved my parents, truly. And I loved Overdale. But I did not love the strictures and rules of the era. Those were times of rigidity – in religion, in schooling, in domestic routines. I could not stand rigidity. I think my father and mother gave up on games as soon as the kids came along. Their only shared activity was a walk together, once a week. Aside from that, they barely communicated. I couldn't stand that rigor mortis. I turned away from it and I became a games player, a fantasist.'

As a fantasist, said Harris, he was robust and attention-demanding – 'When you're the middle child in a large family you learn *to shout* to be heard' – but he was usually ignored. As he tells it, Milly 'humoured' him, but Ivan barely knew of his existence.

'What's his name again?' Ivan would frequently ask, over his newspaper.

'Dick.'

'Oh yeah, Dick, I remember.'

'I made noise,' said Harris, 'because the other option is to accept that you are no one and cease to exist. I could never do that. I had too much going on inside my head, too much I wanted to share.' Dermot Foley, one of the rollicking pre-teen 'musketeers gang' that gravitated around Dickie, remembered the noise more than the sharing: 'Dickie liked a bloody racket, that was all any of us got to know as kids. I don't think conversation was a recognisable activity for him. Maybe it did arise from the indifference of his parents. But it was a reality. From the first time I knew him, all he wanted to do was raise a racket.'

At Overdale, the tendency to shout became a habit of argument. 'I quarrelled all the time, with all of them,' Harris said. 'And when I got fed up I ran away and slept under the stars on the banks of the Shannon, or later at the beach at Kilkee. No one ever came searching for me, that is how I remember it. But, again, when I said that to Noel years later, he said I was talking bollocks. That, whenever I did my Houdini, the fire brigade went out. My memory is of the feeling of neglect – no, that's unfair: call it isolation. And who knows? – maybe it was self-imposed. All I remember is the feeling of loss and anticlimax when I skipped away, and no one came after me. Then I'd sneak home, crawl upstairs and hide in bed.'

On the better days, the days when his young identity crisis didn't depress him, the apple and almond trees of the green house inspired the hollering Tarzan scenarios, authored, directed by and starring Harris. Overdale's garden was long, skinny and claustrophobic: Harris remembered it as the Amazon, the Kalahari and the Canadian Rockies rolled into one: 'I preferred to be outdoors than in, always have, and I knew every weed and knot in Overdale's garden.' Very quickly though, the coastal resort of Kilkee, a couple of miles distant on the Clare coast, upstaged Overdale. Still the cherished summer annexe of Limerick folk, Kilkee was, claimed Harris, 'Limerick's Riviera' in the forties. The Dineen family, like the Harrises and five thousand other Limerick families, relocated en masse to Kilkee for long sojourns every summer. Kevin Dineen, whose path would shortly intertwine with Harris's, remembered forties Kilkee as 'a place of storybook magic, of flat, blanket-white beaches and wheeling gulls all day long, a place outside time'. Harris remembered 'the horizon, which imprinted itself on my mind like paradise. I can still see myself staring out to sea, the grit of the sand between my toes, looking into the blue forever and thinking, Surely to Christ, this is what heaven will be like. There'll be a warm breeze, plenty of laughter on the air, kids being happy, wide spaces, women in corsets . . . and fish and chips.' Manuel Di Lucia, the son of the Italian immigrants who owned the local fish-and-chip shop, befriended Harris on the strand at Kilkee, and grew up playing squash with him on the high-walled hard courts near the sea. 'He felt we were exotic,' recalled Di Lucia, 'because of the food we ate and the games we played. But he fitted in, like a hand in a glove. In fact, he used to say he belonged here. That he should have been born here and, who knew, maybe, but for a confusion of dates and certificates, he was.'

At the start, Harris's time in Kilkee was defined by Milly's dictates, and the ritual summer rental of 'a lodge' – really, a rented cottage – near the beach, which was filled with Harris children. As he gradually grew towards teenhood, the beach town became the rebellious haven, where he sought sanctuary from Ivan and sexual adventures. 'It was really idyllic and innocent,' remembered Di Lucia. 'The main attraction was sports activities – spending the days swimming at the Pollock Holes, which were the rock pools, or bicycling round, then later competing for the local racquetball trophy, which was a version of the game that was a particularity to Kilkee, like haggis is to Scotland. Dickie won that trophy two or three years running. He was naturally athletic, and that's what drew him again and again to Kilkee.'

In late life Harris regarded Kilkee as a mythic hunting ground, the repository of his best memories: 'Did I feel up my first woman there? Or drink my first Guinness? I don't remember. Probably both. But it entered into my blood and possessed me. Wherever I went in life, whatever I was doing in some tropical location or ritzy hotel, I would think of the beach or the promenade at Kilkee and *yearn*. Every man has a spiritual home: that is mine.'

The earliest idylls were always dimly tainted by the threat of summer's end, of dreaded school. All his older brothers and sisters – Harriet-Mary (known as Harmay), Jimmy, Audrey and Ivan – attended St Philomena's Jesuit junior school on the South Circular Road, but even at five Dickie resisted it. 'Frankly, he had no interest in school, *ever*,' says Dermot Foley. 'Primary school especially was a disaster for him, because it was his first prison term. I believe myself he slept through it all.' Harris said, 'I would have done anything to avoid it, and I think the underlying reason was my inability to read fluently. The English language was the modus of communicating every subject, obviously, so I was in trouble before I dipped a pen in an inkwell . . . I just couldn't hack it.'

Harris ultimately toed the line for seven years, then, in a screaming transition, shifted to Crescent Comprehensive, a famously successful secondary Jesuit stronghold. 'I survived by focusing on the sports aspect, full stop. I liked their rugby pitch, that was it, that got me by.'

'By the time he was twelve,' said a Crescent contemporary, 'he had shoulders on him like the bridge of a battleship and a look that had nothing to do with academic life. He was what we then classified as "a messer". He dozed through class, farted for attention, knew nothing. The teachers, God bless them, despaired. Corporal punishment was the great motivator at that time and he was regularly thumped, but he didn't give a damn. He gave the impression that he had come to Crescent to have fun, and fuck the consequences.'

Harris's bravado won loyal admirers. Among the Crescent boys a similarly disposed tight, bright group gathered round him, attracted, said Dermot Foley, 'by his wit and the sense of danger he put out'. Foley, Paddy Lloyd, Gerry Murphy, Teddy Curtain and Harris's cousin Niall Quaid were the core gang. All of them shared an interest in sport, and rugby in particular. 'Father Guinane was Dickie's saviour,' said Foley. 'He was the rugby coach, and a saint at heart. All of us were a bit wild, but Dickie stood out because he slept through the academic stuff. In the real world, he should have been expelled and abandoned. But Father Guinane saw to it that Dickie stayed in the Crescent, basically because Dickie was a good second row and the main concern of the college – though of course they'd pretend otherwise – was maintaining the tradition of turning out a good junior team.'

By many accounts, Ivan and Milly, both sports fans, forgave Dickie's academic lapses on account of his field progress. A neighbour of Overdale recalled the Harrises as 'the sports fanatics of the district. Ivan loved golf, the horses, and all spectator sports. Milly and her sister were trophy-winning tennis players. In fact, it was the Harris family who founded the Limerick County Tennis Club and worked hard for ten years establishing the sport. All of the sons and daughters slotted into one sport or another. Because the boys were big, strapping hulks, they all went into Irish football or rugby.' Apart from Dickie, older brothers Jimmy and Ivan distinguished themselves as Crescent star rugby forwards, and Noel, the baby, superseded Dickie in his love of the sport. Willie Allen, a local lad and favourite combatant from the schools rugby circuit, befriended the brothers during the Crescent days: 'It was a wonder to pass the Harris house and see those rows of blue-and-whites [jerseys] billowing in the wind, five days a week. They were like flags letting the world know that here was a rugby family.'

On the academic front, progress was nonexistent. Harris blithely accepted that he was a dunce. In 1973, in the magazine *Profile*, he summed up his schooldays by recounting the tale of the American journalist who trekked to Limerick in the sixties to research his life story. She knocked on the door of the Crescent and asked the principal if Dickie Harris had gone to school there. 'I'd prefer you didn't mention his name in relation to this school,' was the reply. In the article Harris says the school simply didn't want him, 'so they invented a class for eleven difficult boys.' Dermot Foley concurs: 'It wasn't just Dickie that was bad – there was an entire class of troublemakers, with Dickie at the centre of them. I'll tell you how bad he was: four lines of poetry was too much for him. When he became famous I read about all these two-hour one-man shows, with him reciting poems and singing. Judging by his Crescent days, I just don't know how he did it.'

For Harris, classroom life lingered as 'a faint monotone' and he liked to retell the circulating joke of the early forties that had his maths teacher responding to a complaint by another student:

PUPIL: Sir, Dickie is asleep!
JESUIT TEACHER: For God's sake don't wake him.

Dermot Foley contends this yarn is true and representative. 'The story goes that Father Durnen, the Irish teacher, secretly passed him the results of the intermediate exam, just to help him on his way. Dickie had days to prep himself, and he went ahead and failed it anyway.' Harris confirmed this incident, describing his failure as 'a noble one, given the circumstances'.

From the age of ten, Harris was on the move, following his favoured local rugby teams to matches all across the country. In 1940, he witnessed Garryowen defeat Dolphin in Cork and still thrilled to the details of the game – 'the Light Blues' greatest day' – fifty years later. The passion he took from interprovincial competition and travel was imported back to his own modest games with Crescent and their rivals. Young Munster hero Willie Allen often sparred against him in the Crescent field at this time and recalled him as skilful and unusually strong: 'There are players who *play*, then players who you would describe as whole-hearted, or ferocious, depending on how you see it. Dickie was whole-hearted. He was a great asset to Crescent, because he was *the* man to get the ball in the line-outs. He didn't ever go out in the first ten minutes. He was the sort of player who stuck it like a soldier, even if he was bleeding from head to foot. He got his nose broken several times – but, the way he played, he couldn't have [emerged] without a broken bone.'

Donal Begley, an opponent from the rival St Munchin's, is less flattering: 'He was a great warm-up man, full of vigour in practice but all show. He *looked* dangerous and useful, but when it came to the game he was not up to much. 'I've always reckoned I witnessed the start of Dickie Harris's acting career there and then, in those mid-forties warm-ups. He *acted* the job of being a player far better than he ever played.' Harris himself saw this as typical – amusingly typical – of the ferocity of competitiveness in young rugby in Limerick at the time: 'We were tribes. The Crescent lads banded like the IRA. It was us versus them, with no prisoners in between. But it was all well intentioned. We all, truly, loved the sport for its own sake. When I went up the ladder, and competed in Paddy Berkery's 1947 Cup-winning side, it was the most fantastic time of my life. Two years later I was elected on to the Grand Slam side that swept the boards in the Munster Schools Rugby. Nothing again tasted as sweet. It was the pinnacle.'

The day after Harris won his second Schools medal, he left the Jesuits, without sitting the leaving-certificate examination. The excitement of these days – victory on the beloved playing pitch and a farewell to academe – was overshadowed by events at home. Two years earlier, Audrey, his older sister, had fallen ill with a stomach complaint that was eventually diagnosed as intestinal cancer. After repeated operations and intensive therapy, she died at Overdale in February 1946. Deirdre, Paddy Lloyd's sister, knew her as 'a very beautiful and gentle twenty-one-year-old who never had a chance to live': at the time of her death she had just become engaged to Donogh O'Malley, later a flamboyant and controversial cabinet minister in the Irish government.

'Dickie was beyond consolation,' said Deirdre. 'Jimmy was the closest to Audrey, in age and manner, but Dickie had a deep bond with her. He was also an unusually sensitive fellow, though the bluster of his personality covered it. Everyone took him superficially for a crazy lad. He was the kind of fellow you *heard* coming down the street before you saw him. But Audrey's death, coming in his middle teens, when the world was his oyster, stopped him in his tracks. Despite the so-called money problems of the mills, all of us, neighbours and friends, saw the Harrises' as a charmed home, a stable home. Audrey's death was the first serious setback.'

Jimmy and Ivan, properly graduated from the Crescent, had joined their father in Williams Street, working hard to save the mill. A friend of Deirdre's remembered, 'Outwardly, everything still seemed all right. But Dickie confessed things were not looking good. Ivan's brother [Harris's uncle] had spent a lot of money purchasing special equipment from Germany. It turned out to be a bad investment. The equipment failed, and Ivan and Harris Mills were in the stew. The plan had always been for Dickie to join his brothers running the mill, as soon as he quit Crescent. But, all of a sudden, it didn't look like a secure future for him, or for any of the others.'

According to Harris, his father pushed him towards the business relentlessly – then placed him without apology in charge of hunting the mice that invaded the Henry Street stores. 'To be honest, not one of the brothers had a great head for the milling trade,' said mill worker Michael Davis. 'Jimmy gradually took the helm in the fifties but he didn't really grasp the complexities of the business and it was only a question of time before the whole operation ran out of steam.' Dickie was certainly no asset. Jim Roche remembered, 'I watched his progress with interest. Because of the line-up of brothers, he was low on the list, but eventually he took charge of the Henry Street place for a while, ostensibly to serve his apprenticeship as the mill manager. But we all knew he had no great interest. I recall him standing at the door, out in the sunshine, semaphoring all day long to one of his cronies who was up the street working in another store. It was the *craic* he was interested in, not the hard labour. And the problem was, Harris Mills needed all hands on desk if they were to survive the fifties.'

Camaraderie with 'the musketeers', followed by rugby, followed by the token eight-hour mill shift, became the order of priorities. Dermot Foley observed his friend 'studying hard to be the joker at the mill' while doggedly progressing with Munster Schools rugby. Harris recalled, 'In four years I won three caps [this statistic is under debate], which was satisfying. I measured my life then solely on the pitch. It was like constant battle – all those heroic matches at Thomond Park where we'd kick the shit out of each other and then go off at night around the bars getting legless. I didn't care about the mill, because I was either playing, boozing or sleeping. I was a kid, for Christ's sake! I had no management or business skills. I could barely add up two and two. I had little or no communication with my father, who dwelt in another world. What would you expect?'

In the memory of most who shared his Limerick days, Harris was, during this transitional period, a modest and careful drinker. Betty Brennan, his soon-to-be lover and confidante, observed the boozing as a 'natural extension of his social circuit. For example, on the notorious "away weekends", when he was following some game in Cork or Dublin, he would get drunk like everyone else. But I spent more and more time with him in the late forties and I never saw an incoherent drunk. He was not a heavy drinker. In fact, measured against the typical pub scene of today, he would rate almost as a non-drinker. As I got to know him, he hungered for companionship and someone to talk to. But he wasn't your classic variety "pub person".'

Harris's own accounts contradict the Limerick version. The British actor Ronald Fraser, who would become a lifelong friend, remembered, 'He told me he was pissed from the day he was out of short trousers. I heard this from his lips, and from others in his family. One of his favourite teenage tales was about driving a truck to Dublin, when he was seventeen, on a delivery errand for his father. Harris told me he made his delivery, then made for [the landmark pub] the Bailey, off Grafton Street. His old man told him to be home at seven-thirty *on the dot*! But Harris got well oiled and said, "Fuck it, I'll make it on the back roads in no time." So he set out, pissed as a proverbial, driving this fourteen-foot truck. Suddenly, in the middle of nowhere, ahead, he sees a bridge with a sign saying: "Clearance 12 feet". His attitude is, If I buck up I can make it. And he hits the bridge and lifts it off its pillars. At the other side there's a *Garda*. He flags down Richard, who tells him, "Sorry, officer. You see, I'm just delivering this bridge to Limerick." '

Challenging Harris on the veracity of these yarns, whether for this author or for family and friends, was always a paradoxically frustrating joy. Jimmy Farley, a regular at Charlie St George's pub, insists that Harris had serious alcoholic tendencies from early on, but chose to shroud the truth of pathology in bluster and extravagance. 'I don't doubt that Betty, or anyone else, didn't see the dark side of it – and that itself is exactly consistent with the illness of alcoholism. Alcoholics cover their tracks and build smokescreens. Dickie had the disposition in his blood, and was only lucky that other factors intruded in his life to redirect him. Yes, he was a loud and amusing drunk. Many drunks are. And he got away with murder, because he was charming. Perhaps that was the evidence of his talent on the brew – his charm. Other people would insult you in a pub and you'd knock their teeth out. Dickie could call you a fucking halfwit pig and you'd laugh him off. That's a kind of magic, I suppose.'

Harris's focused analysis, when one cornered him, was self-lacerating: 'I was a rude, bombastic, opinionated, beautifully ignorant loudmouth when I got drunk. I don't know why I pushed it so far – other than the obvious. At the start, I was living the wrong life. I drank to ease the pain, like millions do.'

Though the stories of his early inebriation grew in drama and detail over the years, there was unquestionable humour in some authenticated alcohol episodes. During one delivery trip to Dublin, well witnessed, Harris lost his driving licence for knocking over a double-decker bus in Middle Abbey Street. 'I am bit short-sighted,' he explained to the district court judge hearing the case; to which the judge responded by commending Harris for 'an audacious and historic feat'.

In the winter of 1947 Dickie, the Munster-medalled mouse-catcher of Harris Mills, collided – literally – with an image of himself, reflected in a door in Henry Street: 'My life was haring in circles and I wasn't sure who or what I wanted to be. I was in love with a girl – Grace, Paddy Lloyd's sister – who didn't really love me. I was pining to the moon. I certainly didn't want the mill life, and I wasn't even sure I wanted to play professional rugby, which had been the schoolboy dream. I looked at myself in the door glass and said, "Who are you?" And the reflection answered me back: "I'm the Dickie Harris you haven't found yet. Catch me if you can." Maybe time plays tricks, but, if memory serves, that was exactly round the time I started off in the direction of the Playhouse Theatre.'

CHAPTER 2

Playing House

No purpose-built live theatre existed in Limerick in the 1940s. Since the city's development from a Viking settlement nine hundred years before, theatregoing had never been a major part of the social scene. Visiting troupes did come, usually to play in ill-equipped converted halls or, in the thirties and forties, at the Savoy Cinema. A notable breakthrough came when Dublin's Abbey Theatre Company, one of the world's most celebrated, played the Savoy in the forties. Subsequently, Limerick aficionados had the joy of seeing such notable thespians as Cyril Cusack, Anew MacMasters, Michaél MacLiammóir and Hilton Edwards tread the carpeted Savoy boards, but famine rather than feast was the general menu. Out of such paucity grew Kevin Dineen's vision of the Playhouse and the College Players.

A bakery manager by trade, Dineen was in his middle thirties when, with some friends, he leased a spacious section of building behind the Transport Union headquarters in O'Connell Street, not far from the Harris Mills building. Len, his son, recalled 'playing under this rickety raised stage as my father was hammering it together single-handed, with a lump hammer and a handful of six-inch nails'. The finished theatre seated 250 and was, according to Kevin, 'modest architecture but true at heart'. In 1942 Kevin had founded the College Players, the part-time actors' group that would enact the Playhouse programme. 'The members were drawn from far and wide,' he said. 'Some of them were actors in their blood, others –

36

well – call them non-stop triers.' Apart from Richard Harris, two or three College Players went on to successful, though low-key, stage careers in Canada. The process of selection Dineen decided upon was fussy. 'It was never easy for anyone. We based it on an interview-audition session before two or three of the group's directors, which was followed, if you qualified, by a one-year apprenticeship with the Society of Dramatic Art, which we regarded as a warm-up school for the College Players. Dickie got into the SDA, but never qualified fully for the Players proper.'

Harris's arrival at the Playhouse, in his version, was accidental: 'One day I was bored. I saw a doorway that said, "You too can be an actor", and I thought, Why not?' Another Crescent past pupil, Joe O'Donovan, believes this offhand quip might not be far from the truth: 'To understand him you have to see him as a kid who was *never* relaxed. All the family were active, but he was hyperactive. Rugby, racquetball, tennis, water-polo – he couldn't fill the day in enough ways. When the rugby wasn't in season he joined the Limerick Swimming Club with me, training at Corbally Baths three nights a week. He was just plain restless, and I believe sheer, manic restlessness took him to the Players as if it were just another competitive sport.'

The attraction, Deirdre Lloyd believed, was also the desire for attention. 'He loved the theatre and films and when he went through his phase of being crazy about Grace that's all he wanted to do with her: go to the pictures. He went like he was going to a circus. That was his way of seeing the world: Let's get up off our backsides and have a good time!'

When Harris approached the Playhouse late in 1947 Kevin Dineen already knew him as a lad with theatrical potential: 'I remembered him because he was a son of Harris Mills and had an interesting, wild Irish rover redhead look about him. He was about twelve when I first saw him. I was walking along the beach by the racquet courts where the wall is very high, higher than a two-storey house. One of the great childhood games of daring was to walk across the top of the wall, defying the drop. One day I saw a lad doing it, with a crowd gathered in dumbstruck admiration. I looked again and was horrified to see that the boy was walking *on his hands*. The boy was Dickie Harris.'

Harris started with the SDA 'like a hundred other lads, interested but without any particularly strong direction', said Dineen. The expectation of the Players was a week-to-week hands-on involvement from all young members, in all areas, from cleaning stages to building props, but Harris was not, from the start, entirely committed. The son of one group member recalls, 'He was never disciplined enough to fit in with the College Players' programme. He was an exhibitionist who liked to be centre stage and he had no interest in proving himself. His weakness was the Ink Spots. It often seemed that the only thing that kept him coming was the music that was always on a gramophone there. Dickie adored it. He wanted to be on stage strumming a guitar and singing Ink Spots songs day and night – which was what he did, when he could get away with it. His voice was no great shakes – Noel, who sang with St Cecilian's choir, was the family singer – but Dickie liked the glamour of being Bing Crosby.' Kevin Dineen endorsed this view: 'You couldn't say he demonstrated significant acting skills in the SDA. He simply wasn't tested enough. But he had a flair for the variety end of things. It seemed to me he might one day be a star of the variety theatre – a juggler, a ventriloquist, a magician. To me, he wasn't a charmer, but he was a *charming fellow* and he had incredible energy, which is the reason I supported keeping him on. I was twenty-something years older than him, but watching him work made me feel a hundred!'

With Dineen's affectionate support, Harris did appear in one Players production, Strindberg's *Easter*, in which he served the not-too-demanding role of Sebastian. 'To be truthful, his younger brother Dermot was a much better actor,' said Dineen. 'He was smaller than Dickie physically, but he could command the stage. I remember casting him in a small part in one of our big productions and he swept gracefully across the stage and won that audience. For years I told people that Dermot Harris might well be a theatrical success story. Ironically, he ended up as Dickie's manager.'

Throughout 1948 and 1949 when he was eighteen, Harris maintained a fitful interest in the Players, and in the touring theatre groups that came with greater frequency to Limerick. When Anew MacMasters visited for a Shakespeare Week, Harris, among many Crescent past pupils, offered himself for walk-on, or, as Kevin Dineen described it, 'stand-about' parts. Those, like Dineen, who saw him admired his gusto and wit – not so much as an actor but, inimitably, as Dickie. 'Kilkee was in him in everything he did,' said Dineen. 'I tried to look upon him as a serious trainee actor, but what I saw was the twinkle of devilment, like he was about to handspring at any moment, in the middle of *Coriolanus* or something.' Dermot Foley of the 'musketeers gang' also watched Dickie's first theatre efforts. 'All that stage stuff was a great lark,' said Foley. 'It really was good acting on Harris's part, but not in the way that the College Players wanted. Dickie acted at trying to be an actor. All the time he'd be telling me, "These hams are all boring wankers wearing make-up." The scripts annoyed him, too. Too much paperwork, too much like school! Let's get some action here!'

Fittingly, the real thespian progress was made at Kilkee. The amphitheatre, a natural saucer of rock with stepped walls perfectly suited to play-making, had always been a summer's evening rendezvous point, developing over the years into an ad hoc performance venue. In the forties and fifties, amateur groups started using the amphitheatre for elaborate stagings of Greek and Elizabethan dramas, and vaudeville-type shows. Dineen often sat on the stone steps to watch some jumbled amateur effort and was tempted to bring the College Players to the amphitheatre. 'But it would have been living hell, because it was open-air anarchy. From a spectator standpoint, it was fascinating, a delight. Because you started enjoying some Strindberg and ended up folded over laughing yourself senseless at the dogs peeing on the actors . . . not always, mind, but often.' Jim Roche enjoyed Harris's larking at the amphitheatre too. 'Harris became the lovable local boyo that everyone knew. Long before he was a Hollywood star, he was the star of Kilkee. His gregarious nature ignited other people and his appetite for company was insatiable. In the west end of Kilkee one of the summer hotels housed the Clarelleagh organisation, a Presbyterian and Methodist society. Harris was deafeningly

Catholic, but he was happy to stage-manage an open-air entertainment for them one summer. He really knew nothing about theatre, but his personality drove an amazing show, doing take-offs of American actors and Shakespeare scenes. It was also extremely funny, because the foreign tourists who came expected to get the Celtic blarney, and what they got with Dickie was a dose of James Cagney.'

Of equal interest as theatre was the cinema. In Limerick, the Savoy, a bunkerlike, robust prewar building, accelerated in Harris's affections each year. Johnny 'JJ' Murphy, another Savoy frequenter, knew Harris primarily as a chronic 'drunk-and-disorderly' in the small foyer of the cinema. 'Not to say he was literally drunk all the time, but he arrived like a drunk, banging doors and talking at a higher volume than anyone else. He came mostly, as I recall, for the westerns, like the John Wayne and Gary Cooper stuff.' Manuel Di Lucia believed that Harris's love for 'the baloney of entertainment' saw no distinction between the theatre and the movies, between actor and audience, between fact and fantasy: 'He was always clattering about from seat to seat, laughing and catcalling and making fun of whatever was going on on the screen. He wasn't what you'd call a well-behaved or conventional member of the audience. But you couldn't go against him any more than you could go against a clown at the circus – because being around him was like having your personal court jester in attendance.'

Harris's eccentricity eventually created problems in Kilkee and Limerick, where he was banned from virtually all cinemas. The Savoy banning order seemed particularly amusing when, more than twenty years later, the prodigal son brought the premiere of *Bloomfield* there. Some of the staff, Harris noted wryly, were the same people who had enforced the ban all those years before. It was, he liked to claim, 'touch and go' as to whether the *Bloomfield* star would be allowed past the door of his old alma mater.

At the Carlton Cinema, long gone, Harris embarked on his first Hollywood crush, falling head-over-heels in love with Merle Oberon, playing Cathy in Samuel Goldwyn's 1939 classic *Wuthering Heights*. 'She stopped me in my tracks. Till Merle, the

movies were free-for-alls. I didn't take them seriously. I liked
watching people like Jimmy Cagney and Errol Flynn, but I didn't
really pay attention. Merle was mesmerising. Her imperious look
froze me. Jesus, that passionate mouth, those pert little titties. You
watched her in her ball-gowned elegance and doubted she was
wearing knickers. I loved it that she could radiate such sexual energy
by just throwing a sidelong look at some poor sod. I admired her and
desired her and wished I could be as cool and powerful as her.'
Oberon became his Ideal Woman, the personification of a perfect
femininity beyond Milly and Harmay and Audrey. He wrote away
for a photograph and kept it, along with his secret poetry collection,
in the recesses of his bedroom.

The impact of Merle Oberon's beauty spelled more than just a
sexual awakening for Harris. It changed fundamentally his focus on
entertainment and affected his approach to acting and all areas of
creative life. *Wuthering Heights* became the pivot of his imagination,
and his admiration for the story – a hybrid of Gothic and mythic
drama – dictated his attitude of approach to his early career.
Wuthering Heights became, secretly, the sun and the stars. After his
eventual main success, *This Sporting Life*, he and director Lindsay
Anderson parlayed everything into a remake of *Wuthering Heights*,
with Harris as Heathcliff. The projects was, sadly for all, stillborn.

Despite the temporary interruptions of the Playhouse, Kilkee and
the movies, Harris's main occupation was still rugby. But after his
mid-teens discovery of Merle Oberon the scales tilted in favour of a
lusty interest in the opposite sex. 'I was always a horny bastard,'
Harris later said. 'I just didn't let it rip till I was fifteen or so.' Gracie
and Deirdre Lloyd, Mary Kennedy and other local bob-curled
colleens, continued to see him, however, as the personification of
'niceness'. The raucousness was recognised but, a friend contended,
'Most of it in those early days was a cover-up for his obsession with
Gracie Lloyd. He kissed a couple of available girls at Charlie St
George's and the cinema, but it was only Gracie he wanted, and she
had no interest in him, which drove him nuts.' Deirdre, Grace's
sister, contested, 'He had plenty of dates, so I wouldn't say Gracie
broke his heart. He was never short of admirers among us girls. All

the Harris boys had different facial bone structures, all were very fascinating-looking boys whom we girls talked about standing on corners and in the bars. Dickie looked like his mother, very square-faced and ruggedly attractive. He was known among the girls as a right good catch.'

Harris compensated for the loss of Gracie with breezy, serial relationships that he described as 'warm-up acts', but his first serious relationship – and the model for all his earnest friendships with women throughout his life – was with a newcomer to Limerick, who looked not unlike Audrey Hepburn, called Elizabeth Brennan. Wexford-born 'Betty' Brennan was nineteen when she arrived in Limerick from Waterford on a job transfer from the Munster & Leinster Bank. Brown-eyed, fair-skinned and lithe as a *Vogue* mannequin, Betty came equipped with a sense of adventure to match Harris's, a by-product, she believed, of the independence forced on her by the death of her beloved mother when she was just three. Raised largely by her father, whose guiding influence remained remote but firm, Betty felt herself slipping into a moral and social time warp in fifties Limerick. Ireland then was unarguably in the grip of the moralists, a place of post-colonial paranoia pumped up by the overcompensatory dictates of an incestuous church–state government. The 'moral codes' reigned supreme, facilitating many social abuses, not the least of which was the pervasive sexism that kept women in the uniform of the schoolgirl, the spinster or the house-wife. 'Decent' attire was mandatory; women never spoke out of turn; never challenged husband or father; never went alone into bars. Betty poked fun at the norm: 'I was always a free bird, always out for a laugh, always looking for adventure.' Betty wryly recalled her 'baptism' memories of Limerick: the wagging fingers when she brazenly wore trousers into an all-male bar. 'It just wasn't on for 1951. I think they thought the devil's bride had entered their midst.'

Betty's vivacity hid a reflective, probing character that immediately entranced Dickie Harris when he met her at his post-twenty-first-birthday party in October 1951. 'I knew he was interested in me, but at the start it was Ivan, the mill manager, I flirted with, and it looked like we were the ones who would become "an item". It took a few weeks for Dickie to get up the courage to make his move on me. He wasn't cocky, he was extremely shy.'

Harris recalled the slow-developing love affair as 'a time of tranquillity when I didn't want to go out and get drunk'. Betty agreed: 'My favourite places were the ballroom at Cruise's Hotel, the Stella ballroom or the tennis club, where one could sit and be civil, or just dance.' It was at Cruise's Saturday-night dance that Betty Brennan fell for Harris. He asked her to dance, walked her home to her nearby digs – and the burning romance began. 'I found him strikingly handsome and terribly *kind*,' she remembered. 'To me, he looked like Danny Kaye, with his orangey hair and bright blue eyes. He was also the greatest fun and he loved to talk like no one I ever knew. That was his seductive trick. There was never a silence with him. He would talk you happy.' Harris wasn't a virgin when he met Betty, but she was. Their relationship was consummated – 'perfectly', she said – in the summerhouse on the grounds of a convent on a beautiful spring day.

For Betty the affair was liberating. 'Dickie's energy combined with mine was a potent mixture. We went everywhere together, did everything together, like husband and wife. Occasionally I would lose his attention when he disappeared for a rugby weekend with Paddy Lloyd or Gerry Murphy or Niall Quaid, but that was rare. We were sharers. We shared our time, our dreams, even our money.'

Still idling under his brother Ivan, now at the mill complex, Harris was regularly short of cash. 'I never begrudged him that. We spent our money together liberally, relishing life. The way it worked was, my wages saw us though the first half of the week, his wages paid for the weekend.' Jack Donnelly, recently married to Harris's sister Harmay, was the manager of Cruise's and the hotel became 'a kind of second home' for Dickie and Betty. 'Dickie and Jack were more like brothers, actually. Jack was much older, a small powerhouse of a man with a great discipline and dignity about him. He had a great effect on Dick, and calmed him down. Around Jack, Dick was very well behaved.' One of the musketeers offered the outside perspective: 'Yes, at Cruise's Dick was on best behaviour with Betty. But then he'd come down to one of the pubs like Charlie St

George's and let rip with the lads. At Charlie St George's the company was much rowdier than at Jack's place, obviously. It was all rebel songs and talk about the Brits and the suppression of the Irish, and all that raging history. Dickie loved it, because he said he got his true political education there. So Cruise's was for romance. Charlie's was life lessons.'

With Betty, Harris favoured theatregoing, rather than movies. 'He admired people like Anew MacMasters and liked to take me to the Playhouse productions,' said Betty, 'but to my thinking it was more whimsical interest than real hobby for either of us. But then Dickie could always surprise you. Once, during a Playhouse performance, a character on stage repeatedly came on, starting his lines only to be interrupted by one of the other characters. It was quite an amusing scene, but Dickie added to it. When the incident happened for the third or fourth time, and then the character came on to try it again, Dickie suddenly roared the lines with him, in unison. Those were the kind of moments where you looked twice at him, and his capacity for winning an audience all of his own.'

To Betty, Harris was a magpie mind with a vague interest in books: 'But the literary and intellectual side of him was repressed, or controlled in a strange way. No one spoke about dyslexia, or schooling difficulties, but there were definite issues there.' Harris, for his part, saw himself 'playing a double game' that had more to do with the separate camps acknowledged by the musketeers. 'Yes, I was intimate and trusting with Betty, but some other part of me was absorbed in what I can only call an inner dialogue. Even with the rugby lads, there was always a stepping back. I didn't always like it in myself. It was often confusing, and it caused me agitation. What was I looking for? Who knew? But there was a tape in my head, constantly saying Why? How? When?' The local journalist Gerry Hannan, who got to know Harris in the eighties, wondered whether the character of Limerick life wasn't itself the problem. 'Like so many provincial self-contained towns, it has a lingo and a way of its own. In Limerick's case, the local "way" is quirky, dictated by the notorious Curse of St Munchin that decrees that the locals shall perish while the foreigners prosper. Limerick doesn't like people jumping beyond their station. The Harrises were millers, doing a fair trade, and that was that. Other people were actors, other people were writers. And, on top of that, Dickie's crowd – the musketeers – weren't the long-haired poet types. They were all lads mad for the *craic*. In that picture, it's easy to imagine Dickie as a suppressed spirit, struggling with himself. Whatever artistic feelings he had kept inside himself, because he didn't want Limerick knocking it out of him.'

The private Dickie Harris, the one-part-removed mirror image that kept itself from Betty Brennan and the musketeers, quietly pursued the interest in theatre evidenced at the Playhouse. 'It was always there, always hammering at my subconscious. There was never an open impulse, but it was always going on. For instance, there was a big outing to Dublin with the lads for some rugby international in the early fifties. Lots of booze and laughs. But somehow it turned into a theatre weekend for me. I went to the Gate, to see Pirandello's *Henry IV* by myself. Now that was one tough play for a semiliterate Limerickman. It wasn't *Carousel*.' Harris was slack-jawed in admiration of the story of simple man hiding behind the mask of madness. 'I was *staggered* by that play and it spoke to me very deeply. I felt Pirandello wrote it for me. It sounds corny, but I remember swearing that one day, somewhere, I would perform that play – and it took me almost forty years to make that dream come true.'

Little of this dreamy drifting was shared with Betty. What she most knew was 'the happy rugby fanatic' who – yes – was restless and always kept an eye open to future possibilities. 'We didn't really talk about *our* future, or whether we would stay in Limerick, or stick each other out. We lived from day to day. But there was a feeling of excitement about *his* future that you couldn't put your finger on. I dare say he thought about it more than I did.'

Dermot Foley remembered Betty as 'a right wild one who was *the* perfect match for Dickie'. But Milly – 'Mildew' to Dickie – didn't agree. Before the affair was a year old, Milly's disapproval was made known in an assortment of indirect ways. 'Overdale was off-limits for me,' said Betty. 'Again, you must remember the time and the place and the attitude towards the kind of close relationship Dickie and I shared. We were as close as people can get. He didn't stay at my digs, but let's say he spent more than a little time there. The old woman who owned the place – a ratty old bag – didn't like what she saw at all. To this day I believe she wrote to Milly Harris and complained about our intimacy, and Milly, who positively disliked me, contacted my father in Waterford. As a result, the bank suddenly decided to transfer me back to Waterford. It wasn't a big shock because I sensed it coming. But it was a huge strain on my relationship with Dickie.'

Harris did not, apparently, contest the parental decision. Instead, in his cavalier way, he enjoyed the circulating gag that beautiful Betty had been 'harrised' out of town. Borrowing his brother Jimmy's rattlebag Citroën, he quietly pursued the affair with Betty at weekends. 'We were so close emotionally,' said Betty, 'that the separation hardly bothered us at first. It was just a little inconvenience that seemed to draw us closer, if anything.'

But after a few months Betty was again transferred, this time to Dublin. Time and geography, inevitably, altered realities. 'By then the relationship *was* changing,' said Betty. 'It became harder to maintain the spontaneity, though we tried with letters and phone calls. I suppose I despaired of making a go of it. Really, once I settled in Dublin I began to accept some sort of unhappy closure.'

Harris was less accepting. Reluctant to let go, he continued to borrow Jimmy's or Ivan's car for the four-hour drive to Dublin. 'There was always joy and always surprises,' said Betty. 'On his first visits he stayed at the Avoca Hotel in Harcourt Street, quite a long walking distance from my south city flat. Because of our bad experience with the previous landlady, Dickie was extra-sensitive. So he decided to court the new landlady by bringing her an early breakfast on a silver tray. He brought it from the kitchens of the Avoca and marched through the morning rush-hour traffic with a fully laid-out hotel breakfast. My new landlady was enchanted.'

Harris's outlandish humour went on winning friends. Betty's brother, a seminary student also called Dickie, became one of his most loyal admirers. Though Betty acknowledged that Dickie was 'something of a danger man', Dickie Brennan wallowed in his warmth. A Sunday foursome drive with Betty and a girlfriend, typical of the Dublin social sprees, inspired the future priest to write celebratory poetry still fondly recited by the Brennans today:

From Tallaght then to Templeogue we sped most merrily . . .
Arrived at last on mountain top, it was wonderful to see
Those glens and hills of Dublin which don't flow into the sea
And I think our joy and rapture were well voiced by glad Dickie
As he muttered in his rapture, 'This caps it all for me.'

The epic continues by extolling the virtues of scenery and camaraderie, then conforms to classic Irish lyricism:

Oh 'twas at the Hotel Leinster in that day in fifty-three
That we four to mirth inclined were, and to jollity
Oh, how we quaffed the nectar there, supplied so thoughtfully,
By that wonderful young chappie, Dick, the busy bee!

'It couldn't last,' said Betty, 'because we were simply apart too much. And as time went on I decided that I wanted new work, and a new life. My plan was to earn as much money as I could and go travelling in Europe. It wasn't that I didn't love Dickie. It was just that circumstances were what they were and there was no use crying over spilt milk. I could no more have changed Milly's attitude than my father's.'

Betty Brennan remembered no final break-up blow. 'Whenever we were together it was like old times: fun and activity and few if any rows. But Limerick became my past. I never really knew the musketeers. So the only connections with Limerick were the letters Dickie sent me every couple of weeks.' From the letters, Betty was aware of his continued success with rugby, 'but also that rugby had become a shrinking compartment' in his life. 'I think he was in as much flux as I was. He was revising every aspect of his life, which is what you do when you are in your twenties and more or less alone.'

Harris's devotion to rugby wavered in his pursuit of Betty, but never died. For Dermot Foley, 'It defined him. Basically he loved every moment to be filled with high drama. No personal relationship was ever going to give him that, so there was no way he'd have abandoned the rugby pitch.' In fact, in the dying days of his relationship with Betty, a new placing with Garryowen offered emotional solace. In 1952 and 1953 he competed in interprovincial junior cup matches, under captain Kevin Quilligan, 'serving honourably', according to Foley. Len Dineen, son of the Playhouse director, was just a child at the time, but rugby-mad and destined to captain the London Irish in the sixties. He saw Harris as a 'gifted and consistent player who undoubtedly showed promise, but not, on reflection, the kind of promise that makes an international-class contender'. Forty years later, Harris conceded his weakness: 'I was not emotionally disciplined. If I'd had the objectivity to step back and pull myself together, to decide for once and for all I wanted to be this, or be that, I would have made it as a player for Ireland. I was certain of that. But I wasn't straight in my head. Some days it felt like I wanted some shape or form of "normal" settled life [with Betty]; other days I went out just to get my nose broken.'

Harris's lovelorn letters to Betty in Dublin reveal the division in his personality. Occasionally they ramble on about rugby, but mostly they are charged with the power of his affections, and the frustration arising from their dilemma. Distress and panic resonate from the taunting word games Harris plays, hinting at the delights of rival girlfriends. Years later, Betty looked back on the letters forgivingly. At the time they drove her to despair. Once, she confessed, the stress of resolution – of trying to appease Harris while satisfying her own instincts – precipitated a crisis that culminated in her threat of suicide. 'It was a half-hearted, dizzy threat that started with a row over photographs of an air hostess he sent me, a girl he claimed was his new big love,' Betty said. 'But it goes to show how much heat was in the relationship. It was hard for anyone who knew or loved Dickie not to feel or respond *in the extreme*, because that was how he lived, and what he demanded.'

Ultimately, both accepted the inevitability of the split. Probably both of them wished it, Betty believed, each tacitly acknowledging the roving spirit growing in the other. 'The passion evolved into a great friendship with declarations of endless love going on right till the end. It was powerful, and I believe the power of it was the fact that it was a mutual-support and mutual-education affair. We fed off each other, and grew more than anything in our demand for a life of independence.' Harris still sent photographs, though, after the suicide incident, they tended to be copies of the high-street studio portraits of himself he liked to collect. On one of the last – a handsome smiling full-face picture that already radiated the self-possession of a Hollywood hero – the farewell ode scrawled on the reverse spoke of the measure of his loss and the exacerbated torment of the divided self:

> *Am I a mystic? What mental strife*
> *Plays thoughts upon my mind;*
> *What genie's philosophy of life*
> *Inside this brain you'll find.*
>
> *Is it so strange – to lose the sun*
> *The winter breeze and rain,*
> *The stars at night, the moon so bright*
> *And life of gay, not pain?*
>
> *O God from my life my dream you stole*
> *And left me in this world alone*
> *How can I live without my life?*
> *How can I die without my soul?*

As Betty faded, an anguished gap opened in Harris's life. It wasn't just the absence of a like-minded female friend with whom he could communicate, nor the focus for fresh adventures. Betty's departure underscored his need for poetic expression. With her, he had relaxed and grown enough to reveal some of the precocious roundedness of his developing personality – specifically a feminine side every bit as lively as his rugby-scrum persona. 'The Limerick Dickie set out to conquer was the hard man's Limerick,' says an Ennis Road neighbour. 'It was boxing orchards [scrumping], carousing away at Cruise's or the Hydro Hotel in Kilkee, getting off with the dames, cocking a snook at your elders. But there was another side to him. He had a knack of getting on with all the ould fellas, as well as the young girls. People tend to stick to their peer groups, but Dickie didn't. He moved around. All of us who knew or observed him saw him as an unusual bird, someone who seemed always to be shifting from group to group. For instance, he developed a great friendship with a middle-aged insurance man, Alf Kirby, who would have been a nonentity to the musketeers. And then there were the women. Young Limerickmen, not to say all young Irish Catholics, had arm's-length relationships, because of the [religious] conditioning. Dickie stood out because of his ease with women. Apart from the Lloyds and [Betty], he had concurrent close relationships with many, many local women. You always saw him on a Saturday or Sunday with some attractive girl, laughing and romping, linking arms. But, then again, you'd pass him on the street on Monday morning, alone and hung over, and he'd give you a look of the blackest depression. He was light and dark. You could never say he was ordinary, and several neighbours judged him "the thinker" of the Harrises.'

The perks that Limerick offered – be it the musketeers, wise Alf Kirby or the pageant of the Playhouse – no longer absorbed Harris. Nor did the strained, phony working life in Henry Street. In the opinion of many, Alf Kirby briefly became a father substitute, and it was an open secret that that Harris confided in him, rather than old Ivan. 'The mill was a mess and a bit of a local talking point,' said a local businessman. 'The management was obviously awful and young Ivan wasn't progressing anything. People said Dickie was a joke. He just wasn't cut out for it, but, to give him credit, he knew it and made no pretence otherwise. He just went there when he was bored, just to please his father.' Betty Brennan recalls that Harris's main interest in the mill was as a secret trysting spot, where they romped among the flour sacks. Beyond that, she contended, his professional involvement was 'just going through the motions'. In

Harris's version, his 'devotion' to the mill ended in a head-on conflict with his father. 'There was a labour dispute to do with shorter hours and higher pay. I took the side of the workers, and organised the protest walk-out. My father wasn't surprised by that. By then, he knew me. It was what he'd come to expect. So he just walked up to me in the store and said, "Dickie, you're a pain in the arse. And something else, while we're at it: you're fired." To be honest, it was a happy release.'

Gradually, the indulgent gaiety of cartwheeling youth died. The musketeers started marrying and drifting away. Rugby cronies sworn to lifelong friendships moved to Cork, to Dublin, to London. A few went to the brave new world across the Atlantic. Harris speculated on his options with Kevin Dineen at the Playhouse. Dineen recalled, 'It was clear he'd move away. He wasn't the kind of fella who queues up to wait his turn. Some said he would have stayed with the rugby fraternity and gone the distance as a professional player. But I always thought that was windy talk. The rugby crowd didn't reach the part of him that the Playhouse filled. He was more complex than any of them – and he knew it, and he was speculating on a different kind of life long before tuberculosis flattened him and changed everything.'

The devastating crisis of serious illness befell Harris at a time of peak energy and motivation. Freed from Betty and the mill, he had decided to emigrate to Canada with his cousin Niall Quaid. 'I loved Ireland, I loved all the myth and mystery of it. But I hated middle-class convention and suburbia. I couldn't stand the hypocrisy that came with Catholic tyranny in every aspect of day-to-day life. You simply couldn't relax. You talked about riding women and having a wank, but you did it like a criminal. Somewhere fifty feet away there was always a "man of the cloth" or some fucking judgmental nun breathing down your neck. I'd had enough, and I thought, I'll live in exile like James Joyce.'

The Canadian visa application required a medical examination and Harris knew he was in trouble. 'A few years earlier, when I was nineteen, I was diagnosed with a tubercular spot on my right lung, but I soldiered it out. I had a cough, but I took the medication and took a few weeks in bed, and it passed. So I forgot about it and went on playing rugby, none the worse. But it was always in the back of my mind that there was a problem and whenever I really pushed myself I hit the wall. Something wasn't right, and I knew it was only a matter of time before I went down.' Halfway through training for the 1952 Munster Juniors Cup match, Harris fell ill, but was revived by benzedrine given by Dermot Foley. 'But it was a wing and a prayer. I was six feet three inches tall and when you're that big weight loss turns you into a scarecrow overnight. All through 1952 I was losing weight, and I was down to less than twelve stone for the Cork cup match. By the middle of 1953 I'd lost another stone and a half, and the cough was so bad that someone at the bus stop could have diagnosed TB.' Finally, Milly called Dr Corboy, the local GP, and, after hospital tests, rampant tuberculosis was confirmed. There followed a few weeks of hospital treatment for a badly infected lung, then the jail sentence of long-term confinement to bed at Ennis Road. According to Corby, treatment and recovery might take as long as three years.

Harris was shattered. His Canadian escape route was lost, his rugby life finished. 'It was a crossroads in every sense. The routes open to me at that point were Canada, or a career in rugby in Ireland, graduating from Munster juniors through the inter-provincial seniors. When I saw the writing on the wall with the Canada medical exam, I fooled myself for days, saying, Don't worry, there's always rugby. But deep inside myself I knew it was all over. I never played again after the TB diagnosis. Afterwards, all my life, I regretted the irony. How ridiculous it was, getting a 1953 Munster Cup medal and TB all at the same time. It felt like: Here's a gift, now give it back to me.'

Harris's life went, he said, 'into crash-reverse'. From his point of view he had been strategically loosening the bonds to Ivan and Overdale; now he was housebound. The mill life ended, but so too did the night life. There would be no more women at Cruise's, no more treason talk at Charlie St George's, no more Kilkee play-acting, no more movies. He took to his bed, 'at first in anger and fear', finally 'prostrate with boredom. Jaysus, those endless days.

You cannot comprehend. Just the tedium of it. Four walls, one door, the two changes of bedclothes. The same cups of tea. The same bread and butter. The same newspaper daily. The same everything.' One part of him stoically accepted that the confinement had always been inevitable. 'After the first diagnosis of the spot, I should have gone to bed. I fought it. And I kept fighting it even when I was in the damned bed. I got up when I should have been lying down and to break the monotony I began to drink more than I used to . . . First to forget. Then to remember.'

Milly was a sound though sometimes cranky nurse, and Noel and Dermot particularly were good company – but Harris was inconsolable. So often the soul of the party, he had only the house pet – Harmay's dog – to entertain. 'Time became of great importance to me. Whenever I asked the doctors when I would be cured and might begin doing something useful with my life they'd reply, "In six months." It was always "in six months". Never any more, never any less. And, like two dots on a circle, the two dates never drew any nearer . . . I was dribbling away my youth, identifying with nothing and nobody, achieving nothing.'

Harris remained housebound for nearly 22 months, for six of which he lay inert, 'playing a staring game with the damp Irish walls that caused my TB in the first place'. During this 'catatonic' phase in the middle months, he believed, the shape of an alternative potential future emerged 'like phantoms on the wall in a Robert Louis Stevenson poem'. When Niall and Dermot Foley and others came to visit, all noticed personality changes. Demot Foley felt, 'Everything had been conducted at a gallop till that point. Then it all slowed down to a sort of rigid calm.' As Harris saw it, the changes were profound and certainly affected his 'vibrations' with the musketeers. 'In illness you're a great burden to your friends. In the first week they all come and say, "You'll be up in a month, you'll be up in a week." After a couple of weeks you have fifteen friends, and a couple of months later you have six. And then you've got three, and then you have one, and then you are on your own. They come only at Christmas and birthdays, either looking for or giving presents. So I became a different person in the isolation of my own company.

Invention became the medicine, the comfort, the cure. I invented people out of light bulbs. I had conversations with people inside light bulbs, and I invented hundreds of people coming to talk to me. I [became] the king of England, or I was the Pope. I lay there and *created*. And that is how my acting career started.'

Throughout Harris's life the anecdotal variations in his story-telling were dizzying. Limerick acquaintances such as Gerry Hannan saw nothing uncommon about this: 'A particular type of self-serving story-telling is Limerick's specialty. You don't call the inconsistent interview subject a liar – you call him "colourful". Dickie was "rainbow-hued".' For sure, Harris's imagination was bountiful and it was during these TB days that the banks burst and the river flowed. In his confinement he wrote copiously, filling copybooks with misspelled, surreal notes that were the first lucid indications of artistic potential. Though he was never proficient at art (his constant doodles were basic matchstick men with balloon heads), his mature writing, removed from Lothario love hymns, was often remarkable, boomeranging from Nietzschean *vers libre* to elegiac Dylan Thomas and back. These first structured efforts – some of which would emerge in print in his hugely successful book of poetry, *I, in the Membership of My Days*, published in 1973 – were all the more remarkable because he was not widely read. 'The effort to read started in bed at that time. And my tastes were unusual and narrow because reading took an effort and I wasn't going to waste my time struggling through artsy rubbish just to impress myself. I loved buccaneering adventures, about coral islands and explorers. And the letters of Vincent Van Gogh to his brother became an obsession. I liked the confessional honesty, and I liked pitching myself to try and understand this great tortured genius. That was a magnificent attraction. What was he? Why was he like that? Could he have been saved? When I wrote myself, I was cued by these letters. I tried to write *what I was* with deep, deep honesty.'

One poem written in bed, 'My Blood Reflects Nothing of Me', spoke eloquently about the duality Harris had begun to see in himself, phrased as a hard-drinking hard man tussling with the Catholic suppression of passion:

My blood
reflects nothing of me . . .
But when I bleed
it belongs to her
only then
it is a part of me

'During this period of incarceration,' Harris told a women's magazine in 1965, 'I lived my life at second-hand through the adventure of others, in books. And I decided that, when I was cured, I would like to direct my own scenarios, to bring to life the whole truth of my creation, to look at my life through the telescope of truth. I wanted to bring a little shock, a little disease into middle-class drawing rooms, to lift up the carpets and shake up the dust a bit.' This revolution of thought wasn't evident in Overdale, nor among the girlfriends who stayed in touch by mail, or the musketeers who occasionally dropped by. Dermot Foley reckoned, 'I thought he'd pull himself together and get back in the scrum.' Charlie St George missed his company and his business but felt 'He was a survivor, so I guessed we'd see him again. None of us knew he was that ill. And then, when we found out, none of us knew he would change that much that quickly.'

Dickie Harris was well familiar with the Limerick expression 'alickadoo'. It described the rugby follower who knows about everything, but stands on the wings. The world of Crescent and Garryowen was full of alickadoos. He knew many of them personally, and disliked them. Always a man of action, he had no sympathies with back scratchers and idlers. In the autumn of 1955, as his condition improved, he dodged out of the house seeking only one form of companionship – the fantasy figures of the theatre. He explained to the women's magazine, 'My mind was made up. I did not want a future in the family business. I did not want to grovel for placings on rugby teams. I didn't want to rewind my past. Instead I'd pick up where I'd left it with Niall. I wanted to get out and put a distance between myself and that bed in Overdale.' Out of the ether, it seemed to Milly, Ivan and the musketeers, the decision was made to go abroad and study theatre. 'My parents couldn't understand what drew me to the make-believe world of acting and I couldn't help them out there. Because if they asked me – and they probably did – I'd say, "I haven't a fucking clue." Maybe it was the darkroom glamour of the Playhouse. Maybe it was as simple as just preferring this life of the imagination to the truth of the sickroom. I couldn't qualify it because I didn't understand. I didn't know, that's the truth.'

In the winter of 1955 Harris made written enquiries to acting schools in London – in secret. Ivan, he knew, would not support him; but neither would he block him. Milly, for her part, would be glad just to see her son confident and free again. 'I had that going for me. People were glad to see me out and about – but I was also forgotten and anonymous, which helped the plan.' There was also the fortuitous gift of a small-shares inheritance left by a recently deceased aunt: 'I bought a ticket for the mail boat. What I was left with was enough cash to see me through about a year in London. I saw it that simply: I had one year to succeed or fail. I wasn't stupid. I shook everyone's hand in the clear belief that every one of them *knew* I'd fail.'

CHAPTER 3

Honeymoon on Sixpence

Richard Harris arrived in London at a time that was arguably the lowest ebb of British theatrical and film endeavour. The greatest stage performances of Olivier, Richardson and Gielgud were in the past. And in film as in theatre a postwar 'norm' had been established that refined Victorian melodrama and offended no one. The jolly-good-fellow charm of Kenneth More and Dirk Bogarde dominated, and cheery spirited Ealing Studios thrived. This apparent intertia masked a society ripe for change. The Conservatives had been in comfortable power since 1951, a fairy-tale queen was enthroned, rationing had ended the previous year, council housing was booming – and TV was spreading across the land like bushfire, reporting the alternatives. Britain was, as Churchill promised, a people set free, and in their freedom – and with the spur of an improved quality of life – the mood was afoot for major change.

While British movies dozed, Hollywood was fighting the wars, gamely struggling against the tide of television. Harried into the gimmickry of VistaVision and sci-fi in the mainstream, Hollywood was reorientating and pushing out its best contenders: Brando had just finished *On the Waterfront*, James Dean had wrapped *Giant* and Marilyn Monroe's latest was the seminal comedy *The Seven Year Itch*. But British movie moguls had yet to recognise the need to fight. Before the decade was out Ealing Studios would be finished, and an anti-establishment movement begun in literature and fanned by the neo-realist film successes of Italy and France would utterly change the face of British cinema. Richard Harris, needing to express a duality of character that ill fitted Limerick, would find a perfect home here, at the forefront of a blind, bursting movement to change the world.

But Harris's arrival in London didn't feel like good timing. He stepped off the boat train from Holyhead wide-eyed, unsure of his own emotions in the capital of the colonial empire he had been taught, in history class, to despise. But his heart was full of wonder, not hate. He was alone and utterly at peace in his own company, having learned the benefits of isolation. His own internal universe, he later said, was always fuller than other people's lives. His first urge wasn't the pursuit of food and shelter, rather a desire to see the historical sights. Speakers' Corner was his first port of call and he stood entranced for hours, his few belongings crammed in a grip at his feet. It reminded him of the Kilkee amphitheatre, where unrestricted art thrived. But it was different in a critical way. Limerick was a tight-woven community of seventy thousand people of one race; London was a mishmash and the voice it aired at Speakers' Corner was polyglot. Harris delighted in the many tones and hues of the Park – and missed his check-in time at the YMCA, where he had hoped to spend the first few weeks. Instead, he hailed a black cab and tipped the driver to find him the cheapest decent lodgings. The cabbie obliged and Harris later laughed at the irony of searching for a dosshouse in a cab. 'This weird poise between penury and prosperity was symbolic of my future life.'

He had applied in writing both to the Central School of Speech and Drama and to the London Academy of Music and Dramatic Art (LAMDA). Central was the plum hope and he went there for his audition call on his second day in London. Before he crossed the threshold he was aware that the stakes were against him. He was 25; the average Central student was seventeen or eighteen. Till the end of his days Harris relished the story of his rejection. 'Those were the days of the pretty boy [actor],' he said. 'Fellows like me were not in vogue. I walked in, with all these aristocratic-looking ladies and gentlemen sitting looking back at me, saying, "What are you going to do for us, young man?" So I said, "Shakespeare." I did my audition piece, and they said, "What right do you think you have to enter our profession?" So I looked up and said, "The same right as you have judging me . . ." Then a bell rang and a little man came in and they put me out.' Harris frequently broadcast varying accounts of this story, venting his anti-institution feelings colourfully. Whichever way, he was turned down. 'His Irish accent wasn't particularly noticeable,' said a fellow Irish actor, Joe Lynch, who met and befriended him in London at the time. 'But he had the Irish way about him. He swaggered. He talked louder than "normal people" and he was brash. He made no apologies for himself. You got the impression of a fellow who was happy with himself and was waiting for the world to discover his greatness.'

After an interview, his second choice, LAMDA, accepted him and he was enrolled as a day student. He took a bedsit in a house in the Earls Court Road and sat down immediately to budget his two-year course. The booty from his aunt's shares allowed him £3 10s. (£3.50) a week for food, rent and fees and he wrote home expressing victory. It was just a matter of time now before his theatrical success, fame and fortune found him. If Milly viewed this deduction with scepticism she was probably mollified by assurances that Dickie would not be an actor, but, he wrote, a director. Acting, wrote Dickie, was the door opener; directing was the objective. For Milly, according to Harris, 'director' conjured 'dark-suited gentlemen managing mills', and smacked of respectable industry. But not everyone at home was mollified. According to Dermot Foley, old Ivan regarded unfolding events with a shortening fuse. 'It's just as well Dick was well out of his reach,' said Foley. 'If it had been an acting school in Limerick or Dublin he would have changed [Harris's] mind.' Harris himself later said in surly regret, 'I never got to know my parents, and they never got to know me.' Communication with Limerick assumed a pattern of staccato bursts, dictated by the new nomadic world of Harris's London liberty. 'I recall the first months as wide-eyed hysteria,' said Harris. 'Freedom from TB, from the "valley of squinting windows" that was Limerick suburbia, freedom from Catholic restriction . . . all of it drove me wild. I loved it. I loved new people, new food, new encounters. And the women. The acting world attracted a breed of woman that was new to me: wild women, gypsies, beatnik women. I loved them all because they spoke a sort of poetry, and poetry was what I was about. I wrote down everything I could on matchboxes and cigarette packets. All my thoughts and fears. I didn't smoke then, so I gathered boxes like a magpie and kept a record of who I was shagging and what was happening. I was a love machine at full crank – and LAMDA came second [in my attentions] for a while.' For several months Harris shifted from flat to flat as love affairs dictated, never settling for long.

LAMDA holds no record of Harris's labours, but the actors like Lynch who knew him then talk of unusual energy, his restlessness and his determination. Frank Windsor, a contemporary who would shortly star alongside Harris in a breakthrough movie, voices the general impression of LAMDA-era Harris: 'The minute you met him you thought one word: dynamism. He was not conventional in the sense of a newcomer finding his feet. He gave off an aura of command, like, Look at me! Listen to me! I have arrived!' After six months at LAMDA Harris was bored with the non-progress. James Booth, a RADA (Royal Academy of Dramatic Art) student who grew to know him well on the pub scene, observed, 'His aptitude was based on an unusual confidence that bordered on offensive arrogance and probably had a lot to do with the relief of surviving tuberculosis. Then again, maybe some people are just born with [confidence] in that degree. He was loud and sure of himself and made London his own. His friends weren't only fellow actors. They were musicians and bums. That was something that stood out: he had a need to keep in touch with the average Joe, which a lot of toffee-nosed academy trainees who take their "art" so seriously weren't inclined to do.'

In Limerick, Len Dineen remembered, Harrris had always 'entertained a fixation with the colourful underdog. There was, for example, a big itinerant community, with a lot of drifters peddling wares from door to door. Toasty McKnight was among the famous ones. He was a crooning tramp around the pub scene, always begging a drink, always eating chips and singing in doorways. Generally, people avoided him. Dickie didn't. In fact, Toasty, along with oddballs like Alf, was one of the cherished pals.' Both Dineen and Manuel Di Lucia observed that Harris's fondness for oddball characters was strategic. According to Dineen, the friendship with Toasty was 'a study-and-copy routine' that allowed Dickie to perfect mimicry: 'Dickie was affectionate, without a doubt, but he also turned Toasty into a party piece.' Manuel Di Lucia saw a similar aping expertise at work in Kilkee: 'My father had all the caricature attributes of the traditional Italian and Dickie worked on [him] till he had the mannerisms and the accent to a "T". The family chip shop attracted some undesirables – and that's where Dickie's mimicry came in useful. I remember him creeping up behind some noisy yob and railing at him in ferocious pseudo-Italian, which scared the bejaysus out of the fella and sent him on his way.'

Robert Young, an actor-singer whom Harris befriended at LAMDA, has recorded their early days there as a joyous experience, which neither took too seriously and which was distinguished by late arrivals for rehearsal classes and outbursts of self-assertion from Harris. James Booth recalled other fellow students complaining about Harris's upstart nature: 'You could certainly credit him as being "colourful", if by colourful one means loud-mouthed. He was legendary in his own way even then because he was an attention-grabber as opposed to a serious student. Basically, the word was, he was this most awful dose of hot air who had just blown in from Ireland, and you avoided him unless you had a thick skin, an astonishing sense of humour and a willingness to keep buying pints.'

But Harris wasn't all hot air. Unlike most, he was prepared to put his money where his mouth was in terms of challenging the stodginess of LAMDA's traditionalist, almost Elizabethan cur-riculum. Unprompted – indeed strongly warned off the notion – he decided at the end of his first year to pool finances and mount his own production at a major London venue. James Booth, among many, was astonished by the bravado: 'To be honest, it floored me. He was half trained – and that is being kind to him – and bereft of any substantial financial support, like all of us trying to make our way. But suddenly he decided to launch himself as a producer-director. You have to imagine this gawky kid, half educated, knowing a little bit about Stanislavsky and the Method [acting theory], but not much more, suddenly advertising in *The Stage* to cast a classic at a West End theatre. It'd be the equivalent of some jumped-up kid announcing a rock-and-roll stadium world tour with a banjo and a microphone.'

Even Harris was unclear of his motivation and urgency. 'It felt right, I don't know why. Perhaps it came out of the changing spirit of the times. I was fascinated by the underground element of contemporary cinema. I wasn't educated specifically in where and how the Method came into play in American theatre in the thirties, then in American cinema in the early fifties. I just saw it. I saw how movies looked different with Monty Clift and Brando, and I liked it. It was raw and provocative. Kind of crude, with the smell of real life that contrasted [with] all those pantomime cowboys like John Wayne. In London, in the late fifties, there was an underground buzz happening – that was the buzz that would spark John Braine, John Osborne, Pinter – but it was a slow fuse. I saw it happening, and I wanted to be part of it. But I wasn't qualified. I shot from the hip. I just got sick and tired of old fogeys in grey suits telling me to reread Shakespeare and pronounce my verbs like Olivier. I just said, "Fuck off, I'm doing my own play. Buy a ticket if you want to see how Dickie Harris does it."'

Harris based himself at the Troubadour, his favoured pub-diner-haven in the Old Brompton Road, and set up a corner-table production office with a pint at his elbow and the *Evening Standard* as an elbow rest. Robert Young was his PA, and a half-dozen wide boys from LAMDA served as runners. The Irving Theatre off Leicester Square (now defunct) was chosen as the venue, mainly because its financial difficulties rendered it affordable (it soon became a striptease joint). The play chosen – which he would direct but not star in – was Clifford Odets' *The Country Girl*, also a hit movie starring Grace Kelly and Bing Crosby. On Broadway some years before, the play had won a Tony for the actress Uta Hagen; Hollywood stayed faithful to it, and it went on to earn an Oscar for Grace Kelly. Harris watched the movie, examined the Odets original and the Bill Perlberg screenplay – and decided on a total revamping. His production became *Winter Journey*, something altogether new.

Georgie Elgin, the suffering heroine defending her alcoholic actor husband, underwent dramatic metamorphosis, but the girl's role remained critical. In Harris's judgment, no one at LAMDA matched the part, so he sank more cash into a targeted ad in *The Stage*. Two hundred hopefuls responded, and Harris sat through two weeks of auditions at the Troubadour in despair. 'That was an enormous lesson for me, because I understood for the first time the deception of the acting business. So many people are attracted to it because it appears either easy or ego-comforting. Usually, it's the opposite. But those auditions turned up every variety of eccentric you could imagine. One woman especially horrified me. I told her the play was called *Winter Journey* and she insisted on singing "Winter Wonderland" for me – ten times. Made you wonder about human nature.'

The girl eventually cast was a chance find. Elizabeth Rees-Williams was a first-year RADA student, the daughter of the Liberal peer Lord Ogmore, who had found out about the play from Peter Prowse, a drinking friend of Harris's cast in the male lead role in *Winter Journey*. Prowse had picked up Elizabeth hitching across London and stumbled into conversation about respective career ambitions. The happy coincidence of shared interests brought her to the Troubadour and Harris's audition table.

Elizabeth's sky-blue eyes and the Nordic looks that belied her Welsh background enthralled Harris from the moment they met at the Troubadour, though Elizabeth later recalled that at first he treated her 'brusquely'. Harris himself recalled, 'She was icy or mysterious in a way that mesmerised me. I think I was defensive. I thought, She's lovely, so watch out!' James Booth remembered friends reporting Harris waxing eloquent about his new find, emphasising her 'mesmeric blue eyes and sexy body. In my view, his interest wasn't all professional. Then again, that in itself is a story as old as time on the casting scene.' Booth knew Elizabeth, had shared RADA classes with her, and reckoned her a poor actress: 'Her style, her approach, her sense of herself was outdated. She talked very plummy at a time when the acting world was looking for down-to-earth authenticity. She carried that sense of "the privileged" about her, which was annoying. It was widely known that RADA would drop her. She was lucky. She auditioned for Richard just before the RADA executioners came in.'

To be fair to Elizabeth, her instincts counterbalanced her ambitions and she wrote frankly in her autobiography of her limitations: that she loved theatre, but always knew she was no great shakes as an actress. Even in hindsight, Harris found it hard to judge her, or her thespian capabilities, objectively: 'First off, what did I know? I was a complete newcomer, basing everything on what I'd seen people like Cyril Cusack or the Abbey Players do in Limerick. I was also mad about her from the word go. Both [Peter Prowse and Robert Young] were also crazy about her, so I concentrated on the big seduction. I suppose you could say my first theatrical venture was compromised by that: I adored my leading lady and was more interested in impressing her than impressing the scouts from the National Theatre.'

The Troubadour owners, Michael and Sheila van Bloeman, patrons of out-of-work actors, hosted the all-hours rehearsals that unfolded over the next six weeks. In Harris's judgment these amounted to 'a free-for-all. I barely knew where an act ended and a scene began.' The communal inexperience hardly helped: Elizabeth was nineteen, the rest of the cast all under twenty-five, and mostly first-year students of either LAMDA or RADA. Only Harris's age seniority lent any gravitas to the production.

Revealingly, Harris made light of this hugely ambitious venture in his correspondence home. Neither Dermot Foley nor any of the other musketeers knew about it, and the newer friends from the College Players were not kept apprised of developments. Which was just as well. As it turned out, *Winter Journey* opened midweek and closed before the following weekend. Audience and press interest – and LAMDA interest – was negligible, and in one fell swoop all Harris's directorial dreams, and his cash legacy, were gone.

What followed was a rambling period of 'life in the gutter' that Harris has variously described as heaven and hell. At first he scrambled the 2s. 6d. (12½ pence) a night rent for dosshouse accommodation, then the van Bloemans gave him the marble counter of the Troubadour on which to lay his head. When the improving spring weather invited him 'out of the freezer' he slept under piles of coats on the Embankment. Later he camped in doorways along Earls Court, close to LAMDA, where the formal studies continued, if haltingly. When he collapsed from hunger at the academy, Robert Young offered him accommodation at his small flat in Nevern Place. Here at last was consistent companionship, home comforts and a bed under which to store his poems. 'I was very grateful to Robert, for the hand of friendship extended. That bedsit became "the nest". We had a sink, a two-ring stove, a kettle and two beds with a pillow and a blanket each. It was austerity *par excellence*, and I felt like a king.'

Nevern Place became the laboratory of courtship for Harris and Elizabeth. 'I wined and dined her there, usually asking Robert to disappear for a few hours – and he always obliged.' Within weeks, the love affair to end all love affairs was the talking point at LAMDA and beyond. The key to this passionate mutual attraction was obvious to all who knew Harris and Elizabeth: according to Booth, they were both rebellious spirits, both 'outsiders', and both buoyantly romantic. Harris also admitted to the attraction of the 'forbidden fruit' aura that hung about Elizabeth: 'As far as I was concerned, she was next door to royalty. I was always trying to figure out whether I should call her "My Lady" – which I mostly did.' Another LAMDA friend remembered, 'Their relationship was unusually passionate. Dickie was always grand and demanding in his gestures, but she was also a strong, demanding woman. They should really have fought a lot more than they did – in fact, they shouldn't have survived one another – but, like the best love stories, it just magically worked.'

Elizabeth Rees-Williams did not call on her family for support. Like Harris, she was obstinately independent – if more doubtful of her future in theatre. She continued to audition widely and take whatever work she could get, all the time keeping half an eye on Harris's fortunes. 'From the beginning she adored him,' said the theatre actor-producer Godfrey Quigley, soon-to-be friend and co-star. 'She made a decision that her career ambitions would take second place to his. *He* was the talent, and the personality, and the future. She told me that he was the turning point in her life. And, I suspect, she was the turning point in his.'

Liz recalled the limbo period at the end of LAMDA without regret. The days of scurrying through dingy rooms, making whatever time they could together, were also warmth-filled days of 'making love, playing Sam Kenton records, and always reading. Sometimes Richard worked on his poems . . .' He also took time to introduce her to Joyce and Yeats and the literary discoveries of the TB years. Dylan Thomas became 'an obsession' and he read aloud to her – in his usual stammering, but immensely affecting style – from *Under Milk Wood* and Thomas's poetry notebooks.

What Harris calls his 'starvation period' came to a close when Joan Littlewood and her radical Theatre Workshop Company entered his life. What initially appeared as a chance one-off casting in one of her Stratford productions grew quickly into a long, edifying relationship that outdid LAMDA in every way. 'It was down to luck,' Harris said. 'One lunchtime a friend bought me a cider in a bar, and I overheard two people talking in the cubicle behind us. They were obviously theatricals, and one mentioned that Joan Littlewood hadn't yet filled some parts in a production. That was enough for me. I borrowed fourpence for the telephone call and rang her. She was out, but I spoke to the company's general manager, Gerry Raffles.' Raffles told Harris the role unfilled was for a fifty-year-old. But Harris wasn't deterred. 'I *look* fifty,' he told Raffles – and Raffles smiled at the blarney and summoned him to the Theatre Royal, Stratford East.

Harris encountered Littlewood at a peak moment in her career. Just the year before, Bertholt Brecht had trusted Littlewood with the first production of his *Mother Courage*; its success prompted the emerging Brendan Behan to give her *The Quare Fellow*, recently premiered and hugely applauded in Dublin. A vastly revised version of *The Quare Fellow,* a hard-hitting, purposefully controversial sociopolitical commentary, had been a summer hit at Stratford East and was now transferring to the Comedy Theatre for a bigger staging. Eric Ogle, cast as Mickser, had fallen out owing to illness and it was this role that Littlewood was recasting at the last minute. Harris remembered that Littlewood didn't even bother to audition him. 'She looked at me – the rough cut of me – and heard me speak and said, "Yes, you'll do. You're a Mickser."' The fee was £15 a week.

Harris's part wasn't big – no more than fifty lines in the middle of three verbose acts – but the attention-grabbing nature of the play, a strident indictment of capital punishment, ensured he made his mark. Thirty years later Jim Sheridan, the director of Harris's renaissance movie, *The Field*, commended especially Harris's way with script: 'It's a unique skill. He doesn't just learn his part and leave it to [the director]. He learns everyone's lines and intellectualises everything. That, he told me, was the way he always worked. Some of it was down to insecurity, maybe his dyslexia, but the end result was impressive to anyone who benefited, as I did, from it.' On *The Quare Fellow*, Harris himself was the main beneficiary. 'Littlewood saw that I was "a presence" – those were the words she used to my face – and she promised me more work with the Theatre Royal group, which was actively acquiring new talent at that time. The best part of it for me was the pay. I hadn't a dime. And her group was offering fees above Equity rates.'

By Christmas 1956 Harris had around him the first framework of career and domestic bliss. He had the hopes of the Theatre Workshop and the £6 a week retainer it would yield, the hint of West End acceptance, and a beautiful and sophisticated girlfriend. 'That proved tricky, because we were living like man and wife, but I was holding out [against marriage]. Then [Elizabeth] just popped the question. It was, Let's get on with it! No one lives for ever! And I said, "All right, why not?"' But it wasn't plain sailing. Harris had Limerick to tackle and, much trickier in his recall, the Ogmores. At Christmas he took Elizabeth home to Ireland for the first time and made the introductions. Milly approved of her breeding, but openly disdained her Protestant background. In her memoir *Love, Honour and Dismay*, Elizabeth recorded nothing of the marriage tactics beyond the general remark that neither Harris's family nor his friends cared at all about his London life. 'It was thin ice all the way,' said Harris, 'but I had developed a thick skin [regarding family approvals].'

Back in London he faced the Ogmores in a formal rite of proposal. He borrowed a suit, a fresh shirt, a tie and a pair of Robert Young's shoes. In an oft-repeated humorous version of events, he could find no one to lend him socks. The ensuing meeting with Lord and Lady

Ogmore was, said Harris, memorable for his sweating attempts to keep his trouser legs tugged down, lest the full extent of his poverty be revealed. Lady Ogmore give 'a sort of wail of despair' when the plan for a springtime marriage was announced, and Lord Ogmore insisted that Harris couldn't marry his daughter until he could afford to keep her. 'But I handled that one easily. I was a thespian, dear boy, wasn't I! I could command high fees at Stratford. I had wonderful contacts, you know. Old Ralphie Richardson and Johnny Gielgud and all those splendid theatre queers . . .' There was some substance in this swaggering: within weeks Peter Brook – supported by the playwright Arthur Miller, no less – cast Harris prominently (though in the background) in *A View from the Bridge*. 'Of course I told [the Ogmores] I built that fucking bridge.'

In spite of interfamily grumbles, the wedding went ahead as planned on 7 February 1957 at the Church of Notre Dame in Leiscester Square. Milly had threatened a no-show, but in fact there was a reasonable Harris family turn-out, Ivan excepted. In his place, Ivan sent an envelope containing £25 as a honeymoon gift. The ensuing reception at the House of Lords, attended by three hundred guests, mostly Ogmore friends and family, was memorable for Harris for the ironies. 'It's like a painting by Magritte, when you think of it. Dick Harris from the Ennis Road, this chancer from the oul sod, traipsing around with the titled aristocracy. [Elizabeth and I] were rubbing shoulders with Lord So-and-so and Lady Whatsit and talking horse and hound, and we hadn't a clue. We were living with Robert Young – that was the marriage home – and subsisting, just hanging on the bread line. What we did have, though, was good friendships and high opinions of ourselves . . . so we kept up.' Helen Fahy, an Ennis Road neighbour whose home overlooked Overdale, recalled seeing Elizabeth and Harris on a home visit around this time and observing 'two very slick and rich-looking people. She wore the clothes of a starlet and had silken blonde hair. Dickie strutted like the world belonged to him. They were a fairy-tale couple in our eyes.'

In reality, wedded life was every bit as tough as what had gone before. Littlewood's promise of regular employment with the Theatre Royal had yet to gel, and Harris's income from the likes of

A View from the Bridge was a pittance. Conjuring money from thin air, they rented a small bedsit in Paddington and, briefly shared it with an out-of-work Irish actor, Donal Donnelly. Then, when Liz found rep work in Blackpool, temporary accommodation was found for Harris with the Ogmores at Queen's Gate. At this low ebb Elizabeth came into a small inheritance, which she immediately invested in a lease on 'a poky Earls Court flat above an outsize underwear shop – which felt like a palace, because it was ours and ours alone'. The flat was draughty but roomy, and cost £6 10s. a week. Harris knew they could never continue to pay the rent unless he bolted down regular work, so he pressed Littlewood until she committed, finally granting him the weekly six quid he'd been banking on. 'But it felt like it was too late. Our outgoings were more than eight pounds weekly and, to complicate matters, Lil got pregnant within a couple of weeks.'

According to Joe Lynch, Harris never stopped smiling throughout these trials. 'I think it was what you might call achievement delirium. No one believed he would rise to the top any faster than any of the rest of us who were trying to make it as Irish actors in London. But, inside a year or two, Dickie had put on a West End play, got himself cast in a Behan classic, got himself contracted to Littlewood and married someone we all took to be a princess. Of course he was laughing. The rest of us were still holding begging bowls outside the BBC.' The more Lynch got to know Harris during this time, the more he became fascinated by his 'unique emotional chemistry. He wasn't like the rest of us. He had an emotional hair trigger that worked in a funny way. The slightest encouragement could lift him to near-hysteria, just as the mildest criticism would plunge him into despair. But then he'd twist it. Adversity – like having no money when Lil was pregnant – would lift him up. And then he was unstoppable. His happiness was particularly infectious. You didn't really have a choice with him. When he was on top, the whole world shared it. You just had to give in to him, because he was the ultimate seducer.'

Joan Littlewood's Workshop group was the perfect turf for Harris, centred as it was on innovation, experiment and upending the status quo. Littlewood herself was rebellious beyond even Harris –

London-educated, Manchester-bred, banned from the BBC and ENSA, the armed forces entertainments branch, for her leftist political views. She had started in Manchester street theatre, then set up the Workshop with her life-long partner, Gerry Raffles, in 1945. In 1953 the Workshop took over the Theatre Royal in the unfashionable East End and Littlewood concentrated on revamping the classics, producing, directing and starring. International acclaim came in the middle fifties with an invitation to participate in the Theatre of Nations festival in Paris and a general media acknowledgment that the Workshop had effectively established a London scene akin to the 'off-Broadway' circuit. Over the next ten years three Littlewood shows won the coveted Best Production Award. Her style, and the dictates of the Workshop, were signature designs. The drama spectrum was broad, but deviant from the 'establishment norms'. She mixed Brecht with music hall, social commentary with song and dance, Elizabethan drama with the beatniks. Harris loved it all, found himself 'like a kid in a sweet shop. Jesus! This was Kilkee and the Green House all in one.' There was also, he said, the immediate self-recognition that here he could flex the duality of his nature, the masculine/feminine balance first exercised with Betty Brennan. 'In theory, this was heaven. I could be Tarzan one day, and wear a skirt the next. That was the life I wanted.'

But, once in the Workshop, Harris hit a wall. 'Littlewood was marvellous. I will never withhold the credit – that it was she who taught me everything there is to know about acting. But it was frustrating convincing her to *let me do it*! For a long, long time I was lost in the wings. I was holding up the props [*sic*] like I did on *A View from the Bridge*. And that just wasn't me. I didn't like hanging around. I was too old, for starters.' In September, after four months, Littlewood cast him in her radically truncated modern-dress version of *Macbeth*, booked to tour Europe and Russia. Harris wrote blithely home to Limerick, describing this 'major career breakthrough'. Milly, Harmay and the brothers were, said Harmay's husband Jack Donnelly, 'electrified' to hear that Dickie was already headlining Shakespeare on the London stage. 'I think they had visions of him in neon lights, playing Macbeth or Macduff.'

Harris later told *Profile* magazine, 'I thought: Shakespeare! This is it! This is really it. So I wrote to all my friends in Ireland: You must come! Hurry! Everybody come. Mother, father, brothers, aunts, the rats from the mill. Be up there at the front of the stalls!'

But Harris was the Thane of Ross, appearing briefly in only four scenes. The dishonour, as he described it to *Profile*, was unbearable. In his Limerick-coloured version the Thane of Ross had not four scenes but four lines: 'I had to walk down, say these four lines, wave my arm, go off stage right. So I'm standing at the back, all dressed up in uniform and sword. Suddenly my cue comes and I pick up the sword . . . but I can't remember a damn line. And I can hear my mother in the front say, "Isn't he marvellous?"'

After the London try-outs *Macbeth* left for Zürich, where, in Gerry Raffles's written account, it was 'met with cheers and boos'. Moscow proved better but the general critical response was poor and, for a first-time touring actor, disconcerting. When the troupe arrived home, Littlewood cheered up Harris by casting him immediately in the upcoming *You Won't Always Be on Top*, an early Angry Young Man effort written by a Hastings builder's labourer, Henry Chapman. The play was proposed as a raunchy, ad-libbed diatribe, insubstantial in script, but determined subversion. Harris overlooked any shortcomings in his enthusiasm for – finally – major casting. 'That was one of those circumstances where some intuition tells you trouble is on the way, but your are too busy congratulating yourself for your good fortune to be objective. I should have looked hard at the content and seen that play was bound for trouble.'

It was at this time that James Booth joined the Workshop on a regular basis and got to know Harris well. 'He really could be a bastard and, if you had no patience for understanding, quite dislikable,' said Booth unapologetically. 'He was contentious. He liked to argue about everything from horse racing to the price of a pint. I think it went back to his childhood. I think it was about parental pressure and the dyslexia that he was sick and tired of being bashed for and covering up. On the other hand, there is no doubt in my mind that he had the kind of chip on his shoulder that says something. Till then, he'd had no real big roles, but his manner told you he felt he was the future star.'

While Booth was chalking up this observation, Harris was considering quitting the business. Approaching Christmas, despite the casting in *You Won't Always Be on Top*, he and Elizabeth were all but starving. To pay for a Christmas hamper, they hocked their wedding presents. 'Lil wasn't getting any jobs and we were way overextended. All that kept me going was something I'd been told by [Littlewood]. Lee Strasberg [the cutting-edge American actor coach] had seen *The Quare Fellow* earlier in the year and said my performance was the sharpest he'd seen during his entire visit to London. Strasberg was of the Method school that I looked up to, and I was bowled over by the compliment. That one gesture kept me believing.'

According to Harris, impatience for movement caused him to 'argue and roar' through Stratford East, 'regularly biting the hand that fed me'. He was, he insisted, deeply respectful of Littlewood and Raffles, but 'too eccentric in myself not to be agitated by their lunacy'. In one incident, warmly recalled by all, Harris ended up dumping a sack of cement on Littlewood's head. 'That was a one-off,' said Booth. 'Mostly, Mickser – which was the only name we knew him by – was well behaved with her because he had to be. She held the keys to his future.'

The sparring with Littlewood through that autumn and winter kept everyone on their toes. 'I used to think [Littlewood] was trying to break me, because there was always some decision that seemed to insult or challenge me or annoy me. Like this show piece she suddenly cast me in. I read it and thought to myself, Christ, anything but this! This was a terribly *Britishy* piece of casting, not at all me. I could do accents, sure. But this one was drawing-room *Eeenglish*. I sweated and worried and I didn't think I could pull it off. I went to her and said, "I cannot do this." And she heard me out very impassively and said, "Come to the theatre on Monday, alone."'

When Harris did, Littlewood, seated in the stalls, told him to strip naked on the empty stage. Then she told him to 'clothe yourself in the character'. Peter Hay has written in his *Theatrical Anecdotes* (1989) that Littlewood's genius was that of director as psychologist:

'If she thinks an actor needs putting down, she'll put him down. But she won't come that boss-director [on him]. She is always saying, Don't let yourself be *produced*!' Harris didn't understand her modus: 'I thought she was off her fucking head. But then the ground moved. I was stark bollock naked, talking like Jeeves and thinking, This is the single most liberating experience I have ever had. This is better than sex.'

Ten years before, Harris had joyously romped naked at the Pollock Holes in Kilkee. Manuel Di Lucia remembered his un-Irish ease with skinny-dipping. Twenty years later the actor John Phillip Law, co-starring in the Sri Lankan jungle with Harris on Bo Derek's *Tarzan, The Ape Man*, spoke of Harris's 'brazen resistance to trousers and underpants. It was quite amazing to find all of us comfortable in our Brooks Brothers jungle wear while Richard romped round with his cock swinging at the lunch buffet, saying, "Excuse my balls, it's just such a lovely day . . . !' Harris said, 'Joan Littlewood put nudity into context for me. Just the obvious: that we are all naked under our clothes, and nudity is normality. [Littlewood] defetishised nudity for me, and I thank her for that.'

During the winter, along with *You Won't Always Be on Top*, came casting in Edgar de Rocha Mirianda's *And the Wind Blew* – 'a crease-browed, costumey thing that was quite dull', said James Booth and which Gerry Raffles claimed 'almost closed down the Workshop'. Immediately after came the romantic lead in Pirandello's *Man, Beast and Virtue*. This, in hard terms, was the turning point. Joe Lynch recalled, 'You have to understand that most of the Workshop people, like acting groups everywhere, failed in terms of "star" status. That's not to say they didn't want to achieve it. I believe ninety per cent of the people who join groups like Joan's want celebrity. They want *to be* Olivier or Marilyn Monroe. But they fail. But Dickie didn't. He broke through fast. Partly because his timing was good – it was good to be Irish in London then, with Behan and the "kitchen-sink" drama happening – and partly because he *demanded* attention. After he did *You Won't Always Be on Top* and *Man, Beast and Virtue*, people were talking about him, remembering his name. It wasn't "that big-mouthed Limerick fella" any more. It was ol' Dickie in Pirandello. That was the time, I knew, he had his chance to spring. And he did spring out. He went immediately for television – which in turn led to his movie breaks.'

Drinking pints with Harris at The Railway pub, a Workshop hangout, James Booth heard the master plan unfold: 'Harris wanted television. It was the inevitable next step that would take him to a wider audience and it was also the next step to better money. He was so bloody-minded and ferocious about it. He wanted it all. And he was not without talent, let's remember.'

Harris was appearing in Pirandello at the Lyric Theatre in Hammersmith at Christmas when his TV chance came. It was, he told *Woman's Own* in 1965, a depressed time, despite the progress with Littlewood. He had come to London, he said, 'determined to find my crown', but poverty was destroying him. He was also depressed by the news from Limerick: Rank, the ever-expanding business empire, had been 'ghost-labelling' Harris Mills flour for years; now, sensing Ivan's imminent collapse, they were planning a hostile takeover. 'Neither Jimmy nor young Ivan could do anything about it. I thought Rank were fuckers, because my family had built their own empire and Rank undercut it. There was no support or compassion. It was just ruthless business, and I resented it and took it personally. I vowed to get back at [Rank] and I did. It took me five or six years, but I ended up screwing them for millions of pounds which, given, the injustice of how they treated [my father], they deserved.'

Edgy in anticipation of the birth of a first child, Harris fully immersed himself in Pirandello's Paulino, the vortex of *Man, Beast and Virtue.* Both Booth and Joe Lynch remember Paulino as 'over the top'. But Clifford Owen, the London-born television director recently celebrated for *Johnny Belinda,* sat in the first-night audience and saw magic. He was struck, he later said, by Harris's booming passion and his 'authentic' Irishness. Owen had been commissioned to direct the first play of the Irish-based actor-author Joseph O'Connor, called *The Iron Harp,* for Granada television. The script was sub-Behan, all about perfidy in the IRA during the Troubles, a script of quality that demanded authenticity in portrayals. Owen had already contracted a number of leading London-based Irish players,

among them Donal Donnelly and Maureen Connell, but he had yet
to cast Michael O'Riordan, the blind hero-rebel. From the stalls of
the Lyric, he knew he had found his man. After the performance, he
met Harris in the green room and invited him to an interview at
Granada's Warwick Street offices the next day.

Harris smashed the gas meter at the flat for his bus fare to Granada
and dashed across London only to find himself kept waiting by
Owen. According to *Woman's Own*, when he finally faced the
director after an hour's delay, he screamed in his face, 'I don't know
why it is that so many producers and directors treat actors like
Hogarthian puppets!' Harris later described the encounter less
eloquently: 'I told him he was a fucking pain in the arse and he liked
that. He liked the aggression, and felt it belonged to the part. And that
is how I got the part.' The fee was the standard drama fee – 55
guineas, plus 22 guineas to cover rehearsals – and Harris 'fell on my
knees and kissed the ground at his feet for that loot'.

Of a cast of fifteen, only three performers, all more widely
experienced, received higher fees than Harris (Robert Urquhart, the
star, came out tops, paid 150 guineas), a measure of his growth. But
Harris pretended to ignore the money and concentrated on the script.
'Cliff told me afterwards that when I came into his office he thought
I was weighed down by all the crosses and cares of the world and that
was spot on. And, like Pirandello, I put that energy into *The Iron
Harp*, which had a little of Chekhov in it, I felt. I didn't know about
cameras and television but I had started to know about drama per se,
and I saw I could do a lot with the character, who was a Republican
of the type I was well familiar with.' Harris's comfort, and the
connection he made with Owen, lent enthusiasm that pepped the
entire production. Owen trusted him, and even agreed, on Harris's
request, to casting James Booth in a small role. Booth had one scene
opposite Harris.

Rehearsals for *The Iron Harp* started at the Mahatma Gandhi Hall
off Fitzroy Square on Sunday, 17 March 1957; then the group
entrained for Manchester. On Tuesday a full-dress rehearsal took
place, and Harris's performance – amid the technical maze of TV –
was, according to Booth, 'relaxed, coherent and totally at home'.

Booth elaborated: 'Mickser always liked to preen and pose. I used to mock him: he was the one actor who spent half the day performing for himself in the mirror. His big take-off was Brando – he was always doing Brando in the mirror, directing himself like a movie director. But it was really just prepping, when you look back on it. We mocked him, but when it came to doing television he was readier than any of us. The mirror was really the camera all along, and he delivered his performance at Granada like he was playing to himself in the mirror. I used to say Mickser had a great love affair with himself. Now I realise that that's a great starting point for TV stars. The moral is: get used to mirrors.'

On Wednesday the play was transmitted live at prime time from Studio 6 of the Manchester TV Centre, and Richard Harris's face was flashed across the nation. His part was as substantial as anything he had played with Littlewood, and all the more remarkable because it was, noted Owen, intuitively restrained in the way television demanded. Owen's gamble paid off. The crew applauded, said Harris, the second the tapes stopped rolling.

It was the *Daily Mirror* that first acknowledged a potential international star. For the columnist Richard Shear, *The Iron Harp* was 'an intensely moving document of human beings caught up in war', where the central relationships defined the complex political and metaphysical values. For Shear, Harris, playing an IRA prisoner verbally jousting with his British guard, was the play's highlight: 'His was a first-class performance, rich with the tenderness of O'Connor's words.' Elsewhere, in a sidebar, the *Mirror* advised its readers to watch Richard Harris's progress: 'He is regarded by Granada as a real find – and they have given him the chance to jump from obscurity to stardom.'

Harris relished the notices and took Elizabeth out to celebrate when he got back to London. For five days' work he had earned £80 – more than ten times the Workshop rate. The economics of television were wonderful – inspirational – as were the looks of recognition and admiration from strangers in the street.

CHAPTER 4

Heaven and Hellraising

The overflowing legend of Hellraiser Harris, so efficiently broadcast by Richard Harris himself for thirty years, had its origins in his childhood. It was not, as many have suggested, a PR creation of false but marketable Errol Flynnery. Rather, he was, as Dermot Foley and his school chums insist, 'born to be wild'. In his early teens his nickname 'Prince Dick' owed as much to his attention-grabbing antics as to the supposed wealth of the Harris clan. 'He was incorrigible,' said Foley. 'If there was trouble to be found, Harris found it.' The Ringroses, Limerick neighbours and friends, still recall the horror of the turkey that disappeared off the table on Christmas Eve. And Harris himself admitted to stealing the West of Ireland Tennis Championship trophy on the eve of the final. When his father found it behind a chair in the parlour he exploded in rage and ordered his son to return it. Harris planted it in the loo at Cruise's Hotel and rang Williams Street police station with the anonymous tip-off. This kind of mischief won him attention, but regularly misfired. 'Dickie sailed close to the wind,' said an Ennis Road neighbour and ally. 'But all he was really scared of was making Ivan angry. The family tolerated his larking around – but there were limits. Once he was arrested for being drunk and disorderly in town and was taken to Williams Street police station. After a caution he was released, but the local press carried the story of "Harris Mills son arrested". This was despite his pleas to them not to run it. Ivan read the story and went mad. Dickie never forgave that newspaper for what happened. And I'm not sure Ivan ever forgave Dickie for the public embarrassment.'

But Harris couldn't help himself. 'He was addicted to fun in the way others are addicted to booze,' said Charlie St George. 'And he took the risks that went with it.' He also spoofed the fun when fun was absent. At the start of the fifties his adoration of Merle Oberon extended to embrace numerous dark-haired, Oberon-like visions of Hollywood pulchritude. Among them was Rita Gam, a gorgeous stage actress who had just broken through in Hollywood, acting opposite Ray Milland in *The Thief*. Gam's screen presence was unsubtle but dynamic and Harris was smitten. She was glamour with a raunchy edge, the combination he adored. Limerick's connections with Hollywood were nonexistent and Harris can never have hoped actually to meet Gam or any of his other heroines on the Limerick streets – but then the one-in-a-billion chance happened.

Rita Gam was returning to New York from a European promotional tour when her plane was diverted to Shannon with engine failure. Gam decided to spend a day shopping and Harris found her – by the sheerest fluke – ambling up O'Connell Street. Bold as brass, he asked her to join him for coffee at Cruise's Hotel, where his brother-in-law could, hopefully, coddle and impress her. Jack Donnelly, though, was bewildered. 'My problem with Dickie,' said Donnelly, 'was knowing what and which to believe. It was *always* a drama, and always an outsize tale.' For Gam, Dickie requested 'the full treatment, lay it all on, the linens and the china and the food and the drink.' Gam, claimed Harris, was bowled over by the munificence of this apparently well-to-do Limerick lad. Harris, for his part, had huge ulterior motive. 'I excused myself and slipped away and rang Dermot Foley at his father's chemist shop and asked him to get down there with a camera.' Foley obliged and 'drifted casually into Cruise's, all innocent like', to find his pal taking tea with a Hollywood goddess. The next day Harris arrived at the offices of the *Limerick Leader* with a manila envelope. Earl Connelly, the news journalist on duty, recalled Harris's offer: 'He came in and plonked these pictures on my desk. Here, says he, is a Hollywood exclusive: Rita Gam caught gallivanting round Ireland with her new Limerick companion.'

At Charlie St George's next day, Harris relished the resulting gossip: 'I milked it. And every so often I threw in a new angle, to keep the heat up.' Harris's ace in the hole was the hint that he had slept with Gam. 'That was the bottom line. Everyone wanted to know, since I was "walking out" with her, had I fucked her? They knew I was a randy bastard and they put two and two together. Finally I said, "Well, judge it yourself" – and I was probably holding my balls when I said that.' But, said Harris, the gag backfired. 'I was spoofing all these glorious pornographic details. But then Foley confronts me and says, "Harris, you're a fucking liar. You're telling the world you shagged her on such a day at such-and-such a time and you didn't – you couldn't have. Because at that precise time she was in my father's chemist buying sanitary towels!"'

In London, in the aftermath of the television breakthrough, Harris's yarn-spinning went into overdrive. Joe Lynch envied Harris's lust for yarns: 'Because he had a knack unlike anyone for turning dross to gold with the blarney. Yes, he'd had a first-up television success. But many actors do, and make nothing of it. But Dickie tuned it into the Academy Awards. I met him and congratulated him . . . and he gushed. *Everyone* wanted him overnight. The National Theatre was calling. Hollywood was on the phone. Marlon Brando sent a telegram. It was all rubbish, but it came at you with such enthusiasm that you were nodding, saying, Jesus, Dick, you're in clover. You knew it was bollocks. But he had such neck, you just forgave him everything.'

The power of puffery, gossip and scandal hit home in spring just after *The Iron Harp*. The previous October's production of *You Won't Always Be on Top* had attracted good audiences, but also the interest of the Lord Chamberlain, the government censor. In the course of preparing this down-to-earth play about brickies, Littlewood had sent the cast to real building sites, urging them to beef up on authentic street lingo. Harris met the challenge with relish and delivered what many rated as his finest stage performance yet as Mick the navvy. But the censorship arrangement with the Lord

Chamberlain's office allowed no script 'additions' once a play had been cleared for production. On 31 October and 1 November a representative from the Lord Chamberlain's office attended the show and witnessed Harris's verbal modifications – 'a damburst', said Harris, 'of cock-sucking cunt-licking arse-kicking fuckology'. As a result, Harris, Littlewood, Raffles and theatre licensee John Bury were visited by detectives in January 1958 and statements were taken. On Wednesday 16 April, just days after his television debut, Harris, along with the writer Henry Chapman, Littlewood, Raffles and Bury, was charged at West Ham Magistrates Court with breach of the peace. The charge read that they had 'unlawfully for hire presented parts of a new stage play . . . before such parts had been allowed by the Lord Chamberlain contrary to Section 15 of the Theatres Act 1843'. The maximum penalty was £500 for each of the two 'illegal' performances witnessed, plus closure of the theatre. Harris's amusement turned to rage. 'It was audacious. The thing was, they wanted to get Littlewood. The Workshop was becoming too popular, and it was anti-establishment.' Defiantly, along with the others, he spoke proudly to the press of his 'guilt', declaring a commitment to changing the antiquated rules of modern theatre. A defence fund was launched by Raffles and an open letter appeared in *The Stage*, signed by the posse of champions: Peter Hall, Frith Banbury, Richard Findlater, the earl of Harewood, Wolf Mankowitz, Kenneth Tynan and Henry Sherek. When the trial came, West End actors flooded to the court in protest support.

In court, to a packed gallery, Ian Smith for the prosecution told how the approved plot had been purposefully corrupted; the third act was new and subversive. *The Times* reported Smith 'isolating a scene outside a building bearing the word "Gentlemen" in which a character called Mick [Harris] made a speech in which he appeared to be opening the building. During this speech he altered his voice and the accent to an imitation of what Sir Winston Churchill would have said if he had been called upon to open a public lavatory.' Mr Smith concluded that this interpretation was 'vulgar and blasphemous'. For the defence, Gerald Gardiner QC and Harold Lever MP, both appearing without fees, explained that the play aspired to nothing more than realism: 'These five [accused] persons have no money. The actors receive only £2 to £8 a week and the Company, which is limited to non-profit making, is overdrawn in the bank.' No apology was offered to the courts, Mr Gardiner indicated. The only reason his clients admitted guilt was that they acknowledged 'a breach of law which prohibited theatrical free speech'.

Joan Littlewood was the sole defence witness. She stated that the play was no great shakes but 'for the first time in England I saw written down without taste or discrimination the simple expression of working men on a building site on a wet Monday morning. For the first time I heard the speech of the English people put down with such beauty and simplicity as I've never heard it before.' The magistrate refused to sample this beauty and simplicity aurally, but accepted the guilty pleas and translated them into token fines. Raffles and Bury were each fined £5. Littlewood was fined £1 with costs, and Chapman and Harris given conditional discharges on payment of 11s. 6d. costs each.

At the 'victory' celebration in the bar of the Theatre Royal in Angel Lane afterwards there was standing room only. By its overkill action the Lord Chamberlain's office had resoundingly pushed public opinion in favour of the rebels. 'The Theatre Workshop had never attracted so much press and public attention,' said Harris. 'You couldn't have bought that publicity and for weeks that was all anyone wanted to talk about. It set wheels in motion. The money raised for the defence fund was a surplus, so it went into the formation of a Censorship Reform Committee, which met a week later at the Royal Court and really got the ball rolling for reform. [The whole business] taught me a lesson. *The Iron Harp* got me publicity and attention. But the government court case made me a star.'

For sure, the row gave Harris his first extensive national news coverage and his photograph appeared, smiling gamely between Littlewood and Chapman, all over the press. James Booth, among many, wasn't so sure that the publicity was good for him. 'During *You Won't Always Be on Top*, I brought a friend of mine, the [ICM] agent John McMichael, to see Dickie on stage. I thought he was shaping up well and McMichael could help . . . but, as it turned out, John didn't take Harris up then. Years later, of course, he did, and went on to be a powerful career navigator. But Dickie was blowing with the four winds, and he was as irrational as ever and, when the controversy started, I thought it was bad for him. I thought it distracted him from his learning curve and put false goals in front of him. It laid emphasis on media nonsense, and I'm not sure he ever recovered from the mind-set of trying to manipulate that as his main priority.'

Still fighting debts, with the baby imminent, Harris concentrated on his latest Littlewood work, in George Bernard Shaw's *Love and Lectures*. The Theatre Royal was busier than it had ever been, the audiences more receptive and – sans exaggeration – the big offers were finally trundling in. In May the Bristol Old Vic took him for a short spell playing Tommy Ledou alongside Peter O'Toole in James Forsyth's *The Pier*, a production remarkable mainly for the beginnings of a lifelong friendship with O'Toole – and the marathon alcoholic binges the Irishmen shared. Harris described this period as 'golden days. We kept each other up half the time, we never slept. It was days of chat and yarn-spinning and great, legendary boozing.' At one point Harris and O'Toole had refined their drinking schedules with a precision that allowed them to leave the theatre for a 'booze intermission down at the local' in the middle of the play and get back for curtain-up at the second half. 'But it was always destined to go wrong. One afternoon, we overstayed our welcome at the pub. A breathless kid, a stage hand, dashed in, screaming, "You're on! You're on!" – and O'Toole and I leapt to it. We made it back to the theatre in fifteen seconds and ran in back, through the stage door. It was my turn, but O'Toole outran me anyway, sped through the backstage door, past the crew, on to the stage . . . and took a nosedive, head-first into the audience. A woman in the front row sniffed his toxic breath and shouted, "My God, he's pissed drunk!" O'Toole, of course, was ready for her. He said, "You think this is bad? Wait till you see the other fella."'

The friendship with O'Toole, who called Harris Mickser with a Dublin-accented relish unlike anyone, was a template friendship for

Harris, rarely equalled throughout his life. 'O'Toole was a poet and a warrior. I loved every moment with him. We shared the passion for Munster Rugby and went to Twickenham whenever we could. We shared politics, art, society. He was my brother. I liked to travel, but I enjoyed nothing like an air flight with O'Toole. The Aer Lingus staff especially loved us. The air hostesses were like serial mistresses. It was always, "Hold him up, sweetheart, he's legless" – and they'd nurse us like mothers. The other side of him was the child. "Peter," I would say, "what will we be today?" And he'd say, "Mickser, we're kings."'

Drinking insidiously became Harris's main pastime. 'But no more than many scrounging actors,' said James Booth. 'Harris had a good capacity for booze – but I wasn't far behind. I think he liked the way drink loosened his and other people's inhibitions. And there was the great Irish tradition thing, too, all the late-night get-togethers for tales from home. That's probably what he shared with O'Toole, who was born in Connemara.' In the sixties Harris told the writer Tony Crawley, 'I never touch a drop when I'm happy.' But he added, 'It's a well-known fact that Irishmen are never happy.'

Booth eloquently described life in Harris's beloved Angel Lane, 'aflow with louts and literati attempting to make their way. The railway station next door maintained the nonstop pulse of reality and those who were out of work congregated to cadge fruit from the market stallholders outside. Faustian deals were made and forgotten, borrowed clothes disappeared with the borrower, songs were sung, girls made pregnant, careers billowed and folded.'

Suddenly Harris was beyond all this. Elizabeth gave birth to baby Damian in August, and Harris's paternal concern sent him scouting for a film agent to pump up his cash flow. By chance he was sitting in hotshot Jimmy Fraser's office pitching his case with Stanislavskian sincerity, when Bob Lennard, the casting director for Associated British Pictures – the British equivalent of a Hollywood major – telephoned. Lennard had briefly spoken to Harris after the transmission of *The Iron Harp* and predicted good opportunities in the offing. Now he was testing the grapevine, sounding out the views of quality agents like Fraser. Fraser saw the confluence and the value of the moment and told Lennard on the spot that he was representing Harris. Lennard immediately suggested a seven-year contract, at £30 a week. Harris hesitated, but Fraser set up a further meeting and focused on hard talking with his new find. ABPC, Fraser told Harris, was more than a meal ticket. Maggie Smith, Tony Hancock, Sylvia Syms, Millicent Martin and Richard Todd were all on contract, all scaling the heights. And there was more: ABPC was offering a featured role in an upcoming movie called *Alive and Kicking*, which would be a wholesome slice of Ealing-type confectionary to be sampled worldwide. The opportunity was too good to pass up.

Harris called Ronald Fraser to debate the options. 'He hated the the notion of a long-term contract,' said Fraser. 'What Dick was all about was freedom, and he saw this as a restriction that might anchor him in movie mediocrity. Then again, the money was too good to refuse.' In her memoirs, Elizabeth described the resolution simply: 'We realised that we'd have to start thinking about a life insurance policy for Damian's education . . . so Richard took the contract.'

Harris applied himself to his first movie-making challenge with more emphasis on the studio-posed publicity that attempted to 'soften' him to decent middle-market acceptability than on character acting. Which was fair enough, since his role as the lover (opposite blonde Olive MacFarland) was incidental and required just a day or two's work at Associated British Studios and on Scottish location. *Alive and Kicking* was an unimaginative twist on the same studios' *It's Great To Be Old*, with old-timers Sybil Thorndike, Estelle Winwood and Kathleen Harrison playing mischievous residents of a retirement home who break out, hop on a boat to a remote island and set up an internationally successful knitting industry. The fizz of the comedy, conservatively mounted by producer Victor Skutezky and director Cyril Frankel, was low-key, with Estelle Winwood alone stepping beyond smug granny-playing to provide subtle wit. Harris hardly registered, apart from giving a broadly attractive macho presence to one or two short scenes, and none of the reviews mentioned him. *Films and Filming* merely noted that the movie was oversentimental and waved it away with, 'The movie is as fresh as *Genevieve* in its day, and we wish it the same . . . success.'

Such a success would hardly have helped Harris, who knew the casting was wrong. Politely but firmly, he let Lennard and the executives at ABPC know his feelings: he had studied Stanislavsky and was expert at improvisation; he was reading Shakespeare and studying the classics; he was born to play rebellious key parts.

By Harris's admission and the frank confessions of Elizabeth's writings and interviews, Harris's flamboyant nature, fuelled in equal measure by success and frustration, now became extreme. The relative wealth of the ABPC contract changed their Earls Court lifestyle. Whereas once they had lived on 'a stew made of Oxo cubes and carrots', in rooms that boasted only a solitary king-size bed as furniture, now there was money for minor luxuries. In a matter of weeks Harris paid off many of his debts, decorated their flat exotically – and extended his entertaining circle. The hangers-on syndrome, noticeable, said Joe Lynch, since LAMDA, soared out of all proportion to his wealth, influence or achievement. People 'crashed in' to the family flat weekly and – baby or not – the living room vied with the Angel Lane bar for business. In drink the propensity to brawl unleashed itself, and the nose broken first on the Garryowen rugby pitch was now broken and reset with chronic regularity. 'Curiously enough,' said the journalist Trevor Danker, who met him in London, 'he liked the company of journalists best. Maybe they're the best boozers, I don't know. But he always seemed to have some old hack hanging on to his coat tails like Tonto. And then, at the end of the night, they'd be slugging it out in the gutter over a dumb dispute about Joyce, or the IRA, or the future of theatre or Peter O'Toole's talents versus Richard Burton's . . .'

A brief vogue for IRA-sympathetic movies reanimated him. Working 'the network' on his behalf, Fraser quickly came up with a cracking loan-out offer, shooting for United Artists in Ireland from September to November. The movie was *Shake Hands with the Devil*, a literate first cousin of the acclaimed *Odd Man Out*, co-produced by Marlon Brando's company, Pennebaker. Harris's would be a minor role, tenth billing, but above Irish stalwarts Ray McAnally and Noel Purcell, both of whom he knew and admired. The big attraction, though, was the calibre of the script and the principal casting. James Cagney, Harris's toughie role model from the better days of the Savoy and the Carlton cinemas, was to star, alongside Don Murray and the beautiful Oberon-like newcomer Dana Wynter. The director was Michael Anderson, hot from a string of hits like *The Dam Busters* (1954) and *Around the World in Eighty Days* (1956).

Disengaged from the Theatre Royal but keeping in touch with the goings-on in bi-weekly booze-ups, Harris was relieved to be busy again. With Elizabeth and Damian, he flew to Dublin and joined Anderson's cast at Ardmore Studios, Ireland's first Hollywood-orientated studio venture at Bray, Co. Wicklow, twenty miles from Dublin. *Shake Hands* was, first and foremost, Anderson's baby – his own company, Troy films, had developed the script from Rearden Conner's novel – and from the start everyone was made aware of highest artistic hopes. Only once in recent history had a major American movie been staged in Ireland, and that movie, John Ford's 1952 feature, *The Quiet Man*, hadn't had the advantage of local studio-basing. *Shake Hands* would be the flagship that tested Ardmore's viability and, hopefully, open the door to copious American-Irish movies.

Born within earshot of Bow Bells, Anderson had served his time with the Royal Corps of Signals and learned his Irish history the English way. Despite this, *Shake Hands*, essentially an anti-violence message movie, tended towards distinct pro-IRA sentiments. James Cagney, at that time 54 years old and in happy retirement at his New England farm, had accepted the movie, he said, because of Anderson's script values and because, in the final outcome, the dominant message was love conquers all. 'Brutality for its own sake doesn't interest me,' Cagney told *Picturegoer*. 'I turn down forty gangster roles a year, but this part is different. It proves the uselessness of violence.' Despite the good intentions, *Picturegoer* anticipated an anti-IRA backlash, or an anti-movie backlash, from the active and restless IRA. When questioned about the possibilities of trouble, Anderson sidestepped with the adroit verbal skill of his mentor, Mike Todd, who had taught him the media ropes on *Around the World in Eighty Days*. All publicity, good, bad or suspenseful, would be a positive plus that would help get the message across, said Anderson. 'The main thing I learned from Todd is when to blow your own trumpet. Ballyhoo publicity is important, but only if you've got something special to shout about – and we do.' The movie had 'an embarrassment of talent. The Irish Players from the Abbey Theatre are so good I don't know how I'm going to stop them from pinching the picture fro me.' In *Picturegoer* Anderson listed the top talents, singling out Marianne Benet, John Cairney, Harry Corbett and Ray McAnally. Harris had yet to make his mark.

Harris, whose role of IRA gun-runner Terence O'Brien was substantial, used his time at Ardmore primarily to study the interaction of departments on a big American movie – an arcane process refined over forty years of 'the studio system'. 'I learned that no one individual is any more or less important than anyone else [in film]. It is different from theatre in that way, because the props can literally make or break a scene. A movie is like a painting: it's disparate elements held together with a little surrealism.' Studying the odd phenomenon of 'the Hollywood star' close-up was also edifying. Cagney he found 'extremely gentlemanly and encouraging and free with advice. What I loved about him more than anything was the way he moved. He moved like a butterfly – which wasn't surprising, because he had made all those athletic musicals. I was new and I needed advice and I won the lottery first time out with this Hollywood legend.' Cyril Cusack, Ireland's most celebrated character actor, whom Harris had seen on stage in both Limerick and Dublin, became close friends with Cagney while Harris looked on. Cusack recalled, 'Harris was immensely vibrant and active – so much so that he was distracting. My own temperament is calm, so I was not, let us say, drawn to him. I don't think I thought much of him then, nor indeed did he think much of himself. Frankly, he was more a nuisance, artistically speaking, because all he ever did was bump into people and furniture.' Still, Cusack was charmed by the Harris blarney. 'He told me a sweet story, which was probably apocryphal. Years before, I toured with my own company's production of *The Playboy of the Western World* and took it to Limerick. It had never been seen in the provinces of Ireland and I was very gratified by

Limerick's response. Harris told me that he was prostrate with TB but he crept out of bed, against doctor's orders, and saw the play not once, but several times. He said that that production – and myself – precipitated him into our profession. I took it as a great compliment, though I know he omitted that particular account of his beginnings in later years.'

Despite the IRA sympathies, the paramilitaries' response to the unfolding movie was antagonistic. During preproduction, reported *Picturegoer*, the statue of the Lord Lieutenant of Ireland on the plinth outside the Shelbourne Hotel, temporary home of the movie's brass, was blown to smithereens. Cyril Cusack saw this report as 'scaremongering-cum-cheap-marketing. I wasn't surprised it was alleged, but as far as I know, nothing of that sort happened. I kept away from the hype side of every film I acted in, because I found it all ridiculous. It never interested me. In *Shake Hands with the Devil* the IRA characters were depicted in the heroic-poet mould, which befitted the mood of those times, particularly from an American point of view. And, yes, that probably vexed certain people – even within the ranks of the very same IRA. Mickey Anderson avoided aligning himself with the special-interests groups, but he was tutored with Todd and believed in publicity at any cost, and that came with a price. I think a point came when he forgot about all that nonsense and concentrated on the film for its dramatic values, and then it worked well. [The story], pure and simple, was my point of reference from beginning to end.'

During the nine weeks of Irish filming Anderson kept his head down, refusing interviews and discouraging his stars from parrying with the press. Harris remembered that 'there was an awareness of sensitivities, that perhaps we were spinning a Hollywood yarn from some serious, unresolved troubles. For myself, I was too busy trying to build a career to engage in deep political analysis. But I was a Republican, straight and simple, and I wanted that work to flatter the cause.'

Shake Hands with the Devil had a not inconsiderable budget of £600,000, with scheduled locations around the Wicklow Hills, at St Michael's Lane in Dublin's dockland, and at Ardmore. A total of 742 set-ups were slated – quite extensive for any movie – and a complicated system of running relays to London for film processing and overnight return 'rushes' added to the burdens on the filmmakers. Nevertheless, Anderson brought the movie in on time and under budget, scoring exactly the phase-one business success that Ardmore's bosses, part-sponsored by the Irish government, hoped for.

For Harris a box-office hit wasn't make-or-break, though it would certainly have been desirable in terms of nudging ABPC and Lennard. As it turned out, the film made its money (though Cusack dismissed it as 'not a first rater') – but delighted Harris for the controversies it raised. After the tub-thumping Dublin premiere, attended by President Sean T O'Kelly with Mr and Mrs Marlon Brando Sr, representing Pennebaker, the Northern Ireland censor refused a screening in Ulster. The *Irish Independent* attended the Dublin opening and praised 'an exciting and dramatic movie' where 'the [Republican] case is presented with sympathy and under-standing'. But the Belfast Police Committee called for a hold on the movie's release, and an examination of the issues involved. On 18 June 1959 the Police Committee formally recommended the banning of *Shake Hands* throughout Ulster, just as it had recently forced the withdrawal (said the *Irish Independent*) of *Nudist Paradise* and the fleshy *Isles of Levant*. The boycott, observed Harris, 'hugely increased interest in the film', and within months an idiotically censored version was on release to wide attendances. Few write-ups about the movie did not report the controversies, and Harris relished the mêlée. 'The truth was, *Shake Hands* was just a straightforward thriller plot about a medical student, played by Don Murray, who becomes caught up in terrorism when his friend is killed in a skirmish. It could easily have been a western, or a gangster flick. It was no big deal.' The *Monthly Film Bulletin* concurred, finding it interesting, but 'ultimately the film has all too little to say'. *Films and Filming*, on the other hand, drew similarities with Ford's formidable *The Informer* and hailed 'a notable achievement'.

Harris's work on the film wasn't singled out in any reviews, but what mattered most, by his reckoning, was Anderson's appreciation.

Within months the evidence of the director's appreciation took shape in the offer of another major American movie, this one with the kind of lead casting all the young contenders dreamed about: opposite Charlton Heston and Gary Cooper in *The Wreck of the Mary Deare*, a modern sea epic from MGM.

'His loyalties weren't exclusively hooked up with movies, or television or to Littlewood's Workshop at that point,' said James Booth. 'He was far too intelligent and canny for that. The way we saw it was, his first go at movies worked out OK, but it was no earth-shaker. Many of us started similarly – and then went nowhere. Dickie manoeuvred himself well by *not sitting still*. Arrogance carried him, so that he appeared to be in motion all the time – and that kind of energy begets energy. Casting people were attracted to him, and the whole business of the ball rolling down the hill started. People wanted to be part of it, so he got offered more and more.' Before the MGM movie, Littlewood welcomed him back to her troupe, casting him prominently in a double-role in Frank Norman and Lionel Bart's Soho musical *Fings Ain't Wot They Used T'Be*, staged in March 1959. Harris's part was again down the billing (and smaller than James Booth's), but the show sold to packed houses, transferred to the West End and garnered warm notices for everyone. 'Dickie sang briefly on just one of the numbers,' Booth remembered. 'That was his first professional singing as such, and I remember it because you could never have said his voice was great. He could sing, sure, but he was not a *singer*. There were nights when I wanted to cover my ears and tell him to pack it in, but we were on a run, and we happily went with the flow.'

The run, though, exhausted Harris. 'My inclination,' he said, 'was always to give a thousand per cent' and right then was my "prove yourself" period, and I was operating solely on adrenaline.' Booth recalled the end result of the nerve-draining push: 'He always appeared to be just about to die – literally. Apart from the boozing, his great tendency was towards hypochondria. He was without doubt the worst hypochondriac I've ever met. Almost daily he collapsed, screaming the house down, shouting, "It's a brain haemorrhage, for fuck's sake! I'm fucked! Get a doctor! Get an ambulance!"'

After the musical, with hardly a day off, came Littlewood's revival of John Marston's *The Dutch Courtesan*, where Booth and Joe Lynch observed Harris's confidence as a performer noticeably improving. 'If the movie experience – or the cash and compliments – achieved anything,' said Booth, 'they pushed him to take more risks with projection. I would say he became a more *commanding* performer after his first film experience. Mind you, it also made him a bigger pain in the arse.' *The Dutch Courtesan* received mixed reviews ('When the cast have looked at the script more carefully this play richly deserves a transfer,' said *Plays and Players*), but was significant for Harris's electric stage chemistry alongside Rachel Roberts, the actress with whom Lindsay Anderson would pair him for *This Sporting Life*, the great breakthrough.

The Wreck of the Mary Deare was a supporting lead, offering Harris a chance he grabbed with both hands. Based on the bestseller by Hammond Innes, it was very much a three-man show, the story being a dispute about the salvage of a cargo ship between Cooper and Harris, with Heston as the hero in the middle. Eric Ambler adapted the book with Michael Anderson, and produced a powerful script that made little concession to three-act movie-making. 'I knew it was the best drama piece I'd ever had, and I knew I had to stand up to [Cooper and Heston],' said Harris. 'Working with Cagney prepared me. I wasn't star-struck, but I was also not greatly experienced, as these guys were. I decided to grab a whisky, look 'em in the eye and play it as equals. I also had a little secret. Every time I wilted, I closed my eyes and pretended I was back in Overdale, in the green house, and then it was a lark.'

Heston, later to lock horns in royal style with Harris during *Major Dundee*, started the movie hardly noticing him. When shooting started at MGM studios in California on 9 April, all Heston was interested in was jousting with Cooper. In his published notebooks, Heston admits that he liked the script, disliked Ambler's dialogue and had serious misgivings that 'This [was] Cooper's film.' Harris slipped past, seemingly unseen.

'That was Chuck's style,' Harris said. 'I got to know him better on *Dundee* but he was no kinder. His problem was that he was impressed with himself in a way, say, Cagney never was. He had played in Shakespeare and, to listen to him, you'd think he helped the bard with the rewrites. He was a prick, really, and I liked tackling pricks, so we made some sparks along the way.' As the proverbial greenhorn, Harris was outside the top-table invitations and largely ignored by studio diplomats. In consequence, his long-haul trip to Los Angeles proved slightly depressing. 'Lil and I tried to go to Hollywood the economy way, making turboprop hops here, there and everywhere. It took us forty-eight hours to get there and when we arrived MGM and the Coopers and Hestons really just ignored us. Thus it started – and thus it went on.' As Elizabeth tells it, she and Harris spent their days shuffling aimlessly around LA, trying to orientate and establish the geography. It took days for them to realise that the motel MGM booked them into was a dosshouse in the wrong part of town. The message was clear: Richard Harris was still an unknown quantity, worthy only of minimal attention. The chance to shine was the only luxury being afforded to him.

'The tension of it wiped out Lil and I,' said Harris. 'There was a feeling of make-or-break and we argued incessantly ... about nothing. Really, when I picked a row with Lil, I was wanting to break Heston's fucking neck.' After a fortnight, Elizabeth decided to go home. Harris kept his mind on the movie, fighting for equilibrium as the schedule fragmented under Gary Cooper's regular bouts of illness. 'I spent the off-time exploring Hollywood, doing all the clubs and meeting all the women. But I was disciplined, because I had to be. I knew I might not get this Hollywood chance twice – so I was home in bed by midnight every night.'

Elizabeth was less disciplined. Sailing home aboard the *Queen Elizabeth,* she spent her days and nights in the company of 'a charming RAF officer' and remained faithful to her marriage vows while deciding, emphatically, that the threads had already begun to unravel. In the four-day voyage home, she later wrote, she suddenly became aware of the weakness of her relationship with Harris. She had been living in the shadow of an aggressively ambitious man, voicing no opinions of her own, abandoning all her old friends, even her old, cherished habits. She no longer felt at ease with her husband.

Those who knew his destructive potential might say she was scared of him. But, she wrote, it wasn't fear, just a certain wariness. Hollywood showed her their future; it gave her no comfort.

Early in June *Mary Deare* moved to Elstree Studios in England and Heston and Cooper continued their closed-ranks friendship with dinners at the Guinea and the Piggy in Bruton Place and city sightseeing. Harris, still the outsider, continued to give his everything, and the dedication paid off. Released at Christmas, *The Wreck of the Mary Deare* was a popular, if not a critical, hit, which ran for months on regional screens countrywide. 'That gave me a lot of pleasure, because it was my name on the billings with Coop, and Limerick sat up and took notice. Just to see those thirteen letters, R-I-C-H-A-R-D-H-A-R-R-I-S – it put shivers down my back. Then again, Jackie [Donnelly] and the [Harris] brothers said it put shivers down their backs too.'

None of the major journals remarked on Harris's role as Cooper's nemesis, but the performance was regarded, in the industry, as distinguished, given the disparity of experience. For the *Monthly Film Bulletin*, only the movie's first half was worthy; *Films Illustrated* listed the movie as 'simply adventure for the masses'. 'But that was spot-on for where I needed to be,' said Harris. 'I'd crossed the bar in terms of understanding the market, and I knew I had to project quality but, at the same time, connect with the mass audience. *Mary Deare* was dead right after the other movies. I regarded it as a signpost saying, "Hollywood Straight Ahead".'

Associated British was also pleased with Harris's progress, but already he was voicing unease with the seven-year deal. Payment of the weekly £30 was suspended whenever he worked in theatre, but he worked anyway, choosing to go to Paris in May for Littlewood's production of Behan's *The Hostage*, despite the fact that his part, according to James Booth, was 'miles down from *Mary Deare*, just a nothing walk-on, really'. Joe Lynch said, 'It was go-go-go for him and we were all quite envious. But we also knew his marriage was coming apart because of the pressures, so there was a downside to the glamour.' For Booth, 'the problem was temperament. Richard picked on people. And when he started to get the bigger parts he picked on more and more people and used more savage tactics. From what I saw of him he was very badly behaved at this time – to Liz more than anyone. I was kind of surprised the marriage was surviving at all.'

Without a break, Harris jetted back to Dublin – alone – for another IRA movie, *A Terrible Beauty*. Tay Garnett's film was smaller, less metaphorical or ambitious than *Shake Hands*, but Harris's profile was higher and suddenly, said Cyril Cusack, 'he was hard to miss'. Largely a two-fisted potboiler for Robert Mitchum, *A Terrible Beauty* was set during World War Two and had an acutely pro-IRA plot that offended more viewers than even *Shake Hands with the Devil*. *Films and Filming* attacked it fiercely, giving short shrift to Mitchum and his co-star Dan O'Herlihy, and once again ignoring Harris: 'The producers have miscalculated British audience reactions and in many halls their film will be received with a stony hostility camouflaged as bored indifference.' Cyril Cusack, again playing the peace-loving man in the middle, remembered the production as 'altogether less structured than *Shake Hands*. We were on location around Ireland much more, and the working relationships were less serene. It was a messy kind of picture that left a messy memory.' Friction between the leading lady Anne Heywood and her producer husband Raymond Stross and, initially anyway, between Harris and Mitchum made the production uncomfortable for Cusack and Garnett. Harris disliked Mitchum on meeting him, but warmed to him when the Hollywood star came to his rescue in a pub brawl in O'Connell Street. 'Our relationship changed and we had a great time from then on,' Harris recalled. 'That was special, because we managed to bottle the aggro and turn it into screen chemistry. I was grateful to Bob for putting up with me, because we were kinsmen. His response to the stresses of the business was exactly mine. The creative tension overspills and one is blamed for bad behaviour – but show me an artist, any real artist that you can call a perfect gentleman. It does not, cannot, exist.'

The finished movie, though, frustrated everyone. For Mitchum it didn't even deserve comment. For Dan O'Herlihy it was 'pulp'. For Cusack, 'The title said it all. Very terrible, and not much of a beauty at all.' Ten years later, Harris told the journalist Tony Crawley he looked back on the movie as a complete dud. 'But actors have to learn in some way, and you learn best from your mistakes.'

During production Elizabeth attempted to revive their flagging marriage by paying a surprise visit to the location in Co. Wicklow. She was apprehensive and unsure of herself, she wrote, undecided still if she wished to continue at all. By the time she arrived in Bray, Harris's friendship with Mitchum was thriving and his mood was jolly. Instead of the clash she expected, there were comfortable days in the company of Bob and Dorothy Mitchum, dining, laughing and sharing Hollywood tales. Harris's relaxation wasn't surprising: in Mitchum he had found, said Cusack, 'the Hollywood big-shot respect he felt he deserved'.

By the end of 1959 Harris had four features to his credit and was up in the top-five billing, a considerable feat for a moody late starter. He could boast Hollywood friendships and full pages in fan magazines, and the predictions of Big Success that had begun with a whisper in the *Mirror* were now an unstoppable welter. In Limerick, those of the Crescent gang who remained read about his progress in the tabloids with awe. Dermot Foley couldn't believe it: from street spoofing to movie headlining alongside Bob Mitchum was too much to digest. Foley went to London to see with his own eyes. The old friends met in Harris's new flat at Allen House, an upmarket block in Kensington. 'He was doing bloody all right,' said Foley. 'Because [my family] had a chemist shop which specialised in photography equipment, I sold him a couple of cameras. He was his usual devil-may-care self – but he was also very proud and lordly. Bob Lennard was with him and the conversation was about how long this good run would last. Dickie guessed he might make three or four more pictures. But Lennard told him he was lucky to pull off the first one! I think it was important for anyone working with Dickie to try to keep him under control.'

Sauntering through central London that summer, Harris bumped into Betty Brennan. They greeted each other with the unembarrassed ease of old, true friends. Betty was absorbed in her European Grand Tour, and loving it. Dickie, she discovered, was the fun-seeking, confident wild card of old. The difficulties of his home life that were already leaking into the press were unknown to her: she saw only sunshine. 'He was just as outgoing and optimistic and it was really thrilling to encounter that energy again. We had a chat just like old times, and a kiss, and we said goodbye. He was doing well and I felt delighted for him. I watched him swagger off, never thinking that the only relationship I'd have with him from then on was as a wide-eyed girl in the audience, admiring him in fifty-foot Technicolor.'

Others saw not optimism, but profound darkness looming. Godfrey Quigley, the Irish actor-producer who championed Dublin's Globe Theatre group, the Abbey Theatre's main competitor, enjoyed a companionable summer's afternoon drinking spree with Harris but was surprised by what followed. 'I drank hard myself in those days, so I suppose we were both the worst for wear. We went back to the flat in Allen House and Elizabeth was there being the good and kindly wife but obviously uncomfortable, to say the least, at our state on arrival. She made some innocent but cynical remark, justifiably I'd say, and Dickie lifted up a wardrobe . . . *and threw it at her*! I sobered up quick. I regarded him as a friend, and I liked him . . . But that fury, when it was unleashed, was something to behold. I remember thinking, I'm glad I can open the door and walk out of here. For Elizabeth, with the baby, it's not that easy . . .'

Insecurity and indecision agitated Harris. In the opinion of those close to him, the duality of character so often commented upon was raging out of control: on one hand, the home-loving poet wanted Elizabeth and the steady, unchallenging life of a wage-earning dad; on the other, the talent-possessed hard man wanted far horizons. As ABPC offered more B-pictures, Harris became a spitting viper, suddenly rejecting everything. There were those who believed his lunatic temper would estrange the mainstream moguls and stunt his dramatic career. Others saw the purity of passion that foreshadowed the watershed: within months he found the stage play of his dreams, a role surely fated for him that set London on fire and won the eye of the brilliant emerging film director, Lindsay Anderson.

CHAPTER 5

Gingerly on the Bounty

The Ginger Man was a battering-ram of the new-wave theatre movement that resoundingly won the case for Harris's lead-playing talents and also brought him to the verge of a nervous breakdown. Harris actively hunted that part, sensing an Irish play to outstrip Behan. Set designer Tony Walton, then married to Julie Andrews, mounted the production with director Philip Wiseman, and both felt Harris was right for the secondary part of O'Keefe, but not the lead. The final decision was not theirs, but the author J P Donleavy's. As the actor Ronald Fraser told it, Donleavy 'was a fussy bugger who wanted every comma, every full stop perfectly rendered'. Donleavy was unsure of Harris, but Harris screamed in his face: *'I am the Ginger Man! You cannot cast anyone else!'* Irish-educated and historically eccentric Donleavy finally agreed to the casting. Years later, Harris was still proclaiming his right to the part: so much of the Ginger Man's life and plight was his own – right down to the strains of a mixed-religion marriage to an upper-crust girl. Ronald Fraser was also cast by Donleavy and started rehearsals optimistically, looking forward keenly to a projected six-month West End run. 'But it was hell right from the start. There were awful rows. Dick was trying to manhandle himself into the part, taking it very, very, very seriously. He would rehearse himself for forty nonstop hours, half-pissed, then explode with exhaustion, screaming, "I can't do the fucking thing! I can't do it!" – and storm off to God-knows-where. I was always the one sent to retrieve him from the pub, since I was the

97

one they knew he'd listen to.' This burden had its advantages: 'Dear old Dickie introduced me to my "lifetime drink" – vodka, lime and soda! That was the start of the love *affaire* that nearly killed me many times.' Another actor on the play watched the furies and the drinking bouts in dismay, feeling sympathy for Harris, and for Fraser's nurse-companion role: 'Philip Wiseman was the real problem. He was a lovely man, but he couldn't *direct* to save his life. That was what made it a crucifying experience for Richard, because, if ever there was a play that required a voice of logic at its core, that was the one. Ultimately it was excruciatingly hard *on everyone*, for want of a calm, coherent director.'

With *The Ginger Man* Harris for the first time fully immersed himself in a role, and the consequences shattered his home life. Before the play opened at the Fortune Theatre in September, Elizabeth broke the tension of the long-running domestic chaos by making the choice herself: she left Allen House, taking Damian, and moved back to live with her father. 'Did she?' Harris later said. 'I wasn't fully aware. While preparing for *The Ginger Man* I wasn't even aware what day of the week it was.'

The *Daily Express* was among the first to hail *The Ginger Man*. Welcomed as a ground-breaker in the mould of John Osborne's recent hit *Look Back in Anger*, *The Ginger Man* revealed its greatness in its unapologetic central intimacy. Sebastian Dangerfield, the Trinity student hero amok, was a verbal bastard, at war with himself, the audience and all civilisation. 'Three years ago,' said the *Express*, 'this play about the facts of low life in Dublin could never have been shown because of the censor and because the West End was becoming a cemetery. [Then] Olivier, Gielgud, Coward and Rattigan dominated. Now look what's happening: plays at last that are deep in living . . . tough, uncompromising, and unpredictable.' Donleavy chipped in: 'I expect a couple of rows of audience will walk out each night. But I'm sure for every two that walk out, four more will come in.' Harris's personal reviews, alongside such cant, were uniformly excellent – which was no surprise to Elizabeth, since she had been living on a day-to-day basis watching the true-life emotional thug emerge from the chrysalis of his existential confusion. 'I may have read a review, or I may not have,' said Harris. 'By the time we opened, I was living on Pluto.'

Godfrey Quigley's Dublin Globe group had a reputation for staging oddball classics and Quigley immediately flew to London to take in the landmark show. Quigley knew Donleavy – indeed, 'I personally knew the authentic "ginger man" of the story at Trinity. I socialised with him in Dublin in the most reckless days of my life, so I had what we Irish call a *grath* [love] for the yarn!' Quigley watched Harris over several performances at the Fortune and decided he must stage the play for himself. 'I thought it was the most remarkable play, the equal of Ibsen or Strindberg. I knew, because of its history and locales, it was perfect for Dublin. So I went backstage and proposed a transfer directly to Philip Wiseman.' Quigley believed Harris's energy 'electrified the play as if someone plugged a high-voltage generator into the text'. Others, like James Booth who attended twice, thought Harris one of its weakest links: 'It certainly was memorable as a text, but Harris's performance was too light on its feet. I couldn't see what the likes of Quigley saw, because for me Dickie was *too* wild – Dangerfield needed more control.' Quigley 'loved the madness' and successfully negotiated a transfer of the play, which would import the core talents of Philip Wiseman and Harris. Harris was ecstatic. Elizabeth wrote in her memoirs that he hungered for a triumphant Irish theatrical return, and *The Ginger Man* offered the prize.

The return came sooner than anyone expected. After six weeks, audience numbers in London sagged, so a premature Dublin transfer unfolded. Quigley breathed deep in anticipation of a long, money-spinning run. 'I had my shirt on it, literally. There weren't many times in my life when I went so far out on the limb as a producer. But I trusted the Irish theatregoer, and I really believed that the combination of Donleavy and Dickie was just the wake-up call Dublin needed at that moment.' The lead British casting of Wendy Craig, Ronald Fraser (playing O'Keefe, the part Harris had first been offered) and Isabel Dean was replaced by Genevieve Lyons (Quigley's then wife), Quigley himself and Rosalie Westwater. The production was mounted at the Gaiety Theatre and overseen by the

owner-entrepreneur Louis Elliman, Dublin's 'Mr Showbiz'. First
night saw a packed house, with Dubliners flocking to see the new
Hollywood star, Richard Harris, on stage in the capital.

Quigley was 'delighted' as he came off-stage, but Louis Elliman
confronted him and asked abruptly for cuts in the text. Quigley was
surprised, but not alarmed. Then Harris sauntered past them, bound
for 'a jar or two in the green room', unaware of the crisis looming.
Quigley recalled, 'Louis said he wanted a profane reference to
Dangerfield getting absolution from some church on the quays
removed. He also wanted the song "Down in Dingle Where the Girls
Are Single" cut out. This, I must say, absolutely baffled me. It was a
classic, harmless piece of Dublinese, typical and true. To abandon
stuff like that, for whatever reason, seemed to me a profanity. I tried
to say this to Louis in the most diplomatic way.'

Philip Wiseman was chatting to stage hands a few yards away and
Quigley naïvely called him over to hear Elliman's 'suggestions'. 'I
think I might have made the drastic mistake of not formally
introducing them. I just said, "Phillip, come here and listen to what
Louis is suggesting for cuts."' Wiseman flared up instantly, refusing
to excise a single line for any reason. Elliman, never coy, exploded
back. 'They were roaring into each other's faces. *"If you don't
fucking cut this I'll close the fucking show and, what's more, I'll see
that you never work again."'* Years later, Quigley laughed at 'the
astonishing childishness of theatre people arguing over a storybook
yarn: Louis got completely carried away and kept yelling, *"You will
never ever work in Hollywood!"* – as if he could ever have any
influence in Hollywood.' The row ended in stalemate, with Wiseman
challenging Elliman to go to the media: 'Anything you tell the press
will do nothing other than help the show, publicity-wise, so be my
guest! In a few weeks we'll be playing New York. So start a scandal!
The media attention will be very welcome!'

Before midnight the word was circulating: the show was in the
censorship trough. Harris caught wind, and loved it. Quigley
recalled, 'He'd taken up residence down Grafton Street at the Bailey
[pub]. Now he convened a semipermanent court there, giving
interviews to the world press. *His* play was under fire from the

papacy! This was magnificent! Homeric! Joycean! I remember being dragged off the street, very early the next morning, to pose with him for the posse of photographers he'd drummed up.'

What the *Sunday Times* had described as 'an uproariously funny production' was now, simply, uproarious. The *Irish Independent* reacted with all the hostility Elliman showed: 'The current production is one of the most nauseating plays ever to appear on a Dublin stage and it is a matter of some concern that its presentation should ever have been considered. It is an insult to religion and an outrage to normal feelings of decency. The best course open to all concerned is to withdraw it with the greatest possible speed.'

When Quigley, Harris and the cast arrived for the second night's performance they found the Gaiety in darkness, with a mob blocking South King Street. Inside, Elliman was locked in discussions about proposed cuts with a dog-collared clerical administrator from Archbishop MacQuaid's office, the Dublin equivalent of the Lord Chamberlain's enforcer. Quigley recalled 'a priest from MacQuaid's representing the fascist inquisition-style values of the MacQuaid era, which kept Ireland firmly the Dark Ages. A storm brewed up at that meeting – there was a lot of shouting more fitting a barracks than a theatre – and Elliman told me flat that the play must come off. We refused to change anything. Elliman was so angry that he could hardly speak. He walked out. He allowed us to play that second night, but the next day we were cancelled.'

Harris summoned the Bailey court, recounting every murmur from Elliman's office. 'When the show went on for what was to be its final performance he milked every ounce of pathos from it, adding special emphasis to the concluding farewell scene where the Ginger Man bids adieu on this, his final night in Dun Laoghaire.' Quigley went on: 'I never knock an actor for his egomania. But Dickie's leanings in this direction were, shall we say, over-developed. He liked playing chess with the newspapers, too – in fact, he liked playing chess with everyone – so he saw ample mileage for fun.' Once again Harris summoned all journalists, now to announce his letter to Archbishop MacQuaid, in which he humbly asked for divine guidance in his awkward situation: what could the archbishop suggest by way of assistance? The letter was sent by courier motorbike and the Bailey awaited a reply with well-filled glasses. 'MacQuaid outmanoeuvred him,' Quigley said. 'He sent a note back saying Mr Harris would be advised to contact his personal spiritual adviser if he had a conscience crisis with this play. You have to give it to MacQuaid. He was as much a chancer as Dickie.'

Wiseman, like Harris, pushed the counterpublicity tactic. In a telegram to the *Irish Independent*, the publicly perceived leader of the lynch mob, Wiseman stated, 'Your article concerning the play [we consider] a deliberate attempt to incite a breach of the peace. We are therefore giving you notice of our intention to protect our interests ... and hold you directly responsible for any damages arising from such a breach.' Threats and counterthreats flew, and Quigley paid off his cast and crew and got out of town. 'It cost me £800 or more. My great pal Brendan Smith came for me and put me in his car and took me to a hotel in Dundalk, where we drank a lot of soup over the next few days.'

Harris's soup was every form of alcohol under the sun. Elizabeth spoke of his particular vulnerability to brandy. His tolerance of beer and other spirits was high, but brandy drew the worst from him. Now, to the newspapermen, he was suddenly on the verge of collapse. At his last-night performance the *Evening Press* commended his fine, though edge-of-the-seat, acting: 'He prances and postures like a marionette on the verge of collapse . . .' Harris told reporters, 'This play has ruined me and it has ruined my marriage. I rehearsed it for ten weeks before it opened, and because of it my wife can't stand me any longer.' Godfrey Quigley questioned this depiction of a man on the brink: 'He courted the press with incredible vigour, he was certainly fit and coherent enough for that.'

But Harris entered a Cornish nursing home when *The Ginger Man* folded. He and Elizabeth appeared to accept the inevitability of divorce, but the pain of what he perceived as a double failure flattened him. The boisterous, heartless boyo depicted so often through the years – even by Harris himself – did not fit this picture. Here was a gibbering, exhausted man who could not eat or sleep, rich with acquaintances but lost for friends, achingly lamenting what might have been.

To add to his personal agony, Harris received news from Limerick that Milly was dying of cancer. Devastated, he called Elizabeth and together they returned to the Ennis Road, politely concealing the split. Elizabeth stayed with Harmay and Jack Donnelly, while Harris tended his mother with a comfort that no one else in the family could quite muster. In Elizabeth's account of Milly's final illness she spoke of the mother's request to her son to assume responsibility for the family troubles, which were, in effect, the mills' debts. In Dickie as in no one else Milly saw a wherewithal and energy to save family face. 'But it was by then an impossible task,' said mill man Jim Roche, 'because Rank was dominant in the flour business and monopolised everything because it was cash rich. A family operation was a thing of yore ... The best that Milly or anyone could have hoped was a well-paid sale, lock-and-stock, to Rank.'

Elizabeth returned to London as Harris kept up his bedside vigil in Limerick. Within hours of her arrival home, Harris was on the phone with the news that Milly was dead. She flew back to Dublin and took a train to Limerick. At the funeral and afterwards, the depths of Harris's tiredness touched her. She knew he needed the comfort of a real escape and encouraged him to take any work offer that came along. Fraser immediately found him a TV play, *The Hasty Heart,* taping that week in New York. Harris jumped at the chance, and flew out alone directly after Milly's burial in the family plot at Mount St Lawrence's on 14 December. Two weeks later, revived and inspired by good work, he returned to Europe to romance his marriage back to life. He met Elizabeth in Paris and dined with her at Maxim's, a long-time fantasy of hers. They lingered in a suite at the Ritz, rewriting the terms of a new relationship that would confront all the old problems of his work obsession and their noncommunication. As Elizabeth described it, they settled on a plan for 'a series of beautiful love affairs' with each other, as opposed to basic domestic routine. 'The heart of it is that he isn't cut out for domesticity,' Elizabeth told Ronald Fraser. 'I love him enough, so we'll make it work some other way.'

The new deal dictated that, whenever they were separated, they would meet anew only in hotel rooms; she would wear lilac, his favourite colour, and they would behave like first-time lovers. Elizabeth was happy to be back, but, said Fraser, 'still sensibly wary'. The arrangement lasted several months but, 'I warned her that Dickie was Dickie. He likes chaos, so put your money on more rows to come.'

Sure enough, within a very short time the self-punishing and attention-addicted aspects of his personality had the relationship in turmoil. Part of the new problem was his neurotic obsession with mortality. After Milly's passing, death preoccupied him and – out of the blue – he fixed on the notion that the world would end in 1965. It was a serious conviction. To Elizabeth's utter dismay he formed the 65 Club, with the writer Edna O'Brien and Donal Donnelly among its members. Stationery was printed and a charter for philosophical debates drafted. 'I wanted answers about existence and reality. In the fifties you had some very visionary and very disturbing people upending all the old Christian notions. You had Alan Watts in San Francisco opening the world of Zen to the West. You had George Adamski telling us of his encounters with Venusians and revealing the great secret that the world is a prison planet, seeded by other civilisations. I wanted to stir some ideas. There is more to heaven and earth than is accounted for in anyone's philosophy, dear fellow! So I stirred it. I also *did* believe the end was nigh. Why not? We'd been fucking around with nuclear science like lunatics for twenty years. I had no faith in humanity. I thought we were fucked.'

In the brighter moments came a reawakening of self-advertising. Politics was the headline topic, the bar room – any bar room – the rostrum. In twenty interviews he voiced his newfound political orientations, most, oddly, couched as slings against Liberal and Labour values. Even Lord Ogmore, Elizabeth believed, was a target. 'The House of Lords is just a rich man's labour exchange where the old boys sign on for their £3 a day,' announced Harris. Elizabeth laughed, but tried to persuade him to subtlety, all the time knowing, said Fraser, that she was wasting her time. 'More than anything

Dickie loved to do precisely what he was told not to do, so he had a ball with Elizabeth hassling him.'

Distraction and solace, as ever, came with the work. After months – 'more like years,' said Harris – of inertia, Associated British finally cast him with star billing in a home production, a movie adaptation of Willis Hall's theatrical hit *The Long and the Short and the Tall,* directed by Leslie Norman. Peter O'Toole had led the stage cast (but wasn't in the movie) and Harris, who looked up to O'Toole, was impressed by this and by Wolf Mankowitz's ballsy screenplay. Ronald Fraser, another member of the stage cast, was also aboard. Harris took second billing to Laurence Harvey, unseating fifties favourite Richard Todd to third billing. The bitching one-upmanship that resulted charged the production for Harris. Considerably shorter in stature than Harvey or Harris, Richard Todd took pains to even the score. As cast and crew sweated it out in the mock-up Malaysian jungle at Elstree Studios, Todd discreetly built small mounds of dirt on which to stand in his scenes with his co-stars. Harris spotted the trick and, with Harvey's and Fraser's cooperation, outfoxed Todd by sneaking in little higher mounds for their own use. Nowhere in the movie was Todd eyeball to eyeball with Harvey or Harris. 'The old prat was dumbfounded,' said Fraser, 'and Dickie never stopped laughing.'

A grey parable about the effects of war on a ragtag group of jungle soldiers, *The Long and the Short and the Tall* was entered, along with its contemporary twin *Saturday Night and Sunday Morning*, in the festival of Mar del Plata in Argentina as being representative of 'the spearhead of the new wave of British cinema' – fair indication of substance and worth. The esteemed C A Lejeune declared it 'first-class work . . . It has dignity, humanity and, under the rough exterior, a very tender heart.' But audiences were slower to embrace it. Harris, who played the bullying Corporal Johnstone (with 'just a tabloid verisimilitude', said the *Monthly Film Bulletin*), tended to side with the audiences. 'That era of British film was tricky for me, because British production was coming out of one mind-set and into another. After Churchill, there'd been years of austerity and conservatism and the projection in movies of the stiff-upper-lip of

Eden and Macmillan. Army dramas like *The Long and the Short and the Tall* were still jingoistic, like old Rudyard Kipling tales. In Argentina the audiences preferred *Saturday Night and Sunday Morning*, because that working-class-on-the-edge scenario was easier to identify with. People wanted to be rid of the idea of conscription and war and military discipline. Personally, I found it depressing. I took the role because it was paid work, but I took no great joy in it. The original play was OK, but the movie never developed beyond the play. It remained a play, and felt claustrophobic. I was surprised it did any business at all.'

At home in Allen House Elizabeth played the game of the redrafted marriage, increasingly aware that the Ginger Man – not the play but the character – had not left her life. Harris *was*, as he'd told Donleavy, *the* Ginger Man. All the whim-and-fury mania of the Ginger Man was his, and all the vainglorious indulgence. Home life centred on him and only him, and held its breath while he made up his mind. Joe Lynch recalled, 'Sex and mortality and the movies were all that absorbed him – he often liked to tell you that. He was a loving spirit, but he was the least likely husband and father.' Others saw Harris struggle to come to terms with his strengths – which were manifest gregarious charm, physical stamina and sound arty instincts; and with his weaknesses – the dyslexia (it was formally diagnosed only in 1971), chronic melancholy and outbursts of violence. More than anything, many friends observed, Harris was continuing to position himself for stardom. Cunning and intuitive, he sensed the value of his natural attributes at that period of fundamental societal change, and pushed the rebel heart to the hilt. Joe Lynch felt, 'He didn't start out wanting to be a star, as such. But he found himself in the tide of the rebellious sixties change, and he fitted in. So naturally, he wanted to be part of it, to contribute, and maybe along the way get a better grip, a better understanding of himself. I always regarded his development as intellectual and spiritual growth – and I felt compassion for him, and compassion for the people who suffer under his roof as he tried to make sense of himself and his place in the sixties.'

Out of the critical success of *The Long and the Short and the Tall* came producer Carl Foreman's offer to Harris of a role in J Lee

Thompson's *The Guns of Navarone*, based on Alastair Maclean's formulaic bestseller. His part as a heroic flyer, well down the billing from Gergory Peck and David Niven, was all but invisible, but the merit was in his presence in a populist movie with a guaranteed mass American audience. Within weeks of completion of work on the film – which was destined for excellent box-office and endless television reruns – a fresh flow of American scripts landed on Jimmy Fraser's desk.

Among the phone enquiries was one from the legendary Carol Reed, currently preparing a remake of *Mutiny on the Bounty* for MGM, which was intended to star the Method prince-of-rebels Marlon Brando. Both Reed and producer Aaron Rosenberg had seen Harris's movie work on *Mary Deare* and were attracted, said Harris, by 'my piratical Irish ruggedness which doubtless fitted exactly into their notion of big boys roughing it out at sea'. After an interview audition of curt formality with Reed, Harris was offered an undefined role. 'I didn't need to be told what it was. Frankly, I would have *licked* the deck of the *Bounty* if that would have done the job. Was I enthusiastic? Let me put it like this: I was being invited to star with Marlon *fucking* Brando. All his pictures – right back to stuff like *The Men* and *On the Waterfront* – were the *reasons* I wanted to act and survive as an actor. What he gave to me, at the start, was the theory of acting coming from a place of personal truth. Nothing more, nothing less. I thought, This offer isn't just another American movie. This is American art.'

But *Mutiny on the Bounty* progressed haltingly. Rosenberg had contracted Reed early on, seeing the quirky potential of pairing opposites, but Brando resisted, rejecting what Harris called 'the English epic script ballyhoo', as he had rejected *Lawrence of Arabia*. Rejecting *Lawrence*, Brando had said, 'I'll be damned if I spend two years of my life on a fucking camel.' With *Mutiny*, said Harris, he resisted Reed's 'literary and literate intention simply to redo the 1935 Gable-Laughton classic'. After endless negotiations, Brando finally committed, securing the promise of a new script and winning full casting approval. Eric Ambler was assigned to write the new screenplay – but Brando immediately disliked his approach and called for redrafts, with more emphasis on the mutineers' lives on Pitcairn Island – and crew changes occupied months of preproduction.

During the endless boardroom battles at MGM Studios in Culver City, Rosenberg came to believe that Brando was games-playing with the intention of scuppering the production in order to launch a script of his own about Caryl Chessman, the controversial convicted rapist. Harris knew nothing of this: 'I only knew that it was "war and peace" in terms of the set-up. I knew that Carol was making progress with the Brit end of things, casting his old pal Trevor Howard, and Hugh Griffith and Gordon Jackson and Noel Purcell. But the American end, where the dollars and the green light abided, was something else altogether.'

Awaiting the script impatiently, Harris took root on a bar stool in Dublin. Finally, the package arrived and he got the chance to judge the role Reed – and Brando – had carved out for him. 'I hated it. The part was animated background with an Irish accent.' Harris instructed Fraser to reject the role out of hand. 'That took *cajones*,' said James Booth. 'But, then, Dickie had plenty of experience being a bollocks in his personal life to prepare himself for "star wars".' Elizabeth and others advised Harris of the risk of his posturing, but Harris was unmoved. 'What it boiled down to was bad writing and something that would have ultimately been bad for the movie, and Brando and everyone else. I'd lick the deck . . . but I wouldn't fuck it up. You have to apply some artistic discernment.' Reed and Rosenberg reconsidered, and offered a bigger role, this time as the principal mutineer John Mills, alongside Brando's Fletcher Christian. The advantage gained, Harris now told Fraser to request star billing with Brando. This demand was patently absurd: Brando was peaking with recent victories like *The Young Lions* (1958) and *One-Eyed Jacks* (1961) and was regarded as Hollywood's best property. Rosenberg cabled an immediate 'No', but perked the terms with a more favourable fee. But Harris wasn't manoeuvring for money. As Elizabeth tells it, money per se was of no interest to him: when he had it he was always extravagant, throwing away handfuls on unnecessary antique tables and first-class air fares: 'What mattered to him was major casting and proper respect.'

Harris's compromise negotiation position was the suggestion of equal billing with Trevor Howard, playing the second-lead role of Captain Bligh. Again, Rosenberg refused, stating that Howard was better known than Harris. Harris quickly returned this lob: *he* was presently as well known as Howard had been at thirty years old.

Elizabeth and Harris waited tensely as the scheduled production date, 15 October, drew nearer and Rosenberg declined to respond. Harris now all but accepted the fact that he had blown his chance. Respite from total despair came when Elizabeth was cast in a small role in a Manchester play, but she departed gloomily, feeling every ounce of Harris's misery. In her memoirs Elizabeth wrote of the tension of toiling in Manchester, preoccupied with the fears that *Mutiny* would be lost. Then, one day before Harris's proposed flight to Tahiti to start filming, the call of surrender came from Rosenberg. Said Harris, 'Yes, they'd agreed my terms . . . but for God's sake get on that plane! I rushed out and bought what I thought I might need, added the usual two hundred records and twenty-seven books that make up my usual luggage – and I was on my way.' In her memoirs, Elizabeth recalled that Harris's main item of luggage was not books or records, but a bottle of bourbon.

It was a nerve-racking start to what promised from the outset to be a nail-biting production. When Harris arrived in Tahiti to join Brando, Howard and the crew, no final screenplay was ready and no good ship *Bounty* was to be seen. Brando was still disputing Ambler's work and more writers had been summoned. Charles Lederer was now redrafting, but, said Harris, no end was in sight during the first week in Tahiti. The replica *Bounty*, hand-crafted at a cost of $750,000 in Nova Scotia, was allegedly ready – but that had run into storms en route and might not be on location for weeks. Harris found himself stranded with a company of almost one hundred crew and cast members in a tropical oven, watching $50,000 a day of production funds go down the drain.

On 4 December, weeks late, the movie finally started shooting on the shores of Matavi Bay, without a script. Trevor Howard immediately fell foul of Brando, by accurately delivering his lines while Brando fluffed. Carol Reed hauled patiently, ultra-careful lest his friendship with Howard and the British contingent offend Brando, trying, said Harris, 'to play piggy-in-the-middle with this apparently paranoid [Brando]'. Harris, for his part, 'watched and worked with respectful interest', while doing his best to connect with the moody and reclusive Brando. 'In the beginning I didn't see much of him at all, but it was all right, it was respectful, we were making some progress. But then the December rains came, and everything went pear-shaped again.'

On Christmas Eve Elizabeth arrived with Damian and a nanny, eager to announce exciting news. After Manchester, she had decided to quit acting and concentrate on family. What facilitated her decision was the confirmation that she was again pregnant. Brimming with the news and fighting jet-and-baby-lag, Elizabeth was dismayed not to find Harris at the airport to greet her. Damian had been ill on the journey and the nanny exhausted, but an odyssey lay ahead. Nobody in Papeete, the shanty capital, knew where the production was based. Elizabeth had cabled ahead via Culver City, but Harris never received the information. After a search lasting hours the jungle location was found and Elizabeth collapsed on to Harris's empty bed with Damian, to be awoken hours later later by his loving embrace. '[Elizabeth's arrival and the news] was wonderful for me,' said Harris, 'because I loved kids, really loved them, and I longed for a daughter. I told Lil, "Try to make it a girl, but don't worry if it's another son. Let's make twenty of 'em, and sooner or later we'll get a girl."'

Life in Tahiti – at last with the *Bounty* prop in place – stumbled on, bedevilled by scorpions, land crabs, rats – and a darkening, declining Brando. The Harrises fought gamely to keep up their spirits, said Elizabeth, throwing 'at home' parties in their 'hut home' where Hughie Griffith, Gordon Jackson, Eddie Byrne and Noel Purcell imbibed till all hours. Harris recalled, 'It was quite primitive, in a seventeenth-century sort of way that I loved. I was always a boy-scout mentality, and we were living under the stars like Robinson Crusoe.'

Jogged back to reality on a Hollywood sound stage after Christmas, *Mutiny on the Bounty* became a bloody battlefield of real-life mutinies. Brando was often either absent, or shouting – and Rosenberg suddenly fired Carol Reed. The cause of the dismissal was not, as widely reported, a rift with Brando. Rather, Reed had argued with Rosenberg about the portrayal of Bligh, demanding 'something other than a direct copy of Charles Laughton's Bligh'. The cast, led by Harris and Howard, demanded a meeting with Sol Siegal, MGM's chief executive, with the intention of supporting Reed. But before they could state their case Siegal told them, 'Gentlemen, before you say anything, I want you to understand one thing: that the only expendable commodity in a great movie is a good actor.'

'It was shitsville,' said Harris, 'and no one had the power to do much beyond moan. It began to be a case of, Let's just bite the fucking bullet and end the damn thing – if it *can* be ended!' Lewis Milestone, veteran director of *All Quiet on the Western Front* – made all of 35 years before – took Reed's place and suddenly collided with the reality of a Brando-driven epic. To his credit, he backed down to the inevitable, allowing Rosenberg, Lederer and Brando to do what could only be done – follow Brando's paper trail towards completion. 'Looking back, one admires his "reality focus",' said Harris. 'But at the time it was horrific. We thought, Why the hell doesn't he fight [Rosenberg and Brando]?'

During February Harris spent much of his time extending his trade friendships in the Retake Room, a Hollywood restaurant favoured by the Brits. Brando remained mostly incommunicado with Tarita Teripaim, the Tahitian discovery who became his new girlfriend (and who later bore him a son and a daughter). 'Our lives were separate tracks, except for the rare studio days we shared. But we were still OK with each other, and Elizabeth was invited to bring Damian over to Brando's house to play once or twice.' But Harris's regard for the rebel legend had changed. The excessive rows with Reed and Milestone, and the frequent no-show days, wore him down as they wore down Howard and all the others. Never one to keep his opinions to himself, Harris suddenly flared up during the shooting of a key confrontation scene with Brando's Fletcher Christian. 'He was internalising – which is a Method trick, and it's fine, in small measure. But he was over the top. It was just a mad mumble, going on and on. Finally, I had enough. He was supposed to hit me, and I was to fall. The blow finally came like a damp rag, a little girlie flip on the cheek. I was outraged. That wouldn't knock down a butterfly, I said – and I demanded a reshoot. Marlon did it again . . . and again. All these little girlie slaps. So I just had it . . . and I kissed him on the cheek and hugged him as if he *was* a girl. "Shall we dance?" I asked. He didn't like it at all. He gave me a look like, "You motherfucker! Are you making fun of me?" – and he stormed off.'

After the incident, Harris and Brando refused to appear on set together. In consequence Brando played his Harris scenes opposite a stand-in, and Harris stooped to further insult: 'He used a stand-in, I used a box. So I got a little green box and drew his face on it like he was the Smiley Man and performed to that.' Milestone avoided the dispute, but was forced into the fray on the last day of studio shooting when Brando asked for Harris back on set with him.

'It was quite tense. He asked me, "Would you mind giving me your lines one time?" And I told him no. I gave him the green Smiley box and said, "Marlon, this was you before lunch, and now it is me after lunch. And you can look at that little box to your heart's content and perform, and you'll probably get as much out of that box as I got out of you."' Harris didn't speak to Brando again for more than 25 years.

The marathon went on with reshoots in Tahiti lasting four months, from March till midsummer. Elizabeth and Damian had returned to London, where Elizabeth wanted her baby born, and Harris missed her 'at home' organisational flair. Relief from the tedium came when the British stage director Lindsay Anderson flew twelve thousand miles to discuss a project in prospect called *This Sporting Life*. 'That came out of the blue,' said Harris, 'and it saved my sanity in Tahiti, because I was fed up with Eddie Byrne arguing with Noel Purcell and my left hand arguing with my right hand. Suddenly there was Lindsay with this boyish energy and great smile . . . At last, fun and art!'

Anderson was 38, untried in feature work but with a clutch of substantial creative credits behind him, among them an Academy Award for co-scripting and co-directing the 1955 short *Thursday's Children* with Guy Brenton. His feature debut would be David Storey's rugby novel, which he'd hungered to direct since reading a review of it years before in the *Sunday Times*. The previous year, as funding took shape, he had seen *The Ginger Man* and there and then, he later said, privately, conclusively cast *This Sporting Life*.

James Booth, who knew Anderson, believed, 'Anderson wasn't *interested* in Harris as an actor, he was obsessed. The word was out that this was all about sexual infatuation, that Lindsay had seen the man of his dreams and was ready to – literally – go to the ends of the earth to seduce him.'

At Christmas, Anderson had mailed a copy of Storey's novel to Harris at MGM and received a densely packed, handwritten critique from him. Harris liked the book – for its vibrant and realistic rugby background – and, above all, for the multi-reflections of his own life he saw in the pages. The story, revolving around Frank Machin, a star-of-the-hour rugby player, who struggles for balance between the demands of his team owner Weaver and his passionate desire for Mrs Hammond, his widowed landlady who resists the deception of fame, Harris saw as his own. 'To say it was autobiographical for me might be overstating, but, yes, it connected at the deepest level. Machin *was* me. I always saw it as heavenly intervention.'

While Harris loved the novel, he hated the first draft script that Anderson followed up with. 'He hated it so much,' Anderson said, 'that he didn't even bother to write back about it.' Anderson readdressed from scratch. For him, *This Sporting Life* had always been a charmed project. When he had first tried to acquire the rights, Independent Artists, the comedy-making company of Julian Wyntel and Leslie Parkyn, beat him to it. Independent offered the film to the *Saturday Night and Sunday Morning* director Karel Reisz but Reisz, elsewhere committed, insisted on passing on the project to his untried friend, Anderson. 'So it seemed to be meant for me, and I sank everything into it. With Karel's blessing I commissioned David Storey to develop a screenplay – and from the start I told him to build it up for Harris. I told him, "See *The Ginger Man* if you can, then build it from that."'

The comedian Leslie Phillips, mainstay of Independent, supported the concept of teaming Anderson, Storey and Harris: 'There was a cultural tidal wave coming at the start of the sixties. I knew we had turned a corner in movie-making in Britain and one could either choose to be part of it, or pretend it wasn't happening and lose out. I recall working at Beaconsfield on comedies like *Crooks Anonymous* with Julie Christie, who was just starting. The truth was, we all wanted to be on the next-door sound stage making gritty stuff like *This Sporting Life*. We knew the posh-toff era was dead.' What had crucially changed, said Anderson, was the arrival of a sense of commitment beyond commerce in movie-making. 'There was suddenly social comment, socialist debate, a decent labour movement, a peace movement, real freedom of expression. [A story like] *This Sporting Life* fed on all the changes.'

But Harris was saying no. Anderson spoke to him long-distance in Tahiti, then decided to make a personal visit. The trip to Tahiti took 24 hours' flying time, and Anderson has happily recalled his 5 a.m. arrival at Papette airport where, despite the rigours of filming, Harris met him 'with his eighteenth-century seaman's hair down on his shoulders, bursting to tell me what he thought of the script. Within minutes we were at it, and though neither of us had slept much the night before, we talked and argued right through the next day.'

Harris's intellect delighted Anderson and 'told me instantly that the journey was worthwhile'. What followed was 'intensive, finest-detail brainstorming like I'd never, ever had'. Harris's view was emphatic: that the power was in the novel, and neither Storey nor anyone else needed to 'glam it up with movie razzle-dazzle'. 'So we went back to basics, and started again,' said Anderson.

By the time Anderson winged back to London with a sketchpad outline of a new script, Harris could see the light at the end of the thirteen-month *Bounty* tunnel. The project was already $10 million over budget and six months overdrawn, and Milestone was finally happy to call it a day. But Brando remained unhappy. When the *Saturday Evening Post* ran a feature entitled THE MUTINY OF

MARLON BRANDO, brazenly accusing him of hindering the production, Brando replied with a hefty lawsuit. Implying MGM's inadequacy, he told *Variety*, 'If you send a multimillion-dollar production to a place when, according to the precipitation records, it is the worst time of year, and when you send it there without a script, it seems there is some kind of primitive mistake. The reason for all the big failures is the same – no script. Then the actors become the obvious target of executives trying to cover their own tracks.'

Free at last in October, Harris looked back on the movie as 'nightmarish'. He told the journalist Peter Evans, '*Mutiny on the Bounty* almost made me a drunk and a tramp. It was disgusting. But I survived. I survived and made myself a promise. I promised myself that, however poor I got, I would never again do anything I didn't really believe in.' For some, the much-reported grumbles seemed churlish. Others saw Harris perfecting his personal art of hype: he had clawed his way into the limelight and wasn't about to give over all the column inches to Brando. It took real ingenuity to keep the press rolling, but Harris had the wit and the stamina. Nine months later he still had chins wagging when he blacklisted the gala London premiere of *Mutiny on the Bounty* in favour of an evening with his newfound guru-companion Lindsay Anderson, at a Festival Hall Beethoven concert.

Mutiny on the Bounty was not the outright failure most predicted. Though it differed dramatically from the heroic Gable–Laughton version, its substitute attractions of the island life of the mutineers and finer-tuned characterisations proved worthy. In order to achieve profit, MGM's target gross was $27 million. As it turned out, the gross passed $30 million within weeks, securing a commercial success. Reviews, though, were fire and ice. Bosley Crowther in the *New York Times* cheered 'the sheer magnitude of this enactment' and 'the energy that passionate performances impart to it'. The *Los Angeles Times* encouraged viewers to 'settle back in your chair to enjoy first-class escapist entertainment' (though the reviewer Philip Scheuer disdained Brando, 'whose mumblings left me unmoved'). But the *Monthly Film Bulletin* lamented an overblown production where 'character is deployed not for purposes of human drama or historical accuracy or social conscience, but for showmanship and showmanship alone'. Harris's personal reviews were, at last, highly visible. In the *Los Angeles Times* he merited special attention. And the *Hollywood Reporter* judged him 'fine as the seaman who first sights in Brando's Fletcher Christian decency beneath the fop'.

Before *Mutiny*'s completion, Elizabeth gave birth in London to a second son, Jared. Harris, in Tahiti, had to make do with envelopes of photographs in the mail, but when he returned to LA the family reunion, minus the baby, who stayed in London with the Ogmores, was, he said, 'blissful'. Harris rented Boris Karloff's old house, and the semblance of domestic normality resumed. *The Ginger Man* bogey seemed deflated, even absent, wrote Elizabeth, and she once again held hopes for a calmer life. 'But history was conspiring against them,' said Joe Lynch, who watched Harris's progress from afar. 'A Hollywood movie like *Bounty* is like a volcanic explosion. Richard's name was finally up there on the billboards in letters as big as Brando and Trevor Howard. His credit was *above* the *Mutiny* title, which is the highest of all Hollywood accolades. He was certainly "in the club" at last. But it's common knowledge that that's a tough club, and a hard atmosphere to keep a family – any family, let alone a troubled one like Dick's – going in." Harris, though, remained optimistic. He liked the cachet of acceptance. Liked that he could call up Laurence Harvey for a drink or a meal, or ask Bob and Dorothy Mitchum to introduce him to all the hip new clubs of Sunset Boulevard that savoured Hollywood gods. Harris said, 'There was a lot of grace [in the acceptance] from several people. Guys like Mitchum were always goading me, saying, "Everybody's suddenly asking who the fuck this Richard Harris is." There was lots of warmth and lots of advice, and of course I took none of it.'

The Karloff house was Gothically gloomy, but Harris felt at home. 'I wanted to stay there, but then the owners reclaimed it, and we were pushed out to the Bel Air Hotel, which was harder [to establish] a home life in.' Upset by the sudden move, Elizabeth reconciled herself to the situation. *Mutiny* was on everyone's lips. Her husband was accepted in the Hollywood fraternity. There was much anticipatory talk about this new rugby picture that everyone swore would be an earthshaker. There was fire in her husband's heart and suddenly, she said, she knew this welcome 'eye of the storm' would never be a permanent peace.

The Harrises packed again and returned to Ireland, stopping off in London to collect the baby. Dickie was at his best with the British and Irish reporters, bursting with triumphant plans. The *Ginger Man* fiasco was forgotten. Irish censorship hadn't cowed him. He was, he said, considering an offer to take the play to Broadway. His next movie project would be *This Sporting Life*, with his new friend Lindsay Anderson, whom he adored. He had also formed a development company with a view to producing Liam O'Flaherty's *Insurrection*, about the 1916 Easter Rising. His friend Carol Reed might direct *Savort*, starring Harris, about the doctrine of humanitarianism. 'I want to do so much, and I want to do significant work that speaks for people, whether it is the oppressed people of the world, or people suffering anywhere. I want to portray the truth . . .'

'He came home,' said Godfrey Quigley, 'like a Viking returning, but he had sense of perspective. He told me privately that he knew this whole Hollywood business was tentative, that the *Bounty* was great, but that that was Brando's thunder, not his. He believed he was still on thin ice, and he still had that nervy thing that made even you – in his company – feel edgy. "Calm down, Dick," I would tell him. But all he'd say was, "Life is for living, lad. Plenty of time to calm down when I'm ninety!"'

Homecoming delighted Harris, as it did throughout his life. On this occasion, the recent opening of Radio Telefis Eireann (RTE), Irish National radio and TV, gave him special joy, seeing it, as he did, as a new strike for independence from the colonial past. His pride in broadening Irish horizons was obvious to everyone, but he travelled back to Limerick with real trepidation, aware now that the buffer of Milly was gone, and he would have to cope with the vanquished Ivan and the inevitable demise of Harris Mills, alone.

In Milly's absence, more than ever, he wanted Ivan's approval. But he knew it was an impossibility. Ivan had never accepted his Hollywood visions. With the last-ditch crises at the mills – now operating on a wing and a prayer, fully accepting the imminent Rank takeover – Ivan had less time than ever for his son. Harris later recalled their only exchange that acknowledged his achievements in any way. 'I was sitting in the kitchen telling the brothers about *Mutiny on the Bounty* and all the LA excitement, about Bob Mitchum and Gary Cooper and all the others. Dad didn't even look up from his newspaper, but he said, "Did you meet Betty Grabble?" I said to him, "You mean, Betty *Grable*? No, Dad, I didn't meet her." And he made a noise like, "Uh-ho", as if to say, See, I knew it, you're going nowhere, you are making no progress at all . . .'

CHAPTER 6

Try!

According to Elizabeth and the businessmen who knew him, Ivan Harris remained blissfully unaware of the true devastating extent of his mills' failure. Ironically, the son he least believed in saved him from total indignity. And, doubly ironically, the movie Richard Harris was warming up to, *This Sporting Life*, to be financed by Rank Films, was the device that would facilitate salvation from disgrace. As Ivan's management infrastructure and cash flow disintegrated, Rank took over Harris Mills' production and distribution, leaving only the original mill premises on the corner of Williams Street in Ivan's hands. Rank's intention was to acquire the mill building as well, but Ivan hung on and it was with the financial dexterity of his son, utilising the £25,000 fee from *This Sporting Life* to purchase the building, that Rank outdid Rank and gave the Harrises the last laugh. 'My father might have been unaware of the full failure,' said Harris, 'but he was a man of pride, a traditionalist, and it upset me to see him on his knees at the end. I was delighted that I could help him keep the building, and keep the makings of a small mill going, but it was a small victory.' In fact, Ivan's health declined quickly after Milly's death and he too would shortly die, never witnessing Harris's ultimate rise, never reconciled to his saviour son. Harris told the journalist Gerry Hannan, 'When I bought the building I swore I would keep it, come hell or high water, until time wore away the Harris name from over the door. It was a monument to my father and brothers and my forebears and the work they did. And, by God, I did keep it!' Only in the late eighties, when the HARRIS MILLS boards literally disintegrated above the doorways, did Harris sell the building to Limerick Corporation, for development as a car park.

After the briefest of Limerick holidays – in which he took time to renew his acquaintanceship with Manual Di Lucia and purchase a brick-built home on the coast at his beloved Kilkee – Harris hurried back to Lindsay Anderson in London. Progress on *This Sporting Life* speeded up once the Rank distribution deal was in place, and Elizabeth sighed resignation as the midnight routines of 'prep' meetings began, once again bringing domestic life at Allen House to a standstill. Anderson had now replaced Donal Donnelly, Joe Lynch and every other Dublin drop-in in monopolising Harris's time and devotion. Elizabeth liked him – and welcomed his calm intervention in the latest rounds of husband–wife dissension – but she resented his condescending attitude to her, which she interpreted as intellectual snobbery. More than anything, Elizabeth disliked Anderson's overt rebelliousness, which found its perfect twin in Harris and sparked her husband to press the limits. Together, Elizabeth saw, Harris and Anderson laughed and conspired against all sorts of visible and invisible enemies – against the old institutions of the church, the state and Hollywood. As a peer's daughter, a representational figure, Elizabeth too was fair game, but, said Joe Lynch, she took the jibes with good humour – or the best she could muster – and diverted herself with tending the babies.

For his part, Harris was starting that slow metamorphosis that would drain his generosity and congeniality and produce instead the take-no-prisoners fibre of Frank Machin. He was tunnel-visioned, and, in his own quirky way, spectacularly disciplined. All parrying with the press stopped. One of his last pronouncements was razor-sharp: 'I want to take responsibility for all I do. I don't want to be handed someone else's baby and be told to bring him up. I want my own vision, my own work, my own life.' The symbiotic kinship with Anderson made *Sporting Life* his very own. 'The benefit of so close a relationship was, selfishly, control for me. I understood Lindsay and his interests and needs and intellectual and sexual disposition, so I could predict everything he did and wanted. Yes, there were clashes. Because what he wanted from me personally, in terms perhaps of emotional engagement, I could not give. I gave to a point, but I was who I was and, no matter how I loved him, I would not change myself, or pretend. Lindsay dealt with that and we became very productive as a team.' As the screenplay developed, Harris refused Anderson's request for a 'round table' with the novelist David Storey: 'David was another thing, something separate. I felt if I got to know him I'd like him. If that happened, then in the debates and arguments I might have given in. So Lindsay and I would go away to the coast at Rottingdean and sweat it out together. Then Lindsay would go back to David with our notes. When I finally did meet David, I *did* like him. But by then the script was ready for shooting.'

In the middle of preproduction Harris was offered his biggest cheque yet, to star in the producer Samuel Bronston's history epic *The Fall of the Roman Empire*, scheduled for shooting in Spain that autumn with Anthony Mann directing. The proposed part was that of Commodus, mad son of the Emperor Marcus Aurelius, whose dissipation led to the sacking of Rome by the Barbarians. It was the grandest role in what Harris judged to be 'a colossal script', and he jumped at it, instructing Fraser to work out the deal, and immediately arranging riding lessons to prepare himself for ancient Rome. When Fraser came back with the fee details, an awesome $200,000 – $6 million in today's terms – Harris and Elizabeth were ecstatic. Elizabeth started house hunting. Then a redrafted script, by Ben Barzman and Philip Yordan, arrived – and Harris exploded. 'After some of my best scenes were cut from *Mutiny*, I had drafted a new contract clause that said no cuts, no rewrites. Suddenly, Commodus, the character I wanted, was this revamped celluloid lightweight. I said, No, no, no!' Harris gave Bronston a simple ultimatum: shoot the first script or forget it. Bronston stood his ground and Harris was replaced by Stephen Boyd. Elizabeth's disappointment at the loss of almost a quarter of a million dollars is unrecorded, but, said Harris, the bank manager let them both know how he felt. Having read about the row in the newspapers, he phoned, complaining that Harris's account was overdrawn. Since house hunting was in progress, he suggested to Elizabeth that Harris would be well advised to eat his pride and take Bronston's offer. Harris was outraged: 'I phoned up and told him, "I don't tell you how to run your bank. So don't you tell me how to run my life."'

The script for *This Sporting Life,* meanwhile, had been refined to perfection. Both Harris and Anderson agreed that this was not, as the media described it, a film about sport. Anderson told *Films and Filming,* 'I suppose that the film is primarily a study of temperament. It is a film about a man of extraordinary power and aggressiveness, both temperamental and physical, but at the same time a man with a great innate sensitiveness and a need for love, of which he is at first hardly aware.' That summary resounded, accurately, as a thumbnail of Harris's character, and signalled a film of harmony and truth.

In preparation for the physical trials to come, Harris went back into training – not, as might be expected, with his old friends at the London Irish grounds at Deerpark (where Len Dineen would soon be captain) but on the 'foreign soil' of Richmond. 'I could have gone to the London Irish. But that would have turned it into something of a giggle. I knew I would not become involved with the Richmond people. They are kind of snobs – bank clerks and lawyers. I knew they would ignore me. They never even asked my name – and that was just fine, because I was seething, I was stewing in Frank Machin and I didn't want anyone to distract that.' The realities of the scrum pack after ten years of absence were horrifying: 'Physically I thought I was big enough, but I wasn't as big as most rugby players really are. I hung about the dressing rooms making mental notes on how they behaved. I worked at preparing my body – training runs every morning, muscle-building with weights, clenching rubber balls to build up my hands and wrists – but I was worried in the end that I wouldn't look the real thing in the movie.' David Storey offered reassurance. A former coal miner, three years younger than Harris, he had funded his early art studies by signing with Leeds Rugby League. 'He'd been four seasons with the club's "A" team, earning himself an encyclopedic knowledge of the game. He coached me, and I started trying not just to emulate him, but to *be* him, right down to dyeing my hair black like his.' Anderson was massively impressed by this imaginative discipline. Joe Lynch believed, 'Lindsay fell more and more in love with Dick, because of Dick's dedication. When it came to making the movie, it was a "gimme", it was already "in the can", because of the amount of prep work done.'

For Harris, emotional survival was the name of the game, when shooting began at Independent's Beaconsfield Studios. 'First of all, the script was exceedingly tense, very jerky and full of testosterone. And then the sets were grotty and bleak. After Tahiti, it was tough, but it was also familiar. It was Limerick, really.' Rachel Roberts, a sound acquaintance if not a bosom buddy since *The Dutch Courtesan* at Stratford East, was cast as Mrs Hammond, the unattainable object of Frank Machin's desires. Born in Llanelli, west Wales, and a prizewinner at RADA, Roberts had all the qualifications Harris liked in leading ladies. 'She was very experienced, with the Old Vic and revue shows and every form of drama behind her, and that all helped. She was also a no-bullshitter who didn't mind telling Lindsay when he was wrong. There were no rows, but she would call a halt and calmly explain that this or that felt phoney, and we'd start again. I deferred to her, because of her authority. I also felt a little empathy and sadness for her, because she could be gloomy and depressed, and your heart sank when you looked in those big doggy eyes.' Anderson had huge admiration for Roberts and felt her casting opposite Harris was 'probably the most inspired casting I ever did. The rapport [between Roberts and Harris] enthralled everyone who visited the set. Her technique was very like Richard's. It was clenched and intense and at times even I stood back and just let them at it.' Harris later told anyone who would listen how much he looked up to Roberts: 'She is Welsh, a Celt, sensitive. She knows it all. She's so good you don't have to act with her.'

Frank Windsor, cast in the pivotal role of the dentist to whom Machin is brought at the start of the movie and whose knockout injection stimulates the waves of memory that make the story, enjoyed *This Sporting Life* more than anything he had ever done because of Anderson's unique approach: 'The way Lindsay worked was quite insidious. For example, the dentist scene, which was only a few days' work, seemed of hardly any importance in the script I got. It was quite simply that up-and-coming Machin got his teeth knocked out and is taken to visit me, to get them fixed. But Lindsay saw it as much, much more. It became a motif that he kept cutting back to – the spine of the film, if you will – and said its own piece about man's inhumanity and all that. That for me summed up Lindsay's genius, and why *This Sporting Life* became a recognised classic: every tiny scrap of the script, every small skill any actor had, every "bit of business" was taken by Lindsay and and shuffled into the best possible scenario. The actors all adored him for that care he took, and Richard, I know, felt he was really in his debt for it.'

Karel Reisz, the movie's 'godfather', kept a benign eye on the production and was excited by what he saw of Harris's double nature: 'Those complementary qualities – a huge, commanding presence and a beautifully subtle sensitivity – made Richard an actor in the big, heroic tradition. Above all, he possessed a rare courage that allowed him to explore the heights and the depths.'

What Reisz was observing was a coming of age – not just for Harris but for the new-wave cinema that had grown from the 'kitchen-sink' stage successes of the late fifties, and to which his personal contribution had been colossal. 'Everything had changed in five years,' said Anderson. 'It started when young entertainers like Cliff Richard and Tommy Steele started wearing T-shirts and jeans, and then writers like Alan Sillitoe and Stan Barstow were writing books about the lower middle classes and John Osborne and Arnold Wesker took it to the Royal Court and to West End audiences. It was all an offshoot of the contemporary spirit of relaxation and social awareness. British imperialism taking a knock with the Suez fiasco; the street protesters wanting British troops out of Egypt; the anti-nuclear Aldermaston rallies ... Everything *opening up*. Where Richard shone was his natural openness. One didn't have to mould him or force him to pretend to be an "aware person": he was it. He was as fired up by everything that was changing as I was. The era, the David Storey plot and the man – Richard – came together to create something magical in that movie. I contributed, but I felt like a bystander.'

Off the set Harris's relationship with Anderson deepened, though it would never achieve the serene balance to ensure its lifelong survival. As they intuited a comprehensive hit in *This Sporting Life*, plans were set in motion for other shared projects. *Wuthering Heights*, Harris's boyhood favourite, turned out to be Anderson's fantasy fixation too. Now they decided to mount a production partnership to stage prestige plays and finance big, trendsetting films. 'I want to do *Wuthering Heights*, ideally with Merle Oberon,' Harris told Joe Lynch. But, of course, Oberon was in her late fifties and in semiretirement. In his dreams he would opt for her any day, but, more practically, Julie Christie seemed appropriate casting for Cathy. Harris said: 'I can rattle off the names of six brilliant actors in England – no, seven. But there is only one girl who has any merit at all. And that is Julie Christie.' 'For quite a long time this circular discussion about possible projects became the order of the day,' said Lynch. 'Every time you met him it was, "Lindsay and I want to do this, or that." The world was their oyster.'

When *This Sporting Life* wrapped – inside time and budget – almost everyone, from Roberts to Reisz, predicted a success beyond even *Saturday Night and Sunday Morning*, the first of the new-wave hits. Anderson politely told the press that his film was not new-wave, rather an original: 'Throughout *This Sporting Life* we were very aware that we were not making a film about anything representative. We were making a film about something unique. We were not making a film about a "worker", rather about an extraordinary – and therefore more deeply significant – man, and about an extraordinary relationship [with the Roberts character]. We were not, in a word, making sociology.'

British critics overwhelmingly greeted *This Sporting Life* just as Anderson wanted, as a thoroughbred original. Cecil Wilson in the *Daily Mail* wrote, 'By now the oafish unhero with a gratuitous grudge against society is a stock figure of British films but in this one Richard Harris begins where others left off. The actor comes tremendously into his own as the new British answer to Brando.' That review more than any gratified Harris: unbiased comparison with his template idol, based not on media-hustling but on hard work. The *Daily Mirror*, Harris's original champion, tripped over itself with gushing plaudits: 'Harris [delivers] a powerful, smouldering and superbly gripping performance. I would lay odds that this virile piece of acting will not be bettered this year . . . first league.' Released in America in July 1963 – nine months before The Beatles' 'invasion' – the movie met a proverbial standing ovation. A H Weiller in the *New York Times* called it 'a smashing victory', and echoed the *Mail*'s Brando comparison: 'Credit must go to Richard Harris's portrait of the ravaged Frank Machin. He is a realistically rugged rugby player – the prognathous jaw, the overhanging brow, the dented Roman nose, piercing eyes and massively muscled torso are reminiscent of the early Marlon Brando.'

At the British premiere – in February – Harris accompanied Elizabeth ebulliently, unable to conceal his sense of triumph. Wearing an astrakhan-collared coat 'that seemed straight from Richard Burton's wardrobe', according to the *Mail*, alongside Elizabeth in flowing vampire cape, Harris jostled with an Odeon, Leicester Square, crowd densely populated with Limerickmen. 'The atmosphere throbbed with adulation,' wrote the Irish columnist Des Hickey. 'Other young stars of the new-wave school like Albert Finney and Tom Courtenay were shaking [Harris's] hand. "Richard, you were *enormous*," said Courtenay. Outside the crowds waited hopefully in the rain – and were astonished when the star stood bare-headed on the pavement, shouting greetings to friends and relatives from Limerick.'

This lifetime high, the validation of his belief in himself as man and actor of value, called Harris to reassess priorities. 'So I said fuck off to the big, flashy caviare supper at the Savoy and took the celebration cake, in the shape of a tiered rugby stadium, back to Michael and Sheila van Bloeman, back to the grand old supporters at the Troubadour, where it all began. I saw that gesture as important, as the poetic fulfilment of an unspoken promise. The van Bloemans were the first to believe in me.'

At the party, Harris's star guests included Karel Reisz, Anderson, Storey, Betsy Blair and J P Donleavy. When Reisz and Anderson professed themselves too shy for speech-making, Harris took to the podium, whisky in hand: 'Thank you for coming, my friends. I hope you go back to see *Sporting Life* again and next time pay for your seats. Remember that I get five per cent of all profits . . .'

The 'classical' future career that Harris and Anderson mapped out for selected journalists that night was destined to evaporate, but in the heat of victory everything seemed possible. He told Hickey at the Troubadour party that 'the buzz' around *This Sporting Life* guaranteed more and better Hollywood pictures. 'But I will agree to no picture unless the part is right.' Once again the promises of riches gushed: *Wuthering Heights*, a new *Hamlet*, the Liam O'Flaherty classic, Irish-made movies about the Republican cause . . . Twenty years later Harris reviewed that career crossroads and its opportunities dispassionately: 'I had children and we were living in a tiny flat in London, sleeping together, all of us, in two rooms. And though there was no pressure from Elizabeth I sat down and said, "I've got a choice here. I can do *The Luck of Ginger Coffey* [a quality Irish novel by Brian Moore] – it's a fantastic piece but it will only pay what I got for *Sporting Life* – or I can get a fortune to do *Major Dundee* in Hollywood." And the latter is the choice I made. That choice [to pursue Hollywood] was the right choice, I still believe.'

Before *Major Dundee* or the Hollywood slush-pile avalanche poured forth, Harris sank himself in a release of pent-up social energies surpassing all binges that had gone before. Joe Lynch recalled, 'mad days with a madman. He loved the noise and movement and glitter. I remember being in the flat and suddenly he wanted to sing some song for me. It wasn't good enough just to sing it: he wanted piano accompaniment as well. So he says, "There's a piano upstairs" – and goes trundling off up the stairs and bangs down some poor sod's door and demands the use of his piano. The fellow was shocked but he knew who he was dealing with so he let us in. Harris jumped at the piano and began carolling away for the rest of the night. I think it was hard on the nine-to-five neighbours, to be honest.'

After years of rows and parties, the residents of Allen House finally drew the line. A petition signed by all the residents (except one) requested the removal of the Harrises. The noncontributor was Peter Jeffreys, a printer from Penge, biased because he was Harris's principal drinking partner at the Britannia, the currently favoured pub. By the rules of residency every neighbour had to agree to the eviction of an offender, so the Harrises had a reprieve. Joe Lynch said, 'Harris decided they were a snooty bunch of killjoys anyway and he wanted to get his own back. So he paid a friend of ours, an out-of-work actor, to march up and down outside Allen House with a sandwich board on which was written "Love Thy Neighbour – Signed Harris". It went on for days, and all it did was inflame the situation.'

The neighbours didn't have to suffer for long. Pregnant for the third time, Elizabeth emphatically decided the apartment was too small and commenced a conclusive spate of house hunting. After the family had moved temporarily to a furnished flat round the corner from Allen House, a proper family home, purchased with a loan guaranteed by Lord Ogmore, was finally found at Bedford Gardens. It was, said Harris, anything but perfect – it was upright, sombre, prettified only by two cherry trees, one in the back garden and one in the front – but at least it had kicking space for the kids and lent the Harrises a patina of domestic permanence. For her third baby Elizabeth booked into a private nursing home, 'a well-earned luxury', she said. The night before the birth, Harris boozily serenaded her from the pavement – not exactly the exemplary dad-to-be, but fair to form. But on the day of delivery he was caught short. Visiting for what he expected to be a polite check-in a day or so before the expected big event, Elizabeth suddenly went into labour holding his hand. Jamie was born a few hours later, with Harris standing by, for once.

In the hiatus between the London and New York openings of *This Sporting Life*, Harris and Anderson presented their next – and final – shared production, a stark, radical version of Gogol's *Diary of a Madman* at the Royal Court. It was to mark Harris's withdrawal from serious theatre for 27 years and for a finale it was auspicious, and tragic – tragic because it showed yet again the potential of the partnership. The play, a one-man piece about a poor government clerk who comes to believe he is King Ferdinand VIII of Spain, was restyled by Harris and Anderson, based in part on Patrick Magee's recent rendition of Samuel Beckett's monodrama *Krapp's Last Tape*. 'But it was original redrafting,' said Harris. 'I was working a theme I knew and loved – *my* theme – about the lowly man in love beyond his station, and the torture of intellect.'

The play opened before Princess Margaret, in a disastrous state of tension. The narcissism and confidence fellow actors like Booth saw at Stratford East were nowhere in evidence, and by Harris's admission he was, at first, 'awful in rehearsals and not much better for first night'. Backstage he shook in his boots: 'I stood in the wings gripped with the sudden horror of the ordeal before me. Two hours and twenty minutes on an empty stage without a cue . . .!' Herbert Kretzmer of the *Daily Express* found that first night 'the most tedious evening's entertainment I've endured in the theatre'. 'Then I got it together,' said Harris. 'It was a case of waking up, that's all. I was doing so much work, that it was hard to redirect my focus.' Fighting back, text, set and pace were all tweaked. Within days the critic Clive Exton was applauding 'the greatest thing I have seen in the theatre'.

As *Diary of a Madman* evolved, said Harris, it became, like *This Sporting Life*, increasingly autobiographical – a deeply personal duologue that spun from paranoia to self-aggrandising, with voices whispering from the trough of TB isolation bed, and from the peak of the Bel Air harem. Harris's Askenti Ivanovitch's duologues were Harris v. Harris. Their well-practised fluidity impressed *The Times*:

> In these scenes Mr Harris's playing is superb. He acts like a piece of mobile sculpture. Every gesture is composed as a deliberate displacement of space and the line of his movement precisely reflects the line of his thought. Besides ensuring unbroken contact with the audience, this gives dignity and meaning to a part which might easily have evaporated in self-intoxicated egoism.

Overnight, in the grand slam of movies-cum-theatre success, Harris was an actor-artist, alongside Finney, Burton and O'Toole.

There was more to come. As anticipated, *This Sporting Life* began collecting award nominations. In the late spring the announcement of the Palme d'Or was made and, immediately after an American Academy Award nomination. Harris was especially gratified by the Best Actor Oscar nomination. He told Peter Evans, 'For the first time in my life I have come close to some sort of fulfilment. Until now I've been kicked around, trodden on, beaten down. No more, boyo. No more.'

At Cannes with Anderson, the triumph in acceptance of the Palme d'Or Best Actor slipped into farce. 'I was astonished and flattered to be among these stellar types – and, yes, I was pissed as a newt. Visconti won Best Film for *The Leopard*, which was amazing work. The French actress Marina Vlady won the Best Actress award, which was deserved. And then came little old Dickie Harris's turn. By the time they got to me, there were only two big statues left, and then eleven or twelve little ones for things like Best Sound or Best Wigs. Jeanne Moreau was emceeing and she suddenly called out my name and I ran up to the stage to take this award. But it wasn't an award. It was a little box she offered me. "What's this?" I asked her. She told me, "Cufflinks, that's what the best actor gets." And I thought, Fuck that, I didn't do all that graft for a fucking pair of cufflinks I could win at a carnival. So I leaned across and just took a fucking palm tree statue. And then I said thank you *en Français* and split.'

Two *gendarmes* attempted to retrieve the statue, but Harris nudged them aside and escaped the *palais*. Later the Palme d'Or committee demanded the return of the statue, which was inscribed for Best Animation Film, and Harris relented. The cufflinks in the embossed leather box were duly mailed to him. 'I kept them for years, but they still annoyed me. Who gives *cufflinks* to an Olympic medalist?'

The Cannes Palme d'Or fiasco – spun out year in, year out, over the next three decades as a towering blarney yarn on the talk-show circuit – demonstrated something of the imposed identity dilemma that dogged Harris for the rest of his career. The British tabloids reporting the incident as it occurred headlined IRISH ACTOR IN PUB BRAWL. A week later, in the rosy glow of post-Palme d'Or assessments, the headlines noted, BRITISH ACTOR WINS PALME D'OR. 'I hated that,' said Harris, 'but I suppose I fed into it. The British cliché of the Irish codger was an old chestnut, and it was easy for them to categorise me, because I was larger than life. I was only ever "British" in the papers when I was winning things, or scoring points.'

To those who knew him, Harris's pride in his Irishness had never been compromised. Ronald Fraser called him 'fabulously, *finally* Irish!' And, though he abandoned plans to film O'Flaherty's *Insurrection* in the fluxing dissolution of his partnership with Anderson, he made it clear to friends at the Britannia that his great Irish projects were yet to come. Joe Lynch remembered Harris singing ballads like 'The Mountains of Mourne' and promising his fervent audience that his 'great Irish musical' would shake up the Brits. 'He certainly wasn't anti-British, because he wasn't racist-inclined at all. In fact, the bewildering aspect of Dick was how non-racist and non-bigoted [*sic*] he was. His "Irish secret weapon" was a personal pride-of-identity thing, something to do with gaining acknowledgment from home, and Limerick. In that sense, he never really grew up. He was always a boy, looking for a pat on the head.'

He was a *barnac*, for sure. But he was also now a film star, a commercial commodity. And, as such, he was no longer entirely master of his own destiny.

CHAPTER 7

Try Again

In terms of cinema quality, the early sixties belonged to the Italians. While audiences in America, Britain and France faltered, shifting their interest to TV, Italy's cinema attendance figures remained constant, reflecting the high quality of output since the start of the decade. In the late fifties Italian filmmaking slumped, but in 1961 more than 220 features emerged from the sixty sound stages available and the international awards records show clearly the thrust of expansive intellectual ambition. Only Japan competed in the quantity stakes (547 features in 1961), but American and British endeavours paled in comparison.

America particularly had hit a slide. The studio system responsible for forty years of movie-making had disintegrated and 'runaway productions', with formerly 'in-house' directors and producers chasing the four corners of the globe for independent deals, had become the new modus. According to studio executives, the stars, not the drifting audiences, were the main cause of American decline. Major players like Brando and Paul Newman could command $400,000 per picture. To justify that upfront outlay the studios calculated they needed a box-office gross per movie of $10 million, an impractically high target. The odds were huge, so, the dictum went, fewer risks were taken.

In Britain the rallying of kitchen-sink drama that launched Finney, Courtenay, Alan Bates and Richard Harris gave hope. The Ealing era of parochial smugness was over and a spirit of confidence was manifest in the opening of new cinema chains. The Odeon in London's Haymarket and new Rank and ABC cinemas in Woking, Catford, Sheffield and Southall spoke optimistically of wider audiences. But it was a confidence founded on soft sand. As Lindsay Anderson had predicted in a number of interviews around the time of *This Sporting Life*, the working-class 'rebel cinema' was self-limiting and the consumer-orientated, hedonistic sixties urgently wanted to know: where next?

For Richard Harris personally the answer was simple: the best pictures were coming out of Italy and Michelangelo Antonioni, Italy's most daring director, was already writing fan letters and courting him on the long-distance telephone. Antonioni loved *This Sporting Life* and begged Harris, 'Come walk the backstreets of Roma and find inspiration with me.' The Italian maestro already had a production in mind for Harris: *Deserto Rosso*, his first film in colour, to star Monica Vitti, who three years before had shared the laurels of Antonioni's first international success, *L'Aventura*. The film would be an analytical exploration of a woman's mental breakdown, told in Antonioni's naturalistic style. Antonioni's friends and crew talked of *Deserto Rosso* as being the crown to top an existential hat-trick comprising *L'Aventura*, *La Notte* and *L'Eclisse*, all critically celebrated art films.

Harris's decision to join Antonioni's was seen by many as the demarcation point of separation from Anderson. One actor close to both said, 'Lindsay didn't want him to go. It was quite a tearful, emotional split. They were on the point of announcing something special together – maybe Lindsay's contemporary *Hamlet* – and then Dick said, No, I've had enough personality-management, I want to be free.' James Booth believed Anderson's passion for Harris became claustrophobic: 'How quickly love can turn to hate. They were in too deep together, but Lindsay didn't cop the fact that Dickie hated possessive people, whether they were lovers or sycophants.'

In Italy, Harris embraced, as he always did, new beginnings, new freedoms. As he had done at first with Anderson, he did his homework on Antonioni, and on Italy in general. In London, researching Antonioni's background, he'd been told that the fifty-year-old director was introverted and spoke no English. Neither proved to be true. But Antonioni was a man of many contradictions. Fellow traveller with the antifascists of the Centro Sperimentale, he was a radical every bit as wily as Harris, a jack-of-all-trades film-critic-turned-documentary-maker-turned-*auteur* who rejected commercial considerations but craved a wide audience. *Le Amiche*, which won the Venice Silver Lion, was still regarded as his masterpiece, but he was itchy to beat it with a new, definitive film made in a *vérité* style.

Harris arrived in Rome keen and trusting. But his trust was dangerously naïve in an industry riddled with egomania, dodgy creativity and hype. To begin with, he discovered there was no conclusive screenplay. The chaotic preproduction, operating from a one-room office, immediately reminded him of the early days of Reed's *Mutiny on the Bounty*. 'I looked – and I almost turned tail and ran.' But Harris liked the few pages Antonioni gave him, and enjoyed the director's joyous company over pasta and vino. 'Finally I decided to give in. I didn't want to go back to London. I liked the Italian architecture, the new smells, the sights. So I took the pages, and I took his word and gave it my best shot.' Most engaging of all was Antonioni's description of the character Corrado Zeller, the lover-catalyst in the life of Vitti's Giuliana, whom Harris would play. 'He was a moral wreck, and I identified with that.'

The movie started in confident mode, but Harris swiftly fell foul of Antonioni, who, said Harris, preferred to 'compose' impulsively. Harris tried to readjust and get his balance. He was nothing if not a willing learner and adept at many techniques. But Antonioni was suddenly aloof and evasive. Though the director assured Harris he was improvising as the script 'evolved', interviews with Vitti in a Rome magazine suggested otherwise. After the collaboration with Anderson, said Harris, 'I expected a maturity and mutual respect in the creative process ... good only comes from honesty in a collaboration.' But Antonioni wasn't honest, and Harris flared. In the late sixties, Harris told an arts magazine, 'I believed at the beginning that he would give me this participation, because he is a great artist. I assumed he had respect for my talent because he picked me to begin with. When I got to Italy, I felt quite the opposite. I felt that Antonioni, after about five weeks I think, probably through his own insecurity, found a new formula for making this picture. I think Antonioni's pictures have their own style – but he sort of panicked.' In Harris's view, good films arose from 'an absolutely fifty-fifty compromise between actor and director.' Furthermore, he told the magazine, despite his former blockbusters, he was not 'an action star' and would never allow himself be moulded as such. Antonioni did not seem to understand this, instead treated him 'in the dumb Hollywood way'. But, 'I certainly would not suggest that he's not a great director. He's a marvellous director. He understands Monica Vitti well, and Monica needs to be sort of wound up like a doll, and then let loose – then she goes through all the emotions of acting, whatever she is told to do.'

By Christmas the strain of incompatibility had caused the production to stagger. *Deserto Rosso* was three months behind schedule and Harris was constantly bickering about unrehearsed lines and confusing direction. It didn't help that Antonioni insisted on utilising mainly amateur actors, nor that he avoided using English on set, insisting on all communication being conducted by semaphore. When Elizabeth visited, she saw that Harris's disenchantment had blown the fuses on the film: Harris still called Antonioni a genius, Elizabeth said, but he wanted out.

Hollywood, the perennial burden and challenge, became a sudden welcome intrusion. With Fraser's guidance, the producer Jerry Bresler and emerging director Sam Peckinpah flew to Rome in December with the offer of *Major Dundee*, a western set to star Charlton Heston. Bresler flattered Harris: Anthony Quinn and Steve McQueen had been first choices (in fact, both turned down the role) but Heston had seen Harris in *This Sporting Life* and, said Bresler, insisted the producers book him. Harris wondered did Heston even remember him: in his published diary, Heston details only his initial hesitation; there is no suggestion of his earlier association with Harris. 'I think he basically hated me,' said Harris, 'but at the same time saw what I could do [in *This Sporting Life*] and needed me. I respect that. Meaning, I respect his intelligence in seeing a good thing.' The role on offer – of Confederate Captain Ben Tyreen, who assists rival Union Major Dundee to catch a renegade Apache group – appealed to Harris for its 'human rights and North–South prejudice issues'. Peckinpah was also 'a fascinating, crazy mind . . . but I hesitated, I told them I wasn't sure and I upped the asking price sky-high.' The gesture was a clever one that revealed Harris's grasp of the game rules. In *Dundee*, theoretically anyway, he was selling out to Hollywood – but at a sustainable price. Bresler backed off, telling Fraser that Harris was too expensive and returning to LA, leaving Harris sipping cappuccinos in Antonioni's director's chair. On 12 December Harris was informed that his game had failed: Anthony Quinn would play Captain Ben Tyreen. 'I thought, All right, fuck it, bluff loses. But I'd been there before, and the bluff won – so, you lose some, you win some. I didn't fret about it. But it did piss me off that the only thing to occupy my thoughts when I put my head on the pillow at night was Antonioni and Monica. I thought I might go as crazy as Antonioni if this went on much longer.' But luck raised its head again. On 18 December, Anthony Quinn was declared unavailable and Bresler phoned Fraser to agree a huge fee – $300,000 – for Harris to join *Major Dundee*.

By New Year 1964 Harris was itching to leave the freezing, fogbound location of Ravenna, near Milan. Ronald Fraser said, 'He was giving it 110 per cent till the very end. When he committed himself, he committed himself. I spoke with him on the phone and all he said was, "This may kill me, so keep an eye on the obits."' Antonioni's schedule was upside down, but Harris was booked to start *Major Dundee* on 5 February in Durango, Mexico. Harris stated his case to the Italian, but 'Antonioni resisted me. He cabled Columbia, requesting more time. Columbia refused. Then he demanded more time. His movie was nowhere near finished, he said. But it was finished for me. I just thought he was having one long wank with Monica holding his balls. It went on for ever, and he was enjoying it too much. I waited, and waited and then I said, "Look, what you have is great, so . . . *adios*."' Harris walked off *Deserto Rosso* and booked a direct flight to Los Angeles. 'I just walked out. I left them with the problems of their own creation.

They had to shoot the remainder of the picture without me. Consequently it's not me you see in some of those long shots. They found someone who looked like me and slotted him in.' In the version issued late in 1964 Harris's dubbed Italian voice is unflattering and unconvincing, though his presence has the solid impact of an accomplished, in-control adept. In Italy the film succeeded, fulfilling expectations. In France it was popular. Elsewhere it was hardly seen, though Jean-Luc Godard called it 'the conscious or unconscious summit of Antonioni's recent films'. 'I frankly didn't give a fuck,' said Harris. 'It reached a point where it felt amateurish – the amateur who played Monica's husband, Carlo Chionetti, ended up getting all the praise – but I just lost faith. Later, I looked back on it as an interesting experience in cultural differences. I still held Antonioni in high regard [but] it wasn't where my head was at at that time.'

Harris's own account of his departure from Italy reads like the diary of a nervous breakdown. Through December and January he worked 'around the clock' to catch up on tangled schedules. By the middle of January he wasn't even getting to bed; instead he slept under a quilt on a shakedown on the set, to be awoken at five each day with black coffee laced with brandy – the tipple he most loved, but the one that guaranteed his worst hangovers. On his last night of filming in February, he worked till five in the morning – then threw in the towel. Grabbing a unit car, he dashed across the snow-bound hills towards Milan airport, missed his direct flight and patched together a series of jet hops to London, New York and St Louis – trying to meet Peckinpah's rehearsal dates at Columbia Studios for *Major Dundee*. 'During the London stopover I drank for six straight hours to stay awake. When I made LA, something like seventeen hours later, I was semiconsciousness, but, whether I liked it or not, arrangements were set for wardrobe fittings, riding lessons and a rehearsal talk-through.'

Harris recalled being on Stage 29 at Columbia Studios, daydreaming about the heroes of his youth who had worked here before him – '*It Happened One Night* was shot there, *The Caine Mutiny*, *The Bridge on the River Kwai*' – and then . . . *blackout*.

He later described his collapse in a self-penned magazine piece:

The rise and fall of the siren wail; tyres squealing on a greasy road, rubber-soled shoes squeaking on vinyl floors. A monk in a dark habit is painted on a white wall. No, he's not. He's moving. Speaking. Latin. Schooldays. *Veni, vidi, vici. Amo, amas, amat.* But he's not talking schoolboy Latin. He's speaking the Latin of the Catholic Church. He's giving somebody the last rites before dying . . . I open my eyes. It is not a dream. It is real. That someone is me. "Am I going to die, Father?" I ask him. The priest ignores my question but goes on with his prayers . . .

In the shock of collapse Harris was hysterical, fearing that he'd suffered a heart attack. Heston, who was putting him through his horsemanship paces at the time, was unmoved. In his diary he wrote, 'Dick was . . . stricken is the only word that leaps to mind. I can understand it, I guess. He's been working damn hard with Antonioni and now must feel some pressure on this part because of the riding and the southern accent . . .' Jerry Bresler phoned Elizabeth in London, informing her that her husband had collapsed with nervous exhaustion and was sleeping under sedation. Bresler was calmly reassuring but minutes later Harris himself called Elizabeth, railing at her for not being by his side to look after him. The accusation was, of course, unreasonable: Elizabeth had her hands more than full with the pressures of a new, half-furnished home and three lively children. She stated her case, but Harris was in no mood to listen. He was convinced the collapse was a serious and lingering illness. Elizabeth reassured him the best she could, and took comfort from Harris's decision to pursue extensive medical tests. After his first collapse at LAMDA, when malnutrition had been diagnosed, she wrote, he was always wary, already ready for the next. Now Columbia assigned a heart surgeon to conduct electrocardiogram and other tests. The results, days later, were comforting, though in hindsight probably misleading: it would be fifteen years and many more collapses before hyperglycemia was properly diagnosed.

Heston's relative indifference to Harris's health is understandable. A staunchly 'proper' family man, he possessed a reputation for discipline that was as legendary as Harris's brawling braggart notoriety. It can hardly have escaped Heston's notice that *all* Harris's recent media write-ups were spiced with tales of dangerous abandon. In Italy, for example, it was reported that Harris had experimented with LSD (preceding The Beatles' scandals by two years) and almost killed himself. Harris later admitted this was true. He told journalist–historian John Kobal, 'I felt my mind leave my body. I was in that room but not of it . . . and I knew that I didn't want to be the success I was with all the chains that it brings to a man.' He tried to jump out of a window, but was restrained by members of Antonioni's film crew. 'I'm sure old Chuck [Heston] loathed the fact that I was a druggie and a drunk. When he looked at me, he looked at me like a preacher, or some high-handed twat. I tried to like him, but most of the time I was figuring how to slip some LSD into his coffee. Loosen up, there, pard'ner. Ride a woman, not a horse!'

On *Major Dundee* Heston wore the almost-producer mantle, outranking Bresler, empowered as he was by his recent triumph with *Ben-Hur*. Harris saw the lie of the land and redeemed himself quickly, pursuing earnest conferences with Peckinpah once the worst of his exhaustion was over, and worrying away at the discrepancies in Captain Ben Tyreen, just as he had honed Frank Machin. After days of discussion with Peckinpah and Heston, he royally announced that he had finally 'found' Tyreen – 'a displaced man without roots, and basically I find that was someone [who was] easy to understand. My own family left Wales in 1747 [*sic*] and arrived in Ireland and then generations of my family were Irish . . . and then my father was very pro-British. Yet I am very Irish in temperament. Then my turn came to leave Ireland and my family died off [*sic*]. When you finally land in a foreign country and you stare into strange faces and pass shops that don't mean anything to you, these things make a deep impression on your mind, and you store them. They're like "stickybacks". They stick to me and I can't get rid of them . . . and this alienation is what I attempted to bring to the part of Tyreen.'

With a nervous insurance cover of $4 million riding on him, Harris started filming in Mexico City with a unit doctor in constant attendance, providing daily vitamin injections. 'But it was tough going. After the freezing cold of Italy, there was this appalling desert heat. I remember thinking, I might last a week, but don't count on a month.'

The first day's shoot, he recalled, involved – appropriately – a fist fight with Heston. 'Chuckles', as Harris now christened him, was 'still sceptical and generally a pain in the backside. What was his problem? I had been ill. I was tired. I had barely seen my children, my new son, in months. I came to this scorching location and here was this superstar laying it on hard for me. I was late once or twice for the early-morning calls and he started making a ridiculous deal about it. He got a stopwatch and sat there each day in his trailer waiting for me to clock in. It was like some stupid factory. I soon got pretty pissed off. So I got a load of alarm clocks and set them all around his make-up trailer. And I showed up before the call time and had them all set to go off *on the dot* of the call time. So Heston came in – and suddenly all these alarms went off, a huge explosion of noise. He jumped out of his skin with the shock. I told him it was just me clocking in. But he wasn't amused at all. He had no sense of humour, not a bit. So it made an already difficult production very tiresome.'

On 17 April Heston wrote in his diary that Harris was 'something of a fuck-up, no question', but he later generously revised his opinion: 'I seem to have been unloading all my frustrations over the [scorchingly hot] location on poor Dick Harris. Dick wasn't used to working with either horses or guns. If he was a fuck-up, I was a hard-nosed son of a bitch.'

Peckinpah, both Harris and Heston observed, was no great delight, either. On his first major studio film he was, said Heston, 'going European', and 'shooting the sky'. Heston liked Peckinpah's nerve in departing from the precise script to 'find a mood', but Harris had had enough false poetry with Antonioni. Open three-way rows ensued, spreading beyond the principals. At one point Peckinpah left the desert set and drove off alone into the hills at night, declaring,

'I'd rather sleep with the snakes than with actors.' Harris saw in Peckinpah a fundamental inadequacy and an attitude towards collaboration that, like Antonioni, fell short of total honesty. Harris said: 'I think making a picture is a very serious business. And I think that, if you commit yourself, you must do so in a very serious way. I didn't like [Peckinpah] very much. He didn't prepare enough for me. I prepare very strongly [*sic*] but I found him lacking in application, and consequently he was not getting the best out of his subject, or out of me and Heston.'

Early in April Columbia made an attempt to replace Peckinpah, who had already run a quarter of a million dollars over budget. Fearing the lesser evil of changing horses midstream, Heston objected to Mike Frankovitch, the head of Columbia, and offered his own six-figure salary by way of compensation. Frankovitch was mollified and told him, 'Listen, Chuck, we wouldn't dream of taking your salary! It's a nice gesture, and we appreciate it, but we'll just go ahead as we are.' Peckinpah remained, the movie continued – but the overspend was ultimately docked from Heston's salary.

After the Rio Mescala location, *Major Dundee* moved to Estudios in Churabusco for the final sequences. Heston grew to admire 'this facet of Sam's method: keeping the structure of the scene loose enough to inject ad-libbed lines'. Harris disagreed. On 27 April a laborious bedroom scene with Heston and a small-time actress who spoke no English took endless hours, agitating everyone. It all smacked of autocratic Antonioni and his amateurs and his secret codes, and Harris hated it and started mumbling again about walking away.

Elizabeth's arrival in Mexico and a new on-set friendship with the actor James Coburn kept things rolling. For Coburn, Harris was 'an original, with everything that connotes. He was very clear about his position in the movie industry – clearly someone who was straddling two worlds of art films and blockbusters who felt conflicted. That conflict came out in drink. When he wanted to, he could hit the liquor like no one I knew. We went on the social circuit in our time off, went to bull fights, that sort of thing, making up a foursome with our respective wives.' Harris's tiredness was clearly in evidence for

Coburn. At the Plaza de Toros in Mexico City Elizabeth and Coburn watched in horror as Harris physically attacked a Mexican spectator who knocked over Harris's bag of candy in response to a matador's poor showing in the ring. This summary violence was unnerving to Elizabeth – as was the preoccupation with disease and death, in Mexico more noticeable than ever before. When Lindsay Anderson flew out to join them for a short holiday, the suggestion was made of a spot of recreational 8mm filmmaking. Each would contribute a short film essay about Mexico. Coburn shot bulls. Anderson shot the landscape. Elizabeth shot the peasants. Harris, to universal dismay, shot a child's funeral. 'He could be morbid,' said Coburn. 'Especially when he was tired. At that time he seemed mostly utterly exhausted.'

Elizabeth's concern about their failing marriage hardly touched Harris, in Coburn's view. Instead, Harris involved himself in 'chronically analysing his career with Anderson, myself and anyone else with a sympathetic ear and a strong liver'. The risks and bounties of the stardom he knew lay ahead intrigued him and when he talked about it, said Coburn, it was like he was talking about someone else, not himself. 'He was idealistic, he wasn't stupid. If he had a blind spot it was about human limitations. He seemed to think he could work all day and party all night. Human beings are not cut out for that. There *is* a thing called rest.' The choosing of good candidates for 'the back-up support system' preoccupied him. Fraser he liked, he told Coburn; but he was cynical about agents 'who feast off your flesh like vampires'. Sometime later he complained to several cronies about 'an American agent I had, one of the best. He rang me one day and said, "I haven't seen you in six months. We never meet. We must have dinner!" And I said, "I don't want dinner. You're my agent, not my friend. Your job is to look out for the business, period." They treat you like animals, so they deserve the same treatment.' Now, he reflected, he'd be better off with family members backing him up – Dermot, for example, who was always interested in singing and performing and whom Kevin Dineen had once tipped for stardom. Back in London they would set up shop together. Dermot would get busy learning the accountancy ropes and hunting down the new projects. From henceforth, Fraser and Bresler and Heston – all of them – could deal with Dermot.

Before this new business structuring – posed and planned in detail on the phone between Mexico and Limerick – took place, a call came, from Italy again, suggesting a project beyond *Dundee*. John Huston, legendary Hibernian, widely regarded as Hollywood's Orson Welles successor, with classics like *Moby Dick* (1956) and *The Misfits* (1961) to his credit, wanted Harris for an 'unprecedented epic' in planning. Huston was another Frank Machin fan, and he was lavish with praise. He wanted Harris to play Cain in an Italian-American-financed co-production of *The Bible . . . In the Beginning*, a concept that seemed to Coburn, initially, 'unproduceable'. As outlined by Huston on the phone, though, 'the Old Testament would be reduced to its story components and made linear,' said Harris, 'so it made a kind of sense.' As Harris listened, he was drawn also to the idea that Huston saw the film as 'vignettes', and Harris's role would be short and 'controlled': he would not have the burden of carrying the picture – which was a boon. 'I also loved it that John listened. Neither Antonioni nor Peckinpah granted me that. We talked and exchanged, and I felt good about going back to Italy after the first bad experience.'

Major Dundee finished on 1 May, hugely over time and budget, and Harris flew to Rome, stopping over briefly in London to see his newest son, Jamie. His spirits were now restored and he was sanguine about the completed western – with good cause. Bresler, Heston and Peckinpah continued to slug it out through post-production but the end result, premiered at Chicago's Roosevelt Theatre on 2 April 1965, was a hit at the box office and gave the world its first look at Harris the Hollywood Hero. Eugene Archer in the *New York Times* noted 'an interesting cast, unexpected bits of character revelation and a choppy continuity'. And Philip Scheuer in the *Los Angeles Times* begrudgingly admitted 'no reason to complain about the performances'. Later in London, the film was praised for its 'realistic, almost continental approach' (*Films and Filming*), and at last the Brando comparisons, still on offer in several reviews, seemed contrived and unnecessary: Harris was cutting his own character, clearly growing and stepping out of Brando's, or anyone else's, shadow. 'I felt myself a maturer actor after *The Ginger Man*, *This Sporting Life* and *Diary of a Madman*. The truth of it is, you need a grounding in the classics, you need to work that emotional range, before you can put on a cowboy hat. That is the distinction between art movies and television movies: most of those television actors come from nursery drama schools to the screen without ever breaking an arm, or having their heart broken. How can you project what you don't *feel*?'

In Rome Harris was back on the front pages in no time. Mauro Bolognini was among a group of leading directors setting up a portmanteau movie to launch the society beauty Princess Soraya, former wife of the Shah of Iran, to international stardom. The film was being sponsored by the producer-entrepreneur Dino De Laurentiis and was, in theory at any rate, a no-expenses-spared, blue-chip, glamorous drama. Bolognini courted Harris immediately on his arrival, fixing a dinner date with Soraya in the certain belief that Harris would be bowled over by the sexy princess. But Harris stood Soraya up. The press went wild. 'The facts of the matter were very simple,' Harris later said. 'I didn't want to meet Soraya socially until I had first met the director [they had only spoken on the telephone]. Because if I didn't get along with him, and I did not think much of his earlier pictures, which I'd seen, I had no intention of making this particular film. Now, if I met Soraya before I had made my mind up about working with her and finally decided not to go ahead, people would say that it was because we hadn't hit it off together, which would have been an insult to her.' The accusations of bad chemistry and personal squabbles with Soraya, groundless as they were, made the headlines anyway. Harris wasn't bothered. He knew the strategy of the media, and was happy to reciprocate in manipulating *them*, when he felt the need. 'Fuck 'em, if that's what they feel. Let them write that I'm dating the Pope.'

Hints of a passionate romance with Soraya, which followed on the heels of the first-night stand-off, didn't upset Elizabeth. Since *This Sporting Life* she had watched it all in a detached way, aware, exhausted and immune. The Richard Harris of the press was a barnstorming, horny acrobat, balancing two noncomplementary, improbable lives, drinking beyond human endurance, philandering beyond belief. That the stories were exaggerated she was in no doubt; but there were also obvious, well-familiar elements of truth. Back in London, Elizabeth clung to her Bedford Gardens family routine as the era of Harris-mania began.

CHAPTER 8

On Thin Ice

After his collapse on *Major Dundee* Harris made a serious attempt to control his boozing. On doctor's advice he cut out spirits and confined himself to beer and champagne. He was proud of his courage and the ensuing change of temperament, and spoke widely about it. A year before, he told the British journalist Roderick Mann, he had been drinking with a lunatic abandon. During the American promotional junket for *This Sporting Life* he had grown tired of the nonstop kiss-ass interviews and crept away from the five-star New York hotels to drink 'awful rot-gut with the winos of the Bowery'. He told Mann, 'I spent four days there while the studio was going crazy . . . but it was wonderful.' Afterwards he was 'sick as a dog'. That was all in the past. Now he was reformed, getting fitter, and he could sensibly enjoy the taste of alcohol – which he loved – without pushing himself to the edge. Those who welcomed this declaration as a recipe for an improved, more relaxed marriage ill understood Richard Harris: it wasn't his drinking that fractured the relationship, rather the stress of his chosen career and his ongoing confusion of identity. In other circumstances, all his friends agreed, the made-in-heaven marriage could have thrived. But now there was stardom and a hastening schedule and wider temptations. Very quickly the animal energies that had first attracted Elizabeth became predatory and unmanageably aggressive, and a love that had slid to apathy turned, in her words, to hate.

The actor Franco Nero met Harris in Itri, near Sperlonga, their location for *The Bible*, and found him 'serene, but bursting with a young boy's energy'. Their acquaintanceship grew into warm friendship, but Harris did not share with Nero intimate concerns or any revelations about his family life. Instead Nero – billed as 'John Huston's Great Discovery' – was treated as a bachelor to share bachelor fun with. 'I was really quite innocent and shy,' said Nero. 'This film was to be my Big Deal. I had started at sixteen in Parma, playing with a singing group called The Hurricanes, singing Pat Boone and Frank Sinatra songs and making a little money. But I couldn't speak English, so I just made up these English-American-sounding words to go with the songs.' The removal of his tonsils when he was 21 put paid to Nero's singing dreams. 'They made some kind of mistake and damaged my vocal cords. But it didn't matter because my career plan was to work behind the cameras in documentaries. Vittorio Storaro [the cinematographer who later shot *Apocalypse Now* and *Reds*] was a friend, and with him I went to Rome with a story outline I'd written, looking for a producer to finance us. The producer we met looked at me and said, "You have a pretty face. You are crazy to go behind the cameras. I have a film for you."' The producer changed Nero's original name (Francesco Sparanero) and cast him in a low-budget movie, *The Third Eye*, for Italian release. 'But that was a road to nowhere. The only good that came of it was getting an agent, and that agent miraculously getting my photograph in front of John [Huston]. And so a real film career began, playing Abel with Richard [Harris] in *The Bible*.'

Nero had been a moviegoer since childhood, and knew Harris's name, but the excesses of Harris's publicity had not reached him. Members of the crew pointed out that Harris had fought with Mitchum, Brando, Heston, Antonioni – that no movie of his passed without a fracas – but Nero approached him 'with frank admiration' and was rewarded by a 'brotherly friendship that lasted many years'. Nero remained stoutly defensive: 'I learned that Richard was a private man and I learned he was the most loyal of men. There was no hot-and-cold with him. He was totally consistent with me and very good – except once. The once was when we were filming the death scene, where Cain attacks Abel. Richard hit me with the bone of an animal, a pretty big bone. And he did it very realistically and struck my eye – which caused me some trouble for days afterwards. But that was accidental. If he had a reputation for fighting, I didn't see it. On *The Bible* he was the helpful, sensitive, brotherly pro, and I was an amateur.'

Harris loved Huston, and *The Bible*, even though his scenes lasted just six minutes in an epic that ran for 175 minutes, he ranked as one of his most pleasant movie experiences. In a 1966 interview he said, 'I think it's the best thing I've done. I really do. I found it a fantastic experience, quite remarkable. John Huston is certainly one of the two most exciting men I've ever worked with, a great artist and a great storyteller; so understanding with the actor and so helpful. John is an actor at heart and he let me go, let me get into the part and *do it*, then he moulded it.' Franco Nero, whose expectations of a director were somewhat different given his newness, admired Huston every bit as much. 'He was a loving director,' Nero said, 'who believed in pushing you on to do your best. He was a creative genius.'

Despite the logistical complexity of *The Bible* – Christopher Fry's ponderous script covered the Creation (with Huston as the voice of God), Eden and the Expulsion, Cain and Abel, Noah's Ark, the Tower of Babel, Abraham, Sodom and Gomorrah, Lot's wife *et al.* – Huston hugely impressed the Twentieth Century-Fox boss Darryl F Zanuck, with his management of the budget. 'The production began with Italian cash,' said Harris. 'John had to win over Fox in the first few months. And he pulled it off so well. He cut footage together, showed it to Zanuck, and got the green light to finish in style with Fox finance.' One year after the completion of the Harris–Nero segments at Itri, Nero was surprised to be called back to Rome for more shooting. 'It was astonishing, and shows how huge and complicated that project was,' said Nero. 'John Huston worked like Van Gogh, or someone. His movies weren't just treadmill things. They came together like jigsaw puzzles, and *The Bible* took a long time because of his way of doing things.'

In June 1965 Zanuck called a mammoth press conference attended by 130 reporters to announce *The Bible* as Fox's biggest-ever distribution deal and personally state his admiration for all concerned, an unprecedented personal vote of support: 'On 25 July I will have served three years as president of Fox. I consider no single event more significant than the acquisition of the release rights of this monumental production. As one of the privileged few who has seen *The Bible* in its unfinished form, I would now like the record to show that in my estimation *The Bible* is the greatest example of motion-picture making that I have seen. It is my considered estimation that it will outgross in the theatres of the world any motion picture that has ever been made.'

That was a hard act to deliver, even with the hand of God involved, and, sure enough, on its release in November 1966 *The Bible*'s reception was less than anticipated. Despite its lavish sets, despite the eye-startling 65mm photography by the brilliant Giuseppe Rotunno, despite George C Scott, Michael Parks, Ava Gardner, Peter O'Toole, Stephen Boyd, Nero and Harris, despite the cash and the testimonials, half the world's moviegoers viewed *The Bible* was a well-hyped toga spectacle, of which somewhat of a surfeit existed in the middle sixties. 'It may have been over-marketed,' said Harris. 'In the early days, all I was ever seeing were reports of its magnitude. I read that Luchino Visconti, Orson Welles, [Federico] Fellini and Robert Bresson would direct parts of it, that it would star a hundred Hollywood legends, all that sort of bunk ... and that may have been overkill. I told John, "You know, you'll never get a straight answer from critics or audience about this picture, because you're playing God, literally, and no one will let you get away with that." He just laughed and said, "Doesn't matter to me. God can take a joke, that's all I care about."'

The disappointment was a year away when Harris debated whether to return to London – where all that really faced him was Elizabeth and the ongoing awkwardness with the still-devoted Anderson – or stay in Rome for the Soraya movie, *Three Faces of a Woman*. Finally, after a boozy dinner, he made his choice to stay with the zesty young director Mauro Bolognini. 'Franco [Nero] might have had something to do with it,' said Harris. 'I grew fond of several provincial Italians, and began to like the culture, which reminded me of Irish values.' Harris also grew fond of Bolognini, who at least made the efforts to communicate in English, unlike Antonioni. There was another attraction. The British writer Clive Exton – whose warm review of *Diary of a Madman* Harris loved to quote – was Bolognini's screenwriter.

And then there was Soraya – 'dear, darling, innocent Soraya,' as Harris liked to call her over the years. After the month-long stand-off, all preconceptions he had about the former Empress of Iran disappeared when they met. She was not the brittle, imperious princess he expected, rather a gentle woman of thirty, wounded, he said, by fate. 'Yes, and she was everything else that makes a man weak at the knees. She was sexy, playful and cultured. She also wore her dresses like underwear. Maybe it was the era, but half the time you spent staring down the valley of her titties and trying to pretend you were a grown man with restraint – which I wasn't.'

In 1951, aged just eighteen, Soraya Esfandiari, of mixed German–Bakhtiaria parentage, had married the Shah of Iran in a love match that seemed to win the blessing of the Islamic world. Their life was blissful, until it became clear that Soraya couldn't bear children. Specialists in every field of medicine were consulted and Soraya made no bones about her distress. The problem of her infertility was openly discussed. She and the Shah 'tried four times a night and twice in the afternoons,' she said, to no avail. When French and American fertility experts were imported she told them, 'I'll keep making the omelettes and you figure out how to crack the eggs.' After seven fruitless years the Shah was forced, by the demands of the throne, to divorce her. In a radio speech to the nation reminiscent of Edward VIII's, the Shah spoke of 'sacrificing our love for the sake of the country'. Soraya was pensioned off to live in Europe, where she became a socialite and, in the pop definition, a jet-setter. Her friendship with the Shah remained and, in the eyes of some, her film-star ambitions arose from the desire to impress him, demonstrate her independent worth and seduce him all over.

Soraya contributed to the financing of *Three Faces of a Woman*, and left her personal stamp all over a production that looked, in the final outcome, less like a movie and more like a titillating show reel.

Harris's focus, he later confessed, was 'compromised' in the circumstances of the movie. 'Maybe Soraya's tits were too big and soft, but I wasn't paying attention when I should have been.' Nonetheless, Harris refused Bolognini's first insistence on granting the princess full artistic control. 'When Soraya and I got together, that deal got sorted pretty fast. She knew nothing about films, and I put her right. But she was a good girl, and she deferred to me. She wanted it to be good, but a movie is only as good as its story, and there really wasn't much there. She – and it – were visually flamboyant. That is the best you can say about the movie.'

Bolognini's half-hour film (there were three mini-pictures in one, by three different directors) was both pleasure and frustration for Harris: 'I liked Bolognini immensely as a man. I think he's immensely talented, very sensitive and I like his views. But the Italians have no regard at all for acting. They shoot without any regard for the actor. We are puppets to them. They don't regard acting as a craft, or an art form. They think it's totally dispensable in motion pictures. The theory is they let two or three cameras follow you around a room, rather like documentary shooting . . . and it does become just tedious.'

But the joys of Soraya, and the games of seniority played with her, kept him content. Every day she sent him a half-bottle of Bollinger champagne. On the set he called her 'Soya', like the sauce, which vexed her entourage. When it was requested that he call her 'Your Highness', Harris retorted by demanding that Elizabeth's brother Morgan, who visited with Elizabeth briefly, be referred to as 'The Honorable Morgan'. This absurdity deflated Soraya's gofers and reinstated the good-natured atmosphere. 'In the end, I could always sort her out with a hug and a squeeze . . . which was a relief, since I couldn't get away with doing that with Chuckles [Heston]. Maybe I should have dropped him a note from Rome, saying, Hey, Chuckles, I worked it out. The best way to make a movie is to try to make it with your co-star.'

Wary of getting bogged down with London and Anderson again, he was the magnet of Hollywood, and Hollywood bucks. After Soraya, he stopped briefly in London to set up new offices and review his options, only to be dazed by the volume of scripts. 'That was an eye-opener. I'd been working so hard I didn't see what I'd achieved. *This Sporting Life*, the awards, *Dundee*, Antonioni, John Huston – all in the space of three years.' An offered Broadway show, *Baker Street*, was attractive, because he had decided he wanted some singing roles. And there was also an interesting anti-James Bond parody, called *The Liquidator*, from the director Jack Cardiff, and proposals from Karel Reisz and, again, Anderson. 'What I most wanted to do was something stunningly artistic. My preference was the *Hamlet* Lindsay and I had talked about. But I didn't want to do it with Lindsay, I wanted to be in total control. I wanted to write a new *Hamlet*, a *Hamlet* for the sixties, who faced the dilemmas of the sixties, that awkward collision between materialism and spirituality. There were immense issues within *Hamlet*, fields of discovery no one had looked at. I got hooked on that. That was my daily bread for a long time, and I carried around a little paperback copy along with my notebooks and those two little items kept me sane.'

Negotiating revisions for *The Liquidator*, Harris suddenly swung to a better offer, Rank-funded again, for a Kirk Douglas actioner called *The Heroes of Telemark*. 'I played that like a fiddle,' Harris said, 'because I had ulterior motive. Rank, fuck 'em, were the bankrollers. So I pushed up my fees and they kept saying no, but then always said yes. Finally the fee went sky-high, so good that I had to say OK. I took it, on condition that they gave me a ten-day break for Christmas to spend with the family. I took a lot of joy in calling the shots. I said, I want this, this, this, this and this. And the fuckers said fine. I knew I pissed off Kirk Douglas, but so what? Those fuckers screwed the [mills], that was part of my thinking.'

Duly, Harris started work with the director Anthony Mann in Oslo, then, with just a few scenes in the can, enjoyed stopping the production to fly back to Ireland.

The Richard Harris who returned to Limerick at Christmas 1964 was, to all intents, a pop star. Surrounded by adoring family and back-slapping friends-who-told-you-so, he was everyone's idea of a monumental success. The fans rolled up, haunting the corridors of the Old Ground Hotel in Ennis, Jack Donnelly's new management home, where the family was ensconced for the holidays. At a token press conference, Harris sat between Harmay and brother Dermot (cutting his teeth as assistant on *The Heroes of Telemark*) and spoke of his contentment. He would be buying Creghan's Castle in the Burren, an area of Brontëan moorland, he said. The locale might be perfect for shooting the *Wuthering Heights* he'd promised himself, which, yes, Lindsay Anderson might yet direct. A formal announcement was made of his new business set-up, with Dermot managing his affairs from London and collaborating with him on the selection of projects. He was, he said, writing new poetry in a purposeful way and hoped to make a short film of his poem 'Guns and Drums', crossbred from *Wuthering Heights* and *The Ginger Man*: 'I suppose you could classify it as nostalgic. It is based on the theme of a man against the world and I'll film it in the Burren country . . .' There might also be *Mavourneen*, a satire written by Frank Tarloff and Peter Stone, a Cary Grant collaborator.

Absolute contentment? Maybe not. There was the gripe of the $100,000 promised for *Three Faces of a Woman* and as yet unpaid: 'They'll pay me interest on that, count on it.' And acting had its limitations: 'I'm going to chuck it in as an actor in three years' time, and take more interest in directing and producing. It's good to have ambitions and dreams. And by changing direction I can test my own abilities.'

On 30 December at Ennis Pro-Cathedral family business took precedence. Jamie, 21 months old, was finally christened by the Reverend Kenny, with Jack Donnelly and Mrs Billy Lloyd (sister-in-law of musketeer Paddy Lloyd) as sponsors. The luncheon that followed, with the biggest gathering of Harrises since Milly's funeral, reassured many who doubted the future of Dickie and Elizabeth. 'It was cosy,' said Jack Donnelly, 'but then Dick was moving so fast that nobody could keep up with him. When he arrived that Christmas, it was like Santa arriving. He came – whoosh! – loads of presents and laughs and promises – and then he was back in Norway. Elizabeth probably spent a day or two with him. That's what it was always like, always the dash for the next aeroplane.'

After the New Year celebrations the Harrises flew back to Oslo via London and Richard began work again on what he called

'Kirk Douglas's western on skis'. Harris had rented a luxurious chalet on the 'Bel Air slopes of Rjukan', the location 120 miles west of Oslo. Here, promptly, the entire family went down with a dose of chickenpox – except for Harris, who remained upright, fortified by a new, largely nonalcohol, diet. This 'diet' was just as well, since Rjukan had no liquor licence and the few dowdy nightspots made do with tropical mineral drinks. When the now inevitable fan-journalists braved the climate to pay homage, Harris kept his no-booze pledge. Philip Oakes visited and wrote, 'Given a bottle of whiskey, [Harris] pulled the stopper and sniffed the contents with the rapt expression of a woman anaesthetized with Chanel.' Still, the journalists wanted Hellraiser Harris, so they got him, albeit half-heartedly.

From the start he and Kirk Douglas had not got on. This was Douglas's picture and an important one for him, as it represented an act of contrition towards the director Anthony Mann. During Douglas's earlier epic, *Spartacus* (1956), Mann had been fired in a dispute arising from artistic differences. But Douglas wanted to make up and had promised Mann a replay, once Mann found a good script. The previous summer Mann had called, proffering a screen-play based on the Norwegian wartime underground movement and their efforts against the Nazi 'heavy water' installations that were the nursery for the German atomic bomb. Douglas took the olive branch, and all was well.

But Harris had manoeuvred equal billing, above even Michael Redgrave. From the moment production started, Harris said, he was aware of Douglas's resentment. 'At first he hated me. I knew his reputation for aggression. Richard Brooks, the director, once said, "The trouble with Kirk Douglas is that he thinks he's Kirk Douglas." And that's true. He'd been impressed by himself far too long. I knew I couldn't knuckle under to him. So we had this clash. He could shout. But I could roar as loud as anyone. I told him, "You're too old to start anything. Twenty years ago you could have handled me – maybe – but not now. So don't press your luck."' The journalists who witnessed verbal rows lapped it up. At one point, Douglas had been bragging about his latest girlfriend, a local beauty who had been Miss Norway. Harris chided: 'Oh, yeh? What year?'

By February the waters were calmer, and a relatively trouble-free shoot, religiously adhering to Hollywood disciplines, cheered Harris up. Mann was passionate about the film, which he saw as a notch above the usual syrupy war flick. He had been given the book *Skis Against the Atom* by Knut Havglund and had recce'ed Norway the previous spring: 'I saw the extraordinary visual possibilities of Rjukan. One keeps elaborating and collaborating and eventually the place [inspires] the ideas.' This movie, said Mann, would be as tightly story-driven as his classic *The Glenn Miller Story*: 'I don't believe in "talk" in films. That's for theatre. Here, you will *see* the story.'

For once, Harris was happy to sit back and let the director build part and character: 'When I work as an actor I usually *live* the part I play. Well, this is one of the very few times I'm not going into any deep psychological motivation. Why? The characters aren't important. Here it's the story that's important, almost like a documentary. Mann knows what he's doing.'

For recreation Harris practised the skiing he had half-learned for the movie. His stand-in, Frank Harper, was his closet friend on location, though Elizabeth joined him regularly on the slopes. In the evenings there was *après-ski* in the bar of the solitary hotel, and the talk, when not that of a reluctant hellraiser, was again about death. He told Philip Oakes, 'If I die tomorrow, everything is taken care of.' The Bedford Gardens house, he said, he hated, but Elizabeth liked it, so that was good enough for everyone. 'All I dream about is death. In one dream I was back home [in Limerick] and the streets were full of people streaming in the same direction. I saw my mother crying and I tried to comfort her, but she couldn't hear me. There was a funeral going on and I asked whose it was. Finally someone said, "Richard Harris's." And I shouted out, "No! No! I'm alive!" – but no one took any notice.'

Another repetitive dream was about a plane crash and, said Jack Donnelly, 'it tormented him on that location.' During the shoot, Anthony Mann, who had directed *The Fall of the Roman Empire*, invited his cast to its Norwegian premiere in Oslo. Harris was faced with the choice of a four-hour car journey or a half-hour flight. 'He couldn't afford the time, and he didn't want to insult Mann, so he made the flight with Frank Harper, but it almost killed him. Not the flight itself, which went without incident, but the idea of it. When Dick had those death dreams they drove him nuts. He couldn't shake the Grim Reaper, it was always on his shoulder, always driving him. Maybe it all dated back to losing [his sister] Audrey so young. But it never left him. When he arrived in Oslo he forgot the no-booze diet and enjoyed a few beers with Frank.'

When Elizabeth and the children returned to London, Harris had only work to amuse him. When, during the shoot, *Three Faces of a Woman* opened in Rome, he tried to rustle a print, chasing Bolognini and De Laurentiis, but got no further than hounding down 'a bunch of these social-type write-ups . . . I began to feel I'd just contributed to [Soraya's] home movie collection'. In fact, *Three Faces* found no distributor and though *Variety* previewed it – finding Harris 'fine as the lover [and Soraya] performs ably and exudes undeniable fascination' – the movie vaporised along with Soraya's acting career.

With the kids' departure, the snowy isolation of Norway gave Richard and Dermot the ideal opportunity to reacquaint themselves with each other and plan for the future. 'We decided I would change agents, going over to John McMichael, who was doing well at ICM, and we decided how the London office of "Harris Incorporated" would operate, which would be essentially like any business, but would be driven by art projects, which in turn would be financed by the big Hollywood things like *Telemark*. I didn't want to be a Hollywood deadbeat like Douglas. I wanted to retain an Irishness, and my art. I wanted to be exclusive and unique.' From Dermot's point of view, said Jack Donnelly, there was the consistent concern about impracticalities. 'Dermot saw what happened with Ivan and the mills and knew how an extravagant lifestyle can kill things. He was worried all the time that Dick was too generous and offhand, and the truth is, Dick was. So Dermot's work was cut out. How to manage his brother, and control him, and realise all these sky-high dreams of musicals and Republican Irish movies and all the rest.'

Dermot, and McMichael, started well. Before *Telemark* was in the can, another blockbuster was on offer from Hollywood, with another huge six-figure fee: this one was *Hawaii*, based on James Michener's current mega-bestseller. 'I liked the sound of it for that time,' said Harris, 'because it was a Hollywood studio movie which would put me back in the ballpark, right in the studio's front yard, as it were. Tactically, that seemed important.' What also seemed important was the budgetary outcome of *The Heroes of Telemark*. 'I hold up my hand and say, Yes, sir, some of that was my fault. Yes, sir, I did fight with Kirk and delay things. Yes, sir, I did fuck up a few times on location. Yes, sir, I did it all . . . and it cost Rank something like $10 million over budget and that was just awful for poor old Rank. But I also said, Yes, sir, I settled the account of Harris Mills and Rank Flour. Fuck 'em, I got them in the end.'

Back in London Harris started packing for his busman's holiday in LA and Hawaii. The journalist Weston Taylor dropped by Bedford Gardens and revelled in the Limerickese yarns from 'the hottest property around'. What was the recipe for so perfect a marriage? Taylor asked. 'I get tremendous fun with my wife. The other Saturday lunchtime I went out with a pal to a match. "When will I see you?" she asked. "Tuesday," I said. "And it might be in the police courts."' He was, he said, lucky to have such a blissful domestic arrangement. It was clear, reported Taylor, that he, and he alone, ruled the roost – right down to stage-managing the children's lives: 'I don't send them to school. They have private tutors. The eldest, Damian, has been going to the Tate Gallery every morning with his tutor, or to the National Gallery, or to the Tower of London . . . That is the proper way to educate children.'

The great pronouncement was that he was no longer a hellraiser: 'Can you imagine a hellraiser making arrangements to ship out to Hawaii an entourage including a wife, three sons, a brother, a niece, a secretary and a nanny?'

Taylor recorded that the wild Irish rover was still off the hard stuff, that his life was an idyll. But in Hawaii would come the fall off the wagon and, in its tracks, the violence and tantrums that would end the marriage.

PART II

King Richard

'All nature is but art, unknown to thee;
All chance, direction, which thou canst not see . . .'
Alexander Pope, *An Essay on Man*

'An actor acts, that's all there is to it.'
Richard Harris to the author, 1989

CHAPTER 9

Caprice and Consequences

It is hard to overstate the rosy bonuses achieved by Harris in ten years' acting: the Rolls-Royces, the vases of roses whimsically dyed his favourite lilac, the servants, the gifts, the girls. But it is also hard to overstate the grilling intensity of the limelight, the freedom and privacy that he and others who make the first league surrender. Harris's sense of perspective was acute: 'I saw it as a mountain. You go up, you come down. At the time of [movies like *Hawaii*] I was nearing the peak and the world was at my feet. I was lucky. I was strong and capable and I enjoyed every minute of it – everything, the wine and the women. But I knew it would end and, more importantly, I knew I was, after all, just an artist. An actor, that's all. Not a "legend" or a "star". I enjoyed being paid top dollar. But as I saw the scene changing, especially in the 1980s, I couldn't accept that actors took $7 or $8 million fees. To me, the money paid to so-called superstars like Dustin Hoffman or Warren Beatty was immoral. When it came to the art of movies, the money should have been *on the screen*, in the production, not in the pockets of greedy men.' That, of course, was hindsight, and, Harris was ready to admit, in the middle sixties, that greed, competitiveness, score-settling and every other form of bad behaviour was well within his scope. 'My problem was a temperament that drove me to constant self-abuse and collapse. Intellectually, I was aware of where it was at. But half the time I was so emotionally "out of it" that I didn't know which way was up. Even ten, twenty years later, I would read about things I did or things I said, or friends would tell me, and I'd say, 'Jesus, was it that crazy?' I was a sinner. I slugged some people. I hurt many people. And it's true, I never looked back to see the casualties.'

With sixties hedonism booming, riding the wave was the name of the game. Harris hit LA this time in royal fashion, firmly enthroned as king of West End trendies, friends with Princess Margaret (he purchased her Rolls Phantom V and cherished it), trailed by hand-maidens and servants of all sorts. 'I made for Sunset Boulevard and the club scene and forgot all else,' said Harris. 'The way I saw it was, Make hay while the sun shines. *Carpe diem* – for tomorrow, who knows?' Harris's infidelities were widely known, but in an era of youth promiscuity and masculine chauvinism there was nothing too surprising about them. He had long described himself as sexually hyperactive, and in the LA sorties of this time he revelled in his reputation – more like a kid in a sweet shop than a husband with malicious intent. 'It was a party scene and it grew and grew. One day it was the Whisky-a-Go-Go, the next day it was Plato's Retreat and swingers and day-long orgies. It's hard to see it all in context today, but it was the Swinging Sixties, the Pill, all that, and it wasn't too class conscious. Everyone got a bite at the cookie.'

In Harris's case, there was also the inescapable magnetism exuded by 'the star', and the inevitable pay-off around the A-list social circuit. 'I got to meet everyone who was anyone – Sinatra became a friend, and Sammy Davis and all those Rat Pack guys. I said "Hi" to Cary Grant, met all the legends of the Golden Era and sat on their verandahs to drink martinis with them and talk about who Zanuck liked and who [Jack] Warner bore a grudge against.'

Along the way, unbelievably for Harris, an invitation came to sup with Merle Oberon, the sexual icon who had illuminated his teen-hood. 'She *summoned* me to one of her lavish parties in Beverly Hills. It was like a call from Venus. I remember this fabulous mansion, with these spectacularly landscaped gardens. I remember thinking, Boyo, you've come a long way from Limerick. It felt like something from the Roman Empire. It was magical.'

At first Oberon took no notice of him and mingled with her guests. But 'I had taken a couple of drinks so I walked up to the woman, sat beside her, looked into her eyes and said, "Merle, I have slept with you so many times, dreamed of you, fantasised about you, touched every part of you, kissed every part of you, kissed your breasts and your belly . . . and made love to you in every position that man has conceived."' The actress appeared shocked and walked away. Harris was undaunted: 'I had a feeling, from the way she looked at me. I knew in my heart that I would have her that night.'

The party swung, and fizzled in the small hours, but Harris lingered, tactically positioning himself. 'Sure enough, I finally got her into conversation again, while the maids put everything away. The final guests were gone, and suddenly we were alone.'

Oberon smiled at him, glass in hand and said, 'These fantasies of yours, do you think you would like to make them come true?'

Harris followed her up to the master bedroom, where he stripped and lay 'in a trance of disbelief' on her bed while Oberon disappeared into the bathroom to ready herself. 'I waited breathlessly,' said Harris, 'while my whole life since Limerick passed before my eyes. *Was this really happening to me?*' Oberon came into the bedroom 'wearing a see-through pink nightgown with a slit in the side going all the way up to her waist. She had nothing on underneath and all I could see was these fabulous tits and a gorgeous black bush.' Embracing Harris, she leaned over him on the bed to turn out the light.

'I lay there with her tit in my mouth and stopped her. I told her, "Wait a second. I have made love to you so many times in my mind in the dark in a cold room in Limerick. Now I want to see it all, to touch and experience everything. Just to be sure it's all real.' The lovemaking that ensued, says Harris, was 'fabulous, fabulous, beyond belief'.

In Hawaii, despite the arduous production, Harris didn't apply the brakes. If anything he pumped the accelerator, throttling up a lifestyle that kissed his limited-booze diet goodbye. The weather was heavenly after Rjukan and London, the native women interesting and exquisite and just as he always liked them – plumpish and not too coiffed. He discovered the local version of the cocktail Mai tai, as seductive as neat brandy, and he devoured it, paying no heed to the renewed withdrawal symptoms, which were identical to the dreaded post-brandy rages. With Elizabeth, Dermot and the entourage, he rented a huge house with a pool on Diamond Head Road east of Waikiki, but he was rarely there, spending twelve-hour days instead on the set and vanishing mysteriously into the seductive tropical night. Elizabeth withstood his moonlight whims but the horrors of Mai tai terrified her, and she wrote in her memoirs about fearsome outbursts when Harris dashed into fast-moving traffic on Kalakahua Boulevard and mindlessly attacked passing cars with his bare fists.

George Roy Hill, the director, found Harris 'an interesting force of nature' and felt comfortable with him if, on occasion, despairing of his lack of self-discipline. Educated, like the Ginger Man himself, at Trinity College in Dublin, Hill had an affinity with all things Irish that encouraged constant forgiveness. 'To be honest, I had so much on my hands, covering a script that wriggled like a snake, that I really only gave Dick token time as an individual. I thought he had [emotional] issues, but I had no time to help fix him.'

The 'wriggling script' was nothing short of a literary phe-nomenon, Hill believed, honed from Michener's thousand-page novel and from years of preproduction by the writer Daniel Taradash and the director Fred Zinnemann, who originally planned a double-movie that would run simultaneously or sequentially in side-by-side cinemas across the world. 'That was never really practical,' said Hill. The problem was that Fred was attempting to tell the entire history of Hawaii, from the Middle Ages to modern times, in one mammoth screenplay. In my opinion, film narrative has a time arch, beyond which it becomes self-cancelling. You can skip time, and play with linearity, but you need to hold your characters alive and central, and the [first] version of *Hawaii* didn't have that.' Dan Taradash himself, despite writing the Zinnemann draft, overruled his own work: 'It was impossible for Fred Zinnemann, brilliant director that he was, to do what he had anticipated. [He would have been shooting] without a pause for *two hundred and fifty days*. I just couldn't believe that any artist could stay on top form for that period.' The revised script by Dalton Trumbo concentrated on the establishing of the first Christian church in Hawaii in the 1820s.

When Zinnemann fell out, the intended lead casting of Rock Hudson and Audrey Hepburn was abandoned. Hill, drafted in by United Artists after his recent success with *The World of Henry Orient*, immediately opted for Julie Andrews, whom he knew and trusted, and Harris. 'But I was dealing with an unknown quantity, because these were two very "opposite"-type performers, and I had no idea how they would blend.'

The blend, given Harris's current bipolarity, was appalling. 'I hated her,' Harris said. 'She was condescending and mean. She didn't look *at* you. She looked *over* you. I wasn't any role model, and I'm sure she saw how much I was enjoying myself, and I thought that annoyed her. My patience wasn't great in those days, so there was a lot of cussing. She would say something, all quiet and conspiratorial, to the director. And I would shout, "Did you say something, *Jules*?" – which just pissed her.'

Hawaii was not a critical or commercial hit, but it well served Harris's purpose, driving up his Hollywood status, paying off Bedford Gardens debts and placing him squarely in the business-social mêlée he sought. Out of it, directly, came the opportunity he'd longed for, the chance to romp and sing in a glitzy musical. 'I was making *Hawaii* when I heard *Camelot*, Dickie Burton's Broadway hit, was to be made into a movie. It took me about fifteen seconds to say, "I want that." The only hesitation for me was Julie Andrews, who'd played it with Burton on stage. I thought, If it's her, forget it.'

In a phone call Ronald Fraser listened to Harris express his hopes for *Camelot* and smiled. 'I thought if old Burton decides not to do it, this is Dickie's big break. There was a poetic rightness to it, because he always saw himself as Prince Dick and here he could at last be crowned King Richard!'

For six months, through 1965, Jack Warner, whose studio had purchased the rights, and the scenarist-lyricist Alan Jay Lerner pursued Burton to reprise his stage role. The story yo-yo'ed endlessly and at various times Burton was declared in, then out, of the game. Finally, Burton proposed a fee that was double what

Warner wanted to – or could, given the debts of the studio – pay, and Burton's 'retirement' was formally declared.

Egged on by his London friend and astrologer Patric Walker, who had read the stars and predicted the role of King Arthur, Harris started a four-month campaign of chasing Lerner, Warner and, especially, the assigned director, Joshua Logan. The strategy was never conventional. It started with a handwritten note addressed to Warner, which was fast followed by a confetti of cables, letters and 'I love you' cards. When Logan attended a party in Palm Springs, Harris gatecrashed and delivered a handwritten note, describing himself as 'the out of work actor, King Richard Harris'. Logan ignored him and moved on to London, to start casting British actors. At that point Harris commenced his 'telegram attack', sending more than twenty cables reading, ONLY HARRIS FOR ARTHUR and HARRIS BETTER THAN BURTON and HARRIS WORKS CHEAPER.

When Logan ignored the missives, Harris altered tack, flew to London and dressed up as a waiter to crash a private party at the Dorchester. Here, on a silver salver, he delivered a note to Logan stating, 'Harris for Arthur!'

Harris's serious determination to win the role won the support of others. Nick Roeg, the cameraman-director, was engaged, at Harris's expense, to shoot a screen test based on King Arthur, which was sent to Logan and Warner. Franco Nero said, 'You have to hand it to him, he left no stone unturned. But in the end it came down to John Huston. I know for certain that that is how I got the role, and also, I believe, it is how Logan and Warner decided on Dick. The simple truth is, John Huston recommended us on the strength of *The Bible*. He said, "These boys can be Arthur and Lancelot, they work well together, they have class and confidence, they are true actors" – and that softened the opposition.'

Nero's interview with Logan took place in London. 'But he nearly went crazy when I came in, because I could barely speak English. "This is nuts," he said. "I can't do this with someone like you." But I told him – stammered it out – that I can do Shakespeare in English. And I went on to give him a big speech from *Romeo and Juliet* that

John Huston told me to learn off by heart. John had said to me, "They want romance for Lancelot, so give them the greatest romance ever written!" And I did, and Josh loved it and said, "All right, it's yours." '

The mania to bag Camelot drove a further gap between Elizabeth and Harris and in the hiatus Elizabeth indulged in a brief affair with the nightclub pianist Robin Douglas-Home, nephew of the former Tory prime minister. When she confessed this to her husband, she said, he exploded. 'But that was Dickie,' said Ronald Fraser. 'Of course there was no logic to it, but no one expected any. He was a wild Irishman, whose woman was a possession . . . and that is not spoken in criticism of him, but of all Irishmen, and probably all Englishmen and Americans and whoever else, of that time. That was the state of play. Who could blame Elizabeth for straying? I told him he was a married bachelor, and he should just own up and take his medicine and back down.'

According to Elizabeth in her memoirs, Patric Walker defused the situation. A good-hearted and persuasive man, Walker foresaw career improvements for Harris – and, in his solemn predictions, calmed him. Like The Beatles' soon-to-be 'spiritual leader', the Maharishi Mahesh Yogi, Walker was suddenly elected as man-in-the-middle and constant travelling counsel. Summoned back to Hollywood to begin vocal lessons for *Camelot*, Harris deemed this 'a new beginning' and booked passages on the *Queen Mary* for himself, Elizabeth and Walker. The journey was fraught, said Elizabeth, with Harris throwing nightly tantrums, but once they were in Hollywood a light-heartedness – albeit stimulated by Tinseltown fantasy living once again – improved the situation.

On his first night Harris threw a part for 350 guests, most of whom hardly knew him. Rex Harrison and his wife Rachel Roberts were the star guests, and the Harrises began a chummy family friendship that long preceded the eventual extraordinary romance between Elizabeth and Harrison. The new rented accommodation, the Villa Vesco in the gated community of Bel Air, cost an arm and a leg, so Harris quickly decided to squeeze in an extra movie offer, a Frank Tashlin–Doris Day comedy thriller called *Caprice*.

'I did it on the momentum of the moment,' said Harris, 'and because I was looking for light relief from any quarter.' More unlikely co-star casting than Harris and Day would be hard to imagine, but Harris, initially, at any rate, saw this as a positive plus. 'And then it turned into a bit of a nightmare, because Doris made a mistake. She was the one who asked [Tashlin] for me as her co-star, but she confused me with Sean Connery. They wanted to make a James Bond pastiche, as everyone was making at that time, and Marty Melcher [her husband] had told Doris all about this great Irish hunk that Hollywood was chasing round. Day probably never saw a thriller movie in her life – she seemingly confused me with Sean Connery – and she said, OK, let's get this James Bond guy. And then in comes Harris, red-haired, pink from the sun, big rugby shoulders, big Irish burp, [saying], "How y'doing, baby. Jesus, great pair of legs on you . . ."'

High on the prospect of *Camelot*, Harris worked fast and well on *Caprice* at Fox studios, and at the main city location in the Bradbury Building at Broadway and 3rd Street, a Paris Exposition 1900-style mansion that doubled for the cosmetics headquarters around which the movie plot revolved. Swiss sequences where shot at Mammoth Mountain in the High Sierras, a half day's drive north. Those who predicted turbulence between the egotistical stars were disappointed, though the publicists clung to their hopes. Harris respected Day – 'I liked her, she was fine, she was a ball' – but described kissing her on screen as 'kissing my auntie'. When Day collapsed with back strain late in the shoot the tabloids were quick to speculate inanely on sexual shenanigans: Miss Day's back pains were caused, said one of the movie magazines, 'by the fiery acting of Mr Harris in the love scenes.'

Harris's memories of the movie were 'painless', though he had, he said, found Frank Tashlin 'as odd and intriguing' as Doris Day. 'He had developed a style, much appreciated in France especially, that blended farce with a sort of hip social commentary . . . He was quirky.' *Caprice* started out as satire of the kind Tashlin was famous for in ironic classics like *Artists and Models* (for the Lewis–Martin comedy duo) and *Will Success Spoil Rock Hunter*? But Doris Day upended it by insisting on taking the male-written role, leaving Harris with the 'female' part. 'Something subtle was lost there,' said Harris. 'Tashlin's work looks like shallow wallpaper, but there's irony in it all the way, which is unusual for Americans.' Interviewed in the seventies about the movie, Tashlin described it as an intended attack, like most of his movies, on conformity: 'The nonsense of what we call civilisation, leisure, push-button living . . .' In the movie Day played Patricia Foster (written as the male Patrick), trying to avenge the murder of her father, an Interpol agent. Ostensibly she is probing the world of cosmetic formulas, but her research is a front for a narcotics investigation. Harris played camp Christopher (originally Christine), the mysterious agent who shadows her. 'The problem was the sex-change, because it loaded the movie [for Day], so that it looked like a girlie fun film like *Pillow Talk*,' said Harris. 'It could have been quite different the other way around.' For critics the movie was confusing and incomplete. The *Hollywood Reporter* complained that it 'flits and flutters', while Harris 'does an imitation of Richard Burton which increases one's respect for the original'. Bosley Crowther reported Harris's affecting 'the arts and airs of a very sissy gentleman, even down to wearing the eye shadow'. Interestingly, as far as Crowther was concerned, Doris Day acted 'with masculine muscularity', indicating that her script-reversal notion didn't pay off on any account. Crowther also spotted the Bond association, suggesting that Harris's role was the equivalent of Ursula Andress's in *Dr No*. In Britain the *Monthly Film Bulletin* found the movie 'incomprehensible', while 'Richard Harris seems understandably ill-at-ease'.

Harris's chronic unease was real, and ascended into crisis as the movie wrapped. In the run-up to *Camelot*, Elizabeth suddenly decided she'd had enough of faking it. Harris was drinking recklessly, the rows were rousing neighbours nightly, weekends passed in a querulous blur. Twice on the sound stage at Fox he had collapsed, stalling the production. Excusing himself to the writer Henri Gris, he explained that he had been boozing with Jason Robards, then Lauren Bacall's husband. After a particularly long session, Harris had drunk 'a vodka diluted with water from my swimming pool, full of chlorine, bees, ants and spit'. According to Gris, Harris could 'down two quart bottles in a day and remain beautiful', but after the session with Robards he ended up in the Cedars of Lebanon hospital. Attended by Dr Rex Kennamer, Sinatra's doctor, Harris was dried out and put through an extensive series of tests. Harris told Gris that he had begged Kennamer to help him, fearing he was drinking to excess because of some as-yet undiagnosed terminal illness. 'It's probably true and honest,' Harris later said. 'It took more than twenty years to diagnose my dyslexia formally and even longer to diagnose the hyperglycemia. I did not feel well. Looking back, perhaps it was the punishment I put myself through, because I could never sit still. I used to think I was happiest on the racquetball courts at Kilkee, because there I was sweating like a horse, and that seemed to quieten me. I was in a spin for forty-five years . . .'

In 1966 Kennamer diagnosed a scarred oesophagus, deducing 'inflammation caused by emotional tension', and ordered Harris to get sleep, ease down, cut out the booze. Harris told Gris that he had; he had purchased a food mixer and was making his own carrot health drinks; he would never drink alcohol again.

But it was too late to convince Elizabeth, who, without warning, flew back to London, consulted lawyer David Jacob, and filed for divorce. As Harris reported it, he remained at the Villa Vesco unawares, being looked after by Lupe and Edgardo, the cook and housekeeper. On 23 July 1966 the *Daily Mirror* carried the headline: STAR'S WIFE SAYS: I AM SCARED OF HIM. It outlined Elizabeth's application for two injunctions: to stop Harris molesting her, and to restrict his removal of the children. 'I am frightened of him,' Elizabeth declared in a sworn statement. 'I seek the protection of the court from him.' Her counsel, Joseph Jackson, told Mr Justice Park that this was a matter of great urgency. While acknowledging that Harris was 'a man of considerable talent and exceptional success', Jackson went on: 'Unfortunately his wife alleges he drinks regularly to excess and when he is drunk he goes berserk with whoever is in sight, and she is the victim.' Mr Justice Park agreed to both injunctions *ex parte*, applicable till October, on the understanding that Richard Harris, not represented, could apply to have them discharged.

Harris was shattered, and verbally more expressive of his love for her than ever. He told the journalist Gerard Garrett in Hollywood, 'On the very Friday that my wife saw her lawyers to arrange for the divorce, almost to the hour, I was suddenly certain that our difficult times were over. In fact, I booked an airplane on the spot to go over and bring Elizabeth and the children here for the weekend. When I flew to London on the Friday I swore the airline staff to secrecy. I was planning to go to my local [pub] at the top of Camden Hill and phone, pretending I was still in Hollywood, and tell her to come out of the house in a few minutes. She would have come out expecting flowers or a brass band – she'd know that with me either would be possible – and I would have come out of the trees to surprise her.' Harris did go unknowingly to London, he said, only to be met by a press brigade at Heathrow Airport. Later he expressed his hurt to the Irish columnist Trevor Danker: it was Elizabeth, he said, who informed the press of the impending split, while he was in the air flying to Britain. 'But she was encouraged, or misadvised, I think, that it would make a big splash. It made a tremendous story *on her behalf*. There were the most fantastic allegations made against me. Totally untrue, dreadful things.'

For Harris it was, for once, excruciatingly bad timing. Here he was, on the eve of his fantasy musical, the perfect poetic synthesis of all his art and commerce and ambition – a symbolic crowning, no less – and now he was faced with Elizabeth's desertion and accusations of wife-beating. In retrospect, Harris assumed all the blame: 'It was not callousness on Elizabeth's behalf. She'd had enough. I was womanising and boozing and I was ill. I was probably more emotionally ill than healthy. She'd overstretched herself coping with the children and with me, an overgrown child at play like a maniac all the time. Do I forgive her? There was no [need for] forgiveness. She treated me better than I ever deserved, and then she took one hit too many and packed it in for all our sakes.'

Franco Nero recalled that Harris started work on *Camelot* 'outwardly serene', but 'he was, more than ever, a very, very private man', a man who preferred his own company most days, in spite of the newspaper legends. 'He had a deep love for the part of King Arthur and that seemed to help him through [his problems]. I think he related to the character in some profound way – to this hero who overcomes his own flaws to show goodness and compassion to the world.'

When Henri Gris talked to Harris, alone, in the Bel Air house, Harris admitted serious unhappiness.

'Richard, do you miss your children?'

'Yes.'

'Do you miss your wife?'

'Yes.'

'Would you like to make up with her?'

'Yes.'

'Do you miss your things? Your books, your clothes, your mementoes?'

'No . . . only my cherry-blossom tree. Actually, trees. Plural. I have two.' He continued, 'I won't be back in London for ages. If I try to see my wife and children in London now, I'll end up in jail. I mustn't go near them. Lawyer's orders.'

Villa Vesco had once belonged to the comedian Alan Chase. It was a rambling, leafy estate aglow with the grandeur of ancient Hollywood, with swimming pool and tennis courts and ballroom and seventeenth-century ceilings carted at unutterable expense from Rome. It was several times the size of the Bedford Gardens house, bigger than the previous year's rental in Hawaii, bigger than the terracotta extravaganza in the Roman campagna before that. It was bigger and better than any castle King Richard had yet built – but it was also empty. When the servants were out, said Gris, the only sounds that disturbed the stillness were the latest Brit-invasion records playing on the living-room turntable.

'I thought I had it made,' said Harris. 'The combination of *Camelot* and Doris Day had made me famous at last. But I thought there would be more of us living here . . .'

CHAPTER 10

Didn't We

Camelot, a major milestone for Warner Brothers, Jack Warner personally and Richard Harris had a jinxed history. Born on Broadway in 1960, it followed the hardest of all acts for the same composing team, *My Fair Lady*. Lerner and Loewe painstakingly fine-tuned it for two years but its stage run was, said Lerner, 'plagued by enough misfortune to send everyone connected with it into the desert for forty years'. The set designer Adrian died during its preparation, director Moss Hart suffered a heart attack, Lerner himself fell ill and Fritz Loewe, exhausted by it, decided to retire. The opening night was a flop but the original cast – Burton, Julie Andrews as Guinevere, Robert Goulet as Lancelot and Roddy McDowell as Mordred – clung together and force-fed a hit. *Camelot* limped through two years on Broadway before hitting the jackpot in world tours.

Jack Warner's decision to acquire the movie rights was spurred by the gigantic success of the movie version of Lerner and Loewe's *Gigi*, which won more Oscars (in 1959) than any movie up till then. Warner planned *Camelot* as a big promotional push for the studios, but by the time the artillery of movie-making was assembled – $10 million budget, bankable director (Josh Logan, who had directed *South Pacific*), glove-fit casting – Warner Brothers was on its knees. The movie started in Spain in September 1966 in a relaxed, well-serviced mood – and wrapped nearly a year later in a thunder-rush of money panic.

'It was amazing,' said Franco Nero. 'In our first two months in Spain we shot wonderful stuff, none of which ever reached the screen. In our last one week in Warners' Burbank studios we shot almost one hour of used screen time.'

The trouble was the shifting sands of modern Hollywood. Jack Warner was the last of the great autocrats who answered to no conglomerate. But the days of the one-man-show productions were over. In November, just eight weeks into shooting, Jack sold Warner Brothers to Seven Arts for $32 million and essentially handed over the reins. Though he kept an office on the lot and saw *Camelot* through to the end, his passion faded and its absence gravely hampered the movie.

The perky optimism of Josh Logan as *Camelot* began kept Harris away from domestic autopsies. The first scenes to be shot were those of Lancelot's campaign fights – the *C'est Moi* scenes – and King Arthur knighting him. The unit flew to Madrid, where Nero relished 'lovely weeks among the most beautiful scenery I had ever seen'. Warner and Logan had spared no expense in ground-laying. Months of location checks had identified the best castles and most picturesque medieval sites. Nero had been voice-coached daily by UCLA professor Daniel Vandrargen. At the Burbank studios a hundred craftsmen toiled under the direction of designer John Truscott, assigned to 'reinvent' the story. 'I came into it thinking of it as ultra-romantic in the adult sense,' said Truscott, 'but the director didn't want the picture made that way so I had to lose all my preconceived ideas very fast.' The chocolate-box glamour of traditional Hollywood mythology was abandoned for sets hewn from natural stone 'and beds which look as if they might provide a decent night's sleep'. A fortune was spent creating new, realistic costumes – $12,000 alone went on Guinevere's wedding dress – and a work-of-art Round Table, 38 feet in diameter and 119 feet in circumference, and weighing 3,000 pounds, was chiselled by the master carpenters. 'The feeling one had was of every attention lavished upon the smallest detail,' said Nero. 'It was certainly unlike anything I had done before.'

Harris had only a few days' filming in Spain but, like Nero and the knights, he enjoyed the splendour of Granada and the Castle of Coco in Old Castile. For his part, Logan was uptight. He told *Life* magazine, 'I used to lie awake at night and worry about the complexities. But as the production got under way I began to feel happier. Every day I viewed things with increasing confidence. Basically we have tried to be original the whole way, without recreating anything that has been done before.'

Logan was delighted with Harris, whom he found to be 'methodical and involved', and especially with Vanessa Redgrave, his chosen Guinevere. He had known Vanessa, and the Redgrave family, for many years but had never considered her for King Arthur's bride. Then his young son Tom saw her in *Morgan, A Suitable Case for Treatment* at a New York cinema and insisted, 'Dad, there's your Guinevere!' Logan watched the movie and arranged for a screening for Jack Warner. Warner agreed that Redgrave might be suitable – provided she could sing. Logan flew to London, summoned her and listened to her sole vinyl recording, a ballad on the album of *The Tempest*. He told *Life* he hollered with delight: "She was gorgeous *and* she had a beautiful voice!'

In late October the unit returned to Burbank and Harris moved from the Villa Vesco to a rented beach house at Malibu among the surfer-hippie community. Nero's apartment was at the Sunset Marquee, five miles away. 'We were *the* big production in town,' said Nero, 'and all the superstars came to look us over. Steve McQueen came by, Warren Beatty came, just about everyone you could imagine.' Nero was wide-eyed but still fretting to meet one star – his co-lead Vanessa Redgrave. 'I still hadn't met her, though Joshua Logan kept saying, "You'll love her, trust me, you'll love her."'

Harris hunted the company of musicians. His musical appetite was as eclectic as ever – from Sinatra to Tom Jones to 'Danny Boy' – but the youngsters he mostly hung out with were attuned to Dylan, The Byrds and the early psychedelic scene. But it suited Harris fine. Disdainful of the early youth groundswell – 'I was indifferent to The Beatles, I hated The Beach Boys, they're so *American*' – he felt cosy among socially conscious protesters. A Joan Baez-styled songstress called Kathy Green particularly absorbed him and, said a friend, 'rejuvenated him so that he felt more part of the youth scene than anything'. Green had long chestnut hippie hair, slim hips, bare feet –

and the wildness of Walden Pond in her nature-orientated songs. Harris spent evening after evening with her, romancing her, advising her, arguing the future and promising someday soon to record her work. 'Around that time I started to think seriously of singing as an aspect of my career. I'd always loved it, I sang to myself all the time. But the vibe around Sunset Boulevard and LA at that time was exceptionally vibrant. It was cool to be "Brit", even if I was Irish-Brit. And the scene was full of David Crosby and Neil Young and Paul Simon and Brian Wilson ... All you were ever hearing was about this-and-this act being at the Filmore or the Hollywood Bowl, and bringing the house down. I was hanging round with hippies who thought the scene was *just* about music. It got to feel like music, and only music, would change the world. Movies were old hat.'

The Malibu hippie set, and the $25,000 a week for *Camelot*, restored his confidence. After a wound-licking retreat he was back on the party circuit, the oldest hippie in town, but with the energy of a whippet. He danced, boozed, sang the long nights away – but always made it, bright-eyed, for the set call next day.

Nero joined him on the party circuit, 'but I always said bye-bye at ten or eleven, which, for Richard, would have been the equivalent of lunchtime.' Nero witnessed the ferocious boozing – 'and I don't know how he withstood it, but somehow, next morning, he was there, on time for work and very coherent. It's a paradox, but he was extremely disciplined.' *Life* magazine also observed the heroic boozing. Reporter Jon Borgzinner followed Harris through a vacation weekend in New York, where 'the rambunctious royal' held court at fellow Irishman Malachy McCourt's pub, Himself. Borgzinner wrote,

> Though he postures, swaggers, swills, he fulfils the demands placed on him as an actor with painstaking discipline. At Warners technicians do not stint in their praise of Harris as one of the most careful craftsmen whom they have ever met.

Logan told Borgzinner, 'I felt that I began life again working with Harris.'

After a week or two at Burbank, Nero finally met the queen he was to steal away from King Richard: 'I was walking in a corridor with Logan and this girl in jeans had her back to us. Logan said, "This is Vanessa" and I said, "Hello" . . . but when she was gone I said to Logan, "Are you crazy! She's so ugly!" Logan laughed and said, "Just you wait and see her with make-up and her hair done and all that."' When Nero returned to his dressing room a note in Italian from Redgrave invited him to dinner at her Pacific Palisades house. His Italian girlfriend was in town, but he accepted the invitation anyway and drove his rented car up the coast. He found the house, 'with a pretty woman cooking in the kitchen. I rang the bell and asked for Miss Redgrave and she said, "I am Miss Redgrave!" She was very lovely, and I understood what Joshua meant.'

Nero was comprehensively popular with the women of *Camelot* – he was particularly friendly with Logan's wife – but a deep long-lasting relationship with Redgrave developed within a few months. 'My girlfriend got tired of LA and flew home, so I was alone,' he said. 'Then Vanessa asked me to drive a professor friend of hers to the airport. We all drove out and when we were alone, when he had gone, she said, "Are you working tomorrow?" I said, "No, and you?" She said she wasn't and suggested we do something together. So we caught a plane and went to San Francisco and got to know each other properly.' Just after the movie, Redgrave became pregnant and the couple had a son, though they never married. They remained, said Nero, 'close like a family, for ever'.

While Harris cannoned ever onwards, Nero admitted that the distraction of his relationship with Redgrave deflated his own international career. 'Perhaps I became emotionally rechannelled in a way Richard never allowed himself. After *Camelot* Jack Warner took me aside and said, "I have wonderful pictures lined up for you. They will make you a great star. There is a picture with Natalie Wood, with lots of big stars." But I said, no. Vanessa was making *Isadora* in Europe and I wanted to be with her. I said to Mr Warner, "Thank you, but maybe in a couple of years I can come back . . ."' Nero never significantly 'came back', though he has borne no regrets about his choice. 'I loved Europe. I adored Italy, especially around

Parma, where I was born. My passion was for the little villages I loved, the football team I ran and the orphan children I tended in Italy. In the end, I was not impressed enough by American films. Yes, I loved *Camelot*, I loved the pampering and the fact that they made us stars, but I didn't love it enough.'

Harris remained officially unattached, though never short of companions. The Daisy night club was his favourite disco hangout and *Life* traipsed there in his tracks. Borgzinner wrote in *Life* magazine of him as being 'never happy without women at his feet, an impression he hardly bothers to destroy . . . But, in truth, Harris's lust is for life.'

As Harris squared up to his musical recordings – he had five major songs in *Camelot* – his enthusiasm grew. Eager to match the best in the studio, under the direction of the brilliant musical arranger Alfred Newman, he also wanted to render the songs 'live' during the filming, so as to achieve 'maximum realism'. Such a complicated, risky endeavour appalled Logan, who frantically discouraged him. But Harris was insistent. He had discussed the optimum way of delivering songs on film with Rex Harrison, Professor Higgins in *My Fair Lady*, and was impressed when Harrison informed him that he had delivered all his songs live. When Logan still resisted, Harris headed for Jack Warner's office.

'I jumped on my bicycle – I cycled everywhere around the lot – and pedalled across. I had no appointment, so I had to turn on the blarney to get in to him and when I did I ran up and shook his hand and said, "Thank you so much, Mr Warner. Thank you from the bottom of my heart for allowing me to sing my songs live for *Camelot*. I don't care what anyone is saying about you – as far as I am concerned you are a gentleman!"'

According to Harris, Warner was dumbstruck, not by the brazen approach, but by the implications of 'whoever' was talking about him behind his back. 'It just threw him completely and he grabbed my hand and said, "That's all right, kid. You do your songs your way, don't listen to *anybody*.'

Two weeks later, Harris pressed his luck again with Warner, demanding a major story revision – but this time the blarney failed.

Convinced that Lancelot should never be seen seducing Guinevere, that the intimacy of kisses and embraces in some way 'reduced and humiliated' the dignified aspects of the king, Harris gatecrashed Warner's office and insisted Logan reshoot. Warner listened, and disagreed. But Harris wouldn't let up and started pounding the desk. Suddenly, Warner seemed to concede. He stood up, took Harris by the arm, and led him out to the front of the studio. As Jared, Harris's son, tells the story, Harris panicked in the realisation that Warner might well be about to throw him off the lot. In fact, Warner took him to the gate, turned and pointed to the sign above the entrance. 'What does that say?' Warner asked Harris. '"Warner Brothers",' Harris replied. 'Right. And when it reads "Harris Brothers", you can rewrite *Camelot* any way you want. But not till then."

'I knew I was always taking the Big Risk,' said Harris. 'Right from the start, from Lennard at ABPC, from the *Bounty*. As I saw it, if you don't ask, you don't get. So why not push it?'

When the production ran out of time and was quickly finished, Harris and the others turned their attention to the looping (post-dubbing) and musical tweaking. Once again fussy perfectionism reared its head, contradicting the apparent Malibu hippie insouciance. 'You can change your whole performance in looping,' Harris told *Life*. 'I did 228 loops on *Hawaii*.' Borgzinner sat with him as he indefatigably dubbed new voices on the projected clips, spending a full hour dubbing the word 'Camelot' in one scene, demanding 72 screening reruns to find the exact intonation for the three golden syllables. In the final tearful scene where the king meets young Tom of Warwick, played by Gary Marsh, and warns him to stay away from war with the exhilarating 'Run, boy, *run-n-n-n-n*!' Harris called for twelve reruns, roaring like a lion till his throat became raw and hoarse. Logan loved the twelfth take and swore, 'That's good, Dick. Good.' Brozginner reported Harris as saying, 'No, good isn't enough. It has to be great.'

When *Camelot* finished, Harris waved goodbye to Warner and the lot – taking keepsakes, as he always did. On *Caprice* he had 'stolen' the yellow and black pop-art socks that defined his character. Now, he bought expensive Tiffany's trinkets for every member of the *Camelot* crew, in return for stealing the Warners' lot bicycle and King Arthur's golden crown. He told Borgzinner the gesture was significant: 'I'm only going to play kings from now on.'

The violent jolts in his fortunes – the 'up' of *Camelot* and the 'down' of his marriage break-up – undeniably unbalanced Harris. He later described his frame of mind at this time as 'utterly distraught' – though for *Life* and the fans he made a brave show of it, blithely supporting *Life*'s breezy, heroic portrayal of the Ginger Man, yet again cheerfully breaking his nose, 'while roughhousing with his masseur'. 'It was what they wanted to hear – both the studio, and the audience. That's life, when you think of it. No one wanted me moaning about the loss of the marriage. No one wanted to know about my misery, and the fact that I went out and got pissed to bury it all, and half the time I didn't know where I was and who I was sleeping with. Warners' view was, We give him all that money – so let him shine for us. And you make that devil's bargain and shine, hell or high water. I was fighting a lot – with my shadow. And fucking a lot and all the rest. And the energy had to escape somewhere, so I redirected myself and concentrated for a while on music, which worked for me, because it articulated things I couldn't otherwise express.' During *Camelot*, Columbia Records signed what Harris called 'an option contract' for musical recordings with him – 'But they had in mind a whole load of Dean Martin-style things I had little or no interest in.'

Then the actor Frank Silvera, who ran the integrated American Theater of Being, a nonprofitmaking experimental group, heard Harris's poetry recitations at Malibu and asked for Harris's input for a theatre fundraiser. Harris complied, offering his own poetry readings, and canvassing Edward G Robinson, Walter Pidgeon, Jean Simmons, Yvette Mimieux and Mia Farrow to contribute. 'And it was a turning point, because the singer-songwriter Johnny Rivers produced some of the music for the event and said to me, "You know, there's a kid called Jimmy Webb who writes the kind of songs you sing. I'm going to have him play piano for [the fundraiser], and you should get to know him."'

Harris's rugby career spanned almost a decade. He was sixteen when he played on the first Crescent side to win the Munster Schools Cup in 1947 (above, Harris centre), a victory repeated two years later when his brother Noel also played on the team. After school, he won a coveted gold medal as a member of the Garryowen squad that won the Munster Senior Cup in 1952.

Above, left: 'Overdale' on the Ennis Road, the 'green house' of Harris's boyhood. Much of his early poetry was written here, and it was here he was confined to bed with TB, and first dreamt of escape to a theatrical life in London.

Above, right: Ivan, Harris's father, attempted to train him for management of the family flour mill. Harris got no further than posing for promotional photographs – an early obsession of his – and serving as storehouse rat-catcher.

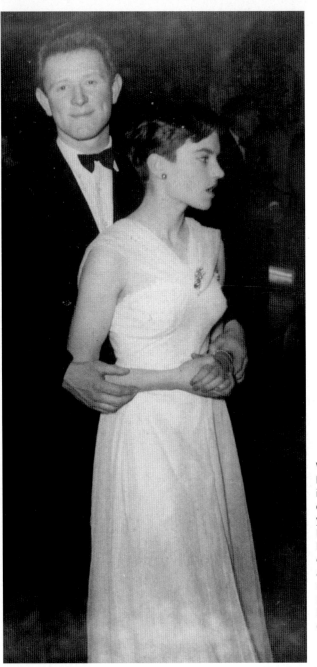

With Elizabeth Brennan, the inspirational love of his Limerick years, in 1951. Harris's mother, Milly, disapproved of Elizabeth's alleged wildness, resulting, says Elizabeth, in her being 'harrised' out of Limerick.

Right: Harris with first wife, the actress Elizabeth Rees-Williams, and baby Damian, pictured in London in 1959.

Below: Harris in Limerick at the premiere of his movie *Bloomfield* in 1970.

Left: At Dromoland Castle in the west of Ireland to promote his first and only directorial feature, *Bloomfield*, with actress girlfriend Linda Hayden in 1970. The failure of the movie threw him into a serious depression.

Above: Two of the stalwarts of Harris's life through the seventies and eighties: Jack Donnelly, his brother-in-law and manager of some of Ireland's leading hotels, and second wife, American model-actress Ann Turkel.

Harris on the road. (Left) The American concert tour of 1972 capitalised on his hit single 'MacArthur Park' and took on the stature of a stadium rock tour. (Below) Harris at his favourite pub in Limerick, Charlie St George's, where, he said, he learned his republicanism. (Bottom) With author Michael Feeney Callan, at work in Dublin on the preparation of this book.

Above: With James Cagney in Co. Wicklow, shooting *Shake Hands with the Devil* in 1959. Harris said Cagney educated him in acting skills: 'He moved with the grace of a dancer.'

Right: With Olive MacFarland in his first movie, ABPC's *Alive and Kicking* (1958), an Ealing-type comedy that attempted – in vain – to present Harris as a cosy, homespun romantic lead.

Above: *This Sporting Life* in 1963 was Harris's artistic breakthrough, affording him multi-award nominations and a deepening and complex relationship with its director, Lindsay Anderson.

Right: Harris with Robert Mitchum in *A Terrible Beauty*, his second international Irish movie, made in 1960. 'I started out hating Mitch,' he said, 'but he stood up for me in a brawl and I learned to love him.'

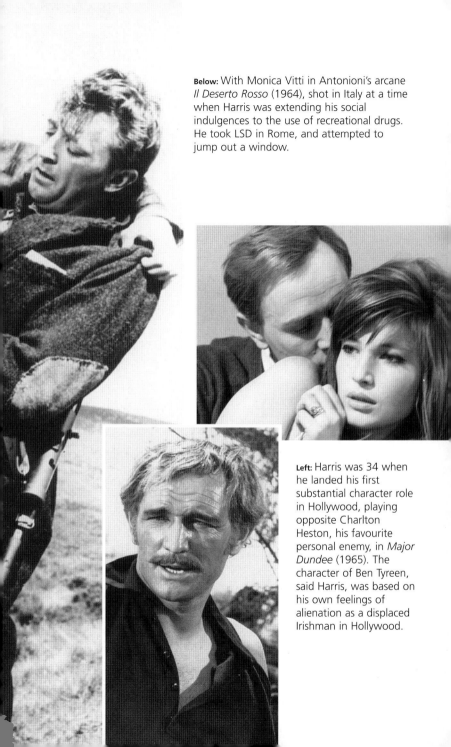

Below: With Monica Vitti in Antonioni's arcane *Il Deserto Rosso* (1964), shot in Italy at a time when Harris was extending his social indulgences to the use of recreational drugs. He took LSD in Rome, and attempted to jump out a window.

Left: Harris was 34 when he landed his first substantial character role in Hollywood, playing opposite Charlton Heston, his favourite personal enemy, in *Major Dundee* (1965). The character of Ben Tyreen, said Harris, was based on his own feelings of alienation as a displaced Irishman in Hollywood.

Above: The first blockbuster: the three-hour long *Hawaii*, based on a book by James Michener (1966). Once again, Harris was unhappy with the casting. This time, Julie Andrews was the object of his wrath.

Below: With Doris Day in the whimsical, clichéd sixties caper movie *Caprice*. Day made the mistake of confusing him with Sean Connery, then the world's number one box-office star, cruising on James Bond.

Above: An improvised rugby match with Connery during the making of *The Molly Maguires* (1970), a movie that proved an honourable failure for all concerned. 'It almost put me out of the business,' said director Martin Ritt.

Right: Harris loved *Man in the Wilderness* (1971), a movie made by the one producer he truly trusted: Sandy Howard. The story was played in near-mime, and Harris enjoyed best the company of co-star John Huston, who introduced him in his free time to the novels of Georges Simenon.

Above: Don Taylor directed Harris and a new(ish) star, Jodie Foster, in the Canadian-set movie *The Last Castle* (aka *Echoes of a Summer*), made as Harris's star started to fade in the mid-seventies. Harris was comforted by his new marriage to Ann Turkel.

Above: The first *Man Called Horse* movie, released in 1970, was a solid success and producer Sandy Howard structured a partnership deal with Harris for a reprise in the distinguished *Return of a Man Called Horse* made five years later.

Above: Bond director Peter Hunt's live action-animation version of *Gulliver's Travels*, released in 1976, was a disaster that Harris lost patience with. 'It's remarkable the thing got finished at all,' he said.

Above: The South African action movie, *The Wild Geese* (1978) was less a return to acting form than immersion in the wild life, alongside drinking buddies Richard Burton and Ronald Fraser. 'We boozed, we smoked weed, we had a blast … '

Above: *Tarzan, the Ape Man*, filmed with Bo Derek and John Phillip Law in the jungles of Sri Lanka in 1980, proved a nightmare for Harris. 'I kept a diary, noting every day I'd left to get it over with. Afterwards, I promised myself I would never make another movie.'

Above: *Camelot* on stage in the early eighties. Harris bought the touring rights and personally earned more than $8 million over four years from King Arthur – more than he had ever earned from any movie.

Left: *Maigret*, made for US television, turned into a major embarrassment in 1988. Harris defended it, because he genuinely loved Simenon's character.

A return to the Oscar stakes in *The Field*, in 1990. Here Harris catches a break in the freezing winds of November, on location in Connemara, Ireland.

With Maggie Smith and Elizabeth Sprigg, fighting mischief as Professor Albus Dumbledore in the record-breaking *Harry Potter and the Philosopher's Stone* (2001). Harris's granddaughter, Ella, was the one who pushed him to commit to the Harry Potter movies, to his ultimate great delight.

Webb was just nineteen, an Oklahoma preacher's son on contract to Rivers at $100 a week. Webb recalled, 'I didn't know Richard, because my head was in my ass for music and nothing else. Working for Johnny, I had the hundred dollars, and a car, which is what I loved best about the deal. My job was to turn out songs for Johnny's other contracted artistes, among them The Versatiles, who later became The Fifth Dimension.' Webb remembered the first impact of meeting Harris as 'gutsy. He had that love for music that all Irishmen seem to possess. We would be sitting backstage during rehearsals and he'd come up to me and say, in his velvet brogue, "Jimmy Webb, play this song", or "Play that song." And of course I would, and he would chirp along like a songbird. He was like my big brother. I felt safe with him. He was very wise and experienced, and I was a little kid.' Formal communication, never Harris's forte, was nonexistent. 'It's hard to explain. He just *was there*, like a lifelong buddy, without all the questions of "Where are you from?" and "What do you like?" He took me everywhere he went. It was comforting. No matter where we went, even to the rowdiest of downtown bars, I knew I'd be looked after.'

Shortly afterwards Webb let his contract with Rivers lapse to sign with Jay Lasker at ABC Dunhill. The changeover was like alchemy. In the space of four months he had two of his songs hit the national charts: 'Up, Up and Away', performed by The Fifth Dimension, and 'By the Time I Get to Phoenix', sung by Glen Campbell. 'I was still the impressionable teenager who didn't really understand the business, but by then I was doin' more than OK.' Harris drifted in and out of sight for a while, and then disappeared from the LA scene. 'There was never any direct talk about recording. It was more like a ritual "getting to know you" dance – and then he vanished.'

Harris's departure was the last-ditch effort to recover his marriage. Back in London, he attempted, again, to romance Elizabeth. 'He was drawn to her and the children,' said the actor Joe Lynch. 'You can't have lived the hard years they shared without some deep bond. She may have hated him then, but she never stopped being in love with him, nor he with her. It sounds like a cliché, but everyone who knew them said it was true.'

Harris rented a flat at 37 Chesham Place, Belgravia, and decorated it with his *Camelot* crown and impulse-bought antiques. It was the semblance of a permanent home designed, friends said, to lure Elizabeth back. But it was luckless place. The columnist Roderick Mann called and found Harris philosophic and subdued: 'Maybe I've changed a bit. All that fighting. I was really just fighting myself. Frustration, I suppose. Now I've learned it's a sign of great weakness to take the discord of your own life and attempt to pass it on. Now I put my melancholy down on paper. You shouldn't regret one moment of sadness: just let others feel it through poetry or music.' It might almost have been conciliatory King Arthur speaking, he who said, 'Might's not right! Might *for* right!' He had, he told Mann, abandoned his Catholicism and replaced it to some degree with Patric Walker's astrology. He praised his astrologer for guiding his life and accepted that his marriage was all but over: 'You can't go back. Only fools go back. The thing is to grow, and be happy with the way you are growing. All of us look up at the sky when we're born and plan one day to reach it. But most give up. They content themselves with standing higher than their neighbour's roof. They forget about the sky they once so desperately wanted to touch. Me, I never want to forget.'

Dermot and John McMichael had lined up two potential pictures – *Nobody Loves a Drunken Indian* and Lerner and Loewe's *On a Clear Day You Can See Forever* – both of which tormented him in the months to come. 'The first one had budget problems that never quit and was made years later with Anthony Quinn, and good luck to him, because it was shit. The second one was worse. Lerner and Streisand stitched me up. They wanted it their way. Lerner never liked my singing, and he took out the best songs from the original Broadway show. Streisand wanted to be Queen Bee. I told her to bark up someone else's tree. She liked to think she was special, but she was really average in every department except the size of her cranium.'

For a while, Harris caroused with Dermot, who was also a hard drinker, and with the myriad Irish journalists who flocked to his door. But then, abruptly, he U-turned from alcoholic idleness.

Demo recording virtually every daily for Lasker in LA, Jimmy
Webb suddenly received a cable from Harris: COME TO LONDON
STOP LET'S MAKE A RECORD STOP LOVE RICHARD.

'I hesitated. I had never been out of the country, hadn't been
anywhere,' says Webb. 'Then I considered the conveyor belt I was
on and said, Wait a minute, why not? I took up the offer and packed
a briefcase full of songs I'd written and took the next polar flight to
London.' Webb arrived exhausted and took a taxi to Chesham Place:
'I remember this rambling, big, elegant house with open fires
everywhere. I was jaded and I recall sinking into a huge bath – I
recall the smell of the English soap, and those crisp white linen
sheets . . .' When Webb had slept off his flight Harris was ready to
work: he wanted to hear Webb's new music immediately. 'He was
absolutely self-assured and in control. He was a man who knew
precisely what he wanted.'

Webb sat at the grand piano in the living room, 'surrounded by the
trappings of a king'. The *Camelot* crown hung jauntily from a great
gilt mirror over an antique Irish refectory table. Turkish odalisque
cushions littered the chairs. There was a seventeenth-century
Venetian bishop's throne, porcelain ornaments, silk fringes. In
Webb's eyes Harris had changed: he was still 'just lovely, a
confident, positive-minded man who was great to be with', but 'he
seemed possessed to do something *now, now, now*.'

Webb banged out 'thirty or forty' songs and Harris sat, paced,
shouted, whooped. 'It was, "I like this one. I'll take that one. No,
pass on that one!"' says Webb. Then Webb performed one of his
own favourites, 'a complicated, rather cumbersome tune I'd written
for The Association, but they'd rejected it, saying it couldn't be
done. Richard instantly lit on it. He jumped up and said, "*That's the
one*. That's the song I want to record *now*." He was absolutely
assertive about it. And it was his intuition, his decision alone.'

'MacArthur Park', Webb's serpentine symphony, was the least
likely choice for a single record follow-up to *Camelot*. Laced with
neoclassical female harmonies, studded with time changes, it
seemed more a show number, best conveyed with lights, dancers and
a live audience. Stacked against the chart hits of the day – the songs

of Jimi Hendrix, The Beatles, The Lovin' Spoonful and The Beach Boys – it was a startling oddity, at seven minutes-plus almost guaranteed to be passed over for pop-radio airtime. 'I raised these concerns with Richard,' said Webb. 'But he was so *certain* of it, it was uncanny.'

Dermot Harris took over the organisation of a new recording deal for Webb and Harris. Columbia quickly fell out, rejecting the proposal to spend $85,000 on 'MacArthur Park' and a nine-song album. 'If it had been just me and a guitar,' Harris said, 'they would have agreed. But Jimmy and I wanted a big production number, with orchestra and all the rest.' Webb's ABC Dunhill stepped in with a funding deal, and Webb flew back to LA to start musical scoring at Sound Recorders, the studio home of Phil Spector and Brian Wilson.

Harris was glad to be working. The best London had offered him that summer was a libel case, arising from remarks made on the Eamonn Andrews TV show. The producer David Newman took the action, but the jury found for Harris and the publicity, said Ronald Fraser, 'really did no good, because it served that stupid hellraising image that Dickie was trying to escape then.' Harris told the *Daily Mail*: 'It's boredom, frustration, *not drink*, that makes me aggressive. I haven't been in a fight since 19 May. I felt so ashamed after the last fight. I swore it would be the last time. The worst thing I do in life is *nothing*. There must always be a new challenge.'

After Christmas, as Webb completed the LA backing tracks, Harris summoned him to Ireland, first to visit his three-storey lodge near the Pollock Holes at Kilkee, then to Dublin. Webb said, 'He took me to all the old places of his childhood. In Kilkee he showed me the amphitheatre, with the wild Atlantic crashing all around it, and said, "Down there is where I gave my first performances." Then he took me to Dublin, with his sister Harmay. They had a big rented house and he said, "Jimmy Webb, I want you to sleep in the bed where I was conceived." I think his objective was to create harmony between us, to make *the link* before the intimacy of the recording process.'

Vocal recording for 'MacArthur Park' and the album built around it, *A Tramp Shining*, began at the suburban Lansdowne Road Studios. Webb had all the sixteen-track tapes ready, assembled and fine-tuned in LA with the participation of leading sessions players like Hal Blaine, who worked on hits by The Beach Boys, Spector, Sinatra, Dean Martin. 'But the fact that I'd cut the orchestral tracks without Richard might have caused some problems. They were a little high for him, but he insisted on maintaining the range and tone ... and I think in the end that paid off, because it helped the emotional intensity of the album.'

The Lansdowne recording sessions proved joyful: 'Every day we left the house in Richard's Phantom V Rolls,' said Webb, 'always with a big pitcher of Pimm's close to hand. Then we went into this little studio and Richard took his place at the mike, with a tall stool to his left and the Pimm's on the stool. Then we started recording, for maybe three or four hours, or however long it took till the Pimm's was gone. Afterwards we reloaded the Rolls and went back to the house. It was a very pleasant ritual.' Harris, said Webb, was never sloppy. 'He could never have gotten through that music in a drunken state. He liked to lubricate his vocal cords, but that was as far as it went.'

Of the songs on the highly innovative album Harris especially related to 'MacArthur Park' and 'Didn't We', which he interpreted as intimate accounts of the break-up with Elizabeth. The lyric of 'Didn't We', laden with regrets, seemed especially apt:

> *This time we almost make it to the moon*
> *Didn't we, girl?*
> *This time we almost sang our song in tune*
> *Oh didn't we, girl?*
>
> *This time I had the answer right here in my hand*
> *But I touched it and it had turned to sand . . .*

Harris played the tracks for Elizabeth, announcing them as personal statements. At the same time he told the journalist Victor Davis, '["Didn't We"] tells of our parting and our three or four attempts to come together again.' Elizabeth loved the songs, but resisted the strategic romantic overture. Webb said, 'I know Richard saw something deeply personal in those songs, but I did not write them about him and Elizabeth. "MacArthur Park" was in my bag for a long time, as was "Didn't We". But it was to our mutual advantage that he personalised them, because he delivered incredible vocal sensitivity – and that, I believe, is what made "MacArthur Park" such a worldwide hit.'

ABC Dunhill's president Larry Newton attempted to stop the release of 'MacArthur Park', considering the airplay problem insurmountable. 'It could ruin the record business,' Newton announced. 'Because a record as long as this takes away potential air time from three other records.' Webb, Harris and ABC's A&R team overrode Newton and 'MacArthur Park', released in tandem with *A Tramp Shining* in April 1968, charted immediately. In four weeks the single jumped to No. 2 on the US *Billboard* listings, with sales of more than 600,000 copies. In Britain it reached No. 4. It has been claimed that its impact influenced The Beatles, whose 'Hey Jude' all of seven minutes and eleven seconds long, made worldwide No. 1 in August 1968.

For the Webb–Harris partnership, the success heralded new recordings and tour offers. In September, 'Didn't We' was released as a single, and a six-record-three-years deal was signed with the newly formed musical division of Limbridge, Harris's London company. 'The music success opened all sorts of doors for Limbridge,' said Harris. 'It was gratifying, because I wanted that company to be like The Beatles' Apple Corporation. I named it after my birthplace, and Elizabeth's – Limerick and Bridgend. I wanted people to say, Harris is not just an actor, he is Jack Warner. That was my thinking at the time. And it wasn't self-serving. I wanted to make musical opportunities for other people, to find talent in writing and producing that I could support and develop.'

'MacArthur Park', as it turned out, proved the making and breaking of what could have been a lucrative and profound collaborative career with Webb. 'I don't know if any of us expected that degree of early success,' said Webb. 'But I predicted the song would chart, and that started a wager with Richard that screwed us up completely.' This wager, dealt from the heart by both participants, would effectively stunt Limbridge's musical hopes. During the recording at Lansdowne, said Webb, Harris had volunteered: 'If this album goes top ten I'll give you my Phantom V.' Webb said, 'I *loved* Richard, so I *loved* the idea of having his Rolls. I didn't *need* a Rolls. I had money and fame, all that. But I adored Richard, I looked up to him – and because of that I wanted *Richard's* Rolls!' The fact that the car was of royal lineage – 'literally had the Royal Household medallion on the grille' – wasn't of special interest to Webb. He just wanted his idol's car. When the album broke internationally, as promised – 'all over the *bloody, fucking world*!' said Webb – Harris offered Webb *a* Rolls but not *the* Rolls. 'Limbridge mailed some catalogues to my New York office showing all the latest available models. I could pick the car I wanted, no expense spared, said Dermot – but that was not the point. What I wanted was our deal. Richard made a promise, and he broke it, he let me down.'

The collapse of preproduction on *Nobody Loves a Drunken Indian* drove Harris into a nervous collapse that left him bedridden for two weeks late in 1968. 'It was a marvellous part,' he told Roderick Mann. 'I banked everything on it and now some fat shareholder in New York has sat on the basket and it's off . . . I foresee a disastrous year for me.' Years later he remembered, 'When a career is moving that fast, every second of the day counts. Everything takes on an exaggerated emphasis so that, when a light bulb pops, the ceiling falls in. I was up, I was down . . . but I kept moving. I thought I treated Jimmy [Webb] just fine, but I wasn't taking stock. I was just running.'

Off balance, Harris accepted a role opposite Michael Caine, an actor he never much liked, in the James Bond producer Harry Saltzman's *Written on the Sand*, later retitled *Play Dirty*. 'And that was a royal fuck-up because Saltzman lied to me. Dermot had inserted clause in my contracts saying an offered role could not be tampered with once I'd accepted. Saltzman signed that contract. But then, when I arrived in Spain, I was given thirty new pages, with four of my main scenes cut to ribbons. I wasn't going to play second fiddle to Caine, any more than I was to Streisand. I told Saltzman, "You are a contemptible, low-life fucker" and I walked off.' Director

Rene Clement supported Harris's protestations to Saltzman, but Saltzman refused to renegotiate. For four days Harris turned up each morning for his set call – then quit for London. Days later Clement left in solidarity, to be replaced by executive producer André de Toth as new director.

Harris's lost £150,000 on *Play Dirty*, but more damaging by far was the negative media reflex. In the various 'reports from location', Harris was described as 'troublesome', 'wild', 'rambunctious' and 'whimsical'. 'Those were upsetting days, because I had nothing to follow up *Camelot* with. So much was expected of me, and all I could coherently offer was a lot of hot air.' Through the winter and spring, the hot air included announcements of a movie about Michael Collins, the Irish rebel hero, for the producer Kevin McClory, and – again – a filmed version of the long-promised *Hamlet*, to be directed by Frank Silvera with a paltry $500,000 backing from Paramount and with Faye Dunaway playing Ophelia and Jimmy Webb supplying music.

None of these projects came to fruition and Harris attended the long-awaited premiere of *Camelot* alone, while Elizabeth was accompanied by her new boyfriend, Christopher Plummer. The reviews, as expected, brightened the air. 'Stunningly beautiful,' said the *Hollywood Reporter*, under a banner headline that screamed: REDGRAVE, HARRIS AND NERO NOW AMONG THE GREAT STARS.

With the Phantom V Rolls row unresolved, Harris holidayed one last time in Mexico with Webb to choose songs for the next album, to be called *The Yard Went On Forever*. Webb said: 'We dug deep in my satchel of earlier songs for that one, which was probably a mistake, when I think back. I think I should have worked up more new material, but events for Richard were moving too fast.' The title track, an arcane anti-Vietnam war song, started with the words:

> *Is everybody safe?*
> *Does everybody have a place to hide?*

The lyric was adapted from Senator Robert Kennedy's last words, said Webb, and yet again label executives voiced reservations, declaring the song too political. Once again, Webb and Harris held out and the track was released as a single – but this time it failed to chart. 'We got it wrong for reasons who can say? I liked it. But it was a bit bizarre, and the public appetite for a certain kind of abstract song was waning by then. In my view, still, the second Harris album was the better one. The real aficionados will tell you that that's their favourite because the songs have a wider range. But it didn't work for Richard. It didn't advance his pop career and, as a friendship, we came unstuck.'

Harris's advance for *The Yard Went On Forever* was an impressive £250,000 and, wisely, much of the money was channelled into bricks and mortar, establishing Limbridge's new office suite at a palatial block on the Victoria Embankment. Some money, too, went as promised into the promotion of new talent. Harris's girlfriend Kathy Green, the Malibu songstress, was flown to London to prepare for recording, though little of substance emerged. 'There's a lot of bread in this game,' said Harris at the time. 'You've got to have guts. When I made my first record my agent, my manager and all my advisers said I was mad, that the pop scene is only for kids. But I'm 37, and there's a lot left [in it] for me yet.'

Though Plummer was the new man in her life, Elizabeth and Harris remained the closest of friends. One shared acquaintance said, 'Liz told me that they were better and closer as a separated couple than as marrieds. She said Dick was never made for domesticity, and she'd just given up. But when she gave up, the real romance thrived.' Joe Lynch said, 'Neither Richard nor Elizabeth knew how to manage that relationship, that's the real truth. Everyone saw what was really going on. She was drifting with the wind, poor thing, moving from Plummer to Rex Harrison, as if she were trying to outdo Dick. Underneath it all, they were so similar in nature, and that's why it was doomed.'

With Harris's keen backing, Elizabeth had started her own design company, and assumed her first major commission decorating the Limbridge suite. She told the *Daily Mail*: 'I've been bursting for something to do, so I've started interior designing. I've got several commissions already ...' Jack Donnelly, always in close touch, observed, 'Dick told the world that all that mattered was movies. The truth was, all that mattered was his wife and kids. He was a softie, but no one really notices softies.'

Cyril Cusack, Joe Lynch and other Irish friends were invited to dinner at Chesham Place. Lynch described Harris then as 'a man in midair, like a trapeze artist between swings'. Cusack found him 'affecting comfort, but sort of wriggling inside his skin'. To the outside world, Harris was the ornery, difficult, defiant King Richard – self-crowned, but with nowhere particular to go. As ever, when bored, he summoned the court, issued the edicts and dispensed the wisdom. With Kathy Green, he said, he had co-written a song that might launch a whole new phase in his career. It was called 'I Won't Go Back'.

CHAPTER 11

Battle Cries!

Elizabeth Harris was granted a decree nisi in London on 25 July 1969. Harris offered no defence to her allegation of adultery with an unnamed actress on a number of occasions in October 1967. *The Times* sombrely noted: 'Discretion was exercised in respect of Mrs Harris's own admitted adultery.' A private financial settlement was agreed and joint custody of the children was granted. Mr Justice Latey observed that both participants had made a number of efforts to save their marriage, the latest as recently as June of that year, but the situation was clearly irretrievable. Years later Harris told *Hot Press* magazine, 'Elizabeth and I would have divorced three or four years previously if I'd conceded to her demands for custody of the children. I said, "No, I want joint custody. I don't want to have to ask you, 'Can I see what's mine?'" Luckily Elizabeth [then] wanted to marry Rex Harrison, so she finally said, "This is the only way I'll get my divorce, so I'll concede to that." And now [in the 1990s] she says, "Thanks be to God you fought for it, because that's what the children needed."'

Elizabeth's love affair with Harrison was in fact a slow-burner that didn't make the headlines until long after the divorce. Outwardly, her close relationship was with Plummer, but Harris knew otherwise and, said friends, turned a blind eye. When Roderick Mann asked him about Elizabeth's mysterious love life he said only, 'It must be hard for the fellow she's going around with now. Because I know she still thinks about me a lot. At a party the other night she said, "This is a dull bore. What it needs is Harris to liven things up." That can't be easy for any man now, can it?'

Harris celebrated – or mourned – the divorce by touring the brothels of Amsterdam and Hamburg, 'fucking for Ireland'. On his return, new domestic arrangements were made, with Elizabeth settling in Wiltshire with Susy, wife of the actor Kier Dullea, and Kathy Green moving into Bedford Gardens to prepare her upcoming Limbridge album. In her memoirs, Elizabeth fondly recalled the dismay of the neighbours who, celebrating what they thought would be the departure once and for all of the loud-mouth Irishman, now had to contend with the shrill outpourings of an American hippie folk singer at all hours.

Harris hauled anchor, finally finding a movie of merit to follow *Camelot* and get him away from 'the blood bath of London'. *The Molly Maguires*, scripted by Walter Bernstein and directed by Martin Ritt, attracted him for its moral and political story of dissent among the impoverished Irish workers in a nineteenth-century Pennsylvania mining town. Ronald Fraser believed that 'After the divorce and the disappointments [of missed movies after *Camelot*] he was very political. It was as if he woke up to responsibility, and tried to be a mature man and not some rake-about-town. It had something to do with the influence of good King Arthur, we all believed.' The evidence of Harrris's interviews of the period lend weight to this. For a while, to be sure, quickfire politics occupied him. He was bluntly against the Vietnam War, though sceptical of the value of the counterculture movement and antiwar films: 'I think one of the things that might ease world tension is a better understanding of people. With air travel increasing, people have greater opportunities to communicate with each other and perhaps this will decrease the possibility of war.' Naïveté, if not out and out devilment, underscored all his grand pronouncements, which flitted from the tax laws to the ongoing dilemma of British rule in Northern Ireland, from American social values to the British establishment. He did not, he stated portentously, support Ronald Reagan's popular governorship of California. 'I cannot accept him. I believe in being politically groomed. He's an actor, so he's not.' Lord Ogmore, finally distanced, was no longer a bone of contention. 'You must have due regard for such men as Asquith, Churchill and Macmillan, who by training and heritage were natural to politics. Or, as in the Labour movement, where people started as miners, then become trade union officials and [learn] politics in a logical way . . .'

On the set of *The Molly Maguires* he was more coherent and disciplined, mindful of the ironies of his role, playing the treacherous Irish enforcer who subverts the miners' fight for status. 'It was the "grey area" of morality that worked for me. Marty Ritt had learned his politics the hard way. He was blacklisted as a member of the Communist Party in the fifties and he learned how to get himself back into the picture the cunning way. So the movie was subtle in so many ways, and I responded to that. People associated it with the Black Panther activists, who were all the rage at that time. People suggested many metaphors and subtexts. But I was happy to see it as a great yarn and it reminded me of *This Sporting Life*, for its honesty.

Playing alongside Sean Connery, then the world's number-one box-office star, Harris established a rapport that developed over the years into a sort of friendship – which, in the circumstances, said something for Connery's forbearance. Connery's reputation merited lead billing; but Harris demanded – and got – his name above the title. 'For the kind of money they're paying me,' said Connery sharply, 'they can put a mule ahead of me.'

The Molly Maguires was shot through the spring of 1969 on uncharacteristically hot location at Lancaster and Eckley, mining ghost towns in southern Pennsylvania. Paramount rebuilt Eckley in all its anthracite glory, at a modest cost of $250,000, and the movie's budget was just $5 million, almost half the budget of *Camelot*. To keep him company, Harris brought his New York boozing pal Malachy McCourt aboard to play, appropriately, an innkeeper. Jimmy Webb was also invited to drop by and he watched in admiration as Harris gave his most intelligent and vigorous performance since *This Sporting Life*.

Harris's contentment in hard labour was reflected in his improved health. As temperatures soared, Connery and a number of crew members collapsed from dehydration and exhaustion, but Harris kept going, inspired, said Jimmy Webb, by the gossip on set that he was bound for a second Oscar nomination. A visiting Hollywood reporter wrote, 'This time he'll get one . . . Harris himself says this is the best role he's played since he won critical acclaim in the rugby league story.'

The Molly Maguires should have succeeded hugely, but it didn't. Photographed with brooding, dark grace by James Wong Howe, scored sensitively by Henry Mancini, it presented itself as a sharp parable that implied continuing injustice in the plight of the dispossessed. But, perhaps for that very reason, said Ritt, both public and critics disdained it. According to Ritt, 'It didn't do any business at all and, though I wasn't completely without employment after it, employment wasn't as accessible to me as it had been.'

Harris got no award nominations, but his reborn movie energies remained. Staying in LA, he met with the producer Sandford Howard and agreed to do his alternative western, *A Man Called Horse*. Howard admits that Harris was not his first, but his *fifth* choice as star. 'The project had a tortured start,' said Howard. 'It started when I was en route from India, where I had drunk the water, unfortunately. I was flying to Japan and became very ill. In Tokyo I was lying there, dying, thinking, I'll get a Japanese doc who doesn't understand I'm dying . . . but this nice Jewish doctor, Dr Birnbaum from the Bronx, arrived. He said, "You've got three days in bed to get over this, so do some reading." So I gathered all the English books I could find and one of them was a western anthology with a story by Dorothy Johnson called *A Man Called Horse*. It had been made already as a *Wagon Train* episode [on US television] but I saw a potential hit movie. When I got well, I acquired the rights for $250. And then I set up a production deal, intending to star Robert Redford. Redford opted to do something else – probably *Jeremiah Johnson*, which was similar territory – so we looked around and found Richard, whom I always admired. We asked three others after Redford. But Richard was the first to say yes.'

Dorothy Johnson, already well known for *The Man Who Shot Liberty Valance*, deferred to the experienced screenwriter Jack De

Witt, then in his mid-sixties, to script Howard's film. Elliot Silverstein, director of *Cat Ballou*, which won an Academy Award for Lee Marvin, was assigned the hot seat. 'But that was a disastrous choice,' said Howard. 'Richard Harris was, well, *all right* to manage, but Silverstein and he just didn't get on at all. I'll explain the working atmosphere in Mexico like this: Richard *fought* with Silverstein; I personally *would have killed* him. He was a rat, and a bad director. He turned in a movie that had such great potential, but it was a dud. We previewed it in Oakland and the test audience hated it. Richard had worked his ass off in the desert, portraying this English gentleman who is captured by the Sioux and takes to their ways, but, when he saw what Silverstein had, he wanted nothing to do with it.' Howard elbowed Silverstein and, with the help of the Cinema Centers manager Jerry Henshaw, a market-shrewd friend, he recut the entirety. 'We salvaged it from the brink,' said Howard, 'and presented something we all liked, and which did good business.' The 'miscalculation' of Silverstein, Howard estimated, added $2 million to the budget – 'and added nearly an extra year to the production'.

A Man Called Horse, when it finally surfaced in 1970, was greeted universally as a noble polemic in defence of the humiliated Indian, two years before Brando's eloquent boycotting of the Oscars – he won for *The Godfather*, but refused to accept the award as a protest against the persecution of settlement Indians – and before other provocative movies, like Redford's *Jeremiah Johnson*, recast the direction of seventies westerns. Harris's presence was no small part of the victory. Once again on disciplined form, Harris shone as Lord John Morgan, the aristocrat who becomes a Sioux warrior. The graphic Sun Vow initiation ritual, in which the white man is hung from a high tepee scaffold by claw hooks in his pectorals, drew controversy and, accordingly, inflated audiences, and gave Harris a box-office to equal *Camelot*. 'It is a story the public has been waiting for,' Harris said on its release. 'This is why it has been successful. Not just in the United States but in Italy, Norway, Sweden, Denmark. Everyone is fascinated because the Indian was a rugged individualist – which all of us hope we are, try to be, and most of us, unfortunately, fail at. The public has never seen the American Indian as he was before the white man. In this movie, we see the truth.' Of all markets, only Portugal rejected the movie, deeming it racist. Harris leaped to the movie's defence, emphasising the months of unremitting research. Everyone involved, he said, had studied the background minutely, including himself. It was fully understood that the Sun Vow had latterly been replaced by the more humane Sun Dance ceremony, but the ritual was precise and historically accurate in context. No gratuitous licence had been taken. Sandy Howard told *Photoplay*, 'We [have gone] so far back in the ethnological background that the Indians have no colour blue. That came afterwards, with the white man. Too many modern-day Indians have not been educated in their heritage. We are trying to add our voice . . .'

Harris's pleasure with the movie, combined with Howard's scrupulous honesty, made for a business partnership that would deliver a *Horse* sequel and other movies. 'Richard and I were similar in our strong-mindedness and our style of straight-talk dealing,' said Howard. 'I treated him fairly and he treated me fairly. That's how Hollywood should be, but usually isn't. After *A Man Called Horse* we said, Let's make some worthwhile films with decent values. We shook hands on it, and we kept to our promise.'

Creatively and emotionally, Harris was suddenly on a high. The deal with Howard, and the evidence of *Horse*, brought him back to the aspiration of the Anderson era, 'minus the personality clashes'. Most importantly, he seemed suddenly to isolate his special suitability for strong, alienated-loner and 'vision quest' roles. 'I couldn't put it in those words, because I would be emotionally dyslexic, or however one states it. But that was *the feeling*. Don't try to be glamorous. Don't be a hippie. Stay inside yourself, and find the power that is individuality – that was my focus.'

The role he went for next exercised this new focus to the hilt: *Cromwell* was a screenplay that had been bouncing around Hollywood for five years or more. Written 'with high hopes if not common sense' by the director Ken Hughes, it had the ingredients of a grand epic like *Cleopatra* – and an mini-epic-size budget in excess of $8 million – but also debated interesting issues about the duality of Oliver Cromwell's role in history. Harris had read the script before *Hawaii* and, he said, pledged himself to it even then, 'despite the fact that I was probably the worst candidate, since I was an Irishman and a nationalist, and Cromwell had attempted genocide in my country'. Harris's enthusiasm had intrigued many prospective backers who saw the power of the paradox, but Hughes ran into the constant wall of market concerns. Said Harris, 'The time was never right. All Ken ever heard was that the days of the epics were over. But those are just excuses. What he had was a fine script, and sooner or later someone would back it – and me.'

Finally, while shooting the children's classic *Chitty Chitty Bang Bang*, Hughes persuaded the producer Irving Allen to mount the film with Columbia backing. Spain was chosen as the cost-efficient, weather-friendly location, Alec Guinness was cast as King Charles I, and Harris was confirmed as Cromwell. 'Until I made *Camelot*,' said Harris, 'no one would positively trust me to play Cromwell. The success of *Camelot* gave Ken the fuel he needed.'

Harris's fee was his best – $500,000 – but his real motivation was art. Cromwell he saw not as the cartoonised scourge of the Irish, but 'as a symbol of integrity, anxious to reform society in the same spirit of King Arthur but forced to arms'. He was not, said Harris, what the storybooks made him out to be: 'He was a quiet, peace-loving chap who was put in the unfortunate position of either inciting an uprising against the king, or abandoning his ideals. He chose to fight and, surprisingly, became an excellent tactician and strategist.' Cromwell's call for education for the masses and an end to the licentious behaviour of the ruling aristocrats impressed Harris. 'I am not saying he had not a black side. I am not denying history. But there was this other side, and that is what I wanted to project. It's not necessary for an actor to *believe* in the character he is playing. With Cromwell, I admire the rigorous self-discipline of the man. I admire his main aim: to take the country out of aristocratic hands.'

In a moment of confluence, Limerick's University Project Committee, campaigning for a third-level college for the city, requested Harris's lobbying help and was happily supported. Harris flew home immediately and joined the action group led by Cecil Murray to address a huge gathering of students, teachers and politicians. He told them, 'I have travelled all over the world and I can see the necessity for education. In every country – Russia, America, even Mexico – the emphasis is totally on education. It is Limerick's time to join in.' If any Crescent Comprehensive Jesuits were in the audience they kept silent. But Harris was at pains to say he had no axe to grind with the Jesuits. Educated in the University of Life, he now appreciated the military order of Jesuit discipline. 'It breeds great individuality,' he told friends. 'I would like to see a separation of church and state. But I would also like to see the Jesuit principles of thoroughness in education more widely embraced.' In future years his educational crusading would become even livelier in supporting the Jesuit system.

Before flying to Spain for *Cromwell*, Harris made the law courts – and the tabloids – again. During a supper cabaret featuring Sammy Davis Jr at the Talk of the Town he became involved in a fist fight. Davis he knew and liked from Sinatra's Palm Springs parties, and Harris rose to his defence when a heckler chanted anti-Jewish remarks while Davis sang the theme from *Exodus*. Harris told Bow Street magistrates' court, 'I found the remarks offensive and distasteful. Sammy Davis is a great friend of mine and I know he is sensitive about remarks that he is Jewish and coloured. I twice warned the man to shut up but he kept on. So I hit him.' Harris also hit Detective Constable Andrew Davanna and Detective Constable George Napier, who had tried to detain him. Fined £12, with £12 costs, Harris considered the penalty worth it: 'Violence is unacceptable, I agree. But sometimes, when you face bigotry, it's the only defence weapon you have.' Sammy Davis Jr, apparently oblivious to the kerfuffle, told the *Daily Mail* from his Park Lane penthouse, 'What more can a man ask of a friend than that he should come to his defence? I didn't really know what was happening . . .'

Two weeks later Harris was in court again, charged with assaulting a traffic warden. Marion McClean, the warden, claimed Harris had obstructed her in the course of placing a ticket on the car of a friend of his. Harris 'danced an Irish jig and embraced' her: 'It was as if he folded his arms very tightly in front of him – and I was squashed in between,' said Ms McClean. This time the sentence was six months' conditional discharge. The magistrate Kenneth Barraclough – obviously a fan – observed that the actor was clearly showing 'misplaced friendliness', but cautioned Harris: 'You must not think that everyone enjoys being hugged and jigged around by a film star.'

Just before departure, Harris indulged in 'the biggest gift I've ever given myself', purchasing Tower House, a listed quasi-Arthurian pile in Melbury Road, Kensington. The house stood tall against its dowdy neighbours, almost intimidating, said Ronald Fraser, in its Gothic-like, fussy façade, 'missing only the gargoyles and pantiles'. The journalist Trevor Danker said, 'It was a great Victorian extravagance, a bit of King Arthur bravura. No one would seriously want to live there. But that's what he wanted, that's why he pursued *Cromwell* and all those regal trappings: he believed himself to be the King of Kensington.' The irony of socially conscious Cromwell, the enemy of aristocracy, gifting himself a fantasy palace Harris ignored. 'I loved it because it was an eccentricity,' he said. 'It was built by the architect William Burgess who built Cork Cathedral and it was the focal point of Kensington for me when I arrived in London. I used to see it like something from a Grimms' fairy tale, and whenever I had no place to sleep, on a summer night, I would hide away in the bushes – because it was all overgrown and derelict then – and have the greatest rest of my life, just like sleeping in the garden in Overdale.' Harris also enjoyed the fact that he had 'snatched the house away' from Liberace, who had made an offer of £70,000, which was beaten by Harris's £75,000. 'I found out in the *Evening Standard* that he was interested, and they published his offer . . . but he didn't get the deposit down fast enough, and I pulled it from under him, poor sod.' Danny La Rue's claim that Tower House felt 'spooky and haunted' didn't perturb Harris: 'I love ghosts. I depend on them to guide me through.'

Harris treated his new home with obsessive fervour, bringing in Victorian designers to reconstruct many neglected architectural aspects of the 25 rooms. Burgess's original design drawings were unearthed at the Victoria and Albert Museum, and the stone- and plasterwork was reconstituted to match them. The original plan had been for 'a model residence identical to fifteenth-century design', and legend had it that Burgess built Tower House as a shrine to Chaucer. 'I was faithful to that kind of dream thinking,' said Harris. 'I even booked the building firm who'd undertaken the decoration a hundred years before. I wanted Burgess to be proud of us.'

Harris stayed in Spain through the autumn for the marathon *Cromwell* but the nature of the movie – heavily populated, clanging with battles, packed with character scenes of highest intensity opposite Alec Guinness – burned away energies somewhat depleted by Tower House. 'That was a hell of a production logistically. The Spanish army loaned out four hundred trained soldiers to recreate hand-to-hand battlefield fighting, but it was constant retakes, constantly on horseback, constant heat, the discomfort of armour. Everyone got burned out and I marvelled at how Ken Hughes kept going. I saw it as an immense jigsaw puzzle, and, as the weeks went by, it was harder to keep it straight in my head. It wasn't intimate, like *The Molly Maguires*. It was – literally – the English Civil War, and it felt like it every minute.'

Towards the end it was obvious that Harris was near to breakdown. When the time came to shoot the execution of Charles I, he flipped. He described the breakdown – a combination of intemperate drinking and overlong stress periods – as a 'terrifying experience'. He awoke in his hotel at dawn in a cold shivering sweat: 'I actually thought we were about to cut off Charles I's head, for real. I was shouting down the telephone, "We must give him another chance! We must think twice about this!" I was convinced we were doing it for real.'

The production nurse was summoned, and a psychiatrist called in. Harris's hysteria was uncontrollable and, according to himself, he was held down 'by people kneeling on my fucking chest – it was that bad'. Harris was tranquillised, and slept nonstop for eighteen hours as the production stood down. 'It was a replay of *Major Dundee*. I never could see that stuff coming. It just hit me – *bang!* – and I was under.'

In the opinion of some, like James Booth, Harris was prime material for professional analysis and therapy, but rejected it. He later told a magazine, 'I studied psychotherapy in America for years. I became part of a school. And I found that the most fantastically damaging thing about modern thinking is: let us discover why, why, why. [Analysis] can be good for people who are damaged, seriously mentally damaged. It can be a useful medical therapy. But in America it's just a rage, a fad.' Harris's self-analysis in Spain was simple: once again he had overstretched his physical and emotional capacities. The remedy was: take it easy.

'My trouble always was the recognition of my weakness, and then the risk-taking buzz that made me just go for whatever it was [that challenged me] anyway. I could not say no to the forbidden fruit. I loved its taste. The illegal item was the best item. The wrong woman in my bed was the best woman. The rude comment far funnier than the nice remark. If I hated myself, in the final analysis, I'd say, Yes, you needed therapy. But I didn't. I thought too many people were too joyless, and I loved being joyful, and giving joy where I could . . . so I did, and damn the consequences.'

The varied successes of *The Molly Maguires*, *A Man Called Horse* and *Cromwell*, ranked on top of the continuing steady sales – if not pop triumphs – of his records, made it impossible for Harris to slow down. 'One woke up each day with a phone call, saying, Hey, Dick, do you want to fly to Prague to meet so-and-so producer-man? Or, Hey, do you want to record with Phil Coulter, who loves you? Or, Hey, how about meeting such-and-such in Acapulco? It was hard, in those circumstances, to lie in bed and say, No, I think I'll read the *Express*.'

Grammy nominations (for Best Contemporary Singer and Best Album) put the emphasis back on the music business and both Dermot and Harris himself felt the signs were right to strike the music market again while the iron was hot. The problem now, though, was Jimmy Webb's nonavailability. 'I looked at other options, and there were plenty. Leslie Bricusse, [who had written the stage success *Dr Dolittle*], had written *Scrooge* for me as a musical. And the Las Vegas International Hotel offered me the ridiculous fortune of £150,000 for a cabaret show centred on "MacArthur Park" and the *Camelot* songs. My main feeling was, I am an actor, not a singer, but I liked good cabaret acts. I liked seeing Frank [Sinatra] and the boys do it so well. It was sexy, and it was a great privilege to hold an intimate audience with your voice, as it were. So I thought I might set up a cabaret, open it at a smaller Vegas venue like Caesar's Palace or the Sands, then take it on a world tour. Phil Coulter always wanted to do that with me [as musical director], and, in the end, that's what we got to do.'

For an instant, tantalisingly, the long-dreamed-of *Hamlet* project seemed to be on. This more than anything kept Harris from the Greek islands holiday he promised himself after *Cromwell*. All of a sudden, all the ingredients were slotting together. The industry trusted him as never before. Respected, influential champions like Hughes, Logan, Ritt and Sandy Howard took his corner. Suddenly the components came together. Mia Farrow was announced for Ophelia, Peter Ustinov for Polonius, George C Scott for Claudius. The writer Gavin Lambert commenced work on the script with Harris, developing 'the modern voice' for an intended two-and-a-half-hour Paramount movie. Executive Arthur Lewis delivered the best coup, giving Harris, who had never professionally directed before, the green light. Harris, said Jack Donnelly, found it hard to conceal his enthusiasm. He had talked about the project for so long, come so close with Anderson and Silvera, but never this close. He was forty years old; now, he knew, was his last credible chance. Locations were scouted at Holy Island, off the coast of Northumberland, and a skeleton crew assembled. It was *that* close. Harris told the magazine *Today's Cinema*, 'If I had to choose between working another twenty years as an actor or doing *Hamlet* and ending my career, I'd take *Hamlet*. I feel that strongly about it.' But that pronouncement came in with the Kiss of Death. Within weeks, *Hamlet* faded, a victim of studio boardroom squabbling, destined to dwell in the ether for ever, like *Wuthering Heights*.

John Kobal was among the journalists who regularly met Harris and warmly recorded his progress. He talked with him in LA, New York, Norway and England and found him, as he approached middle age, battle-worn but full of fight. In his notebook Kobal wrote,

He speaks rapidly, punctuating his sentences with facial commas and periods. There is a shrug about him, an air of dogged optimism, self-assurance, a touch of smugness. He is part idealist, part romantic. There is also about him the feeling of size, of large-scale bonhomie, and of the sincerity of what he believes in. What he believes in is himself. He looks his age, but has an adolescent intensity which makes him look youthful. He moves like a dancer, delicate, introspective – but can also 'turn it on' when observed and encouraged. He knows himself so well as to use his real self for his public self. His bouts of drinking and brawling were played up in the press – for sales. Which he understands. What he doesn't understand, or says he doesn't, is the betrayal of people he trusted with himself, with his 'private' self – as when he told Roderick Mann something regarding his wife, off the cuff, and Mann printed it. He no longer talks to Mann because of that. In this grown man, there are traces of the gawky boy.

Weston Taylor was another journalist Harris accused of betrayal. The Irish journalist Trevor Danker recalled, 'During that period Dickie was drinking heavily – not as heavily as his brother Dermot, who could really down them, but still overdoing it. Both of them, Dickie and Dermot, were great romancers, with women all over the place. Weston Taylor wanted to do a piece and he came to the Savoy, where I had been drinking with Harris. By the time he got up to the suite to see Harris, Harris was well jarred and spluttering all over the place. He would drink for days without even eating and be quite ill. When Taylor talked to him, I don't think he was fully aware of what was going on. So he blabbed and blabbed about Elizabeth and her blossoming romance with Rex Harrison and about the kids.'

Taylor later wrote a double-page spread detailing his talk with Harris and making spiky references about Elizabeth and her new life. Harris instructed Wright & Webb, his lawyers, to sue, but the case was settled in a High Court with an apology. The transcripts of Weston Taylor's notebooks and tape make revealing reading – not in their mouthy invective, but in the confessional candour that showed a vulnerable and regretful man, and a man obsessed by his craft to the detriment of all else. References to Elizabeth are overshadowed by his passionate concern for the children and by his interest in the movie world. His comments on David Lean's Irish epic, *Ryan's Daughter*, fill rambling pages of text, overshadowing even health issues: Harris considered *Ryan's Daughter* 'a mighty work', and revealed he would have given his right arm to play Robert Mitchum's role. Beyond that, his comments about Ireland suggest deep, ongoing self-analysis: 'There is an image of the Irish projected . . . The [Irish] have qualities which are admirable to me and most exciting. What happens is that when they move out of Ireland to New York they have a great fear of being absorbed into the nation they have moved to. And by doing that [*sic*] they are inclined to project their individuality too strongly and therefore become professional Irishmen.' The boozy asides were contradictory and provocative: 'I find the Irish people live from Friday to Friday. There's no ambition. They amble through life. They freewheel with great abandonment. They're not ambitious because [in Ireland] there's nothing to be ambitious about.'

Despite his public stance of protectiveness towards his and Elizabeth's privacy, lingering discord rippled around their respective social circles, now bluntly divided, and beyond. Harris's loathing for Rex Harrison and the romantic 'opportunism' that he saw in his former friend was the cause of the disquiet. He had plenty of work opportunities to absorb himself in – the planned music tour, a new book of poems he was assembling for Random House, an Israel-based movie to substitute for *Hamlet*, even the renovations of Tower House – but all he thought about day and night was Harrison's intrusion on his territory with his children. 'I was never in a good place psychologically about all that. It was a bee sting – right?' In October he departed for Israel to shoot his next movie, *Bloomfield*, under the direction of Uri Zohar. Within days Zohar was removed from the film and Harris took over as director, discharging the pent-up *Hamlet* energies. The film was finished in February, and Harris rushed back to London with the eager intention of seeing his sons. When he telephoned Bedford Gardens, he was informed that

Elizabeth had taken Jamie on a cruise with Rex Harrison. Harrison had just instructed his solicitors to issue a statement announcing his separation from Rachel Roberts, and Harris understood the implications. He immediately went to court, demanding the return of Jamie, in keeping with the terms of the divorce settlement. He told Mrs Justice Lane in the High Court: 'The boy needs continuity of schooling. I am afraid that, even if Jamie returns shortly, my ex-wife will take him away again.'

The judge took Harris's side: 'She should come back and be made to understand that this kind of thing won't do.' An order was issued for the former Mrs Harris to return Jamie within 48 hours. Harris's lawyer, Stephen Tumim, left the court saying Harris was 'overwhelmed with concern' about Jamie. Elizabeth duly returned, but in March Harris applied for her committal to prison for contempt of court. She had failed to file a general undertaking not to take the children out of the country again, which, Harris asserted, was contrary to the divorce agreement. Elizabeth's solicitors apologised and offered to give the undertaking, and, by mutual consent, the application for imprisonment was dropped.

Harris turned back to postproduction on *Bloomfield* and the restoration of Tower House as Elizabeth made arrangements to become the fifth Mrs Rex Harrison. The marriage took place shortly afterwards, at Alan Jay Lerner's Georgian mansion on Long Island. Harris was not among the guests.

CHAPTER 12

Blooming Poetry and Dying Blooms

Bloomfield arguably marked the end of Richard Harris's serious artistic striving for almost twenty years. After, he made two careful films – *Man in the Wilderness* and, for television, *The Snow Goose* – but then began a cycle of staccato, half-intellectualised work that only rarely threw up a movie worth watching. Half the problem was weariness – his was among the most productive and varied of all sixties star careers – and half was the kind of disillusionment typified by the experience of *Bloomfield*.

The movie was unquestionably a *Hamlet* replacement, made possible by Limbridge's account-shuffling and Harris's investment of his own fees into the production. Producer John Heyman, a devoted Harris friend, set up a co-op scheme in which ten individual investors and a number of leading banks – among them the House of Rothschild, Fund of Funds and Henry Ansbacher & Co. – pooled resources. The budget was tiny for a film of its type – just $2 million – but it was all Harris needed to fulfil the ambition of his TB bed: 'to direct my own scenarios, to bring to life the whole world of my own creation, to look at my life through the telescope of truth'.

Wolf Mankowitz, best known for *A Kid for Two Farthings* (1955), a schmaltzy yarn about a Petticoat Lane boy whose pet goat has the magical powers of the unicorn, wrote the script, and Uri Zohar, an experienced Israeli, was commissioned to direct. But Harris had ulterior motives, recognising, as he did, the momentous opportunity and the terminal failure of *Hamlet*. In its essence, *Bloomfield* was, or

206

had the potential to be, an allegory of fine style. Mankowitz's subthemes of innocence and enchantment laced this tale of a schoolboy's dreamy adulation for a tired football star, just as they did in *A Kid for Two Farthings*. 'It wasn't rugby, but it wasn't far off,' said Harris. It also provided a forum for dissecting idealism, disillusionment and middle-age inertia.

When Harris arrived in Israel he virtually took over the production. Always the willing scribbler, he unravelled and rebuilt the screenplay to his own liking, changing three-quarters of the dialogue and running-order sequences. Not since *This Sporting Life* had his input on script revision been so intense. Accompanying Heyman, he scoured Tel Aviv and Jaffa for locations, refusing the heavy costs of sound stages and utilising instead apartments, front gardens and hotel rooms. Even his own suite at Tel Aviv's Dan Hotel was annexed.

As he had done for *This Sporting Life*, Harris went into heavy training for his role as the footballer, working eight-hour shifts with trainer Josef Merrimovitch, and jogging everywhere. He also devoted much time to rehearsal with Kim Burfield, his young co-star. As Eitan, supposedly Israel's greatest football star, approaching his last game at the age of forty, Harris needed to portray peak physical fitness and a jaded spirit. Kim Burfield, playing Nimrod, the youth who befriends him and discourages him from 'throwing' the big game in return for a well-paid retirement, also bore the weight of a complex, two-hand plot. 'I saw it like a two-actor stage play,' said Harris. 'Very intimate, close-lensed, passionate. It wasn't something you could play with cameras, like the Italians did. You had to get the drama pin-sharp.'

Uri Zohar partnered this process, but didn't last long. When Harris took over lock and stock, according to technicians on the movie, progress became jumpy and confused. 'I was learning as I went along,' said Harris. 'But I'd also been studying my art for fifteen years. How many doctors study for fifteen years?'

On 2 February 1970 *Bloomfield* was finished and Harris flew to London for postproduction, then diverted to Dublin when he learned from Jack Donnelly that Harmay was seriously ill. After an unsuccessful operation, Harmay died. Donnelly and Harris, brothers in spirit, were inconsolable. Death was never far from Harris's thoughts and he mourned his sister volubly, lamenting the curse of the Harris womenfolk, all taken prematurely. The spiritual soother of a return to Catholicism was out of the question, he said. 'It would be hypocritical,' he told Jack Donnelly. 'I live life as I believe it. You have to be honest with yourself, and only in being honest with yourself can you honestly say, "Our Father, who art in heaven . . ."' Part of him refused to accept Harmay's passing. In his notebooks, he commenced one of his most poignant poems:

> *When I see in my feel*
> *the picture of your history*
> *fade with the sailboats of my mind . . .*

> *When I feel*
> *what you have felt*

> *When I see what you have said*
> *Then I will believe you are dead.*

Dublin and Limerick found him more temperate than usual. Questioned by a Limerick journalist about his love life, he expressed apathy. 'Someone interesting' for companionship would be nice, but for companionship only. Hollywood women were 'Dreadful, dreadful, dreadful'. He despaired of finding a woman who could absorb him, but 'I had dinner with Romy Schneider in Tel Aviv a few weeks ago. We began eating at eight o'clock and we finished at four. When we finished I suddenly realised, "Christ! We've been talking together for *eight hours*!" That's the first time in my life I've ever spoken to a woman for eight hours.' Schneider, happily married to the German actor-director Harry Meyan, was 'just a pal' and he stressed that he was no longer on the lookout for love. 'I've found that I like living on my own. I like being able to do what I want when I want. I will never marry again. I will never again put myself in a position where I can be faulted after ten years. The one tragedy for me is that I haven't got a daughter. I shall never have one now and I would have loved one to spoil. I would have brought her up so well. Sons can make their own way in the world, but a daughter . . .'

Deirdre Lloyd, the old friend from the Ennis Road, was jokingly blamed for his lack of a daughter. 'He said it was all my fault,' said Lloyd. 'One dark night in Limerick in the early fifties I was walking down a laneway with a girlfriend and we heard a rush of footsteps and suddenly this big man was on top of me, shouting rape. I turned round and gave him my knee where it hurts. He rolled in agony on the ground – and it was Dickie – and from then on, he said, he wasn't able to produce the goodies to make a daughter.'

In London, as he started the edit of *Bloomfield*, a long *Sun* interview unveiled Harris's uncensored new philosophy: 'Sure, making love is good for you. Just like satisfying any bodily appetite. You feel hungry? – eat. You're thirsty? – drink. You feel frustrated? – make love. But don't *fall in love*. That's too time-consuming. It saps your energies.' All reference to Elizabeth and the past was avoided. He would not comment on Elizabeth's romance with Harrison, but the hurt was clear and it clouded his attitude to all women: 'Most of the women I've had affairs with in the past are my friends now. But people are so dishonest to one another in bed. They sustain one another's illusions with half-truths. Women play games when they're making love. Just as they do at all other times. The trouble with women is that women need men. Women are far more in search of the reassurance that a man can provide than vice versa – even in this day of supposed equality.'

The chauvinism was, said friends, a smokescreen. 'He felt deserted,' said Ronald Fraser. 'He can be very childish. He expected Elizabeth to wait by his side for ever, but of course she had her own needs. That period almost destroyed him. Losing [Harmay] added to it. If he wanted to get off the booze, which he was always promising, it certainly wasn't a conducive situation.'

Bloomfield took his mind off his loneliness. It all felt too hurried, too money-starved, but he gave it twenty hours a day that spring. Two young Irish songwriters, Bill Whelan and Niall Connery, had submitted demo tapes to Limbridge the year before, one featuring a ballad called 'Denise' that excited Harris. On impulse he commissioned a soundtrack from the boys, one of whom, Whelan, would go on to score the musical-dance epic, *Riverdance*. He also summoned Lindsay Anderson for editorial advice, and Kevin Connor, himself soon to graduate as a director in children's fantasies like *The Land That Time Forgot*. Harris even went so far as to employ a computer-linked audience to test the rough cut. Ninety minutes of roughly assembled storyline was shown to fifty people, who pressed buttons when they were bored or felt the movie was overrunning. Harris studied the print-outs, discussed the results with Anderson and Connor, and recut – and recut.

The veteran cameraman Otto Heller, who had guided Harris through the Tel Aviv shoot, died suddenly during this editing phase, depressing him. 'So many little and big things went against me,' Harris said. 'But I kept one aspect in the centre of my vision: innocence. I tried to keep Eitan and Nimrod true all the time. I tried to hold onto magic.'

Some comfort came from his new love affair with the blonde Linda Hayden, a fringe actress whose popularity grew through the seventies in sexy British comedies, and with the tide of applause that came with the side-by-side premieres of *A Man Called Horse* and *Cromwell*. In combination with *Camelot*, still running in theatres all over Europe, the two new movies knocked all opposition flat, rocketing Harris's face and name on to bus shelters and hoardings everywhere. Columbia spent what was then a colossal £25,000 on London store-window displays, saturating Oxford Street with posters of Cavaliers and Roundheads. Selfridge's was the promotional flagship, laden with tie-in merchandise and boasting a Cromwellian banquet hall installed to serve traditional period dishes. In the music stores, Harris's promotional posters were for 'The Ballad of a Man Called Horse', a tedious theme song even Sandy Howard thought little of, but which sold well on its association with a hit movie.

The aggressive campaigning paid off, and both Harris movies overtook *Woodstock* and Lerner and Loewe's *Paint Your Wagon*, the current main contenders. In its first seven days, *Cromwell* took

£20,000 at the Odeon, Leicester Square, then an all-time record for Columbia. At the Plaza, *A Man Called Horse* took almost £10,000, doubling the opening average. Harris's personal reviews were also impressive. For Marjorie Bilbow, Harris's Cromwell was 'an unforgettable performance that demonstrates once again that [Harris] is at his magnificent best in a role that demands both strength and sensitivity'. The same week *Photoplay* classed him 'superb' in *A Man Called Horse* and speculated excitedly on his coming movie, *Bloomfield*.

Already, Limbridge was boastfully announcing the projects beyond *Bloomfield*. Assuming triumph for Harris the director, Limbridge stated that the rights to a stage play, called *Dylan*, had been acquired and would be the next directorial effort. Other small-budget art movies were also in the pipeline and Terry James, a new musical director, was working with Harris on a succession of major projects to follow his upcoming world tour. Jack Donnelly said, 'Dermot was over the moon for Dickie because so much was happening on so many different fronts. It looked as though Limbridge would become a world-beater. Dermot and John [McMichael] were working round the clock, literally, to keep up with it all, and the only downside was the boozing, which kept them all too hazy at times. But Dermot kept telling me, "Dick is only starting. Watch what happens next."'

In Limerick, Dermot Foley had become president of the Limerick branch of the International Lions Club: 'When I read about Dickie's "personal film", *Bloomfield*, I immediately thought, This is his chance to do us a favour! I called him in London and asked right out, Will you do a benefit special premiere in Limerick? Dickie likes it straight. He was always a quick-decisions man. I asked, and he said, "No trouble."'

With *Bloomfield* finally finished to Harris's liking, the home-coming to end them all was planned like a military operation. Dermot Foley, however, recalled it as 'a cross between a religious visitation and the Keystone Kops'. Foley had asked Harris to muster some star guests, so Harris laid on a charter flight from Heathrow for Roger Moore, *Avengers* star Honor Blackman, Bee Gee Maurice

Gibb and his wife Lulu, actress Imogen Hassall, Linda Hayden and a score of others. Harris booked his guests into the luxurious Dromoland Castle for the premiere evening, followed by a weekend of riding, golf and revelry. 'It looked good on paper,' said Foley.

Events unfolded dramatically. At Heathrow, the premiere party was delayed forty minutes because of a bomb scare. For Lulu this was 'a little disconcerting'. Others threatened to mutiny, but held on. According to the press, as they arrived at Shannon for the transfer to Dromoland, 'hundreds of screaming youths' lined the concourse, and the streets beyond. Later, at the Savoy Cinema, the battleground of Harris's early histrionics, the streets were cordoned off for crowd control. Harris duly arrived, in floor-length suede coat and multicoloured Indian scarf, followed by fifteen hundred guests, among them the minister for posts and telegraphs and the minister for justice. Harris was modesty exuberant, relishing this trophied homecoming he had long dreamed about.

But, in the auditorium, Limerick burst his bubble. As everyone settled expectantly for the momentous twitching of the curtains and the lights dimmed, a stern announcement was suddenly made over the speaker system: a male caller to William Street Police Station had just given a warning that a bomb had been planted in the cinema. The mass evacuation, led 'with panache', said Foley, by the minister for justice, took everyone's mind off movies. One hundred Gardai and Special Branch officers combed the cinema before the all-clear was given. Harris said later, 'I can think of fifty fuckers who made that call, and none of them had anything to do with the IRA or the UVF.'

Bloomfield, finally unveiled, was a major disappointment for Harris. Though it earned a Golden Globe nomination, no two reviews concurred and the American critics generally savaged it. The *Hollywood Reporter*, never a Harris fan, accused the actor of unforgivable self-love and flatly called the movie a failure: 'The story basks in its own self-importance since the actor-singer-poet-director (and soon to be novelist) at the helm has again allowed his prodigious energy to be refracted through a project which misses the mark as significant dramatic experience and panders to obvious moral truths.' The *Monthly Film Bulletin* poured scorn on 'an embarrassing debut for Richard Harris as director', and *Films and Filming* called it 'unremittingly, lumberingly awful'.

The death of *Bloomfield* – booed off screen at the Berlin Festival, where Harris booed back – spelled the death of one facet of the public Richard Harris. Already wary of himself in the mirror of the press, he now slammed the door on candour in all his artistic aspirations. No more were the hopes of *Hamlet*, *Dylan* or a possible *Borstal Boy* movie discussed. In their place came an offhand brashness in relation to movies and, at the same time, the ferocious insularity of the long-haired poet. 'He was totally fucked off by it,' said Ronald Fraser. 'He said to me, "No one *saw Bloomfield*". They had Dick Harris *up to here* for twenty years. And then Dick Harris offered them his throat, and they cut it wide open.'

Harris's place of solace was the partnership with Sandy Howard, as far away from Limbridge and Limerick as possible. Good timing and good fortune presented *Man in the Wilderness*, the ideal antidote in a movie so diametrically opposite to anything Harris had done that it seemed, in concept, like a brand-new genre. Sandy Howard knew new work was the remedy for Harris's anguish. 'Richard isn't a quitter. You learned that very quickly when you really got to know him. *Man in the Wilderness* was *the* medicine. My friend Jack De Witt had again written this truly extraordinary script – which was virtually a movie in mime, a silent movie – and we heard Richard was taking a break from everything in Tunisia, so we decided to fly out and offer him this gift.' Howard had 'discovered' the story of the frontier trapper left for dead in the wilds of primitive America, when he was hunting locations in the Dakotas. 'It was almost mystical in how it came into my life, because these backwoods guys just told me a yarn – and there was the movie. Immediately I thought of Richard, because this was about a loner whose strength is his isolation skills, his inner spirit. I knew this *was* Richard.'

En route to Tunisia, Howard and De Witt survived a hijack attempt by militant Muslims, but 'it was just a bit of rumpus up the front of the plane that we didn't think twice about it – which goes to show how Jack and I – and Richard, by the way, when it was his turn – lost ourselves into everything we did.' Over drinks and dinner in a 5-star Tunisian hotel, the movie was discussed and, as Howard imagined, agreed on a handshake.

Harris embarked on *Man in the Wilderness* as an exorcism, divesting himself of dialogue disciplines and calculation, relying solely on physical fortitude and instinct. It was shot in Almeria, Spain, doubling for the Dakotas, and Harris played Zachary Bass, based on the real-life tale of Hugo Ass, who struggles against nature to survive, tackling heat, cold, hunger and bears. 'I think it helped that I made him a full partner on it,' said Howard. 'But that's not to say that he was not an appreciative and respectful collaborator anyway. He was always a very giving man to those who respected him. I know it's a cliché, but he was first on set in the mornings, and last to go home at night. Making him a partner copper-fastened it. It made certain that he showed up each day, fast and sober.'

Harris 'adored' the movie, he said, because of director Richard Sarafian's care, and because of its authenticity: 'I like Bass because he doesn't beat nature, he joins it. There is no fight to survive today as there was once in the old West. This is living, because it is close to dying.'

Refreshed in the summer, and lured by the appeal of an offer to film Paul Gallico's classic novella, *The Snow Goose*, Harris returned to England long before he'd planned. 'I knew that little book as a wonderful, delicate parable, like something by Laurie Lee. I had the greatest love for it, and, when I read the script, the literary part of me caught fire. Probably the silence of *Wilderness* contributed. That, and the fact that most of [what was otherwise on offer] was big-budget spy junk.' Paul Gallico's wartime classic about a hunchback Dunkirk fisherman who gets involved with a shy girl and the wounded goose symbolic of British tenacity had been pitched for filming for thirty years. Gallico had always resisted offers: "Because those other producers wanted to do their own *Snow Goose*, not mine.' Then the American Hallmark Hall of Fame made its approach, in a co-production arrangement with the BBC, and with a script reverence that satisfied Gallico. Harris, in turn, delighted in the script, once again a polar opposite to the De Witt *Man in the*

Wilderness. For Innes Lloyd, the BBC producer charged with overseeing the production, Harris's enthusiasm was for 'immersion in the character of the cloth-capped gypsy outsider, the man outside normal life, doing his own thing. I think it was, in the phrase, *where he was at* at that time. I'd heard all about his great stress with [the failure] of *Bloomfield*, and that his career was at *the* crossroads. There was a lot of significance laid on the fact that he was "lowering" himself to do television, which, let's face it, he hadn't done since [*The Iron Harp*] fifteen years ago. But that all missed the point. In my experience, he was nothing other than pleasant. He didn't contribute to the screenplay – the director Patrick Garland and Paul Gallico did all that – but that spoke of Richard's satisfaction with the piece, and his equilibrium. As far as he was concerned, the literary qualities of the drama are what attracted him, and then this immersion in the old-man role. He struck me not as a star in trouble, but as an actor – an actor's actor, the real thing.'

During the six-week shoot at Frinton on the east coast of England Innes Lloyd saw Harris 'hard-working – but quiet and reflective. We had no booze nor women problems. His one excitement was rugby. I remember being on the train with him coming to Frinton, and all he really wanted to get fired up on was rugby league and chitchat about the upcoming internationals. He seemed in some ways eager to escape all the showbiz rubbish of his life, and he was excellent company on a man-to-man basis, very self-educated and eager to discover things.'

Both *Man in the Wilderness* and *The Snow Goose* earned Harris good reviews. 'A work of simplicity and purity,' said the *Los Angeles Times* of *Man in the Wilderness*, commending the 'authority' of Sarafian and Harris's 'eloquence in what is virtually a mime performance'. *The Snow Goose* – 'deeply satisfying' for Gallico, Garland and Harris, according to Innes Lloyd – also received unqualified raves. Cyril Cusack called it, 'Undeniably among the best things Harris ever did.'

Harris was professionally appeased, but restless. In quiet rooms, in the gloom of his own company, he was, said Jack Donnelly, constantly at war with himself – smarting from the humiliation of

Bloomfield and the loss of *Hamlet*, worn out by the high maintenance of relationships like Linda Hayden (one of many at the time), mourning Harmay, mourning Elizabeth, missing the kids. 'He always tried to keep up with the kids,' said Donnelly, 'and he took the greatest pleasure in a day out here, and a weekend there with Damian, Jared and Jamie. Damian was a great football player at school, and that gave him much joy. The other boys were wild dreamers, he used to say. He monitored them all very closely and often said to me, "Jackie, I'd be happy just to pack it all in now and take the kids and start again on an island somewhere."'

Throughout the remainder of 1971 he drank as he had never drunk, brawled as in the sixties – and occasionally quietened himself to concentrate on the poems and songs he was contractually committed to. In October he finally joined the Derry songwriter Phil Coulter to record Coulter and Bill Martin's 'My Boy', a poignant, personal-statement tear-jerker penned especially for him. The song spoke of lost marriage and a man's fervid, hopeless devotion to his son. Entered in the Radio-Tele International Grand Prix at Luxembourg in late October, where Harris represented Britain, performing live on stage for the first time, the song became a Harris staple and a minor hit.

He continued to sing, jigsawing together a new album in the absence of Jimmy Webb. *My Boy*, the album assembled under Coulter's supervision, was one of his best-realised popular records, a reasoned blend of catchy tunes like his self-penned 'All the Broken Children', Webb's leftover 'Beth', and labyrinthine symphonies like 'Requiem,' another Webb mini-epic that Harris declared his all-time favourite song. *My Boy* was, by his design, 'a concept album about a marriage' and remains the nearest expression of autobiography that Harris has ever given his fans. 'Beth' might easily have been Elizabeth; 'Why Did you Leave Me?' was a self-explanatory heartbreaker; 'This is the Way', the aggressive defence philosophy that rejects angst. This last song, by his new musical guru Johnny Harris (no relation) and John Bromley, possessed an almost distressing primal energy that obliterated the lingering romance of Webb:

I have lied, cheated when I could
And worse than this, it felt so good . . .

Fighting is just a way of life with me

Jesus is just a word I use to swear with
This is the way I live my life . . .

The sleeve notes, written by Harris as song preludes, were succinct, though stained with the fluttering self-pity that tainted *Bloomfield*. Their uncompromising honesty – warts and all – provided a sampler for the richer, less commercial, poetry to come.

Limbridge's labours were now attracting submissions from aspiring songwriters all over the world, and Harris had his pick of wide-ranging material. Dermot, supported by Terry James and Johnny Harris, carefully shuffled through it all, selecting, editing, arguing possibilities for the song bank that would support the upcoming musical tour. Among their superior finds was the young, hip Canadian Tony Romeo, who supplied a second concept album, *Slides*, autobiographically based on the holiday adventures of a gypsying teacher who loses his job because of his Thoreauvian, nature-loving style. *Slides* was the purest pop, purer even than Coulter, delivering three near-perfect ballsy ballads in 'I Don't Have to Tell You', 'How I Spent My Summer' and 'I'm Coming Home', as well as yet another Webb-style slice of Gothic romance in the title track. But the album, on ABC Dunhill's subsidiary Probe label, failed to make the charts and Harris finally – unreasonably for many – called it, 'Rubbish, misconceived. It was a ballad style that was Barry Manilow, not me.' The singers he professed to love and aspire to, he said, were the perennial Sinatra, Tom Jones and Kris Kristofferson.

After the long build-up, in 1972 the music tour finally took precedence. Trevor Danker, who met and drank with him regularly said, "It was something he needed to get out of his system. He wasn't a kid, but he had that kind of kid pop image still going, which was miraculous, really. Knowing Dick, he said to himself, "Let's take it on the road and have a laugh with it." And that's what he did.'

After a try-out in the English provinces, Harris's roadshow trekked through major American venues, playing Chicago, Minneapolis, Columbus, LA and several cities in the Midwest. With four big albums – and *Camelot* – to draw from, there was no shortage of material to fill a two-hour solo show, though Harris admitted at the time that he was as terrified as he had been in the solo hours of *Diary of a Madman*, facing the lonely spotlight. 'I wasn't a singer, which made it interesting, to say the least. But I could and did sing. [Coulter and James] and all of them moaned all the time that I couldn't keep rhythm, but I didn't give a fuck. I was there to deliver the song, and, as far as I was concerned, it was the orchestra's job to keep up.'

Dermot, several chummy London journalists and a variety of girlfriends kept him company on the road in an entourage not dissimilar from a rock set-up. A friend who joined the tour recalled, 'Those were raving, mad days, you can imagine. It was no different from any rock band scene, with the star being mobbed and sucked up to. Dick enjoyed it, and he especially enjoyed the women on offer in every city you visited. Bear in mind, he was a bachelor, and bear in mind his appetites were enormous, so he took everything on offer.'

In one incident, another friend recalled, Harris missed his on-stage cue. The band started playing the opening chords of 'MacArthur Park', but the spotlight raked an empty stage. Panicked, the stage manager sent the friend on the urgent errand to *'Find Harris, for Chrissake!'* The friend did find Harris – in his room, naked, with 'a priceless black beauty' on hands and knees before him, giving him oral sex. The friend grabbed Harris and hurried him into jeans and kaftan as the pulsating orchestral strains hammered the floor under them, launching into the umpteenth bar of the song's rambling overture. Harris finally made it up on stage – 'a good five minutes into "MacArthur Park", pulling up his zipper'.

'The younger fans stormed the stage after the performance in St Louis,' wrote Richard Evans of the London *Evening News*, who joined the tour. 'And in the more sedate setting of New York's plush Philharmonic Hall they lined up three deep at the foot of the stage, hands outstretched, to acclaim and touch their bearded hero.'

Afterwards, said Evans, the star took a group of the faithful to a nearby bar – appropriately called the Ginger Man. 'Why?' Evans queried a swooning group of teenage Kansas City girls, who had hired a bus to make the pilgrimage. 'Is it because he's a movie star?' 'It's just *him*,' was the harmonised reply. 'He's so *real*. He's a human being. There's nothing phoney about him. He's someone you can identify with, because he doesn't give you all that showbiz schmaltz.'

Still, Evans declared himself flummoxed. Harris's songs and the poems he read on-stage were hardly teen-dream stuff. They were litanies of divorce, of death and of politics. One poem, 'There Are Too Many Saviours on My Cross', was bare-faced politics, damning the violence in Northern Ireland and condemning *both* sides. This, above anything, was the hot spot of the tour, and, on his return to London, Harris issued a seven-inch recording of the poem on vinyl. It was hyped like a pop song, a Limbridge press conference on his return announcing that the proceeds from 'Saviours' would go to 'the victims of injustice in Northern Ireland'. Few reporters present were impressed, and a welter of questions was fired at Harris, reminding him of his Republican sympathies and asking about his concern for 'the other side'. Harris flipped, rose to his feet and shouted back, white-faced with rage, 'Are you questioning for one second the motive of all this? Are you doubting me? Are you looking for an argument? This money will go to *all* families of people who have been killed.'

The moment was significant. Harris had, he later said, indulged 'the games of media and commerce' for too long; now there would be no more games. Now he would say what he felt, write it, broadcast it whenever he felt like it. Overnight he became a self-declared political crusader, splurting out the instincts, prejudices and self-education of thirty years every which way. Boldly, he announced that, yes, he was a supporter of the IRA in its battle for a unified Ireland. 'I will not apologise any longer for my roots and my soul. I am what I am. I did what I did. I do what I do. I say what I feel.' John Lennon-style, he started lobbying and agitating, avoiding the middlemen and going for 'hard targets'. He wrote to the Irish *taoiseach* [prime minister], declaring his commitment to Irish unification, sent his poetry to Downing Street (to no response) and issued a statement that he was preparing 'a film on internment without trial in Northern Ireland, which will be an exposure of the British Nazi-style brutalities'.

Ablaze in his Irishness, he returned to Dublin at producer Kevin McClory's request to help mount a one-man show at the Gaiety, old home of *The Ginger Man*, in aid of Dublin Central Remedial Clinic charity. This homecoming presented yet another Richard Harris, a man vastly changed from the louche hippie of *Bloomfield*. During 1972, he told a press conference, he had gone through huge personal changes. He had been offered 22 movies, all rubbish, and turned them all down. 'I can't be bothered. Now I have bigger fish to fry.' Later, in a quieter setting, he told the journalist Trevor Danker unapologetically, 'I really hate journalists. They always write the story *they* want to write. They steer the conversation *their* way. You can't win. In the circumstances, better to pose oneself as an activist than an actor – because the issues confuse them, and one stands a better chance of emotionally surviving it.' Still, he had juicy gifts for the pop press: his new love affair, he finally confessed, was with Nina Van Pallandt, formerly half of the Danish singing duo Nina and Frederick. She was currently in LA, completing her film acting debut in Robert Altman's *The Long Goodbye* with Elliot Gould, but soon they would be back in each other's arms. Danker asked him if he would revise his opinion on the possibility of another marriage: 'Marriage is archaic,' he snapped, but: 'This relationship [with Nina] is not just a case of being good friends, it's a lot more than that.'

After a profitable Gaiety night – in a one-man show designed by Sean Kenny and mostly self-directed – Harris was, for the first time since *Bloomfield*, ready for the overdue public autopsy of his movie directorial debut. Seated in front of a half-pint of Guinness in Neary's pub in Dublin, he admitted to Kay Kent that he would love the chance to direct again. Kent observed 'his eyes lighting up with enthusiasm [at the mention of directing] for the first time that day'. There was joy, saw Kent, but also objectivity: 'I never want to act as well as direct again. I was *terrible* in *Bloomfield* . . . in the acting *and* in the direction. Although I knew what I wanted to do as a director, I just didn't have the time to prepare properly. I like the idea of directing myself, because I love the poetic expression you can get with movies. But it'll never happen like that again.'

As announced, Random House issued his first book of poems, *I, in the Membership of My Days*, late in 1973. It consisted of 38 free-verse pieces with a binding theme of defiance in the face of imperfection, disillusionment, loss and death and comprised the best of his jottings dating from Overdale in the early fifties. The best, most applauded, poems were his musings on the death of Ivan and Harmay – and the Rabelaisian 'song' for crippled Christy Brown, author of *My Left Foot. The New York Times.* among several broadsheets, admired the work; but Limerick itself, said Harris, 'couldn't make head nor tail of it and basically had a good laugh. Someone told me some [Limerick] schoolteacher told his class to read the poetry to find out how poetry shouldn't be done . . . which is just sour-grapes bollocks.' In the first few weeks, the book sold 22,000 copies, said Random House, rendering it, in the publishers' eyes, 'a comprehensive success'. Harris had, he said, been paid 'a six-figure sum', which covered an option for a collection of short stories and the novel *Flanny at 1.10*, which he had been working on for some time and which was 'almost complete'.

Jack Donnelly saw the poetry as a gesture of 'casting a tow line back to Limerick. A lot of the moving around was beginning to wear him out. The poetry was a love letter to Limerick and Ireland in general, and I thought he was saying, "Here I am, the real me, take me back and let me settle down . . . Give me a bit of peace." '

Changes *were* evident – he seemed to dress more stylishly, shave and crimp himself to a more youthful elegance, talk more calmly and purposefully – but there was still a glass in his hand and one woman or another clinging to his arm at Neary's or the Bailey. Joe Lynch recalled a journalist at the time telling Harris 'he'd finally started to look "normal and calm enough" to settle down and lead a "normal" life with a "normal" wife to push him around'. Harris laughed in the journalist's face. 'I believe there's a balance in everything and a reason for everything, and the bad and the good you do all comes back to you. It's a sort of boomerang effect. I may have caused a lot of unhappiness with my bad temper and my drinking and my wildness in the past, but at least none of it was deliberate; and no one has to stick around to be a victim and accept the sort of nonsense I gave out. Yes, I think people get what they ask for, in a strange sort of way. And I'm glad that no one can do anything to me. Because I'd never allow myself to be anyone's victim, however fond of them I might be.'

CHAPTER 13

Ann

Booze and continual one-night stands kept his equilibrium (the Nina affair was over within a year), but still, addictively, he worked Hollywood. Rod Taylor, firmly among the Harris friends, recalled the Mexican location for *The Deadly Trackers*: 'It was convivial, let's say. I think Richard had the hots for one of the native actresses, Isela Vega, but he didn't get anywhere. Not to worry: both of us enjoyed the friendly local hostesses to the full. But that was the extracurricular work. The day job was *the* thing.'

The Deadly Trackers was patchwork, an unlikely production recovered from the debris of an abandoned Richard Harris–Sam Fuller movie and largely glued together by Rod Taylor, a subtly macho actor, Australian by birth, whose Hollywood rise in the sixties paralleled Harris's. Taylor had stumbled upon the movie – as ambitious a piece of metaphorical morality as any of Harris's westerns – when Fuller and Harris came unstuck after four weeks in Spain. 'I didn't start with the production. In the beginning it was Richard and Sam, and it just didn't hold together, because Richard hated the script. All I heard was that Sam had been impossible. Richard couldn't stand it and then Fould Said, the producer, took the whole deal back to Mexico, changed the story and put the famous "boy genius" director Barry Shear in to direct, and save our bacon.'

Fuller and Harris, at equally tipsy stages of their respective careers, had disputed the storyline centred on a sheriff's pursuit of the outlaw who murders his wife and son. In Mexico the character of the antagonist was completely rewritten to Harris's liking and *Riata*, Fuller's original storyline, was all but ditched. Fould Said's great skill was his innovative approach to location shooting, which had distinguished itself in the cult sixties TV comedy-thriller series *I Spy* and movies like *Across 110th Street*, and for which he ultimately won a special Academy Award in 1974. 'Cinemobiles' – self-contained production wagons that were, in effect, mini-studios – were the key to Said's technique, and he employed them to brilliant effect in salvaging *The Deadly Trackers*. 'It was the production manager Sam Manners that really saved it,' said Taylor. 'He was the one who recommended me as the perfect screen enemy for sheriff Harris, and he was the one who kept all the disparate elements together in a movie that must have looked, for a long time, like a dog's stew.'

Harris had previously met Taylor at a party at Zsa Zsa Gabor's home where, said Taylor, they 'fell in love'. 'We were kindred spirits. We'd both had our dark days and come through shining, and we both loved movies for what they were. When we joined up in Cuernavaca, our shared values is what made the whole thing move.' Taylor, like Harris, still thought the script 'awful in parts' but 'Richard made one want to fix it, and we really broke our balls for it. He went on his knees before me and paid compliments to my work on [John Ford's] *Young Cassidy*, which was all about Sean O'Casey. He forgave this Aussie imposter doing O'Casey because I was great, he said.'

A paid-up member of the Screenwriters' Guild, Taylor contributed many new scenes to invigorate what was essentially a chase yarn: 'I think what the story lacked was a decent account of the villain's villainy. So I wrote in some scenes, with Richard's blessing.' Harris, not rookie director Shear, and not Said, claimed Taylor, was the principal creative force that made it possible to complete the film. 'Richard dominated and I provided what was expected of me as the co-star antagonist. We had our ego clashes – but in the course of fighting creative battles, never personality clashes. I know Richard tended to jump on some people's asses, because that's the way he was. That's the way I am, come to think of it – I fight with two fists when someone hasn't done their homework – but Richard only raged on that movie because there was so much to be straightened out.'

According to Taylor, both actors 'stayed off the piss from Monday to Friday. Every Monday morning we had this secret code. We held up four fingers to each other, which meant four days left. On Tuesday it was three. On Wednesday, two. On Thursday it was one. Which really meant we had just one day till the piss-up started on Friday night. It was a grand time – from Friday till dawn Monday. We put down a lot of booze. But we never let the tequila interfere with our work on the battlefield.' Harris had 'a self-checking mechanism', said Taylor, that limited excess and revealed his professionalism. 'On those weekends, whether we were enjoying the local women or the tequila or not, we worked on that script. It was the only free time we got, really, because the locations were gruelling and we had a lot [of rewriting] to get done.'

To their credit, and Sam Manners's, the production remained on time and on (reduced) budget. Warners financed the production and, surprisingly, allowed Harris to supervise the tricky, cost-restricted postproduction that utilised a little of Fuller's second-unit footage, and musical out-takes from old movies to counterfeit the unaffordable (given the budget) score. Musical segments by Jerry Fielding from *The Wild Bunch*, Pat Williams from *Hardcase* and Richard Markowitz from *The Last Tomorrow* gave the movie a cobbled-together, awkward unity that everyone, said Taylor, did their best to ignore. 'Considering what we started with, and the project's history, I thought the end result was good. Against that sort of adversity, you measure true talent. And, in the circumstances, Richard should have been very proud of himself.'

Nobody agreed. The *New Yorker* billed the movie 'an incoherent, blood-soaked chase story', notable only for the value of Cine-mobiles. For Harris personally the movie was as near as he would ever get to a directorial follow-up to *Bloomfield*, and as such its failure cut deeply. His almost total dismissal of it in later years revealed, said some, the profound degree of disappointment in its failure. To add to the directorial upset, there were also some of the worst ever personal reviews to deal with. The critic Tony Ryans mocked an 'obstinate' aping of Brando – 'complete with Method pauses, grunts and flailing arms . . . Harris swamps the rest of the film with his studied machismo and Shear is left to trail along behind, his function reduced to recording.'

In the bleakest depression, Harris stumbled back to London and into another no-hope swamp – *Gulliver's Travels*, directed by the recent Bond director Peter Hunt. The story pedigree was the big attraction – and the script, said Harris, was 'a sweet, childlike working' – but Hunt's financial backup was shaky and it hardly helped that, after animation of the 'little people' sequences in Belgium, the production company filed for bankruptcy. *Gulliver* stopped in mid-production, enraging Harris. 'Incompetence I cannot stand. Also deception. Unfortunately those are the prime players in movie-making. Forget talent. Talent is negligible in the stakes. Talent, in truth, ranks down at the bottom of the scale . . . On *Gulliver* it was humiliating, because we started and stopped, and the rest of the time I was sitting in hotels, waiting for a call with the suspicion that the producers and financiers were out on a golf course somewhere, planning some apartment block they wanted to build.'

In the opinion of Harris's business associates, his loyalty to his audience stayed intact while violent cynicism about the industry took hold. At the time, Harris was quoted as saying, 'I can tell you what the next Steve McQueen movie will be and I can tell you exactly how he's going to play it – the same way he's been playing it for fifteen years. In the motion-picture business you cannot have tremendous artistic ambition. And that's why I couldn't care less any more.' Joe Lynch said, 'He really couldn't. In an elevator with him you could feel it. You felt he was saying, "Fuck this star crap. Fuck the studio time call. Fuck the 'suits' with their rip-off deals. Fuck the box office. Let me get back to the jungle."'

Harris sat down with Dermot at Limbridge for a re-evaluation. A friend said, 'He was in serious financial problems, bordering on bankruptcy, so the sit-down was the American equivalent of "going Chapter 11". They had to rewrite the accounts, or everything would be lost. At that time, as I saw it, all Dick had was the royalties from the music, and the cuts he had in Sandy Howard's movies.' As a result of the discussions, Harris divested himself of most of the material trappings he had gathered over the years. He rarely used the lodge at Kilkee, so that was sold to Manuel Di Lucia for £14,000. Tower House, the haunted Arthurian folly (he claimed he was tired of the ghost of a boy who 'pestered' him), was sold to Jimmy Page of Led Zeppelin for £350,000. A new plan was laid to shift this money into a wide range of investment properties around the world – houses in suburban areas where the price tags were moving upward. As Harris told it, he and Dermot concluded that the high-flying Hollywood life was over. 'We decided to put 50 per cent of every future film fee into property around Los Angeles, and that is what we did.' The scheme was enough to restore him, temporarily at any rate, to movie-making.

A new home was sought, and found with the help of Kevin McClory, who had made his wealth in a court settlement with Ian Fleming that granted him shared rights in one James Bond story, *Thunderball*. Since co-producing *Thunderball* (and earning $20 million on its back), McClory had been living in a six-bedroom timber-frame home on Paradise Island, off Nassau in the Bahamas, near the home of the millionaire Huntingford Hartford. For years, McClory had been advising Harris to consider tax-free Paradise Island as a home base, but Harris always sidestepped. Finally, McClory claimed, he 'found Harris drunk in a Dublin gutter and put him on a plane to Nassau'. Harris dried out at Pieces of Eight, the McClory home, and succumbed. With McClory's assistance he purchased Hartford's ten-bedroom clapboard residence on three acres, a quarter of a mile from McClory's, in the shadow of the Holiday Inn.

Harris's tax-haven hideaway, which was to become a spiritual home to rival, even override, Limerick, was a storybook paradise: rolling scutch lawns surrounded by sweet-scented bougainvillea and casaurinas and cabbage palms, a coral beach, a private jetty with a power boat to take him across to the amenities of Nassau, just five minutes away. The purchase price was £200,000. At first Harris told Jack Donnelly and Ronald Fraser he would be bored to death in the isolation of the Bahamas, but very quickly he adjusted. Paradise Island became, he said, his salvation: 'It was my bunker, the place where I hid my creative soul.'

Richard Lester's movie *Juggernaut*, shot side by side with John Frankenheimer's *99 and ⁴⁴/₁₀₀% Dead*, took him away from the lobster lunches at Captain Nemo's on the Nassau dock, and back into 'the investment hustle'. 'That was a kind of turning point, that was the moment I started the blockbuster-mentality shit.' Lester's film, shot with a guest-star-heavy cast at Twickenham in the mould of so many 'star vehicles' of the seventies, and John Frankenheimer's, shot on location around LA, were 'performed in automatic-mode', said Harris, in which 'the biggest effort I made was reading the cheques'. Frankenheimer's movie, though, provided a bonus beyond all expectation. At the start, Frankenheimer told Harris his co-star would be Jacqueline Bisset. 'And I loved her. I thought she was a great actress, and the cutest, most sophisticated little beauty around. I was a fan. I told John, yes, get her for me, and I will do your movie. But he didn't, he couldn't, and I almost walked away. But he begged me not to. He said he had someone altogether new in mind, who would blow my socks off. A total "find". I said, "I don't believe you" . . . but he delivered on his promise.'

There are, in classic Harris style, at least two accounts of the circumstances of his meeting with Ann Turkel, the 26-year-old brunette whom he adopted as acolyte, then substitute daughter, then lover, then wife. In the most popular account recorded by Simon Kinnersley in the *Daily Mail*, Harris was flying to LA on a 747 when 'the girl in seat 2B caught his attention'. By the time the plane had crossed Newfoundland they had agreed to meet for a dinner in LA. After that, said Kinnersley, 'their relationship quickly blossomed'.

The alternative version is less romantic. Frankenheimer had screen-tested a variety of newcomers for the part of Buffy, the object of the hero's sexual dalliance in *99 and ⁴⁴/₁₀₀% Dead*. Part-time model Turkel from Scarsdale in New York State, inexperienced but strikingly handsome, he liked best. On the phone he told Harris, who, in Frankenheimer's account, bitterly objected. The role of schoolmarm Buffy, said Harris, was too substantial for a new actress. On top of that the girl suggested – Turkel – was 'everything I deplore in a female'. Harris later told *Photoplay*: 'It is true. I said, She's too tall, too thin, and she is a brunette. I prefer blondes. She's also not very sociable.'

When Harris finished Lester's sea-rescue movie, *Juggernaut*, he flew to LA and watched Frankenheimer's screen-test footage. 'I was more certain than ever that this was a bad idea. I saw it through, and was convinced it was a classic case of the casting-couch business. But John persisted and begged me. I gave Ann ten days of hell while she waited to find out whether or not she was going to be in the picture.'

Frankenheimer – whose casting instincts had proved powerfully accurate in hit films like *The Manchurian Candidate* – finally convinced Harris and filming started, with Turkel working overtime to try to impress the star. What made matters harder for Turkel was her hero-worship of Harris. *Camelot* was her favourite movie and, she told crewmen quietly, she had revered pin-up King Arthur for years. Harris detected her 'sincere commitment' – though not, he said, the idolatry – and swung to the polar extreme in his behaviour towards her: 'Once we began filming, through guilt, I became attentive and helpful to her, explaining camera angles, how to read her lines and so forth. I must say she was a good student. But there was never a hint of romantic notions at the start.'

Turkel struggled. She had long fantasised about getting into movies but had, she told a magazine interviewer, seriously doubted her chances with Frankenheimer. Once tested, her friends had promised her, she would be cast and adopted by Hollywood for ever. On the movie set, Turkel was less confident, but kept her hopes. According to her, she knew of Harris's bad press and prepared herself the worst. But day by day the working relationship improved. Late-night shooting recaps became candlelit dinners. Harris studied her inquisitively, and smiled, and relaxed. 'She was great, because she was tolerant and patient,' said Harris. 'She was the best company, very beautiful, very attentive – but not a great talker. I later got the full picture, about how in awe of me she was. But at the time it came across as shy and impressionable, and really very engaging.' Harris 'knew' she liked him, but their intimacies, he said, were restrained and guarded for quite a long time during the filming.

Finally, six weeks into production, they found themselves seated by the pool of Harris's rented LA home, perusing script pages. Harris asked her, 'Annie, do you think there's something going on between us that we don't know about?'

Ann replied blushingly, 'I think there might be.'

'I was one surprised Irishman,' said Harris later, insisting that the relationship was 'the most unlikely of all my life'. Prior to Frankenheimer's casting, Ann Turkel had been 'almost married' to David Niven Jr, head of Paramount's European division, and 'heading for the life of a Hollywood society beauty'; such a background, such expectations, ill-prepared her for coping with poetic, disenchanted, hard-boozing Harris. But the chemistry worked – especially after Harris introduced her to his sons on holiday in the Bahamas at Christmas. Ann got on well with all the boys – she was closer in age to Damian than to Damian's dad – and she described her Bahamian baptism as 'love at first sight'. The islands would make a perfect future home for them, and she can have been excused for thinking that introductions to the family suggested noble intentions on Harris's part.

'But I really wasn't ready for another marriage. What was happening with Elizabeth [and Rex Harrison] was depressing. I wished her well, because I loved her always, but I'd lost confidence in marriage. I told Annie that. I told her I did not trust the institution of marriage. I told her I couldn't see the point any more.' Instead, Harris's proposal was that they should go on as they started, in a mutually edifying partnership where he played tutor and she was confidante, companion and comforter. 'I believe you are born to live alone,' was his favourite comment at the time. 'I don't believe any two people can adapt to suit one another. That idea is a complete fallacy. You've got to work out your own rhythms, and if someone doesn't fit in you've got to say, "Right! That's finished!" and then move on.'

But Ann's arrival changed his life, though he was slow to admit it. His energetic drive – property investments apart – suddenly returned, and he was anxious and interested again about movies and movie-industry gossip. 'It's easy to put it down to the middle-aged old fogey trying to impress,' said one friend. 'But, when you met them together, you saw a kind of equality that changed your preconceptions. He definitely tried to impress her – what man doesn't with a new woman in his world? – but he was more interested in impressing himself. Maybe it was her idolising him as a movie star. Maybe, up close, he saw himself as a great screen legend in a way that was new. Dickie wasn't the kind of fellow who looked in the mirror and said, Gee, there you are, you Hollywood hulk . . . He was too insecure for that. Ann came up behind him and brought it all back together. She was the one who hugged him and told him he was the bee's knees.'

At this opportune time, Harris met with Sandy Howard to formalise a venture partnership for new movies. In all Howard proposed a $25 million slate of production, expanding his existing production company in partnership with executive Terry Morse and distribution-marketing experts Charles Boasberg and Milt Goldstein. Howard had no fewer than eight new films in sight, four to star Harris – on a fifty–fifty profits split. Among the new movies, over which Harris would have full creative control, was *Return of a Man Called Horse*, budgeted at $3.5 million, and *The Last Castle*, a Canadian co-production whose financing necessitated shooting in Nova Scotia. The actor-director Don Taylor was retained by Howard to direct this small-scale weepie (released as *Echoes of a Summer*) and was introduced to Harris shortly after the venture deal was agreed. Taylor found Harris 'very sober and very excited by the new partnership and the productions lined up. He gave the impression of being very interested and demanding and unwilling to leave any stones unturned'.

Against the backdrop of productivity and new businesses, Harris suddenly began talking about marriage. At Christmas, the first gossip columns stirred: the word was, Harris would marry Ann in April. The cavalcade began again, with reporters tagging him – and Ann – everywhere. The experience was new for Ann, whose erstwhile background was the restrained, formal world of middle-market fashion houses and occasional designer launches (her father was a clothing manufacturer), and whose brief time with David Niven Jr had been lived firmly in the background.

In April Harris flew to London to record the album of *I, in the Membership of My Days* under the direction of Terry James, producing, and arranger Johnny Harris. All his sons contributed, reading poetry from his book, and the narrative line was beefed up with a number of slight songs, some traditional, others (notably 'I Don't Know') gracefully penned by Harris himself. This was turnabout time, the adieu to pop songs and the beginning of a number of concept spoken-word albums, which would win much acclaim, though poor sales. (The spoken-word *Jonathan Livingstone Seagull* won him a Grammy; Kahlil Gibran's *The Prophet* was to follow.) Apart from compilation rehashes issued by budget labels, Harris's chart-oriented musical career was over.

Ensconced at the Savoy Hotel in London, another of the spiritual sanctuaries that would endure till the end of his life, Harris and Ann dodged incessant press enquiries about their future plans. The expected marriage date came and went without announcement and finally Harris met the press in his suite and gruffly said the marriage was off. 'The postponement is partly because of my filming and recording schedules. But it has also dawned on me that, although we've been around together for six months or so, we don't really know each other. Until now I've seen Ann only for a few minutes in the morning, before I go filming [concluding scenes for Lester's *Juggernaut*], then for a few minutes in the evening, before I go to the recording studios, and for another few hours in between, in the lulls.'

The *Daily Express* pressed him on a change of heart, but Harris was adamant that they would eventually get married. He had even told her father, during a telephone conversation – and cautioned him at the same time: 'I've made no bones that I'm not good news for any girl. I told him, "If I was in your place I'd have a contract out on Harris's head in five minutes." All he did was laugh. But as it was a phone conversation I don't know if it was through clenched teeth or not.' His expectations of the marriage were stated boldy: 'Ann is an old-fashioned girl who wants marriage, and I'd like a daughter.' Nursing 'the worst hangover of my life' during his exchange with the *Express*, Harris sipped a remedy cocktail of brandy, port and soda and defined his fail-safe marriage tester: 'I'm now taking five months off to hole up in the Bahamas and we'll see how we get along being in each other's pockets twenty-four hours a day.'

After a visit to Cashel, Co. Tipperary, where Jack Donnelly was now managing the luxurious Cashel Palace Hotel, Harris geared up for the two Sandy Howard pictures, to be shot in Canada and Spain. Donnelly found him 'very subdued now, with a new slant on things, thanks to Ann. He likes to walk with her. He seems less frantic. He reads a lot more, and gets joy from just sitting over a slow evening meal. Those days of dashing to the next gig are gone.'

Harris joined Taylor in Nova Scotia in a fixed mood. 'We saw the movie exactly the same way from the outset,' said Don Taylor. 'There were no arguments, not even any heavy debates. Bob Joseph, who wrote the stage play on which it was based, had flown down to Nassau for a couple of days before we started, to make sure we were "on the same page". Then we all reassembled in Canada to do it. It was as good as that.' Taylor had discovered an exceptional child star some years before and had cast her in his version of *Tom Sawyer*. Now he opted to use her again, as the dying girl around whom the story revolved. 'Richard thought my casting was the big thing. Jodie Foster was the kid and he positively adored her – and also the little boy we had, Brad Savage. He had an unusually good way with children. They drew the best out of him, because he was a child, really. Children showed the scope of his sensitivity, the side of him people try not to see because of the bad press. Jodie learned a lot from Richard Harris.'

Taylor faced up to 'the booze issue' at the very start: 'We sat down and talked about it and he didn't deny it. Yes, it had delayed productions and caused troubles in the past. But he gave me an undertaking. He was as good as his word. When we flew to Canada, we had no problems at all. It was a fragile movie, because there wasn't much money in the budget, and Richard responded so well to that. He was comfortable with the people. It was a family experience, and a good art-house end result.' Taylor recalled the contentment of all cast and crew, and their satisfaction with the objective achieved. He remembered the first showing to Sandy Howard's distribution team: 'When the movie ended and the lights went up, it was obvious that everyone was moved. This simple, tragic everyday story of a dying kid shook up everybody. But then reality strikes. The distribution guy said, "It's a jewel – but do we know how to release it?" – and we didn't, really.'

Echoes of a Summer was many months in postproduction and limped into market release after a premiere at the Cork Film Festival in June 1976. It achieved no coordinated cinema release in Britain and was not widely seen until its TV premiere seven years later. It took its place alongside *Juggernaut* and *99 and $^{44}/_{100}\%$ Dead* as one of a string of middle-seventies disappointments that reshaped industry and public perception of Harris and drove him, again, towards bankruptcy. In *Juggernaut*, Harris played a bomb-disposal man hoisted onto a transatlantic liner to save the passengers from a terrorist device. The movie grossed well enough, but it was neither better than nor different from any of fifty Photofit same-plot movies that clogged the contemporary market. Frankenheimer's was yet another thriller, land-based but all at sea in terms of suspense and denouement, where Harris, blond-wigged, played a charmless thug commissioned to ensure the election of Bradford Dillman as an underworld *capo*. Frankenheimer called it 'probably the worst movie I ever made', and its only redemption, it seemed, was the polite good notices directed towards Ann. David Niven Jr, her influential ex, commented chivalrously, 'Considering it was her first film, she was very good and is sure to get future parts. I thought she looked lovely.' Little more, in any quarter, was offered by way of commendation for any of Harris's recent movies.

Ignoring the bad press, Harris marked his satisfaction with Ann's performance by giving her a gold, enamel and diamond butterfly, her favourite good-luck symbol, on a neck chain. And then in June, left-footing the attentive press, he married her in a private ceremony in Los Angeles. Harris was unusually tight-lipped about the occasion: 'She is a good talker. When we exchanged our marriage vows the magistrate asked, "Do you take this woman to be your lawful wedded wife?" And before I could utter a word, Ann said, "*He does*!"'

Outwardly calm, Harris felt himself 'approaching some watershed that might drown me. It's that difficult stage in an actor's life. I am not a young man. I am not an oldie. I don't want to appear ridiculous bedding some seventeen-year-old, and I certainly don't want to be the guy with the walking stick.' A measure of his discontent, despite the marriage, was his decision to go into therapy with Ann. A close friend said later, 'They fought too much too quickly, and that was one of the deal-breakers. Ann said, "Either we work this out together in counselling, or we call it a day." Richard really didn't want to let her go, because he'd had so many women, and she was the first since Elizabeth who brought dignity to him, the first he wanted to impress sincerely.' Harris said, 'Neither of us needed [the counselling]. But we're so individualistic. So we said, "Let's go examine transactional analysis", which I became an absolute freak on . . . but there are really no answers.'

The binding force in the relationship, said Jack Donnelly, was both the individualism and their kindred gypsy spirits. Both loved to travel at the drop of a hat. Both, said Harris, were 'excitement freaks' prone to bouts of boredom and ever ready to tackle them. Paradise Island became their home, but Ann insisted on keeping her flat in Scarsdale on the thirteenth floor of a slick apartment building. 'We had a contract,' Harris explained. 'and one of the things she insisted on was maintaining her apartment, because it kept her family ties. Her grandmother is there, her mother and father, her brothers and sisters. And being Jewish they have that tremendous affinity.'

Ann's strength of character, and her independent spirit, kept Harris on his toes. 'The days are never long enough for her,' he complained, but he encouraged her as she renewed modelling contracts and announced her own plans to make a record, hopefully with Peter Frampton: 'It's funny, because I was discovered for *Vogue*, singing. A college friend asked me to sing at a Mary Quant fashion show and an editor from *Vogue* called me afterwards and asked if I'd thought of modelling. Now I'd like to do both, and act as well, if the roles come along.' Ann's comfortable integration into Harris's 'heart circle' impressed him too: all the kids liked her, and she took time with Damian and his new girlfriend, advising her on contacts that might help her break into modelling. 'Her generous spirit always surprised me,' Harris said. 'There is often the difficulty between new wives and old, and I'd made it clear to Ann that I saw Elizabeth as a lifelong friend. But she had no issue with that, or with the boys. She treated them like brothers, really, and I admired her sense of proportion. Sometimes, it was too much, too precocious, and she made me jealous. But that is part of a woman's armoury, isn't it? They make you jealous to drive you wild in bed.'

Late in 1975 Harris rejoined Richard Lester in Almeria for four weeks on *Robin and Marian*, an important, career-defining movie for Sean Connery, whose post-James Bond progress had been, till then, variable. Harris's role as, appropriately, King Richard in this inventive story of Robin Hood's last days suited him because, 'I liked Sean [Connery] more than many actors. I liked his consistency as a friend and as a man. There aren't many actors I look up to as role models, or what have you, but Burton, O'Toole and Sean are worthwhile. They are the kind of people who shake your hand, and mean it.'

Sandy Howard was someone else whom Harris looked up to, and, after Connery's film, he was eager for a headline vehicle of his own, in reprising his role of Lord John Morgan in *The Return of a Man Called Horse*. 'The movies with Howard gave me special fulfilment, because I didn't have to grovel and fight with him. It was like Lindsay, in a way. There was an equality, and trust. My attitude when I worked with him changed. I felt, Now if a picture I do fails it will be because *I* failed in the conception of some element, not because some studio has changed its mind. There was a feeling of . . . more freedom.' In *The Return of a Man Called Horse*, directed by Irvin Kershner in South Dakota, Mexico and Wiltshire, that sense of freedom worked the alchemy, turning a fairly average 'replay screenplay' into a powerful sequel, widely welcomed and noticeably successful in its first weeks at the box office. In America, especially, *The Return of a Man Called Horse*, was praised for its daring. The *Los Angeles Times* called it 'hauntingly beautiful' and remarked upon Harris's performance as 'one of the best of his career'. But the movie stalled in the Midwest. 'It fell foul in the more conservative markets because of its violence,' said Howard. 'I regretted that, because it had the potential to be one of those rare sequels that work, like *The Godfather*. But there were other negatives. The first *Horse* movie worked because of its authentic nature. Kershner cast the second one with Jewish actors playing western roles and, in one fell swoop, killed the point of the exercise. I hated a lot of what I saw, especially the too graphic violence of the Sun Vow ceremony. I felt it was exploitative, cashing in on what we'd achieved in the first one . . . But I felt one of the better things about it was Richard, because he seemed at home in the middle of it all, and also seemed to be in a comfortable place in his head.'

To Howard, and even to members of the Limbridge circle, Harris and Ann had, to some extent, shut themselves off in their private, hermetically sealed paradise. 'I wanted a movie for Ann and I,' Harris said. 'Whenever I said that to agents, the response always was, Oh, he's doing a Dickie Burton [with Elizabeth Taylor]. But I genuinely was interested in Ann's capabilities. There was always a buzz around her, always a feeling of the *possibilities*.' Jack Donnelly said, 'Professionally, Ann wasn't calming for him. If anything she drove him, day and night, which was good to see, because there'd been a time, after Harmay and *Bloomfield*, when we worried about him. He laughed a lot with her and he doted on her, like a father. That was an affectionate phrase he often used: "My little girl". He stopped gallivanting because she put a ten-mile limit around him. What she wanted was a proper decent married life – but she also wanted this career alongside his.'

Lew Grade and Carlo Ponti, working in partnership with Fox in Britain, finally gave Harris and Ann the substantial co-starring role they both sought. The movie, to be directed by George Pan Cosmatos, would be another *Juggernaut*-type seventies mega-thriller, called *The Cassandra Crossing*, to be shot in Rome and Geneva. 'I remember getting the green-light call,' said Harris, 'and thinking, We have one shot at this. We're now the Mr & Mrs Act, so this better pay off. I'm sure I encouraged Annie. I also probably scared the shit out of her.'

During the early days of the Cinecitta shooting of *Cassandra* the couple sneaked away for a romantic weekend in Paris, where Ann saw an African fertility talisman in a shop window. It was woven from elephant's hair that allegedly ensured fertility for the wearer. She urged Harris to buy it for her and she wore it – 'round my waist, because that's nearer to the womb'. The charm worked. By the time they flew back to Rome, Ann was pregnant.

CHAPTER 14

Back in the Wilderness

Italy had never been lucky for Richard Harris, and his return to Italian-based filmmaking maintained the tradition. *The Cassandra Crossing* was a bandwagon plague-on-a-train disaster movie overwhelmed by stars – Sophia Loren, Martin Sheen, Ava Gardner, O J Simpson, Burt Lancaster, John Phillip Law, Lee Strasberg – and overfussily mounted by its creative overseer-producer, Carlo Ponti. In Ponti's description, Cosmatos, his protégé, was 'a moving movie encyclopedia', who had learned, by way of commercials-making in New York and Rome, every trick of cameras, light and modern movie technology. Cosmatos, was also an unashamed movie fan who had been an assistant director on *Exodus* and admitted that 'Everything I know about directing I learned from watching movies.' *The Cassandra Crossing*, in its strained, potted plotline and roadshow performances, upheld the inevitable promise: despite the big budget and the pin-up faces, it unfolded like yesterday's dough. Harris sensed the trouble from the start, and, years later, winced at the memory: 'I'm a Limerick lad. So it was a wet dream to be acting with Ava and Loren in their corsets and bras. But the way it came together put my back up. All those disaster movies – you always hoped someone, somewhere would take some time to put a little *Macbeth* into them. But somehow it never worked, ever. In the end, I never saw the movie, I couldn't watch it. From then on, I avoided watching those seventies movies. I preferred to get a video, and watch the Lindsay Anderson work.' John Philip Law, who became very friendly with Harris on this and a later *Tarzan* movie, was more forgiving: 'Let's say it was an honest effort. With honest mistakes.'

Harris played Dr Jonathan Chamberlain, husband of the Sophia Loren character, and key lead role, but Ann, playing a student hippie plague casualty aboard the Stockholm-bound Transcontinental Express stole most of the attention on and off the set. 'For a start, she was pregnant,' said Harris, 'so there was all that coddling. It was very blissful, daydreaming about the daughter we wanted and how perfect it was going to be. But I used to think it was harder for her than for everyone else, because all of them were pros and she was Mrs Harris. She was carrying all these emotional loads, but I was proud of her. She stood up to it brilliantly.' Stress, though, took its toll and during the shooting of her principal scenes, in which she collapses with plague fever, Ann became ill for real with stomach pains that worsened over the course of the next fortnight. She put on a brave face, but Harris became seriously worried when he heard her crying and, overruling her objections, took action: 'I put her on a plane from Rome to New York and got her back to her gynaecologist. It was clear that there was something really wrong, and we hoped and prayed the pregnancy was safe. But she miscarried on the aeroplane. I tried to block it out of my mind, but I knew it was coming, because she was in such agony for fourteen days.'

The devastating disappointment momentarily flung them closer while, paradoxically, distancing them. 'It's hard to explain,' said one close friend. 'He desperately wanted a daughter and Ann recognised that and wanted nothing more than to give him a daughter. He was, at the same time, devoted to her, he loved her. So she was feeling guilt, and he was feeling unable to assuage that guilt, because of the longing for a daughter. When you spoke with him, you spoke in circles. He was crushed, but he was angry. Ann was crushed too, and she was angry in a different way. The only consolation was the work.'

Harris comforted Ann by devoting himself to projects exclusively designed for her. He had already signed with his old employer, the director Michael Anderson, to star in *Orca – Killer Whale*, a *Jaws* spin-off dressed as an anthropological nature movie. He pleaded with

Anderson, but there was no suitable role for Ann. In compensation, he jumped on Alistair Maclean's *Golden Rendezvous*, to be directed by Ashley Lazarus, on condition that Ann be cast prominently alongside him. Concurrently he turned to writing his own screenplays for her. In a short space of time no fewer than four were chalked up. 'I'll produce them myself,' Harris told *Photoplay*. 'The first will be called *The Case of Patrick Silver*. The next one is tentatively titled *Hit Me* and I'll produce, with Ann starring, hopefully alongside Kris Kristofferson, who is an actor we both really admire.' Kristofferson, Harris said, had become 'something of an obsession' for both he and Ann 'because I somehow feel a kinship with him. I find his life and mine have extraordinary parallels. We started off big together, we were very productive, highly intelligent people. I had a book of poetry, had songs published, gold records and acting, just like him. But then I lost it all by my consuming passions. I damaged my talent because I couldn't come to grips with the disappointments that were laid upon me by producers and heads of studios.'

None of the self-created movies mooted got off the ground and Harris later took full responsibility: 'I was a loose cannon. Who would trust me? I was a casualty of twenty years [*sic*] of photos in the paper with some big-titted scrubber [*sic*], with a glass in my fist, telling the world, Fuck off! I crucified myself. And then, when it came to walking humbly back and saying, Gee, could I have ten million dollars to make this . . . doors shut in my face.' Not all of the gloom, though, was of his own making. 'So many "friends" let me down. I helped so many people . . . But you don't go round, saying, Hey, I gave him a thousand dollars when his wife left him. You keep your counsel. But my generosity was often thrown back in my face.'

Even Sandy Howard, he felt, had let him down. Harris had always been a very vocal promoter of his own work, but as far back as *The Molly Maguires* he had been arguing about lack of support in pushing his name and his movies. Indeed, *The Molly Maguires* had evolved into a public fight. The Paramount boss Robert Evans had accused Harris of indifference to marketing, declaring him 'aloof to any promotional ideas that might have helped box office'. Harris angrily denied this: as far as he was concerned Evans 'dumped' *The Molly Maguires*. 'They told me they planned a premiere in New York and asked me to indulge a promotional gimmick where my pal [Malachy] McCourt and I would go on a drunken binge. I was willing to lie in the gutter for those fuckers. But then [Dermot] rang and we were informed that Paramount decided to drop the premiere. Those idiots had no respect.'

Sandy Howard strenuously denied Harris's accusation that he'd abandoned promotion of *Echoes of a Summer*. 'Richard was wrong. Yes, we had distribution difficulties, but that's the film world. You live with it. I did five pictures with Richard and the only movie we argued over was *Echoes*. No matter what it was, we couldn't get it right. He insisted on singing the title song and he sang it flat. I kept saying it was flat, but he kept saying otherwise. He murdered it – but I forgave him.'

'I saw my life and career replayed in the late seventies,' said Harris. 'Damian was eighteen, and attending the National Film School in London and talking about all these movies he wanted to make. Ann was being taken seriously as an actress, but was hitting all those walls I hit early on. She was "too this" and "too that". It was frustrating, and it also was unsettling. I'd lie in bed, looking at the ceiling, thinking, Is that it for me? Is it Damian's turn for success now? Or is it Ann's?'

'Developing Ann' remained the goal. Under his advice she turned down minor parts in *Rollerball*, *The Man with the Golden Gun*, *Rafferty and the Gold Dust Twins* and *The Bank Shot*. 'I'm sort of tutoring her,' Harris admitted at the time. 'I give a lot of time now to guide her acting career, because she's ready. Lee Strasberg, who's supposed to be the bastard talent-spotter, did a scene with her in *Cassandra Crossing* and he says she's the best raw talent he's seen. And I agree.' Twenty years earlier, Harris pointed out, it had been Strasberg who spotted him on *Borstal Boy* – so there was real reason for optimism. 'When I married Ann I seemed to get custody of a child. Now the maturity and strength she's bottled up before is all coming out. We have terrific fun together. The basis of our marriage is friendship. The husband is often the stranger in many marriages, spending his time in pubs and so forth. But Ann and I can talk.'

In the *Guardian* Ann described her recovery from the miscarriage and the progress of their marriage: 'Richard says I have to establish my own identity. He says he couldn't be married to anyone who couldn't produce. At the moment photography is my own form of creativity. I didn't start off to be a photographer, but I knew something about it from modelling. Then Richard started looking so incredible I had to shoot him. Now I'm hooked on shooting him. *Time* magazine even published one of my pictures of him . . .'

Orca – Killer Whale took them to Canada and a long, photogenic shoot in freezing Arctic waters. Developed by the writer-producer Luciano Vincenzoni, whose extensive research inspired Dino De Laurentiis to shuffle a $6 million deal with Paramount, *Orca* committed the sin of making a disingenuous denial of the *Jaws* cash-in link. Harris truly liked the script – which was a zoologically accurate, *Moby Dick*-like account of a whaler's determination to capture or kill *Orca orcinus*, the killer whale, and rejected all *Jaws* connections: 'I get really offended when people make the comparison. [In *Orca*] the characters are real people, three-dimensional people whose lives become inexorably laced into that of a brace of mammoth mammals of the sea. It must never be dismissed as just another disaster or frightener movie. The end result is more breathtaking than either director Michael Anderson or Luciano Vincenzoni or I and Charlotte [Rampling, his co-lead] or anyone else ever imagined.'

Harris, at 47, insisted on performing his own stunts in snow and icy water and 'almost died a couple or three times'. When the picture transferred to the gentler climes of Malta, for shooting at the gigantic movie tank at Rinela, Ann stayed in Hollywood. Harris lovingly kept in touch, with daily, sometimes thrice-daily, phone calls. The five-week separation, he said, was as stressful as the Arctic locations. 'It was dreadful,' Ann agreed. 'Our phone bills were astronomical, over ten thousand dollars *a week*! Once we were on the phone for four hours from Los Angeles to Malta. After I'd hung up, the operator called me and said, "I just wanted to let you know that you've beaten Richard Burton and Elizabeth Taylor's record on the phone."'

Both *The Cassandra Crossing* and *Orca* benefited from Harris's eloquent support – *Orca*, significantly, taking an impressive $3,546,500 in its first weekend of American release. Neither film swayed the critics and, though Harris loudly professed himself indifferent, there was evidence of artistic stirrings that just would not lie down. In the autumn of 1976, Warner Brothers threatened legal action against him for reneging on an oral agreement with the producers of *The Squeeze*, finally shot in London with Stacey Keach under Michael Apted's direction. The movie was a fast-paced, gritty gangland yarn, but, said Harris, 'I was moody. I wanted art again, just art. I kept looking at these script pages about car chases and exploding bombs and saying to myself, What had this got to do with Frank Machin?' A few weeks later he negotiated himself on to Ingmar Bergman's *The Serpent's Egg*, to be shot in Sweden. The joy died fast: weeks before Bergman's picture was due to start, Harris collapsed again and was returned to Los Angeles for more unresolved medical tests. 'The fates were against me. Again and again I had some *Hamlet* in my sights, and I always ended up with the booby prize.'

Despite the ongoing medical concerns – 'which drove Ann up the walls, she couldn't sleep!' – Harris was still living the gadabout life of a teenager, staying up late, drinking vodka for breakfast, filling up with fast food when he missed a meal. In February, shortly before *The Golden Rendezvous*, the *Guardian* had him happily 'consuming a breakfast fry-up and still drinking heavily', though Ann's influence had, he said, reduced his intake and moderated his general behaviour. 'I wasn't really trying to change my habits,' Harris confessed years later. 'In movies like *Return of a Man Called Horse* I looked fucking great half-naked. My bones were good – these rugby-player shoulders, firm thighs, great legs. So no one took the collapses seriously. Even the doctors would say, Jesus, you have a great body! No problems here. It was like the joke of the dying old guy, saying, I told you I was ill: they just wouldn't believe. But then, neither would I.'

Alistair Maclean's *Golden Rendezvous* Harris again rated as 'rubbish'. Seventeen seagoing weeks and $6 million were spent shooting this creaky hijack tale, and though the producer André Pieterse started out singing the praises of the Harris–Turkel teamwork – 'They resemble the way Humphrey Bogart and Lauren Bacall interacted together' – the movie ended in a fury of bickering and litigation. When postproduction was completed at Pinewood, no one could make head nor tail of the plot, so an additional six-minute explanatory opening sequence was shot. Harris tried to put the grim experience behind him, but it wouldn't go away. A year later, when the producer Euan Lloyd brought him back to Pieterse's native South Africa for a genuinely electric adventure yarn, *The Wild Geese*, writs were served at Johannesburg airport, accusing Harris of subverting the movie and depleting government-invested funds. *Golden Rendezvous* was already under investigation for the alleged misuse of funds intended for the black cinema industry, but Harris erupted in rage when Rand Court Judge King cited Pieterse's contention that Harris, and Harris alone, had delayed the production by 44 days and cost the film a further £800,000. According to the court papers, Harris was destructive and had allegedly consumed a bottle of vodka a day during the confined shooting on a ship in the Indian Ocean. Harris denied all the 'absolutely defamatory' claims, counter-claiming for £25,000 in unpaid fees that Pieterse owed him.

An out-of-court settlement more or less buried *Golden Rendezvous*, but Harris turned with glee to *The Wild Geese*, 'the Christmas present of the seventies': 'I'd been plodding through sewage, and then, at the end of the tunnel, there it was: a romp with the boys, a night on the town! Was *The Wild Geese* a movie? I thought it was a summer holiday.' The reason for Harris's delight was simple: two of his great boozing idols, Ronald Fraser and Richard Burton, were cast alongside him in a movie set in the sun. 'You must remember,' said Fraser, that we also had Roger Moore, Stewart Granger, Jack Watson and Helmut Berger – and we were all friends. Most of us grew up together in the theatre and movies of the time. There was a competitiveness, yes. But there was also just the great club warmth of friends on an outing.' The outing was to

Tshipise, a town in the northern Transvaal on the Rhodesian border, where the unit took over a vast, self-contained township peopled by black actors. Temperatures soared to 110 degrees and the much-voiced fear was that Harris, Burton and Fraser, all ferocious drunks when the mood took them, would stymie the production. Fraser said, 'Euan Lloyd was going around worrying, saying, "I know Harris can be a bit of a nuisance and Burton can put back a few too. And Fraser might have a few as well! We could be in trouble here!"' Euan Lloyd's first-choice casting had been Burton and Moore with Robert Mitchum and Richard Widmark – 'an altogether safer chemistry', Fraser opined – but the volatility of this particular brew, properly stirred, promised fascinating on-screen sparks. Andrew McLaglen was charged with directing, shooting a script by the multi-awarded Reginald Rose, author of *Twelve Angry Men*. 'All the ingredients were there for a great picture,' said Fraser. 'It was just *us* that was the problem.'

As Harris told it on the talk-show circuit, he kept his promise to Euan Lloyd and stayed sober. Coached by 'decently disciplined' Roger Moore, he in turn watched over Burton, telling him, 'Whenever you feel like a drink, do like I do: jump up and down.' For the remainder of the production, claimed Harris, he and Burton were to be seen daily hopping like kangaroos. Ronald Fraser said, 'That's bollocks. We were never sober. And, when we were, we had a couple of rented houses in the complex, with nice gardens – and *weeds*. My gardener was mowing the lawn and came in with five or six bags of cuttings. I said to him, "What the hell are you doing, bringing this stuff into the house? Take it outside." But he said, "It's not for burning, Doc. It's the stuff you roll in a paper and light."'

Harris, Burton and Fraser indulged, rolling, according to Fraser, 'deadly joints of Durban Poison, which was utterly blissful and made us all think we were gods'. The high-powered grass gave a totally new complexion to the grilling heat, the flies, the reckless-action mercenary plot. 'We were all so happy, convinced we were doing Shakespeare,' said Fraser. 'The producer was looking at us, wondering, "These guys *should* be trouble, but they're all angels! What happened?" Then again, for all we knew in our condition, he might have been saying, "How quick can I wrap this and get out of South Africa before we're busted?"'

The long, hot shoot was marred for Harris only by the unshakeable illness that confounded the unit doctors who frequently looked him over. 'Burton would say, "Maybe it's a hangover." But it felt worse than any hangover, and the illness came at odd times.'

The Wild Geese was best remembered by Harris as the film that deepened his relationship with Burton, whom he 'idolised till the day he died: *there* was talent!' The movie itself – about an assault mission led by Burton to free the imprisoned leader of a central African state – was unoriginal, but successful enough in its middle-market targeting to inspire talk of a follow-up, though Harris would not have been involved since his character, Rafer Janders, died in the movie.

The disappointment of Ingmar Bergman buried, Harris returned to the Bahamas, refused to take stock and forged on, jumping at the cheques and the opportunities to push Ann's career. Whatever concerns he felt about his worsening health were buried in booze, and in a new predilection for top-quality cocaine. In the late seventies, after *The Wild Geese*, cocaine became 'a social necessity' for him. By his own admission he spent a fortune on it, and it almost killed him. Jack Donnelly recalled, 'He knew he wasn't well and he was constantly going into these comas. It was a long time before the doctors sorted all that out. The first step was getting him off the drink. So he was told to stop drinking and that would relieve the comas. No drink, and the comas would stop. So he took the drugs to stop drinking.' Ronald Fraser said, 'He wasn't improving, so he went back to his doctor to sort it out. He said, "What's the fuckin' trouble here? I'm not drinking and still the comas. What's wrong? I want it sorted out." The doctor asked him did he take drugs and Dick said, "No, never touch the stuff." And the doctor was bewildered, he could not sort this out . . . So he asked Dick what he took in place of alcohol and Dick said, "Oh I use that white stuff, up me nose. And I smoke some weed, that kind of thing . . . But I never take drugs. I wouldn't be caught dead taking sleeping pills or aspirin or any of that muck."'

Another journalist friend recalled, 'Dermot and he were bad influences on each other. Dermot had a huge capacity for careless drinking, day and night. It was the booze that brought down Dermot's marriage [to Cassandra, who later married the actor Pierce Brosnan]. And I think Richard tried to keep up with him, but just couldn't manage it. Dermot's seemed to be the stronger metabolism. Not, though, as it turned out in the end.'

The comas – and sometimes fits – worsened. During a stopover in LA to prepare for Roy Boulting's swan song, *The Last Word*, Harris went into a serious coma that Ann mistook for a heart attack. Once again he was rushed to the Cedars of Lebanon, just as he had been at the start of *Major Dundee*. The cardiogram results showed a sound heart, but there was clearly something chronically wrong that needed resolution. As Harris awaited the results of further tests he returned to a rented Beverly Hills mansion and flushed $6,000 worth of cocaine down the toilet. Inside eight years Dermot would be dead, from a heart attack induced by heavy drinking. Harris already saw the signs and knew he must change his lifestyle. 'Dermot had more guts than me,' he said later. 'I didn't want to go through drink and drugs.'

While they were on holiday in the Bahamas at Christmas, a doctor friend of Elizabeth's urged Harris to check into a New York clinic for more blood tests. It was here, finally, that the life-threatening hyperglycemia, the root of years of suffering, was revealed. A rigorous diet-and-medication treatment was prescribed and Harris squared up to a reorganised life, with all fat and sugar eliminated from his meals and a daily routine of vitamin supplements, overripe bananas, oatmeal and Evian water. Initially relieved that the mystery of his bad health was cracked, Harris 'celebrated by getting pissed. It took me two years to understand that I wasn't Superman and those doctors meant what they said. I was so happy to be diagnosed, that I was two years celebrating.'

In the mopping-up process of change, Ann was the first victim. For months, since *The Wild Geese*, there had been rumours of Harris's annoyance at her reputed involvement with a 22-year-old gym teacher. An intimate relationship was denied, but the aching reality of a change in the dynamic of their marriage could not be. 'Actually, it was very sudden,' said Fraser. 'In her eyes it was salvageable, but he seemed to want to move on. He hated Beverly Hills and she liked it. Most of the time he stayed there it was only to satisfy her. It was probably her influence that brought about the transfer of Limbridge offices from Alembic House [on Victoria Embankment] to LA. It was kind of new, relatively, to her. But Dick had had a lifetime of it and he loathed all the falseness of that place.' The other major factor was the medical diagnosis, many friends believed, that Harris saw as a 'reprieve', inviting him to reconsider the quality of his life and rebuild. 'It was a case of clearing out the cabinets and starting again,' said a friend. 'Anything that caused him stress had to go.'

Ann tried repeatedly to break through the stone wall that Harris suddenly built around himself, but all she found was the die-hard loner that all his lovers ultimately got to see. He was aggressive in his unease – a mode of behaviour adopted whenever he wished to cease negotiations in any area. The man who had said, 'I function best by myself' was reverting to form, sloughing off the skin of marriage, pushing her away. The tripwires of the failure were clear: the baby hadn't happened; her career was, at least tentatively, up and running; there was little more, apart from friendship, that they could offer each other.

In Harris's opinion selfishness ended his first marriage, selflessness the second. He had, he said, become just a minder for Ann, and her need to stay up late and boogie through the night just exhausted him. The music she listened to, the books she favoured, bored him. As did her image of him. She had fallen in love with King Arthur, then woken up one day to find a tired, middle-aged actor in bed beside her. She couldn't come to grips with a man addled by himself, by his misjudgments and by the limitations of his artistic potential.

A Bang Not a Whimper, the movie that would have co-starred Ann and Kris Kristofferson (it was apparently retitled from *Hit Me*), was abandoned. In April 1979, just five years after the wedding, the formal undoing began. Harris consulted Raoul Feider, one of New York's top divorce lawyers, and a flat $1 million pay-off offer was, reportedly, made to Ann. She refused point-blank and asked Harris to try again. She loved him, and she would do her best to be the wife he wanted.

The separation had already begun. While Ann stood her ground in Beverly Hills, Harris stayed at Manhattan's Regency Hotel to prepare for a clutch of good-wage movies that would keep him busy. Already in the can was *The Ravagers*, a post-holocaust romp that no one, least of all Harris, noticed. Ann featured in it and it was their final shared movie. Next up was *Highpoint*, a slap-bang-wallop thriller by Peter Carter, to be shot in Toronto with his first wife Elizabeth's ex, Christopher Plummer. Harris was happy just to get out of town, get on a plane and shake off the scandal-hunters. Many versions of the break-up were now in circulation. Britain's *Daily Mail* blamed it on Ann's affair with Shaun Cassidy, twenty-year-old brother of the singer David. 'All the gossip said just one thing,' said Ronald Fraser. 'They were leading different lives and there was no point pretending any more.'

Harris skipped the option of confrontation after *Highpoint* and flew back to South Africa on the producer Phillip Baird's invitation to do *Game for Vultures*, based on Michael Hartmann's controversial novel about sanctions busting. American James Fargo, director of Clint Eastwood's popular *Every Which Way But Loose*, also enticed Harris, and the presence of Joan Collins, whom Harris liked and worked well with, was another bonus. The script was good and Harris's best endeavours were briefly aroused. With Fargo, Baird and Collins he participated in long round-table discussions to add humour and punch-up the political aspects. Joan Collins recalled, 'My character was really not an essential part of the story but a lot of humour grew from the improvisations with Richard Harris. Nicolle [my character] was the main woman and I wondered how I could make her more interesting. I think Richard and I succeeded in bringing a touch of deeper characterisation to these roles.'

Game for Vultures, despite all its political echoes, failed miserably, just like *Highpoint* and *The Ravagers.* 'I don't even recall those movies,' Harris revealed, explaining for all the extent of his unease and the chaos of the time. Something happened. I slid away from myself somewhere, or maybe it was just a fashion shift in the industry. It was all that disco era, all *Saturday Night Fever* and Stallone and The Bee Gees, and I had no place in it. It was the same for Burton and O'Toole. Their careers had been mighty. And then, where were they? I felt like a dinosaur, and the scripts I was being offered were rubbish, playing disco managers, that kind of garbage . . .'

The one real opportunity of professional redemption might have been Roy Boulting's LA movie, but Harris was emotionally unwell and Boulting elderly and jaded. *The Last Word* had elements of *It's a Wonderful Life* – in it Harris tackled City Hall in an effort to stop the demolition of a ramshackle apartment block – but script-by-committee, the notorious Hollywood murder weapon, destroyed it. Like *The Last Castle* – indeed, like all the late-seventies films, excepting *The Wild Geese* – *The Last Word* never found an international distributor and further emphasised the imminent end of Richard Harris's career.

By the end of 1979, against all advice and wisdom, Harris was sedating himself in booze. Avoiding Limbridge and Howard, dodging the business meetings he knew would only regurgitate the problems and rows, he sought solace, sometimes with Elizabeth and the boys, often with Jack Donnelly, in whatever hotel Donnelly was managing at the time. The new domestic pattern of hop-skip-jumping from plush Dublin hotels to plush London hotels (with the Savoy always favoured) to Nassau, which was to continue till the end of his life, now dictated his days. With Donnelly, he liked best to reminisce, and his talk was usually about the great days of the Hydro in Kilkee, of remembered girls and fist fights at the chip shop. When he spoke of Ann – to anyone, friend or press – he spoke in the emphatic past tense: 'When you marry a girl so much younger than yourself you start to lose your identity in trying to be what they want you to be, and in trying to keep up. My relationship with Ann was very *Pygmalion*. She was only a very naïve young girl when I met her but she grew into a mature woman. In the end she was demanding so much of me that it was threatening my own career. I quit singing and my acting was sliding. But I got sick of being a part of her life rather than of my own. I couldn't be bothered to keep acting out the parts she wanted me to play at home. She was taking me for granted. I'm too big for that. So I took a walk and left her.'

He told the journalist Simon Kinnersley, 'I've changed a lot recently. I'm not prepared to take on the responsibility of someone else any more. But I'm quite willing to share. I wouldn't mind going back to a series of hot, traumatic affairs . . .' He was speaking from the location of his newest movie, an off-beat psychosexual mélange that started filming in Paris, the city of dreams.

CHAPTER 15

Your Ticket Is No Longer Valid

The love of cinema, once an inferno in Harris's heart, was almost dead. *Your Ticket Is No Longer Valid*, prophetically titled, fired the killing shot.

Marty Baum, Harris's LA agent, found the project, being developed from an obscure Romain Gary novel by Canadian producers Robert Lantos and Stephen Roth, and sent the screenplay to Harris in Toronto during *Highpoint*. Harris liked shooting in Canada, liked the verdant landscape, especially in the summers, when it reminded him of Ireland, and he liked the core of the proposed story, all about male impotence. In a careful gesture that was a throwback to the meticulous sixties, he asked to see the original novel and hunted it down himself when the producers failed to deliver it. As Lantos and Roth had pitched it, the movie was slight; but Harris saw possibilities for the first time in years. With a lot of imagination the movie might, just *might*, measure up to the *Sporting Life* league and blanche out some of the damage of *Bloomfield*. When Lantos spoke of the picture as a potential *Last Tango in Paris*, Harris was further enthused. The meeting with the director George Kaczender was also reassuring. The chemistry was right and, against the odds, Harris's approach was suddenly reminiscent of the Lindsay Anderson era. He researched Kaczender, whom he had never previously met, and watched a copy of his popular hit, *In Praise of Older Women*. Harris only half-liked the movie: 'It appeared to me to have fragments of such cohesion, and then such sloppiness [but] I

252

put it down to editing problems.' Kaczender excused himself, explaining that the film had been taken out of his hands in postproduction. According to Harris, Lantos then promised Harris full creative participation in the still incomplete script for *Ticket*, which would be shot not just in Canada, but in Paris and Nice.

Still unsure that the story and the people measured up, Harris hesitated. To help his decision he sent the script to Eugene Landy, the radical LA psychologist famous for rehabilitating the troubled Beach Boys genius Brian Wilson. Harris met with Landy and compiled 52 pages of notes. These he handed to Kaczender and the producers for discussion. No discussion ensued. The essential teamwork, requested from the start, was faulty, but it didn't prepare Harris for what he later described as Lantos's 'ultimate betrayal of his trust'.

Harris agreed to do the movie, which he considered 'a last shot at art' provided Lantos, Roth and Kaczender accepted his suggestions for revisions and his usual recent contract clause of cast approval. Lantos then informed Harris that George Peppard, the *Breakfast At Tiffany*'s star, would be cast as his co-lead. Harris liked Peppard, whom he had met while Peppard was shooting *The Blue Max* at Ardmore in Ireland years before. 'Richard and I were like brothers,' said Peppard. 'We'd struck a really good friendship, getting blind drunk together in Dublin. I had the utmost regard for him as a masterful actor, an actor of the first order. I was attracted to this film because of him. But, to be truthful, my career was in the gutter at that time. No one in Hollywood would touch me with a stick, so I was pleased when these producers came along with a script with potential.' The make-or-break casting in the script, Peppard observed, was the girl, the 'highly charged sexual magnet who resolves Ogilvy's [Harris's] sexual neuroses'. Both Peppard and Harris were insistent that this role be carefully cast. Lantos showed Harris three photographs of prospective young actresses, among them a newcomer called Jennifer Dale. After discussions, Harris approved Dale in the role of Laura, the twenty-year-old Brazilian heroine. What Lantos neglected to tell Harris was that Dale was his girlfriend, and that he had already cast her. When Harris found out he confronted Lantos, who played dumb. Dale, said Lantos, was his *ex*-mistress – which was untrue.

Your Ticket Is No Longer Valid began shooting 'under the nervous direction of Kaczender, a man who doesn't like to go to war', according to George Peppard, in the autumn of 1979. After several days Harris had his first scene with Dale, which was a lovemaking scene. Harris, already depressed by the apparent insincerity of the producer, was horrified to find Dale directing him. 'The young lady, carried away by her position, began to explain to me in front of the entire company what the scene was about and where the camera would be placed. All my fears came out in that one moment, that her situation with Lantos was not over. It was an intolerable situation for me. I blew. No question about me letting off steam. I told her that she may be a very, very brilliant director and a very brilliant young lady, but I signed a contract with Mr Kaczender to direct the picture . . . and then I walked away to my trailer.'

George Peppard, who had no scenes with Dale, became quickly aware of Harris's upset. 'Lantos called me aside after a few days, the girl beside him, and told me Richard was being a problem, that the movie was in trouble. They begged my assistance and expected me to help. They were a little surprised when I told them I was on Richard's side. He was, I knew, very professional, and it was obvious to me that the girl was inappropriate for the story. She was the wrong actress in every way: wrong attitude, wrong persona, exuding nothing of the sexual energy the part called for.'

The film disintegrated. Lantos made gestures to placate Harris, agreeing to rewrites. But Dale remained in place, deeply offending Harris. 'I know the accusation could be made that I played by the same rules, that I pushed Ann [as an actress],' said Harris. 'But my creative instincts always came first, I believe. I knew when it wasn't possible or right – as in *Orca*. But this situation was abuse.'

Harris says he worked harder than he had done since Antonioni on *Ticket*, sometimes as many as eighteen hours nonstop per day. But Kaczender's control was 'negligible' and the collusion of the others sickened him. When Ann came to visit the Canadian location in an attempt to discuss their marriage deadlock, Harris jumped at the distraction. But the visit went awry. Harris told *Cinema Canada*, 'The hotel room had a winding oak stairs to the bedroom. Lantos called to talk to me . . . and heard a noise from the bedroom and accused me of having somebody up there listening to our conversation. I told him there was a lady up there. He said I had somebody listening for evidence. I asked him, "For what evidence?" He then accused me of tape-recording our conversation. It was sheer paranoia. He said the atmosphere wasn't congenial to discussion about the script. I shouted up to Ann and she eventually came down and introduced herself as my wife. It was like Watergate, it was ridiculous.'

The paranoia destroyed any qualities that the movie might have yielded, George Peppard believed. 'Richard showed no signs of lethargy, but the film he signed to do, that film *I* signed to do, wasn't the one that got made.' Harris retreated as he saw his great 'last chance' go up in smoke. 'I started backing off, and it felt terminal.' But he rallied when Marty Baum and John Van Eyssan, chief of production for British Columbia, saw a rough cut of various scenes and embraced him. Van Eyssan told him, 'You are going to win an Academy Award, finally. This is a stunning performance.'

Lantos, meanwhile, continued to cut the film. He told *Films and Filming*, 'I think a lot of people will hate it, but absolutely no one will walk out of the theatre after seeing it and be indifferent towards it, or not talk about it. Because for the last half-hour you will be in a state of shock.' At the public test screening in Montreal three months later, the audience was shocked – by boredom. Harris raged: 'It was unrecognisible.' Peppard perceived 'a mess. This was the kind of movie you can't jazz up. You had to let it run its time. It's not like a big commercial film where everything jumps along. It needed depth and space. It could have been wonderful, the subject was good, but they turned it into a stupid, hip film centred around this colourless girl.'

The emphasis on Ogilvy's sexual identity problem – the power of the story – had been elbowed out in favour of a glitzy projection of Pin-up Dale. Harris explained to *Cinema Canada*, 'I had this wonderful idea about the finale. At the end my character decides to commit suicide. Before he does he takes off his hairpiece and he looks like a grotesque caricature of a human being, with the little band-aids that keep the hairpiece in place. The director wondered whether the scene would be advisable, given my "image". I didn't care about "image". He said [my idea] was staggering, but Lantos had objections. It transpired he objected to the [implied] homosexuality. His objections were based on the fact that it would lower Dale's appeal to the audience to see her fall in love with a man who's gay and wears a hairpiece and high-heeled shoes – which was the plot to begin with.'

Harris tried to buy back the film. It had cost $6 million, of which his fee was his now regular $1 million. Marty Baum supported Harris, promising to raise $5 million on his own bat to reacquire 'every single bit of footage, the soundtrack, continuity sheets, everything'. Lantos resisted the purchase offer.

'I was destitute,' said Harris poetically. 'I rang them time and again, begging them. I offered to fly to Montreal at no cost and offered to pay for re-editing if they gave me the opportunity to assemble the picture as it was in its proper form. If I could just recut, and take out fifteen or twenty minutes . . .'

While Lantos was away in Europe, Roth conceded and sneaked Harris back to Montreal to facilitate some re-editing. But then Lantos returned and, said Harris, 'went berserk'. Lantos later told *Cinema Canada* magazine that Harris had 'sabotaged' his movie – then went ahead and released his 'Dale version'. Harris fought till the bitter end, belatedly taking three pages in *Cinema Canada* to state his case. The 'brutalisation' of the movie, he said, sickened him. He had done his best against loaded odds, and a wonderful opportunity for producers and audience had been lost.

Much more, of course, had been sacrificed. *Ticket*, even George Peppard acknowledged, *could* have been Harris's reissued passport to committed movie endeavour. Instead, with apparent finality, it closed the door.

'*Bloomfield* and *Your Ticket is No Longer Valid* were the real tragedies for Dick,' said Ronald Fraser. 'All along he was trying to get back to the pace he set with *This Sporting Life*, and those were the ones that seemed to be the opportunities. Dickie Burton gave up, too. And Peter [O'Toole]. Finally, you accept that it's just a business for traders. That no one really cares about much except money. I think that's why so many movie artists are boozers and druggies. They call you "artist", but they want you to be a prostitute.'

Nothing more than an act of friendship brought Harris to John and Bo Derek's *Tarzan, the Ape Man*, shot in the jungles of Sri Lanka the following year, 1981. 'I love the Dereks,' was his all-embracing explanation of his involvement. John Phillip Law co-starred and witnessed strange goings on. 'I didn't like Bo as much as Richard evidently did,' he said. 'But I had a lot of time and respect for John, who was a fair dealer. John's approach to making the movie was to take a needle and stick it right through the globe of the world and see whereabouts is the absolute polar extreme from LA. He wanted to get as far away from Hollywood as he could. I think Richard rose to that joyfully. That part of it was fine for me, too. I'm one of those outdoorsy camper types who'll muck in and go native anywhere. But Bo tried to bring western civilisation with her. Food was brought from LA, which of course went bad en route and poisoned everyone. Then one day I opened a door beside the make-up room in one of the unit bases and found five hundred toilet rolls from Bloomingdales! That was Bo's private stock of LA toilet paper.'

John Derek was ostensibly director, but Law watched Bo take charge. 'She was on a roll after [the hit] *10,* and was cashing in. John let her go out of control and Richard didn't really give a damn. He let her get away with it too, I think because he was jaded and angry with life and everything . . . and he *hugely* overplayed his part. Me, I hugely underplayed. In between was room for Bo to do whatever she wanted – and what she wanted was to do the dazzling star thing.'

Throughout, said Law, Harris tried, but couldn't shake the booze. 'He was such a good guy and so well liked by all the natives, a gentleman in his heart. But every now and then he'd hit the bottle bad and be really, really, really ill. Production was held up several times when he overdid it, and collapsed. It was very worrying, but then he'd pull himself back together, scraping himself together, and forge on.'

'I kept a diary of the days,' said Harris. 'I was contracted for forty-two days' work. And I look back on that diary, which reads: "Forty-one days to go till completion . . . only forty days to go . . . only thirty-nine days left . . ." I realised it was the end of the line. I didn't want to make movies any more. The whole process just annoyed and bored me. That was it. That was the moment it ended for me. I said, spiritually, I am out of here. From now on, a new life.'

Tarzan cost $8 million, though Law said, 'I'll be damned if I saw more than $3 million spent. They must have dug a hole and done something with the rest.' But Harris was, he said, sufficiently rewarded. Law contends, 'He and I came out very well financially – that was [the reason both of us had] for doing it in the first place – but we were equally delighted to get back on the plane for New York and just forget about it.'

The expected divorce application, on the grounds of incompatibility, had already been filed in Nassau and Harris wanted temporarily to avoid the confrontations of the Bahamas or Beverly Hills. Jack Donnelly said, 'It was all raw and tender. He was vulnerable in a fight with Ann and they'd said enough. He just wanted to move on.' But in New York he received a frantic business call, summoning him back to LA. The touring stage production of *Camelot*, starring Burton, was in serious trouble and the producers reckoned that Richard Harris, the original celluloid King, might be their salvation.

Harris was only 'vaguely aware' of Richard Burton's health problems. Since the previous June, Burton had been back on the road, reviving his 1960 creation. But his health had been deteriorating all along. Apart from fighting alcoholism, he had continual agonising pain in his right arm, diagnosed as a pinched nerve. Most of the time on stage he couldn't lift the sword Excalibur and his arm swung lifeless. In April the tour arrived at the Pantages Theater in LA, but Burton survived only six performances. He was admitted to St John's Hospital in Santa Monica, where two days of tests revealed a degenerative condition of the cervical vertebrae in the spine. Surgery was advised and Burton, underweight and exhausted, was sent to bed to build himself up for the operation. It was clear that his touring days were over, but the show was booked months in advance. 'The producers called because I was the obvious replacement,' said Harris, 'but their timing couldn't have been worse. I was at the point of deciding I wanted to secure the divorce, go to Nassau and write like Hemingway for the rest of my days. Life might be good again. A beer on the beach at sunset, a few naked women in the bay . . . But then I was told Dick [Burton] asked for me. So I told the producers, "If it's true let him call and ask me personally." And he did. He said, "Dickie, you'd be doing us all a favour." And he was my friend, so I said yes.'

Harris flew to LA on 3 April and held a press conference to introduce himself as the new King Arthur. In view of the production crisis the tour director, who had long since departed for London, was summoned back. Frank Dunlop, founder of the Young Vic, was forced to address the show from scratch. Harris said, 'Richard [Burton] and I approach the part in a totally different way. He plays it as a man born to greatness. I play it as a man with greatness thrust upon him. It is a fundamental, but vital, difference.'

Rehearsals were, surprisingly for Harris, invigorating. Though still prone to fainting spells, he lapped up eight five-hour work-throughs and seven two-and-a-half-hour musical sessions, harmonising well with Meg Bussert as Guinevere and Richard Muenz as Lancelot. The grace and grandeur of the old battlehorse came back to him. King Arthur was his pop heyday; it was gratifying to relive it.

Burton underwent his operation successfully and flew back to his home in Switzerland to recuperate, bidding adieu to *Camelot* for ever, and Harris opened, wrung with anxiety but bang on schedule, on 13 April. It was his theatrical comeback after an absence of nearly twenty years.

Variety, among many others, loved the rejigged show and approved of the new King Arthur: 'Harris plays the role for laughs and is a more pixyish king than either Burton or William Parry [Burton's understudy, who would remain Harris's understudy].'

Credit for the new *zing* wasn't all Harris's, though: 'Perhaps the best thing that has come out of the problems caused by Burton's illness was the fact that director Frank Dunlop came back for more rehearsals. Aren't road directors supposed to keep an eye on the show even if the star *doesn't get sick?*' The criticism seemed petty against the obvious triumph: crammed houses, standing ovations, myriad extended tour offers in Asia and Australia.

Harris signed with a new British agent during *Camelot*, indicating a reborn theatrical impetus. 'But it was desperation, too. Because it was reaching a point in movies where I was unemployable anyway in the eyes of some people. My concern then was money. Dermot and I talked about our options all the time, and he had the problem of my realities. Because I wasn't interested in films any more, and income had got to be found . . . because no one lives on fresh air.' Harris later confessed to 'two occasions in the seventies and early eighties where I was so financially stretched that I sold jewellery.' Jack Donnelly thought this unlikely. 'He lived well, and he was the kind of person who wouldn't give up a nice lifestyle . . . so that alone would motivate him. Even if he never wanted to make another movie, he'd get out of bed and write a book, or make a record or . . . whatever it took.'

In the circumstances, *Camelot* held him together. Arrangements were made to take the show to London, and the Apollo Victoria was booked for a limited season the following year. Talks of other London stage work began. In his recent years on the road Harris had written his own stage play, called *Miscast in Carrickfergus*, for which, his agent announced, a venue was being sought. The story was 'vintage heyday autobiography, about me, about Dylan Thomas and Richard Burton and Peter O'Toole, about a kind of corruption, where somebody is born with a gift which is native to their environment in Wales or Ireland and then, to express it, they have to emigrate and be absorbed by another culture, a more sophisticated society, where the gift is chipped away.' The poignancy of personal anguish was unmissable. 'There was a lot of depression at that time,' said Ronald Fraser. 'Elizabeth had written a super play, too, and people were saying it was about her love life, though I doubt that's true. But Dick was trying to sort himself out, really, like doing "the psychiatrist" on himself with analytical writing. He was a gifted writer, a great letter writer, too.'

After seven weeks at the Pantages, *Camelot* hit the road for a gruelling summer tour fractured by Harris's health problems. In Detroit, Harris collapsed in the middle of the first act. When the call for a doctor in the house went up, Harris said, 'Twenty-eight doctors queued up, examined me and asked for my autograph.' Hospitalised again, he was informed his condition had deteriorated: 'I had the impression of a very pleasant, not especially concerned, doctor standing by my bed, telling me, "I think, if it goes on like this, you have about eighteen months to live." I asked him what I had to do [to survive], and he said, "Stop the piss" – so I did.'

On 11 August 1981 at the Jockey Club in Washington Harris ordered two bottles of vintage Château Margaux and shared them joyously with his musical associate and friend Terry James. 'They tasted', he said, eyes shut tight to the memory, 'like nectar.' He didn't recall the year or the price of the wine (he had never been a connoisseur); all he knew was that it was the best alcohol he ever consumed. Proud of his discipline after just a few weeks, he told the *Indianapolis Independent News*, 'I could sail the *QE2* to the Falklands on all the liquor I drank. I'm off it now, and I'm a very dull man.' For Jack Donnelly, the commitment was astonishing: 'I never thought I'd see the day, but he made the pledge and it lasted him for ten years.' In the early nineties, Harris returned to 'the odd glass of Guinness', which remained his daily companion till the day he died.

The American touring success culminated on Broadway, where Harris had never played, and which, with his renewed discipline and relative health, he relished. Burton had started the tour at the Lincoln Center, but Harris's 'homecoming' version almost doubled ticket sales. His widely applauded opening at the Winter Garden was coordinated with a 'semi-live' taping of the show for transmission by Home Box Office, the cable television giant. Harris declared himself ecstatic, but jaded. 'We taped our show in the middle of his run in January,' said Cathy Fitzpatrick, HBO's associate producer. 'It was a nightmare. First and foremost there was a row with Don Gregory, the tour producer, who came to see what we were doing and immediately clashed head-on with Richard. And, when I say "clashed", I mean war. For a minute, I thought someone might get killed.'

Harris, Gregory and Mike Merrick, the other tour producer, had been on bad terms since the summer. Cathy Fitzpatrick said, 'Richard was, to me, personally very charming, but he was ill, that was obvious. It was a freezing, terrible winter, to make things worse. The flare-up began when Richard appeared late for a run-through call. He'd requested time off, but Gregory ignored him and called him anyway, since he was needed for camera checks. It descended into a fist fight, with Marty Callner, the director, trying to get between Richard and Gregory. Richard walked out and refused to proceed with the shooting unless Gregory was removed. That was really tricky, because we were doing it in sections, and quite a lot was with the live Broadway audience.'

Harris and Gregory avoided each other during the next fortnight as Harris struggled to keep pace. 'He was very, very tired,' said Fitzpatrick, 'and his voice failed. We lost quite a few days with him, which necessitated a new schedule that overran considerably.' Harris delighted in HBO's patience. Michael Fuchs, the HBO chief, called to cast an eye on the settling storm and professed himself confident in Harris and in the quality of the production, HBO's most expensive show ever. 'Whatever Richard didn't get done vocally at the Winter Garden he caught up with in dubbing in LA,' said Fitzpatrick. 'I watched him working there and was impressed by his immense care in creating the vocal mood, especially for "How to Handle a Woman".'

Marty Callner had 125 TV specials with the likes of Steve Martin, Diana Ross and Victor Borge under his belt and gave the taped *Camelot* his all. One hundred and twenty camera filters were tested to find the perfect "softness" for the mystical atmosphere. Eventually a $2 pair of womens' tights did the job. Forty thousand pounds of dry ice was employed to achieve a suitable misty romance. In the end the unedited footage ran to 116 hours, which was finally cut to two and a half. On its HBO screening in September, the *New York Times* applauded 'a memorable majestic and troubled king ... [Harris] skillfully elevates a serviceable musical to surprisingly moving drama'.

The moving drama of his personal life raged on. Still resisting the divorce, Ann continued a determined partnership with director Barbara Peters, whom she had met during an unseen low-budget Roger Corman flick called *Beneath the Darkness*, with the intention of developing her own productions. The M & J Production Company, said Ann, would concentrate on self-scripted films, starting with *Brother, Sister*, written jointly by Barbara and her. With great self-assurance she sidestepped questions from the press about the inevitability of a final split with Harris. On the contrary, she insisted, Harris would star in Barbara's film, *The Indian Who Sold Brooklyn Bridge*, which was allegedly in advanced preproduction for M & J.

Harris's viewpoint was different. He'd had enough and, though the Bahamian courts insisted on one last try for reconciliation, he dismissed the possibility. After 421 performances of *Camelot* – 'to 421 standing ovations of fifteen or twenty minutes' – he ended in a blaze of glory and returned to the Bahamas 'to put the whole business of the marriage to bed for once and for all'. Ann visited him, but there was no peace pact. He told the journalist William Marshall, 'I have given Annie a new plan for our marriage. From now on I'm dedicated to living my life as Richard Harris, egomaniac. I have told her we will spend roughly one week out of four together. If she doesn't like that, it's the end of our marriage.'

It was. In September the divorce was finalised, once again with an undisclosed, but, said Jack Donnelly, 'very substantial' settlement for Ann. Harris celebrated as only Harris would – cheekily and dangerously. Back in London for talks with Dermot and Terry Baker, the new agent, he ran into Susie Burton, who was in the process of divorcing Richard. 'I asked her out for a date,' said Harris. 'But she refused me, saying she didn't think it would be proper. I said, "Why not? I'm used to replacing Richard."' Susie Burton's response was unreported.

Harris had clearly won a new lease of life with *Camelot*. Certainly the industry offers became more flattering. A big-budget tour of

James Hilton's *Goodbye, Mr Chips* and a musical cable special of Dickens's *A Christmas Carol* both interested him, and though he later dropped out of both, the bottom-line economics galvanised him. The combined fees for him personally, he worked out, would be in excess of $3.5 million. 'I can't do that well in movies,' he told the *Los Angeles Herald Examiner*. Later he said, 'My back was against the wall, both professionally and emotionally. And then I looked again at what *Camelot* did for me. It brought order back into my life. I went to bed a little earlier, and was forced to watch my diet, cut out the booze, reorganise. At that point it seemed clever to take stock and build my life around the advantage I had, which was the public's view of me as the one and only King Arthur.'

Inspired, he negotiated to purchase the touring rights of *Camelot* from Alan Jay Lerner. 'I thought, I've given a chunk of my life to this King Arthur. I've been good to him. It's time for him to be good to me.' The deal was the canniest and best-rewarding of Harris's life. In subsequent touring over the next six years, *Camelot* would earn $92 million – outdoing Rex Harrison's box-office for *My Fair Lady* – of which Harris personally grossed nearly $8 million. He took great pride in this stroke of business genius, telling friends and strangers alike with equal candour about the multimillion *Camelot* rewards that finally liberated him from the tyranny of movie-chasing. 'I'm in a wonderful position now,' was his standard recital. 'I can make a movie if I want to. I don't have to feel *I have to*. What *Camelot* has given me is "fuck off" money.'

Before opening with a new British cast at the Apollo Victoria in November 1982, Harris took Sandy Howard's invitation to join a third *Horse* movie in Mexico – 'because I felt like it, period'. The script was of little interest, and the resulting film showed Harris's extreme apathy towards movies at this time. 'It was a mistake for both of us,' said Sandy Howard. 'I let Richard down with *Triumphs of a Man Called Horse*. It was misconceived, and I put the wrong people on it. The source material was sound – Jack De Witt had again written a really good script for us, just before he died – but most of the other people on the production were wrong. John Hough, the director, did his best. But the script we ended up with, after all those production committee rewrites, was shit and I pushed Richard, and in the end felt we misused him. He's too good for that sort of idiot movie. I feel sorry for that.'

Triumphs – rightly – made no money and finished the cycle of *Horse* movies, but Harris didn't care. He opened *Camelot* in London to good notices but lousy business. Announced to run till May, the play folded after a couple of weeks. Harris pocketed his fee and jetted back, alone, to Nassau, comforting himself with the heavy slate of upcoming foreign *Camelot* tours.

The house was lonelier now, mostly stripped of Ann's possessions. But he had all the company and comfort he needed, he told Jack Donnelly, in his staff – and Jamie's 'drunk and disorderly' charge, which hung, framed, on the verandah beside his favourite wicker chair.

CHAPTER 16

Field of Dreams

These months of Bahamian seclusion – uninterrupted by romance or booze – represented one of the longest periods of reflection since the start of Harris's hectic career. Genuine reassessment, not the usual bullying reaffirmation, was the order of the day. 'He was immediately a different man without the drink,' said the actor Godfrey Quigley. Many other friends echoed this. Undeniably he matured, and took time to look at his life without prejudice. To friends and foes he confessed that there was much of the past that was unknown to him. Burton, for instance, had told him of their three encounters before *The Wild Geese*; Harris could recollect only one. It had all been great fun, good laughs – but at whose expense? It struck him that he had lived most of his drunken life not for himself, but for an audience. He had overplayed the game expected of him. 'After all, your life is your memories. So what life have I had?' he complained to Jack Donnelly that Christmas.

Camelot put him back on the road in a series of tough whistle-stops through Australia, North America and Japan. A lesser spirit might have been crippled with the boredom of early-morning flights from town to town, the same faces in the company, the same hoarse songs. But Harris took endless pride in it. All the same, he would not, he pledged, 'work it to death like Yul Brynner did with *The King and I*. When the magic goes and I don't get a buzz from singing "How to Handle a Woman", I'll stop.'

In this phase of his celebrity, the one conspicuous and dangerous change was the mood of the media. Having curtsied in his court for years, the worm turned. The contradictions of the limelight years – and his media naïveté – came back to haunt him. In 1973, during his poetry period, he had pinned his colours to the IRA. A planned anti-internment movie, he'd claimed on more than one occasion, had only been elbowed to 'give a chance' to the newly formed Northern Ireland Assembly. But he wouldn't stand down. When the Tory Opposition leader Edward Heath visited Nassau, Harris and Kevin McClory had taken a full page ad in the *Nassau Tribune*, demanding an end to internment without trial. Heath's response was a press conference in which he advised Harris and McClory to 'ask their friends to stop murdering people'. Incensed, Harris was the poet-activist again, releasing a statement through Associated Press, damning 'the deliberate policy of discrimination enforced in the British-occupied areas of the artificial state'.

Shortly afterwards, his attendance at a dinner for NORAID – a fundraiser for the IRA – had severe repercussions. In the middle of negotiating a role in Jack Higgin's *The Eagle Has Landed*, which featured a wartime IRA man dropped into Britain to kidnap Churchill, Harris was forced to quit because of threats to the producers. Fearing reprisals, Harris readjusted his stance, publicly declaring that he was not a NORAID supporter, and had been misrepresented in his particular brand of Republicanism.

Then came the Harrods' Christmas bombing of 1983. In Florida for *Camelot*, journalists pressed for a reaction and Harris stumbled into a minefield of contradictions. The IRA action was 'horribly wrong, but understandable,' said Harris. In his view 'that arrogant lady, the British prime minister' wanted to keep the trouble going. 'Do you think she gives a shit about those innocent people getting killed? She says, "Perfect, great, now [the IRA] are going to lose support in America."'

This misdirected knee-jerk resulted in an avalanche of hate mail and the worst coordinated negative press Harris had ever experienced. Horrified, he tried to fight back. But many newspapers, including his original champion, the *Daily Mirror*, went into all-out attack mode, implying, if not outrightly accusing him, of treachery, deception, media manipulation and proactive association with the IRA.

When the *Republican News*, Sinn Fein's newspaper, advertised Harris's endorsement of the IRA, a firm, unconditional stand was finally taken. He was not, he announced, an IRA supporter at all: 'The Harrods' bombing put an end to all that.' In former years, he admitted, he had been 'hoodwinked' into attending a NORAID dinner, but he had long since lost any sympathies for the cause. His statement ended: 'I could never condone or excuse IRA violence in any form.'

But the miscalculation and response winded him. Jack Donnelly saw him 'profoundly upset, because he'd shot his mouth off. There were many times when I'd said to him, "Be careful, Dick, because [the media] won't always stay for supper. They won't hang around for you to explain in fine detail what you mean when you splurt out this or that." With the IRA row he saw the media in a new light. "I thought they understood me," he said very innocently. But I told him that that's not the way it goes. They build you up, and they can tear you down.' Chastened, Harris drew up the drawbridge and withdrew from political commentating, though the consequences of his naïveté left their mark. Throughout the eighties a Special Branch *Garda* officer in plain clothes kept him company whenever he went on the town in Dublin. In social encounters, the officer was introduced as 'Sean' or 'Declan', without the true biography. As far as Harris's guests or cronies knew, 'Sean' was a pal of yore who liked the theatre, and a pint. Nationalist politics were rarely openly discussed.

After a year of self-questioning on the road with *Camelot*, Harris felt the need to repair the swan-song disaster of *Triumphs of a Man Called Horse*. To the surprise of many, he agreed to the lead role in *Martin's Day*, a small movie shot in his beloved Canada. For once, the elements came into proper alignment, and the movie was substantial. Directed for UA by Alan Gibson, the movie reunited Harris with his old friend James Coburn, but was mostly distinguished for its exceptional photography by Frank Watts and for the performance of Justin Henry, the child actor from *Kramer vs. Kramer*. *Variety* found it wanting, but Harris devotees like Joe

Lynch and Ronald Fraser found the portrayal of a simple-minded criminal who kidnaps a child, then goes in search of his own childhood, among the finest of his career. Unfortunately, since no cinema chains in the UK showed any interest, distribution was negligible and Harris seemed, said Lynch, all but forgotten by the audiences who had first discovered him.

On the surface, Harris didn't appear concerned. By the middle eighties, in his own widely disseminated description, he was unassailably rich (thanks to *Camelot* and the payback on Dermot's property investments in LA), reformed and self-assured. But the background story was different. Elizabeth's divorce from Rex Harrison and subsequent marriage to Lord Beaverbrook's grandson Jonathan Aitken – an unstable union from the beginning – upset him, as, much more, did the circulating word of his youngest son Jamie's drug addiction. In the heat of marital rows, Elizabeth found comfort again in company of her ex, and together they addressed a plan to help Jamie. Harris had bought and furnished an apartment for his son, but they discovered to their horror that Jamie had sold 'everything except the doors on their hinges' to support a heroin habit. In the intermittent breaks from *Camelot*, Harris regularly met Elizabeth in London and Dublin to try to rehabilitate Jamie. 'It's a decision he had to make himself ultimately,' said Harris. 'As a parent, you can support and give love, but the addicted person has to choose, himself, to quit. Fortunately, Jamie did.'

The anguish over Jamie was leavened somewhat by the progress of the other boys. Jared had started out declaring an interest in law, but turned to theatre and, after a variety of study courses, found employment with the Royal Shakespeare Company. Damian, as he had promised, graduated from film school, acquired an agent and made his move towards directing, ultimately debuting with an admirable version of Martin Amis's *The Rachel Papers* in 1989. 'All the boys made me happy because of their distinctive individualism. I was their friend, not their dad. Each educated me, more than the other way round. Jamie's spirit was angelic, totally extraordinary, and [in his addiction troubles] he paid the poet's price. Jared always looked like me, physically and psychologically. He was wild and free and acting from the day he was born. Damian was more mature at age twelve than I was at thirty. He showed me the meaning of discipline, and I thought, always thought, he had huge dignity. All my children were the greatest works of art . . . and I have Elizabeth to thank, because she gave them life and she gave them her spirit.'

In the winter of 1985 Harris and Dermot were back on the road in America with *Camelot*. During a visit to Scranton, the university town in Pennsylvania, they had dinner with and befriended Fr Panuska, the Jesuit president of the university. An immediate affinity was established. Despite their personal educational ups and downs, all the Harrises had a special place in their hearts for the benefits of Jesuit teaching methods. Dermot had been educated at Rockwell College in Tipperary, another Jesuit stronghold. The brothers agreed they had no regrets and told Fr Panuska that they wished more Irish students had access to Jesuit education. Dermot was fervent and articulate about the tragedy of Irish youth battling a class system and low living standards that made higher education impossible for so many.

When the tour moved to Chicago, to another rapturous welcome, Harris was in fine form but Dermot was tired. 'He almost never missed a performance,' said Harris. 'He was my anchor on the road. When the storms blew, it was always his face in the dressing-room doorway, saying, "Cool it".' In Chicago Dermot fell ill with chest pains and returned to his hotel to rest while Harris trod the boards. During the evening, with his condition worsening, an ambulance was called and he was transferred to hospital. When Harris took his curtain call he was told of Dermot's collapse. He grabbed a coat and hurried to the hospital, his make-up still intact. 'By the time I reached Dermot's bedside in the intensive-care unit it was too late. I collapsed. I couldn't bear to see him. I took one look at him, and I asked them to draw the curtains. Then I sat with him for an hour, with the curtains drawn.' The heart attack had been massive, the damage irreparable. Dermot passed away in the early hours.

Returning to Limerick with his brother's body, Harris was, said Len Dineen, 'a completely different man. More into himself, more remote than he'd ever been. To Limerick folk, he had always been just plain Dickie. But time doesn't stand still. Everything changes, and people forget.' The funeral mass at Our Lady of the Rosary church on the Ennis Road, not far from the family home, was well attended, but Harris told Dineen he was disappointed at the turnout. Another Limerick friend felt 'he was unrealistic. The part of him that never stopped looking for Limerick's approval wanted some fanfare that would have been inappropriate anyway. But ... it was his brother, whom he idolised, so perhaps it's understandable. Nothing, no bunting or bugles, would have been good enough, because it was Dermot he was burying.' Elizabeth flew in from London, and Dermot's two children by his marriage to Cassandra stood by. Pupils from the Crescent, pals, rugby cronies and a few old girlfriends stood out in the crowd. 'It brought me to my knees,' said Harris. 'A woman came up to me and kissed my cheek and shook my hand. And then I looked deep into her eyes and I knew who she was: she was a girl I had held in my arms and kissed forty years ago. But she wasn't a girl any more. She was an old lady. And I was an old man. She stood there before me, all wrinkled and aged, her hands, her belly, all shrivelled, and I was thinking, Look at her. I once hungered for those lips, I once dreamed about those breasts, I once lay awake pining for her. And she was looking at me, thinking, Look at him. His hair is dyed, his skin is sagging, he's old and tired.'

Dermot's loss took the fizz out of touring *Camelot*. With his friend and manager removed from his side, Harris no longer wanted to be on the road. After the funeral he took Concorde back to New York and worked out his contract, but he had 'wrung it all dry. I saw no purpose in the loneliness of the road without Dermot. Elizabeth and I were closer, and I was friends with Annie, whom I talked to all the time on the phone. But the blood was gone out of it. What do you do when your partner is gone? Do you sit on a bed in Boise and count the shillings you earned last night? I couldn't do that, so I wound it down.'

In December Harris launched a scholarship fund at Scranton University in his brother's memory. Fr Panuska was astonished by the generosity and commitment. 'I am moved by this remarkable intention by a person whose acquaintance with Scranton, and the

University of Scranton, is so recent,' he said. Harris said the duty was due. The fates had taken him and Dermot to Scranton in the closing days of Dermot's life, to remind them both. The rallying of support among the new Jesuit friends at the time of Dermot's death was also deeply inspirational. They had taken it on themselves to look after the funeral arrangements, and counselled Harris, and been there to talk to in the long, difficult nights.

The Scranton Fund, it was agreed, would sponsor at least one Irish scholar's attendance at the university every year. For nostalgia's sake, the first student would be a Limerick boy, from the Crescent. After that, students would come from all over Ireland, North and South. 'It will be good for education and the arts, and for cultural integration,' said Fr Panuska. 'Mr Harris is a visionary man.'

Back in Ireland Harris worked exclusively for months promoting the fund. His aim, he said, was to raise the $500,000 needed to perpetuate the scholarship. 'It's time nations started to understand nations, and education and educational-cultural exchanges have to be the way forward. I am not a politician. I am not an activist. But, as a human being, I owe it to those who deserve it to use what powers I have on their behalf.' He had little trouble finding high-level supporters, among them the *taoiseach* Charles Haughey, who pledged himself as patron, and Cardinal O'Connor, the Archbishop of New York. Aer Lingus, the national airline, agreed to fund flights, and 'the hit list' of imminent supporters, said Harris, included Vice-President George Bush, Rod Stewart and the actors Carroll O'Connor and Gene Kelly.

The church connections prompted questions about his religious rebirth and, in the heat of the moment, Harris declared an epiphany: he was 'a born-again Catholic' with a mission to accomplish in honour of his wonderful brother, who had been 'like a son to me'. He went on: 'There is no doubt that I've trod an exceedingly immoral path, a Rabelaisian drunken life, through nonbelief. Now I have become so Catholic you wouldn't believe it. I've become a traditional, conservative Catholic. I believe the church dogma should not be changed. I believe in what Pope John Paul advocates. I don't believe in the ordination of women. I don't believe in abortion.

Contraception I would argue about. I don't believe the Church should change in this almost Sodom and Gomorrah world we now live in.'

Comprehensively reformed? The journalist Lise Hand of the *Sunday Independent* interviewed him at the Berkeley Court Hotel, Jack Donnelly's latest management assignment. Armed with a brace of modified questions as befitted 'Richard Harris Mk 2', she found herself wriggling round his suite instead. She wrote, 'Some things never change. Once a rogue, always a rogue, despite all protestations to the contrary.' The interview was tough going – 'only because it's difficult to take notes when a big, strong man keeps trying to wrestle you to the couch or insists that you haven't seen the whole suite until you've seen the bedroom'.

Donnelly saw him as 'a lovable rogue. He *had* changed after Dermot's death, but a rose is still a rose . . .' For the interviews, unlike Hand, who managed to keep him seated and sated, Harris was in mood for resignation, not re-evaluation. 'We are all unfulfilled,' he told *The Times*. 'Look at Olivier: all he ever wanted to be was the world's greatest actor. Yet privately he always envied Richard Burton's life – the wine, the women, the waste. And all the time Richard and I were envying his discipline.'

The gloom foreshadowed *Maigret*, a TV movie comeback of sorts, shot in Paris, London and Tenerife by HTV in association with a small American production company. Harris feigned enthusiasm, declaring himself a fan of *Maigret* and author Georges Simenon ever since John Huston had introduced him to the books on the set of *Man in the Wilderness*. He had read, he said, 60 of the 104 Maigret novels and had always wanted the role. The movie's budget was small, just $3 million, but Harris's presence elevated it above the run-of-the-mill. George Weingarten, the American producer who launched the project, had been introduced to Simenon by his friend Graham Greene. Ever cautious of bastardised versions of his hero, Simeneon resisted until told that Richard Harris might play Maigret. 'After that,' said Weingarten, 'it was all downhill. Simeneon saw Harris as an actor of quality in the first league, a historic actor.'

Harris played the role 'for peanuts', because of the cachet of Simeneon. 'Maigret is a legend, and it's not often one gets challenged to play mythical characters.' But his application seemed pedestrian: 'I chose a soft hat, a duffel coat . . . and size-15 shoes for my own size 9½ feet. My theory was to try something different, the way Larry [Olivier] or Guinness did it, to take a personal "prop" and build it like that, from the feet upwards.' Sure enough, the oversize shoes suggested a cumbersome shuffling ditherer – but they also, for the very first time, projected virile Dick Harris as an arthritic, stooped man, making improbable love to a grey-faced, wrinkled Mrs Maigret. The critics, to a man, hated it. 'Ersatz,' said the *Western Mail*. 'Awful,' said the *Saturday Post*. The *Daily Mirror* poured scorn on Harris's Oirish brogue. After destroying Maigret, they ventured, why not go the distance: 'How about Sherlock O'Holmes? Paddy Mason? Hercule Guinness?' The *Express* moaned:

> Some actors in their frenzied endeavours put on a funny nose, wear a silly hat and adopt a limp. The role springs to life. Others struggle with the inner workings of the character through rehearsals. Harris appeared to be in an anguished conflict between the two styles. The result was catastrophic.

'I've reached a point where I don't care about critics,' said Harris. 'They don't, maybe can't, read sixty Simeneon books. I did.'

Alternating between suites at the Savoy and the Berkeley Court, Harris continued raising cash for the Scranton Fund (£100,000 raised in the first year) and seeking 'connections' to assist the careers of Damian, Jared, Jamie and Ann. 'They'd kill me if I said that to the press, so I do what I can do when they're not paying attention. My prediction is that Damian will direct classics, Jared will out-act me and Jamie will be a producer. I just feel it. Annie? I want her to get her feet on the ground. What Strasberg said is right: she has the [acting] talent, if she wants to go for it. But she's a woman, she's fickle. I could kill her for some of the time-wasting junk she involves herself with.' Ann's once high hopes of her own productions styled for Harris, he felt, were fated to begin with: 'It's a murderous industry. I came into it like a gladiator, and still it flattened me. Annie is too soft.'

In support of Scranton, he joined Menahem Golan's movie adaptation of *The Threepenny Opera*, called *Mack the Knife*, with co-stars Raul Julia and Julie Walters. Then, again for HTV, *King of the Wind*, a Christmas-market period piece in which he played King George II. In London, queried about his role in *King of the Wind*, he puffed on an unfiltered Benson & Hedges and told reporters, 'I've no idea about my character. They put a wig on me and said, "Your name is George", and here I am. I really only came [to London] to go to the theatre. I went to the preview of Dustin Hoffman's *Merchant of Venice . . .*'

The insouciance and boredom were troubling to many who knew him. One Irish-based producer remembered calling him at the Berkeley, where the phone in his room was answered by 'a dreamy-voiced woman who sounded about seventeen. I wanted to propose a project, which was sound and well funded. It was not, I told Richard, a million miles in quality or scale from *This Sporting Life*. "Really?" said Richard. "Well, here's something. *This Sporting Life* was made a million years ago, so, if you take my advice, you'll go and get a day job and stop disturbing a man taking a rest."'

The very personal student production of *Julius Caesar* at Scranton, preceded by a month-long drama class in which Harris was tutor and critic, kept the tenuous connection with drama going. 'I called it *A Work In Progress* and all the door takings went to the Dermot Harris Scholarship, which was already serving its first Limerick student. I have Dermot to thank for keeping me at Scranton and allowing me to unscramble myself. What did I do? I did what I did during *Maigret*: I read all the time. Shakespeare, just Shakespeare. It was ambrosia, really. I would wake up on bad days, and the Shakespeare reminded me why I am who I am and why I did what I did with my life.' Weeks later he was telling the journalist John McEntee that he still could do *Hamlet*: 'Think about it with Jose Ferrer, and Cyril Cusack as Horatio: you get the idea of what I'm after? It could be tremendously exciting.' But few producers were listening any more. 'I had no misconceptions,' said Harris. 'In the whole world there was probably one producer who held me in any regard, and that was Noel Pearson.' Pearson, Dublin's acknowledged successor to 'Mr Showbiz' Louis Elliman, wasn't interested in *Hamlet*, but his reputation through the eighties was for staging inventive, oddball productions that took good receipts. An associate of both men said, 'Noel liked Harris and refused to see him, as most did, as a has-been. He went to New York and had many meetings with Harris about various theatrical ventures, because he felt there was an omission, that Harris had not quite gone full circle, that the best was yet to come. For a while it looked like they might get T S Eliot's *Murder in the Cathedral* going at St Patrick's in New York, with Paul Schofield co-starring with Harris. That was Noel's kind of grand thinking – and Harris loved him for it. But it was too big an undertaking, and Harris's reputation was too low, so it never got past the discussion stage.'

In truth, the casting opportunities were all but gone. Harris's reputation as a tough man with a resolute creative attitude had overwhelmed him. On top of that, in the view of Joe Lynch and many others, he had 'failed to make the critical metamorphosis into late-middle-age roles.' He was nearly sixty, celebrating his birthday on 1 October 1990, but the raging against the dying of the light was still in overdrive and his promotional handouts still had him as fifty-six years old. He was, undeniably, lean and light on his feet. But his face had the hollows of age and his eyes spoke of elderly experience.

Through 1989, the year of *King of the Wind* – all of one day's work – he concentrated almost entirely on family, nursing Jamie, advising Ann on her new relationship with the up-and-coming South African tennis professional Gary Muller, and courting Elizabeth. He had a semipermanent girlfriend in New York – 'a wealthy, self-sufficient career lady whom I see regularly' – but was more often than not on the telephone with Elizabeth, currently operating a PR agency whose many clients included the new, star-attracting Halcyon Hotel in London, where he sometimes stayed. On Elizabeth's birthday he surprised her with a gift: 'I love giving her surprises. After she'd opened her birthday presents I suggested we go to the hotel for a meal. She was moaning, saying we'd have to get a taxi because we wouldn't all fit in her old banger, a knackered Renault. When we got outside I let two taxis pass – I love winding her up – and that started to get her temper up, she started accusing me of being an idiot. I waited until she was about to explode and handed her the keys to . . . a new Mercedes 190 parked across the street. How I enjoyed the look on her face!'

The columnist Nigel Dempster speculated on a permanent reunion in remarriage. Harris said no: 'I'm a modern example of the feudal lord. I'm the caretaker, the overlord of these people. I'd kill to protect my family. I'd smash their opponents. I don't impose my will, I'm not creating a dynasty, but I watch over them. That includes Elizabeth. Anything I have, she can have. I'm not as close to my second wife, Ann. I don't feel the same sense of protection towards her. She never became a Harris because she is Jewish.'

At the Berkeley Court he locked himself away for days in depression. Jack Donnelly, downstairs managing the lobby, worried about him: 'His life is so different now. He needs a woman, and [Elizabeth] is always somewhere around. But there's nights when he can't keep still. It's almost worse when he's not drinking, because nothing calms him. Mick Doyle [the Irish international rugby player] sends him rugby video tapes, and he watches those. He collects rugby jerseys and memorabilia, but . . . it's upsetting to see him at a loose end.'

At the darkest hour, with nothing to divert him, the fates intervened. Through the early summer of 1989 he had been scribbling on three projects: the interminable, never-to-be-finished novel, now called *Saul G*, a follow-up poetry collection called *Fragments of a Broken Photograph*, and a half-realised script about the return of King Arthur that he hoped to get into production with his sons. No offers were on the table – except Noel Pearson's invitation for a bit-part role in his upcoming Granada Television-funded production of a modern rural Irish stage classic, *The Field*, by John B Keane. The part on offer, of the village priest, was just window dressing in a film that would star the pre-eminent Irish stage actor Ray McAnally. Harris was dismissive of the role, but favourably disposed, because of Pearson. 'I wanted to be helpful to him, but it was an insult. I knew

McAnally had made the main role of Bull McCabe his own on stage, but I felt I could do it better. In fact, I told Noel as much, but he just laughed and said, "Well, that's the way it goes, sunshine."'

Pearson's production of *The Field* was blue-chip pedigree. Aside from the Keane association, its core creative team had already made a notable impact with their recent film of Christy Brown's *My Left Foot*, which won Academy Awards for Brenda Fricker and Daniel Day Lewis. Pearson's director partner, Jim Sheridan, was the current toast of Hollywood, and the partnership was viewed as the natural successor to the David Puttnam–Hugh Hudson team who had scored so well a decade before with another outsider, *Chariots of Fire*. Pearson's strength was the kinetic acuity of Sheridan, a New-York-theatre-trained newcomer to film who viewed *Robocop* - directed by Paul Verhoeven – as 'my idea of a decent European–American movie.' 'Traditionally, in Irish film, we lose the plot,' said Harris at the time. 'Our theatre is a theatre of internalised reflection, of the inward journey, which is hard to convey in moving images. So when we make movies they're inclined to be landscape photography with a lot of old men mumbling.' That summation perfectly posed the challenge of *The Field*, a bucolic western tale of land obsession and murder told on stage in a terse, claustrophobic three acts. 'Ray McAnally was the driving force from the start,' said Jim Sheridan. 'He, in effect, created the role in 1965 and he believed in it passionately as a major film, so it really was his. We'd had him in *My Left Foot*, but in *The Field* he would be the star.' McAnally, who had risen to eminence in many fine television roles over thirty years and had won a BAFTA nomination for his part in *The Mission*, viewed *The Field* as a ticket to wider movie recognition. At 63, he said, he felt himself in need for 'something scholarly and important', and *The Field* answered the criteria. John B Keane saw McAnally 'as a newcomer' in terms of a wide movie audience, but felt 'he had earned the role.'

As Sheridan worked the script, targeting a wider audience and better distribution chances by introducing an American character to the rural Irish action, Harris bemoaned his failure to be taken seriously as an actor, even in Ireland: 'No one trusts me any more. I spent half the movie *Maigret* arguing with people, and I was accused of causing big on-set rows. But what they won't tell you is, I fought for Simeneon. I fought for the maintenance of quality. I don't believe in lying down on the job. I've seen these so-called "nice" actors. Very able fellows like Ian McKellen and Kenneth Branagh. But they're like bank managers. So sweet and careful. Who needs them? We are suffering a plague of good taste. Give me Sean Penn and Mickey Rourke any day. They project *danger*. That's what makes acting – and life – interesting.'

Ray McAnally's death from a heart attack at his Wicklow cottage in June threw *The Field* into turmoil and reversed Harris's decline. 'It was terrible,' said John B Keane. 'Everything could have gone so wrong from then. Ray was [the character] Bull – and then we had nothing!' Harris immediately roused from inertia, listening to his old instincts, recognising an opportunity. Diplomatically, gracefully, he made the call. Pearson stalled: 'The thing was, Granada just didn't want him for the role. Put it down to bad reputation, fashion, whatever. But they said no, we can find someone much better.' Harris was upset: 'They said they didn't want me. They said I was old hat. They wanted Brando or Connery. Brando's make-up man, whom I had known for years, actually rang me on Marlon's behalf and asked who these Irish people approaching him were. I told them they were a bunch of layabouts who couldn't be trusted. I was galvanised. I did everything in my power to stop them getting someone else.'

Pearson's profound belief in Harris carried that day and in August, after eight weeks of discussions, Granada agreed the recasting, with John Hurt and the American actor Tom Berenger playing co-leads. The emotional impact on Harris was literally life-transforming. In May, when his friend Frank Sinatra visited Ireland for his first concert tour there, Harris had openly lamented his lost career. In the autumn, squaring up to his biggest lead casting in twelve years, he was thirty again. As he scoured bookstalls for research materials on life in the west of Ireland, tightened up his daily vitamin diet, exercised with long walks and leg stretches, no mountain seemed too high. When Terry Baker told him of theatrical producer Duncan Weldon's offer to stage any play of Harris's choice in Glasgow after

Christmas, just a month after the *Field* shoot, that offer too was embraced. The media moratorium was displaced, and all at once he wanted to talk with anyone who cared to listen, just as in the Bailey court days after *The Ginger Man*. 'This [*The Field*] will be mighty. It's the best screenplay I have ever read. [Granada] never even heard of Tom Berenger, but they saw the light and saw reason and took me. *This Sporting Life* was my *Hamlet*. *The Field* will be my *Lear*. This will be historic.'

The Field began shooting in October in the village of Leenane on the Galway-Mayo border, in a mood described by assistant director Kevan Barker as 'pure hell'. Barker, whose recent credits included work with Merchant-Ivory and a host of first-rank stars including Maggie Smith and Julie Christie, found Harris to be everything his bad press implied. 'Maybe it was profound insecurity, but it made life a nightmare. The clichéd definition we'd had of him before production was certainly borne up: he was larger than life.' On day one, in fact, Harris didn't show. Ignoring call sheets, he arrived many days late on location, sporting a newly grown Father Christmas beard that 'shocked' Jim Sheridan. 'But we got used to it,' said Sheridan. 'Richard had created a version inside his own head, and we went along with the beard.' At the end of the first day's shooting, Harris fell ill, suffering a hyperglycemic attack, which he blamed on the unit chef's lasagna. 'He threw a tantrum just as he was about to settle down to important scenes with [actor] Sean Bean,' said Barker. 'He did a wobbly, accusing the chef of putting sugar in the lasagna, which drove the chef through the ceiling.'

Director Jim Sheridan, mild of manner and open to the prompting voice of experience, struggled to keep the peace. 'It was endless uphill work,' said Barker. 'Tom Berenger just walked away in disgust when Richard flared, but it was humiliating for many of us.' In Barker's opinion Harris contested Sheridan's direction and continually strove to put over his own directorial concept. John B Keane, however was 'delighted' with Harris's furious energy. 'He told me he'd been looking for a script to measure up to this for years,' said Keane. 'It got to be a little embarrassing, in fact, because he repeated it so often. It got to the point where I wanted to say, Stop it, Richard. You'll frighten me. I'll never write again.' Keane had asked Sheridan to cast his brother, Eamon, himself well known to Irish theatre audiences, in a role, and Eamon kept the family informed of day-to-day location progress. 'Eamon was asked to sum up the experience of working with Richard and he came up with a royal line: that there went a circus of a man!'

To all, like Jack Donnelly, who shared Harris's everyday life, *The Field* was a nigh-miraculous gift to him. Not only was it an unqualified art film with intelligently calculated populist leanings, but the role of Bull McCabe, a stentorian, frustrated nonconformist, fitted sixty-year-old Richard Harris like a glove. All of the insecurity Barker saw, all of the anger of neglect and miscalculation, all of the angst and intolerance were *both* Bull and Harris. Barker said, 'Richard *lived* Bull McCabe. He was obnoxious. But then so was the Bull. It was a performance that came much more from self-revelation than theatricality. It probably worked so well because it was Richard finally taking off the mask and letting it all hang out.'

The Field cost $7 million, of which Harris received a relatively paltry £100,000, proportionately among his lowest fees ever. At the wrap party in December, however, he forked out $1,000 to cover crew booze, while staying resolutely dry himself. 'It wasn't about money anyway,' said Jack Donnelly, 'because *Camelot* had him home and dry. But *The Field* mattered more than anything to him because it was an Irish film. He told me, "This is something that only comes along once in a lifetime. It's full circle. The only thing that'd be more resonant would be a movie about Garryowen or Old Crescent."'

Elated though 'utterly fagged out' after *The Field*, Harris chose not to back-pedal. His usual Christmas holiday on Paradise, mostly in the company of Jack Donnelly and the kids, often spilled long past New Year. This time he was up and at it as soon as the festivities were out of the way. By mid-January he was back in the newspapers, embroiled in a row with the Glasgow Citizens' Theatre, with whom he had agreed to appear in a play that was intended to take him back to the West End stage. Theatrical impresario Duncan Weldon's blank-sheet offer during the summer had resulted in weeks of talks, before a joint decision was made with the Citizens' Theatre. Harris had considered Anouilh's *Ring Around the Moon* and James Goldman's *The Lion in Winter* before finally remembering the play he'd seen and loved at the Gaiety in Dublin forty years earlier, Pirandello's adventure in madness, *Henry IV*.

The dispute with the Citizens' Theatre arose when Harris rejected the proposed translation. He had prepared his own translation (by Julian Mitchell), but director Peter Prowse insisted on his resident writer's version. 'I hated it,' said Harris. 'They updated the play and it became very camp. It wasn't the Pirandello I remembered, so I withdrew.' Prowse attempted to go ahead without him, recasting in a hurry. 'All hell broke loose,' Harris told the *Evening Standard*. 'The press said I failed to turn up, that I'd let them down, that it was all my fault. But it wasn't and *I* didn't get into any public rows.'

This heroic restraint in refusing to indulge the row suggested a true rebirth, and the reason for it was the fulfilment of *The Field*. Calmly, almost unnoticed, Pirandello progressed, now entirely under Harris's management, with a new director, David Thacker, and a new cast assembled in London. A woman friend, the Greek actress Aliki Michael, described Harris during the February rehearsals as 'quite emphatically self-assured, very much his old self, very calm, deep and inward-looking'. In due course the play started on tour, opening in Cardiff to generally good notices. But Harris felt there was more yet to do. Aliki Michael said, 'He was very obsessive with the material and had taken on the author's role. It seemed to be a new attitude he'd adopted, which was, Everybody has had their chance with me, now it's my own turn to do it right. In the middle of a conversation he drifted off and I complained. He apologised very courteously and said, "Do you know, it's just dawned on me that I've spent more time in my life dreaming than thinking. I think I missed my life: it passed me by while I wasn't paying attention".' When Michael offered the comforting suggestion that he had plenty of time to set things right, he replied, 'No one has plenty of time. It's important to do what you're doing like it's your last chance.'

In his effort to do things right the new, improved Richard Harris turned Pirandello inside out. Sarah Miles, his initial co-star, withdrew in mid-April claiming 'personal reasons' that Jack

Donnelly believed had to do with 'never seeing eye to eye'. By the end of the month David Thacker was gone, to be replaced by Harris's new choice, Val May. Thacker's departure was excused as a case of 'artistic differences only'. Whether he liked it or not Harris found himself fighting a rearguard action in the press: 'No, I didn't lock myself in my dressing room and refuse to come out. But the set *was* wrong [so] I registered my objections by going on stage and ranting and raving . . .'

The reward for obsessive perfectionism came in May, when Harris conclusively retook the 'legitimate' West End with Pirandello. The *Evening Standard* celebrated 'a return to sparkling form' and all the leading reviews offered superlatives. 'What was especially fascinating about it,' said Joe Lynch, 'was Dick's self-restraint. In previous years a victory like this would have bored you to death with himself blaring how wonderful he was. This time he just let the work speak for itself.' John McEntee of the *Standard* agreed: 'He was tamer, he didn't want the grand media limelight and he seemed to just want to quietly bask in the achievement.'

The bushfire talk of imminent awards became rampant. A mid-1990 call to reshoot part of the completed *Field* showed Harris again at full creative charge, leaving no stone unturned, and when the movie was released in the autumn the fruits of hard labour were there for all to see. *The Field*, like *This Sporting Life,* was essentially art-house, and in that aspiration it discharged itself admirably. But Sheridan's parallel intention to open the borders to mass-market appeal failed and audience figures, especially in the US, were poor. With a box-office gross of just $1.5 million, *The Field* disappointed investors while comprehensively satisfying discerning critics. By year's end, in spite of the losses, there was talk of BAFTA and American Academy award nominations, and in the early spring came confirmation. Jack Donnelly believed, 'He was beside himself with delight.' But Harris was phlegmatic: 'My reaction was, It's about fucking time . . . not arrogance, but impatience. A lot of being overlooked through the years was my own fault. I'd messed around. *The Field* was Ireland, and you don't piss on your own doorstep. I got some control. I held it together. It was time. It felt good.'

Harris didn't travel to LA for the Oscar ceremonies, but Donnelly saw him 'comfortably optimistic'. His chances seemed doubly good since the fellow contenders – De Niro, Gerard Depardieu, Kevin Costner and Jeremy Irons – were, in this instance, representing manifestly lesser work. Only Costner's Indian epic, *Dances With Wolves*, was viewed as a serious runner, but, as it turned out, Jeremy Irons won for *Reversal of Fortune*, an undistinguished B-movie. Harris hid his disappointment in graceful retreat, allowing a broadsheet interview or two, tersely congratulating Irons, then holing up in Nassau. Aliki Michael later found him 'muted. His reaction was not to talk about it much at all, and to counterbalance by concentrating on the many new offers that were coming his way as a result [of *The Field*]. "Sure, I knew I hadn't a chance," was his way of dismissing it. But it was easy to see he was covering the hurt and that he'd really badly wanted the award.' Jack Donnelly felt angry for Harris's loss: 'The award was overdue. We felt he should have won it for *Camelot*, or *A Man Called Horse* – so many different terrific performances. The saddest part for Dick was his belief that time was against him. He was always going on about it, and, after *The Field* it was worse than ever. The only positive aspect of it was the respect the film brought him. All these industry people he hadn't heard from in years called up to congratulate him – Lindsay Anderson, Dick Lester, all of them. We even noticed it when he came to stay at the Berkeley Court. There was a time in the eighties when the phone never rang, when no one was looking for him. Suddenly, we were inundated. Half the time the switchboard was under special instructions not to bother him. It felt like 1965 again.'

CHAPTER 17

Exit M'Lord

The nineties, the era of unified Europe, of the common currency, of the IT tsunami, of satellite television and globalisation, came down on Harris like a biblical plague. Always the individualist, the piratical outsider, he found himself at a loss. The Ireland he grew up in was a cowed and self-apologetic place, where emigration for employment and the subtle tyranny of theocracy dominated. The Ireland of the nineties was the world of culture trendsetting, of U2 and *Riverdance*, and the multibillion-pound European fund investments that built an overnight infrastructure to match the US. In the sixties, when his career took off, Ireland produced the same number of movies per annum as Uruguay: fewer than two. Against this background of paucity, his Hollywood achievement towered like a colossus. By the late nineties, as many as forty films a year were produced, reflecting the Western economic confidence that fed globalisation and the American-led threat of monoculture. Against this backcloth, on the evidence of efforts like the touring *Camelot* and *The Field*, he was an anachronism, a minor cinema figure trapped, like John Osborne or Richard Burton, in the bolide flash of the Angry Young Man, as if in aspic.

Always comfortable with pencil and scratchpad, he was irritated by the technologies of the new age. At his best in the square ring of Jack Warner's personal office, the 'conference call' ethos of the corporate behemoths that had replaced the big studios left him stranded. He was innately resistant to conformity, and so the notion of an unfolding, homogeneous world without frontiers translated for him as a world without national identity of personal individuality and depressed him. At a low moment in 1989, he had described himself to Sinatra as 'a dinosaur'. To Jack Donnelly, after the seesaw of *The Field*, he confessed himself spent. 'What I need to do,' he told Donnelly, 'is find an heiress with an island in the Pacific where I can write poems all day and make love to the servants all night.'

Despite a deepening tendency to depression, though, he retained what his son Jared described as his great strength: his skill at 'networking', at isolating the key components of whatever art or game he chose to play, and zooming in on the G-spot. Just for a moment he seemed deflated and tremulously close to a sincere retirement, but the progress of all his sons in the industry – Damian had just completed his first Hollywood-style feature, Jared was absorbed with the RSC and Jamie was working as a trainee assistant director – propelled him on to the Hollywood party circuit with a formal, almost institutional sobriety. Joe Lynch was astounded to see him rise with the multitude at the American Film Institute's Salute to Kirk Douglas 'not because, like everyone else, I'd heard again and again all those yarns about him knocking Kirk sideways in Norway in the sixties, but because he resisted those gatherings like death itself. He always said "They're bullshit, ass-kissers." But there he was, in his tux, standing up and blowing kisses to Kirk and telling him how great he was. Maybe *The Field* taught him a thing or two. Maybe he smelled the awards again, and thought to himself, This time I'll play it their way.'

Whichever way he reasoned it, Harris made a blunt decision in the aftermath of *The Field* to overcome his personal apathy and the momentum of the decade and devote himself to film as he had never done. In the next ten years he would make no fewer than 22 films, a level of productivity unmatched by any of his prolific contemporaries, whether Costner or Sean Connery, and certainly beyond the output of his heroes Burton and O'Toole. Lindsay Anderson saw him pitch out the year after *The Field* and saw the significance of his modus: 'The first thing he jumped at was a trio of big Hollywood stories, with a Sam Sheppard play thrown in. It was so typical of him in his heyday, because he understood more than any actor I've known how this is a business, and you must be seen to be profitable to the accountants. In the sixties we tried to do the same, but we never pulled it off. Richard went on to do it by himself, but he usually came unstuck by shooting his mouth off at some executive like Jack Warner. In the nineties he knows better.'

Harris's submersion in the torrential nineties began with a near-cameo in a preordained Tom Clancy hit that served to allow him to restate and clarify his matured political credo. *Patriot Games*, a formula right-wing CIA tale in Clancy's Jack Ryan series, was a financial success grossing more than $83 million that could have been substantially better. Clancy's novel concerned a splinter IRA group's plot to murder the Prince and Princess of Wales; in Philip Noyce's movie, the terrorist target becomes a fictional cousin of the queen. Harris, as the voice of Sinn Fein, the IRA's political wing, condemns the splinter group's activities but the opportunity lost is the one of contextual relevance. Clancy's novels, despite their bias, display revelatory behind-the-scenes accuracy; Noyce's fictional-isation loses out at a time of historic importance, when the legitimacy of Sinn Fein's stance began opening the way for the Good Friday Agreement and the enduring ceasefire. In the middle eighties, Harris said, 'I learned my lesson. The only politics I wish to express is the politics of poetry, which is truth.' *Patriot Games* denied him that truth, but served to keep him in the running with the big players.

Clint Eastwood had admired Harris since the sixties, though their paths had never crossed. In the run up to *Patriot Games* he approached with the offer of a leading role in his new directorial project, *Unforgiven*, a western designed, like *A Man Called Horse*, to deflate the Hollywood-West mythology. Harris, whose effusive opinionating in the area of assessing the opposition hadn't much altered, regarded Eastwood as 'as one of the few Hollywood heads worth the money' and signed up with alacrity for a role that was to prove every bit as apt as Bull McCabe. Neither Harris nor Eastwood is on record admitting to it, but the part of English Bob, the famous gunfighter who now lives off his publicity, seemed tailor-made and not a little affectionately wry. Eastwood's goal was tribute: to the

West as it truly was, to the changing tides of Hollywood realism, to
Don Siegal and Sergio Leone, both recently deceased, who had
moulded his own screen cowboy image in movies like *A Fistful of
Dollars* and *Two Mules for Sister Sara*. But the greater joy was
Unforgiven's feeling of hard-edged biography, that in essaying the
three central roles – the suppressed, avenging hog farmer Munny,
played by Eastwood himself, the reactionary sheriff, played by Gene
Hackman, and English Bob – director and cast had drawn from
personal realities and transcended caricature by presenting themselves. In a complex, arcane morality tale set in the town of Big
Whiskey, Wyoming, take-no-prisoners English Bob is not a lot
different from the the unchecked Arthurian-braggart Richard Harris
circa *Camelot*. Almost everyone who reported the film spotted this
and saw much to praise, and Desson Howe in the *Washington Post*
crystallised the film's power, saluting 'the grim wryness' of Big
Whiskey and Harris 'as a murderous English shyster breezing
through the town [bringing] his been-to-hell-and-back presence
to bear.'

At the end of the decade Harris spoke of the unavoidable moment,
after *The Field*, when he realised age had caught up with him: 'From
the age of forty-five [since *Return of a Man Called Horse*] onwards,
I always dyed my hair. When it came to playing Bull, I let the dye go
and grew it naturally, and of course I ended up with an overall white
stubble. And then the white stubble became a white mane, and I
looked at myself in the mirror and said, 'Dick, you're sixty. You're
an old man. Let it be. And from then on I was Dick Harris, the white-
haired old-man actor.'

The surrender was cancelled by the defiance of the telling and in
the early nineties he struggled with himself and his image more than
he had ever done. In the hiatus before *The Field* and the honeymoon
afterwards he continued to romance a series of younger women
fervently, employing his old tricks of charm, grace and poetry, even
going so far as to hunt down copies of *I, in the Membership of My
Days* in secondhand bookstores, the better to spice the mating ritual.
During *Henry IV* he entertained what he called 'his last great
romance', with a cast member he refused to name. 'But it's

ridiculous now, I'm past it,' he would tell Jack Donnelly, then hesitate, and think, and wink, and add, 'Maybe.'

Randa Haines's close character study, *Wrestling Ernest Hemingway*, about two old codgers (the other played by Robert Duvall) sparring for youth, was yet again an extension of his reality, allowing him to play off his age dilemma with humour. Shot in Florida, it marked a notable first – the first time Harris had allowed himself to be directed by a woman. At the time Jack Donnelly prophesied blithely that 'It will never work', and he was almost right. Coming on the heels of the previous year's Matthau–Lemon minor hit reunion with *Grumpy Old Men*, Haines, famous for hard-edge successes like television's *Hill Street Blues* and the movie *Children of a Lesser God*, steered her cast into a subtler mirror-dance of senility, in which 'Oscar' and 'Felix' vibrantly reflect each other's immutable shadow self, without any ultimate resolution. Rita Kempley in the *Washington Post* found it "profound" while Roger Ebert saw sub-structure befitting Hemingway himself (the Hemingway in the title refers to the Harris character's boast that he once wrestled the writer). Ebert wrote,

[The characters] don't have much to do. Even more important, they don't have anyone who much cares what they do. Still, they keep on plugging, nursing their dreams of romance and happiness. Even when there is no longer an audience for it, a man must still behave according to his code.

According to Harris's code, he – predictably, given his internal unease – picked holes with Haines's work. Comfortable to romp in the nude on set (and on screen), as the movie wrapped he was suddenly displeased with everything – except his own performance. 'It sickened me. And when I saw [the rough cut] I thought it was destroyed. I called Robert Duvall from Nassau and I told him to get on down, that we needed to fix it. But he said no. I couldn't believe it. I liked him a lot. A great actor, with great instincts. But he said no. He said, "Dick, has no one told you life is short? Why do you bother to even watch what [the directors] do with our work? Why torment yourself? Give it to her. Forget about it, and move on. And in the future, don't bother to look at the movie when it's finished. You did your job. Be happy with that." '

Two further American productions occupied him in a desultory way through 1993. The first, an ambitious, though missable modernist western called *Silent Tongue*, written and directed by Sam Sheppard with the trademark claustrophobic internalising that made his *Fool for Love* so special, was memorable mostly for the tragic sudden death of co-star River Phoenix at a Sunset Boulevard nightspot shortly after completion. The subsequent segment of TNT's stern Bible series that cast him in the lead of the two-part story of *Abraham* was similarly mechanical and unnoticed. Jack Donnelly, in his last days of management at the Berkeley Court, found it hard to keep tabs on his prodigal in-law at this time. 'He hops around more than ever. He's at a stage where he doesn't like to look back, so keeping busy keeps him hopeful. Who knows? The next one might be the Academy Award.'

Nassau apart, Harris's havens were Canada and South Africa, countries he loved and whose audiences had remained loyal to him. Since the seventies, whenever options afforded themselves, he would ask Terry Baker, 'Can they do it in Ireland, or Canada, or South Africa?' In the middle nineties, after the release of Mandela and the end of apartheid, South Africa rewarded his fidelity with the offer of the landmark remake of Alan Paton's humanist classic, *Cry, the Beloved Country*, the country's first post-apartheid feature. Harris professed himself deeply touched: 'One has visited and seen the injustice, and coming from a country where [injustice] is integral, where we have fought our own wars and now see justice in sight, it's a great privilege to be part of the awakening.' Paton's novel was famously made, Hollywood-style, with Sidney Poitier, in 1951. The new version, directed by native Darrell James Roodt and financed by the independent trendsetting distributors Miramax, diverted from formula, taking the first two-thirds of the Paton novel to create a powerful open-ended polemic about faith and humanity in a place of decadence. Mandela himself, attending the New York opening on 23 October 1995, commended a 'work of art' where 'the talent and creativity that was virtually unrecognised under apartheid is able today to shine, combined with the skill and experience of compassionate friends of South Africa such as James Earl Jones and Richard Harris'; yet even that towering compliment only partly pinned the uniqueness of the film and the extraordinary ensemble-acting achievement. Paton's story of the lives of two men of separate caste and beliefs intertwining in the fate of their sons spoke of biblical parable, and in the Roodt–Jones–Harris version the power of parable elevated the movie beyond geography and politics to speak for the ages. Harris professed himself 'gratified' by the experience, and gracefully, appropriately, conceded analysis to the critics, who, unanimously, rose in ovation. The *San Francisco Chronicle* summed up the consensus that the movie was 'a glorious tribute to the workings of a faith that does not blind, but opens up the human spirit'.

Harris's unavailability for media discussion spoke of a true withdrawal. In 1994 Jack Donnelly was knocked down by a car in Dublin and sustained serious injuries, but rallied. Not long after *Cry, the Beloved Country*, he died quite suddenly, severing the last true umbilical tie to Limerick and the past. Joe Lynch spoke with Harris at this time and found him 'very introverted. His life now is the children, who aren't children any more. Like all of us, he has a hard job furnishing this new world called old age.'

Drifting on the market currents, Harris took what he could, lest boredom drive him to a standstill and despair. Ten years before, he had wondered about the 'in-built self-destructive aspect' of creativity and the fate of artists, from Thomas Chatterton to Hemingway, who ended their own lives: 'It's understandable. Every living thing serves a purpose. Like the scriptures say, to every thing there is a season. So you take what you have, and you make yourself useful. But what happens when you are no longer useful? When you're either disabled physically, or mentally, or emotionally? The answer, always, is: you adapt. Adapt, or perish. There are terrible burdens people carry all over the world. Illnesses, injustice, starvation. But they endure, and we should take strength from that. The key word is "hope". You must hope for something. You must dream. And for that reason, I always daydream. I always build castles in the sky. I did it in Limerick till it drove my parents insane. It got so bad, my father wanted to pay me to leave the Ennis Road. It hurts me to think I never reconciled with him, that he never understood that I had the kind of temperament that would have perished if I hadn't dreamed my life away. I don't want to be a Hemingway. I don't want to go down to depression. I want to be looking at women in lust till the day I die and I want to be sipping Guinness till the day I die, and I want to have a scheme, or a play, or something in my sights, till the day I die.'

In 1990, Jamie had observed, during *The Field*, that movies meant less and less to his father and Terry Baker confirmed this: 'All he really wants to talk about is something like *King Lear*, which is a passion now.' By the middle nineties, those close to him, like Donnelly, believed that his only movie impetus was a desire for the formality of an Academy Award: 'He'll never openly admit it. It's always contradictory. But it's there. He also feels he should be knighted, that he's served his time.'

Harris muddled on – through *The Great Kandinsky*, a BBC film about an escape artist in an old folk's home, through *Savage Hearts*, a Bristol- and Bath-located low-budget thriller that featured his son Jamie, through *Trojan Eddie*, an Anglo-Irish B-picture, through *Smilla's Sense of Snow*, a metaphysical Danish-set B-picture, through *The Hunchback*, a made-for-television Dumas revamping, through *This is the Sea*, another portentous Irish tone poem, through the New Order Russian-made *Barber of Siberia*.

These films, made in quick succession kept him on aeroplanes, in hotel rooms, meeting new faces, eating exotic food – in short, comfortably in flux. There was no time for building new friendships to replace the lost, precious little time even for reflection. He stayed trim, maintained his daily 23-vitamin-supplement non-sugar diet, but, after more than a decade of abstinence, allowed himself now a daily Guinness or two. 'You need to stay lubricated, just to remind yourself you are still living and breathing.'

A rare interview granted to the journalist Penelope Denning in the middle of this buckshot schedule found Harris recumbent, yet agitated, at the Savoy Hotel. Stretched across a sofa and staring at the ceiling for protracted periods, he explained that he hadn't seen *Trojan Eddie*, nor intended to. He had even refused the special New York celebrity screening of *The Hunchback*. The experience with Haines and Duvall on *Wrestling Ernest Hemingway* put paid to all that. Fiddling with the zip on his jeans, 'as if to confirm that flatness and firmness of his stomach', Denning noted, Harris seemed mostly keen to restate the impervious nature of his status, quoting the advice Duvall had given him: 'You're very wilful. You know your power and you have constructed your life, and nobody can advise you.' But behind the bluster were the apparent ulterior motives of revisionism and theatrical intent. He hated, he said, actors who lacked discipline, citing an unnamed co-star on *The Hunchback* who boozed all night and came on set fifteen minutes late. Yes, he had once be so inclined, but, 'when I started my career I was obsessive. In the mid-1970s I didn't want to do it any more . . . and I just walked away.' The one regret was never having done *Hamlet* – 'the only regret I have in my life' – but that would soon be fixed by his new plans, to mount either *King Lear* or *The Merchant of Venice*. 'They're going to be vastly different. We've got to stop genuflecting at the altar of Shakespeare. Stratford, for instance, is like an assembly line. When I did the Pirandello I found I wanted to say something about people in our profession who are exposed to the public, how our personalities keep changing. The Pirandello was all about the reinvention of ourselves and the masks we continually change when we are confronted by different situations . . . I'm wearing one now . . . We can't help it. That's what we are.'

In the course of the conversation, Denning reported Harris's 'contempt for the English' and the undiminished temperamental hair trigger. 'When I suggest that Harris's hell-raising did little to rebuff [the] Irish stereotype, the breakerdown-of-doors quivers with rage. What do I mean by that? What about Richard Burton and Peter Finch, he says, finger jabbing like an electric drill . . .' but in seconds the rage has died, 'unpredictable as summer thunder, and just as harmless.'

The sudden death of Terry Baker, of a heart attack in a London street, left Harris without another champion and obliged him to change masks yet again. Nudged away from theatre, he sought, and found, suitable movies in his favourite climes – *To Walk with Lions*, a modest *Born Free* sequel, shot in Africa with Ian Bannen and Honor Blackman, and the heyday Disneyesque romp called *Grizzly Falls*, shot in Canada.

By the summer of 1999, filming Ridley Scott's earnest *Gladiator*, a ferocious re-enactment of the death of the Emperor Marcus Aurelius and subsequent, disastrous thirteen-year rule of his deficient son Commodus – the events charted by Gibbon as the start of the fall of the Roman Empire – Harris again wore the mask of the arch professional thespian. *Gladiator* was expansive (at least in art direction and special effects) and *verité* violent but, as Philip French adeptly noted in the *Observer*, the movie was at heart a literal remake of Anthony Mann's 1964 *Fall of the Roman Empire* – the Bronston-produced version in which, 35 years before, Harris had been offered the role of Commodus. Now, portraying Commodus's father, said French, Harris displayed 'an uncanny resemblance to Alec Guinness in Mann's picture'. During the production, Harris gave a rosy account of his reasons for taking the role. Every movie in the last ten years, he said, had been, in principle, his last one. He had no more appetite for films, and wished for retirement. But there was still within him the Limerick child who viewed the world of movies with 'a sense of awe'. Scott's production had just been 'so vast and astonishing – the sets, the scale, the battles, everything' – that he had been seduced.

Gladiator's success was of the Hollywood superleague variety, wreathed in worldwide award nominations – including a staggering clutch of Oscars (it won both Best Film, and Best Actor for Russell Crowe) – and grossing almost $456 million at the box office, though many critics were disdainful of what Roger Ebert called its '*Rocky* on downers' simplicity of storyline, and the faux-Shakespearean tone of dialogue. For Harris, though, it was closure on the missed Bronston opportunity that had, he admitted, all been down to 'a lot of stupid shoot-from-the-hip posturing'.

Having completed eight exhausting weeks on *Gladiator* in Malta and London, Harris appeared determined to quit. In the closing weeks of production his 'slugging partner' Oliver Reed, with whom he enjoyed an uneasy friendship, died suddenly on location in Malta. Friends professed Harris 'shocked and unsettled'. It wasn't hard to understand the resonant connections of image, temperament and anguished artistry, but Harris rejected all comparisons: 'I intend to die in bed at 110, writing poetry, sipping Guinness and serenading a woman.'

Approaching his seventieth birthday, he had slotted himself into the lordly life he felt befitted his accomplishments. Without wife or constant companion, he opted for the Savoy Hotel as his personal castle, its staff his consorts. 'I like the round-the-clock comforts,' he'd said years before. 'I like it that I can call up for a sandwich at 4 a.m., or find someone in the lobby willing to talk about the [rugby] interprovincials in the middle of the night. I like fresh sheets, and I like efficiency around me. When you're at the Savoy you have a personal staff of hundreds.' For this dedication of service he paid £6,000 a week and felt it was cheap at the price. 'If you're paying the mortgage on a home you can't ask the bank manager to fetch you a pint.'

In his seventieth year he committed some days to an unreleased movie called *The Royal Way* for the director Andrei Konchalovsky and participated in the American Film Institute's salute to itself, *100 Years: 100 Stars*, but was otherwise unresponsive to movie offers. Then, on the heels of *Gladiator*'s high profile and higher box-office gross, came Warners' offer of the major role of Professor Albus Dumbledore in *Harry Potter and the Sorcerer's Stone*, the film debut of the current children's-literature phenomenon created by J K Rowling. The approach came via Harris's new agent, but he rejected it out of hand. On his seventieth birthday he had partied till dawn, not hitting the sack till 7 a.m., and apologising profusely to Elizabeth, who chastised him for his no-show for a planned country break. 'I didn't want to do the Potter thing,' he said. 'I'd made my mind up that it was over for me, that I didn't need any more early-morning call sheets and all the hassle. I didn't need the money – so why else would I do it?' But then Ella, Damian's eleven-year-old daughter by a recently dissolved marriage, begged him otherwise. In a phone conversation she told him the plot of the Rowling book in passionate detail and swore she would never speak with him again unless he took the part. 'What could I do?' moaned Harris. 'I wasn't going to let her down.'

Excess has always shadowed Hollywood's monolithic successes, from *Gone with the Wind* to *Titanic*. None has emerged hype-less and full-formed, and, true to history, the Harry Potter series started with a Barnum-like parade of press teases and casting summits. The eventual selection of newcomer Daniel Radcliffe to play the *Oliver Twist*-like Potter succeeded months of casting on two continents by director Chris Columbus and producer David Heyman. Stuart Craig, the inventive set designer of *Gandhi*, was deployed to invent the visual wizardry of Hogwarts, the magic academy at which Potter is transformed from a done-down foster child to a young Merlin. The *Hollywood Reporter* announced a budget of $126 million – parlously close to the no-hope investment of tainted monsters like Costner's *Waterworld* – with $40 million assigned for marketing.

In the end, it came down to storytelling and performance and on both counts the movie, and Columbus, scored. 'Hewing as close to the spirit of the literary work as any movie can,' said the *Reporter*, *Harry Potter and the Scorcerer's Stone* (retitled '*Philosopher's Stone*' in the UK) surpassed the highest expectations worldwide, opening the Christmas season for Warners in November 2001 and soaring to earnings in excess of $317 million, rating it second only to *Titanic* as the most successful box-office movie of all time.

Personal reviews seemed academic and though they were mixed the fulfilled objective, in terms of conclusively winning the juvenile audience, thrilled Harris. 'I am glad Ella liked it,' he said, though the equal gratification of substance, of a movie of artistic merit, unquestionably remotivated him. There were critical American dissenters, disappointed perhaps that Steven Spielberg hadn't, as initially announced, taken the reins and added his distinguished blush, but others, like Philip French, saw transcendence: '*The Wizard of Oz* offered comfort to American children during the late years of the Depression . . . Harry Potter affords hope of magical powers available to the brave, the decent and the resourceful in our own anxious times.'

Harris jigged himself for a final sprint. While Harry Potter was in postproduction he flew to Malta to join the cast of the umpteenth remake of *The Count of Monte Cristo* – a modernised but breezy version that at least refreshed Dumas's great tale of escape and revenge for a new generation – then signed for Don Boyd's Merseyside gangster flick, *My Kingdom*.

Even beyond the Everest of Harry Potter, *My Kingdom* was the crowning twilight gift. Don Boyd, the resilient British independent producer-director whom Alexander Walker once described as 'a one-man film industry', had started in fringe theatre, with his own group, Incognito, when he was nineteen, in 1967. Thereafter he was an assistant to John Schlesinger, and worked with Altman and Godard before launching into small-budget directing in the eighties. None of his feature films had been big successes, but he was the driving force behind the production of the celebrated *Scum*, formerly banned by the BBC, and had significant hits with an adaptation of a Donzinetti opera, starring Amanda, one of his three daughters, and with the intimate documentary *Donald and Luba: A Family Movie*, anatomising the break-up of his parents' relationship. *My Kingdom*, written with the *Guardian*'s crime reporter Nick Davies, Boyd had conceived as a showcase for Merseyside, an area of inherent drama, he believed, which had been poorly served on film. It was also a lateral reconstruction of *King Lear*, Harris's last great passion.

As Boyd tells it, he met Harris at the Savoy and found a quick, harmonious partnership that lasted until Harris read the final draft script. Then heyday Harris reared his head again, engaging his own screenwriter and, said Boyd, concocting 'a happy ending' for the grim tale of a mobster who loses control to his daughters. The movie duly started on location in Liverpool in a welter of knock-down screaming matches that must have seemed, to anyone who'd known Harris, like a lip-synch'd replay from the dying days of *Mutiny on the Bounty*. Boyd found Harris intractable, but a peace agreement based on early-morning script conferences and late-night post-mortems kept the show – rockily – on the road. At one point, according to Boyd, Harris went so far as to try the notorious 'Gloria Swanson line' from *Sunset Boulevard*, overstepping the director to announce, 'I'm ready for my close-up' at a moment when the scene favoured not Harris, but the co-star who happened to be one of Boyd's daughters. 'I told him, "This scene isn't only about you. It's about her" . . . [and] he really gave it to me then.' The other members of the cast, said Boyd, ran for cover when the rows flared.

If anything, Boyd related, Harris's rage was a glory to behold and it surely must have been, because it was the final blaze of a dying ember. Boyd found the overall experience 'nightmarish' but, ultimately, 'wonderful'. From Harris's perspective, Boyd's movie was the greatest late-life honour, the long-dreamed-of opportunity to usurp Shakespeare, and turn four centuries of dramatic tradition on its head. 'He had notes about everything,' said Boyd. 'Not a line of dialogue escaped his attention' – but it couldn't have, because, in one way or another, he had been preparing and honing it all for forty years.

My Kingdom, released haltingly to what the *Hollywood Reporter* called 'the specialist market' in the gap before the final Harry Potter was, for the Harris camp, an unmitigated success that showcased an exceptional talent – externally and internally, in performance and instinct, in presence and spirit. Playing Sandeman, the Irish crime lord whose kingdom comes unstuck as he tries to redistribute power and cash following the murder of his wife, Harris rose to the grandeur of Lear and, as promised, surpassed expectations in an act of deft iconoclasm. 'Harris commands the screen,' wrote Kirk Honeycutt in the *Hollywood Reporter*, 'using his frailty to suggest the ravages of a life of corruption and ruthlessness.' In the *Observer*, Philip French found Harris 'formidable' in an 'ingenious relocation of *King Lear*'. Harris, who no longer looked at the final cuts, looked at *My Kingdom* and found it hit the spots: 'It appears to work on different levels – which is something you don't see in cinema any more.'

Harry Potter and the Chamber of Secrets, the swan song, filming through the spring of 2002, once again under Chris Columbus at Pinewood, occupied and excited Harris in a way that surprised even Columbus. The historic box-office of the first one, and perhaps the *My Kingdom–Lear* idyll, seemed to have touched and invigorated him. 'It was perfect,' said Harris, 'because I only shot for twenty days over six months. This was marvellous. Shoot one day, then get three weeks off. Perfect for an old man.' The real joy, though, was the chance to see Ella reap the rewards, cast, as she was, in a small role round the Hogwarts' banquet table, in sight of the untouchable Dumbledore, overseeing all, like a cross between King Arthur and Merlin, perched on the highest podium.

In March, as Harris shot his many and varied scenes – more verbose and plot-laden than the scenes in the first Potter – many remarked on his pallor and sluggishness. One crew member recalled that he seemed sedated, but in fact he was ill, and had been staving off the worst of it for months. On the phone to Ann Turkel in New York he complained of successive flu bouts that confined him to his bed at the Savoy. 'When we talked on the phone,' said Ann, 'we simply didn't know it was so bad. I remember saying to him, "But, Richard, you've had the flu ten times in the last year."'

Caringly instructive to Daniel Radcliffe and the kids of Hogwarts, most of whom kept their distance and regarded him with awe, Harris still had a sting in his tail. Cast and crew delighted in his willingness, no matter what, to call for another take or question the lighting. Yet, when old troupers like Alan Rickman or Dame Maggie Smith complained earnestly, he would tell them: 'Look, there's a war in the Middle East, floods all over England and bombs being thrown all over the world. There's real life going on out there. This is all just make-believe crap.' Daniel Radcliffe recalled Harris's lingering advice: 'He told me to live my life the way I wanted, not to someone else's plan. Do the work you want to do. Please yourself.'

In the early summer Harris retreated to the Savoy and all but vanished. It had been his regular evening habit to visit the downstairs bar, the American, for a bedtime pint drawn by the head barman Salim Khoury, or his specially annointed cocktail, the Camelot Fizz, blended from good red wine and soda water. Now, abruptly, he was nowhere to be seen. Almost daily for years, said Ann, she had spoken with her ex by phone, no matter where either of them was located. Recently she has been dividing her time between New York and LA, where, with Madonna, she attended Kabbalah classes and had begun the process of relaunching herself as a model-photographer. Her first major spread, all of sixteen pages in the July issue of Italian *Vogue*, was a breakthrough she wanted to share with Harris. But by mid-summer the calls were erratic. Finally Elizabeth, herself ensconced in a new life with fiancé Jonathan Aitken, consulted with the boys about taking action. 'Something had to be done,' said Elizabeth, 'so we just went to the Savoy and banged the door down.'

Harris's condition had deteriorated, Howard Hughes-like, behind closed doors. Emaciated and too weak to stand, he was also too weak to fight off Damian's insistence on summoning an ambulance. Harris's Savoy departure has become the stuff of hotel legend. Because of the gurney, and the haste of emergency, the paramedics used the hotel's main elevators, situated near the main lobby. As they exited, with Harris outstretched, the actor shouted to the guests taking tea nearby, 'It was the food! Don't touch the food!'

The diagnosis of Hodgkin's disease, an insidious lymphatic cancer, started Harris on a reluctant course of chemotherapy that lasted several weeks. Throughout, attended regularly by his sons and Elizabeth, he kept a brave face and when Chris Columbus and producer David Heyman visited he warned them not to recast the next Harry Potter, scheduled for filming the following March. Mindful that Sean Connery and Christopher Lee had been their original first choices, he told them, 'Call either of them and I'll kill you.' All of the close family, including his Dublin-based brother Noel and Damian's new baby daughter, visited in the last weeks, but Elizabeth judiciously kept the severity of Harris's condition from Ann, with whom she had developed a close friendship. Finally, on Wednesday, 23 October, Ann too was summoned and flew overnight to London. 'I wished I'd been there sooner and was with him for longer,' she said, 'because by the time I got there he was so exhausted that I didn't want to tire him. So we just talked quietly, as we always did, and he told me he loved me. I love Elizabeth [too], and her children are like mine. Elizabeth's sons are my surrogate brothers, my pals, my extended family. I don't know how I would have got through this without Elizabeth.'

In shifts and together, Ann, Elizabeth and the boys kept Harris company through Thursday night, but on Friday afternoon he waved them away, saying he wanted to sleep. The group moved to the connecting sitting room and they were there when Harris lapsed into a coma, then passed away at seven o'clock in the evening. Ann recalled that 'the last thing I said to him was, "Don't go yet. It's not your time to go to the other side. Stay here with us." But, who knows? He might just have seen something more interesting on the other side, and gone to check it out. He was always an adventurer.' In the hospital morgue, Elizabeth, Damian, Jared and Jamie took a moment's privacy for reflection and a prayer. 'And then it seemed so morose,' said Jared. 'We thought, This isn't the way he'd like it, all quiet and sombre. So Jamie slipped outside and got a Guinness and wet a finger and moistened his lips. And that's how he went – as he'd love to have gone – with the taste of a good pint on him.'

In the last months and years of his life, Richard Harris, the star risen and set, had blazed once more in the incandescent glory of his best days. He had failed to capture the elusive Oscar that Elizabeth believed meant much to him, and had – maybe understandably, given his vociferous politicking – failed in his hopes for a knighthood. But, no matter, when the need dictated, he had stolen the honours he felt were his due and signed himself in all correspondence 'Sir Richard Harris'. The Coal Hole commemorated his multi-achievements by nailing a brass plaque with the slogan 'M'Lord' above his snug, and in the corridors of the Savoy, his final Camelot, he was inexhaustibly 'Sir Richard' or 'Your Majesty'. At the time of his passing, his tenacity, and his value, were enshrined in movies. A number of yet-to-be-seen films – a *Julius Caesar* adaptation, an Italian art-house picture called *The Apocalypse* and another international venture called *Kaena: The Prophecy* - stood in line. And *Harry Potter and the Chamber of Secrets*, his gift to his grandchildren, opened in the UK in mid-November with record advance ticket sales of £3 million and subsequent opening grosses that took it beyond its predecessor and into the movie history books.

'There were many odd aspects to Richard,' his friend Rod Taylor offered in analysis of Harris's compulsive and, finally, winning nature. 'The key is, he always wanted it right. He always wanted the Garden of Eden. We all do. Richard was just one of those guys who, no matter how you shook him, wouldn't stop trying.'

Harris, doubtless, took consolation, exultation even, in the roundedness of his journey and the magic of his farewell. In the very last scene in *Harry Potter and the Chamber of Secrets*, to all intents his appreciative adieu to us, his audience, he addresses Hogwarts' gathered clan and passes the decree permitting a holiday from homework. The camera pulls back from the febrile, cheering faces, swoops over his regal shoulder and zooms up from the fairytale castle into a blemishless starry sky. He has given us reason to laugh, then exited in a sprinkle of fairy dust.

Afterword

The ghost of Richard Harris didn't lie still. In death, as in life, there was the *frisson* of controversy. At first, harmony and conciliation surrounded his passing. In a coordinated interchange with the press the extended family announced the imminent homecoming for burial at Limerick's Mount St Lawrence's. But within hours a contradictory story suggested instructions for cremation, with his ashes scattered off Paradise Island. Immediately Limerick was up in arms. Corporation officials argued and objected, news journalists found friends and foes ready to plead, or haggle or condemn. The only indisputable truth was the request to be interred wearing the red jersey of Young Munster, the beloved rugby team that had some years before granted him honorary membership, and whose progress he and Peter O'Toole had followed avidly. Behind the confusion were the echoes of his great existential dilemma and the rage against mortality. 'I have never known anyone so sincerely lustful for life nor so utterly disdainful of death,' Lindsay Anderson once said, and there was the suspicion of a kind of denial behind the headline arguments.

Harris himself admitted that the death of his sister Audrey, when he was just fifteen, profoundly wounded him. Years later, attending the funeral of his mother at Mount St Lawrence's, he had hidden behind a tree, weeping, rather than witness the burial. At Dermot's funeral, in the same graveyard, he had huffed and puffed like a bull, complaining about the turnout, blinkering himself against the reality.

Some of it, of course, was the unending tussle with Limerick, the hopeless war against conformity, which was really just the war against his shadow self, the loving, sensitive, even obsessive, family man. At the heart of that was the filial cry for attention and approval. In 1962, aged 32, in full vigour and health, with the peak of *Mutiny on the Bounty* behind him, he had holidayed briefly in Limerick and knelt at his sleeping father's side, praying for acceptance: 'I always wanted him to open up his arms and smile at me and say, "You did it, son. No one held any hopes. But you took life by the scruff, and *you did it*." '

As it unfolded, the mystery of his final destiny became even cloudier. After brief services in London and Dublin, a major memorial was held at the Jesuit Church of the Sacred Heart on O'Connell Avenue in Limerick on Saturday, 30 November. Elizabeth, Jared and Ella led the mourners, kept company by his three surviving brothers, Billy, Ivan and Noel, Munster rugby hero Mick Galwey and former *taoiseach* Albert Reynolds. Peter O'Toole, the last surviving of his close theatrical friends, pleaded illness and cried off. But the shortage of faces from the worlds of arts and entertainment was counterbalanced – as Harris would have wished – by the impressive rugby turnout. The offertory gifts were a rugby ball, a Young Munster jersey and the Munster Schools' Junior Cup, borne by a member of its current holders, the old alma mater, Crescent Comprehensive. Ella led the eulogies, reading a poem her grandfather wrote when he was twelve and another, written at the time of Richard Burton's death, and reworded. It began, 'Richard Harris is dead, only if we want to believe it . . .'

The six hundred people who clogged the Crescent streets around the church and the phalanx of attendant journalists seemed appeased. The Limerick reconciliation was made. The chamber of commerce announced plans to erect a memorial, possibly a bronze bust, in permanent tribute. But there was no burial at the family plot at Mount St Lawrence's.

In the days that followed, rumous were rife. The family officially announced that the cremation had taken place and Harris's ashes had already been taken to the Bahamas. But, reported the *Irish*

Independent, if the key rumours were to be believed, Harris's last wishes were a joke at the taxman's expense. It was true that he had negotiated for himself partnership points in the Harry Potter movies, and it was evident, given their success, that new fortunes were yet to be reaped. 'There are even suggestions,' said the *Independent*, 'that Harris is to have his remains smuggled secretly back to Limerick to be spread locally, or perhaps even at Kilkee . . .'

Those who understood the power of the west, and the magical marriage of Limerick and Kilkee, and the immutable passion of the *barnac*, knew which rumours to believe.

The Films

Including made-for-television films.

Alive and Kicking (Associated British-Pathe, 1959)
Director: Cyril Frankel.
Screenplay: Denis Cannan.
Part played: Richard Harris uncredited in most production notes.

Shake Hands with the Devil (United Artists, 1959)
Director: Michael Anderson
Screenplay: Ivan Goff and Ben Roberts
Part played:Terence O'Brien

The Wreck of the Mary Deare (MGM, 1959)
Director: Michael Anderson
Screenplay: Eric Ambler from the novel by Hammond Innes
Part played: Higgins

A Terrible Beauty (United Artists, 1960)
Director: Tay Garnett
Screenplay: Robert Wright Campbell, based on the novel by
   Arthur Roth
Part played: Sean Reilly

The Long and the Short and the Tall (Warner Pathe, 1960)
Director: Leslie Norman
Screenplay: Wolf Mankowitz, based on the play by Willis Hall
Part played: Corporal Johnstone

The Guns of Navarone (Columbia, Great Britain, 1961)
Director: J Lee Thompson
Screenplay: Carl Foreman, based on the novel by Alistair Maclean
Part played: Barnsby

Mutiny on the Bounty (MGM, 1962)
Director: Lewis Milestone (and Carol Reed, uncredited)
Screenplay: Charles Lederer (and Eric Ambler, uncredited); based
    on a novel by Charles Nordhoff and James Norman Hall
Part played: John Mills

This Sporting Life (Rank, 1963)
Director: Lindsay Anderson
Screenplay: David Storey, based on his novel
Part played: Frank Machin

Deserto Rosso (Academy-Connoisseur, 1964)
Director: Michelangelo Antonioni
Screenplay: Michelangelo Antonioni and Tonino Guerra
Part played: Corrado Zeller

Major Dundee (Columbia, 1965)
Director: Sam Peckinpah
Screenplay: Harry Julian Fink, Oscar Saul and Sam Peckinpah
Part played: Captain Benjamin Tyreen

The Bible . . . In the Beginning (Fox, 1965)
Director: John Huston
Screenplay: Christopher Fry
Part played: Cain

I Tre Volti (De Laurentiis, 1965)
Director: Maro Bolognini
Screenplay: Tulio Pinelli and Clive Exton
Part played: Robert
(Note: Harris appears in one part of four-segment film)

The Heroes of Telemark (Rank, 1965)
Director: Anthony Mann
Screenplay: Ivan Moffat and Ben Barzman, based on the books *Skis Against the Atom* by Knut Hauglund and *But for These Men* by John Drummond
Part played: Knut Straud

Hawaii (United Artists, 1966)
Director: George Roy Hill
Screenplay: Dalton Trumbo and Daniel Taradash, based on the novel by James A Michener
Part played: Rafer Hoxworth

Caprice (Fox, 1967)
Director: Frank Tashlin
Screenplay: Jay Jayson and Frank Tashlin
Part played: Christopher White

Camelot (Warner Bros-Pathe, 1967)
Director: Joshua Logan
Screenplay: Alan Jay Lerner, based on the musical play by Alan Jay Lerner and Frederick Loewe, itself based on the novel cycle *The Once and Future King* by T H White
Part played: King Arthur

The Molly Maguires (Paramount, 1970)
Director: Martin Ritt
Screenplay: Walter Bernstein, suggested by the book by Arthur H Lewis
Part played: James McPharlan

Cromwell (Columbia, 1970)
Director: Ken Hughes
Screenplay: Ken Hughes
Part played: Cromwell

A Man Called Horse (Cinema Centers, 1970)
Director: Elliot Silverstein
Screenplay: Jack De Witt, based on a story by Dorothy M Johnson
Part played: Lord John Morgan

The Snow Goose (BBC-Universal, 1971)
Director: Patrick Garland
Screenplay: Paul Gallico
Part played: Philip Rhayader

Bloomfield (Fox, 1971)
Director: Richard Harris
Screenplay: Wolf Mankowitz, based on a story by Joseph Gross
Part played: Eitan

Man in the Wilderness (Columbia-Warner, 1971)
Director: Richard C Sarafian
Screenplay: Jack De Witt
Part played: Zachary Bass

The Deadly Trackers (Columbia-Warner, 1973)
Director: Barry Shear
Screenplay: Lukas Heller, from a story by Sam Fuller
Part played: Sean Kilpatrick

Juggernaut (United Artists, 1974)
Director: Richard Lester
Screenplay: Richard De Koker, with additional dialogue by
    Alan Plater
Part played: Fallon

99 and ⁴⁴/₁₀₀% Dead (Fox-Rank, 1974)
Director: John Frankenheimer
Screenplay: Robert Dillon
Part played: Harry Crown

Gulliver's Travels (EMI, 1977)
Director: Peter Hunt
Screenplay: Don Black, based on the novel by Jonathan Swift
Part played: Gulliver

Robin and Marian (Columbia-Warner, 1976)
Director: Richard Lester
Screenplay: James Goldman
Part played: King Richard

Echoes of a Summer (United Artists, 1976)
Director: Don Taylor
Screenplay: Robert L Joseph
Part played: Eugene Striden

Return of a Man Called Horse (United Artists, 1976)
Director: Irvin Kershner
Screenplay: Jack De Witt, based on the character created by
   Dorothy M Johnson
Part played: Lord John Morgan

Orca – Killer Whale (EMI, 1977)
Director: Michael Anderson
Screenplay: Luciano Vincenzoni and Sergio Donati
Part played: Captain Nolan

The Cassandra Crossing (Fox, 1976)
Director: George Pan Cosmatos
Screenplay: Tom Mankiewicz, Robert Katz and
   George Pan Cosmatos
Part played: Dr Jonathan Chamberlain

Golden Rendezvous (Rank, 1977)
Director: Ashley Lazarus
Screenplay: Stanley Price, based on the novel by Alistair Maclean
Part played: John Carter

The Wild Geese (Rank, 1978)
Director: Andrew V McLaglen
Screenplay: Reginald Rose, based on the novel by Daniel Carney
Part played: Rafer Janders

Game for Vultures (Columbia-EMI-Warner, 1979)
Director: James Fargo
Screenplay: Phillip Baird, based on the novel by Michael Hartmann
Part played: David Swansey

The Ravagers (Columbia, 1979)
Director: Richard Compton
Screenplay: Donald S Sanford, based on the novel *Path to Savagery*
    by Robert Edmond
Part played: Falk

High Point (ICM, 1984)
Director: Peter Carter
Screenplay: Richard Guttman and Ian Sutherland
Part played: Kinney

The Last Word (No distributor listed, 1979)
Director: Roy Boulting
Screenplay: Michael Varhol, Greg Smith and L M Kit Carson, based
    on a story by Horatio Hareberle
Part played: Danny Travis
(Note: Released in some markets as *Danny Travis*)

Your Ticket is No Longer Valid (CFDC, 1981)
Director: George Kaczender
Screenplay: Leila Basen and Ian McLellan Hunter, from the novel
    by Romain Gary
Part played: Ogilvy

Tarzan, the Ape Man (CIC, 1981)
Director: John Derek
Screenplay: Tom Rowe and Gary Goddard, based on the characters
    created by Edgar Rice Burroughs
Part played: James Parker

Triumphs of a Man Called Horse (VTC, 1982)
Director: John Hough
Screenplay: Jack De Witt, based on the character created by Dorothy
    M Johnson, Jack De Witt and Miriam De Witt
Part played: John Morgan

Martin's Day (MGM-UA, 1984)
Director: Alan Gibson
Screenplay: Allan Scott and Charles Bryant
Part played: Martin Steckert

Maigret (HTV, 1988)
Director: Paul Lynch
Screenplay: Arthur Weingarten, based on the character created by
    Georges Simeneon
Part played: Maigret

Mack the Knife (Cannon, 1990)
Director: Menahem Golan
Screenplay: Menahem Golan, based on *The Threepenny Opera* by
    Bertholt Brecht and Kurt Weill
Part played: Mr Peachum

King of the Wind (HTV, 1990)
Director: Peter Duffell
Screenplay: Phil Frey, based on the novel by Marguerite Henry
Part played: King George

The Field (Avenue, 1990)
Director: Jim Sheridan
Screenplay: Jim Sheridan, based on the stage play by John B Keane
Part played: Bull McCabe

Patriot Games (Paramount, 1992)
Director: Philip Noyce
Screenplay: Tom Clancy and W Peter Iliff and Donald Stewart, based on the novel by Tom Clancy
Part played: Paddy O'Neill

Unforgiven (Warners, 1992)
Director: Clint Eastwood
Screenplay: David Webb Peeples
Part played: English Bob

Wrestling Ernest Hemingway (Warners, 1993)
Director: Randa Haines
Screenplay: Steve Conrad
Part played: Frank

Silent Tongue (Trimark, 1993)
Director: Sam Sheppard
Screenplay: Sam Sheppard
Part played: Precott Roe

Abraham (TNT, 1994)
Director: Joseph Sargent
Screenplay: Robert McKee
Part played: Abraham
(Note: Self-contained segment of TNT Bible series)

Cry, the Beloved Country (Videovision, 1995)
Director: Darrell James Roodt
Screenplay: Ronald Harwood, based on the novel by Alan Paton
Part played: James Jarvis

The Great Kandinsky (BBC, 1995)
Director: Terry Windsor
Screenplay: Julian Dyer and Terry Windsor
Part played: Ernest Kandinsky

Savage Hearts (Buena Vista, 1995)
Director: Mark Ezra
Screenplay: Mark Ezra
Part played: Sir Roger Foxley

Trojan Eddie (Buena Vista, 1996)
Director: Gilles MacKinnon
Screenplay: Billy Roche
Part played: John Power

Smilla's Sense of Snow (Fox, 1997)
Director: Bille August
Screenplay: Ann Biderman, from the novel by Peter Hoeg
Part played: Andreas Tork

The Hunchback (no distributor listed, 1997)
Director: Peter Medak
Screenplay: John Fasano, based on the novel by Victor Hugo
Part played: Dom Frollo

Sibirskij tsiryulnik (a.k.a. The Barber of Siberia) (USSR, 1998)
Director: Nikita Mikhalkov
Screenplay: Rustram Ibragimbekov and Nikita Mikhalkov
Part played: Douglas McCracken

This is the Sea (Universal, 1998)
Director: Mary McGuckian
Screenplay: Mary McGuckian
Part played: Old Man Jacobs

To Walk with Lions (MGM, 1999)
Director: Carl Schultz
Screenplay: Sharon Buckingham and Keith Ross Leckie
Part played: George Adamson

Grizzly Falls (Providnce, 1999)
Director: Stewart Raffill
Screenplay: Richard Beattie, based on the story by Stuart Margolin
Part played: Old Harry

Gladiator (Dreamworks, 2000)
Director: Ridley Scott
Screenplay: David Franzoni
Part played: Emperor Marcus Aurelius

The Royal Way (no distributor listed, 2000)
Director: Andrei Konchalovsky
Screenplay: Andrei Konchalovsky and Larry Gross

Harry Potter and the Philosopher's Stone (Warners, 2001)
Director: Chris Columbus
Screenplay: Steven Kloves, based on the novel by J K Rowling
Part played: Albus Dumbledore
(Note: released in the US as *Harry Potter and the Sorcerer's Stone*)

My Kingdom (First Look-Sky, 2001)
Director: Don Boyd
Screenplay: Don Boyd and Nick Davies
Part played: Sandeman

The Count of Monte Cristo (Buena Vista, 2002)
Director: Kevin Reynolds
creenplay: Jay Wolpert, based on the novel by Alexander Dumas
Part played: Abbe Faria

Harry Potter and the Chamber of Secrets (Warners, 2002)
Director: Chris Columbus
Screenplay: Steve Kloves, based on the novel by J K Rowling
Part played: Albus Dumbledore

Julius Caesar (US, TV, 2002)
Director: Uli Edel
Screenplay: Peter Pruce and Craig Warner
Part played: Lucius Sulla
(Note: Two-part television miniseries)

The Pearl (No distributor listed, 2001)
Director: Alfredo Zacharias Jr
Screenplay: Alfredo Zacharias Jr, based on the novella by
   John Steinbeck

San Giovanni – L'Apocalisse (Italy, TV, 2002)
Director: Raffaele Mertes
Screenplay: Raffaele Mertes and Francesco Contaldo
Part played: St John/Theophilus

Kaena: The Prophesy (no distributor listed, 2002)
Directors: Chris Delaporte and Pascal Pinon
Screenplay: Chris Delaporte and Tarik Hamdine
Part played: Opaz

The Theatre Productions

Early walk-on parts in Kilkee and Limerick are not listed. Neither is his student production of Julius Caesar *at Scranton University* (see page 275 for details).

Easter by August Strindberg. At the Playhouse, Limerick, 1947. As Sebastian.

Winter Journey (based on *The Country Girl*) by Clifford Odet. At the Irving Theatre, London, 1956. Directed by Richard Harris.

The Quare Fellow by Brendan Behan. At the Comedy Theatre, London, 1956. As Mickser.

Macbeth by William Shakespeare. At the Theatre Royal, Stratford East, London; Zürich and Moscow tour also, 1957. As Ross.

You Won't Always Be on Top by Henry Chapman. At the Theatre Royal, Stratford East, London, 1957. As Mick.

And The Wind Blew by Edgar de Rocha Miranda. At the Theatre Royal, Stratford East, London, 1957. As Monsignor Gusmao.

Man, Beast and Virtue by Luigi Pirandello. At the Theatre Royal, Stratford East, London, and the Lyric Theatre, Hammersmith, London, 1958. As Paulino.

Love and Lectures (the Bernard Shaw–Ellen Terry Letters). At the Theatre Royal, Stratford East, London, 1958. As Bernard Shaw.

The Pier by James Forsyth. At the Bristol Old Vic, 1958. As Tommy Ledou.

Fings Ain't Wot They Used T'Be by Frank Norman and Lionel

Bart. At the Theatre Royal, Stratford East, London, 1959. As Sergeant Collins and as George.

The Dutch Courtesan by John Marston. At the Theatre Royal, Stratford East, London, 1959. As Malheureux.

The Ginger Man by J P Donleavy. At the Fortune Theatre, London, and the Gaiety Theatre, Dublin, 1959. As Sebastian Dangerfield.

Diary of a Madman by Nikolai Gogol. At the Royal Court Theatre, London, 1963. As Aksenti Ivanovitch.

Camelot by Alan Jay Lerner and Frederick Loewe. United States tour, 1981–2. Apollo Victoria Theatre, London, 1982. Also worldwide tour, including Japan and Australia, 1986. As King Arthur.

Henry IV by Luigi Pirandello. British tour and Wyndham's Theatre, London, 1990. As Henry IV.

The Records

Based on UK album and single releases.

Singles

'MacArthur Park'/'Paper Chase'. RCA 1699. Released June 1968.

'How to Handle a Woman'/'I Wonder What the King is Doing Tonight'. Warner Bros 7215. Released August 1968.

'Didn't We'/'In the Final Hours'. RCA 1733. Released September 1968.

'The Yard Went On Forever'/'Lucky Me'. Stateside SS8001. Released November 1968.

'One of the Nicer Things'/'Watermark'. Stateside SS8016. Released March 1969.

'Fill the World with Love'/'What a Lot of Flowers'. Stateside SS8032. Released November 1969.

'Ballad of a Man Called Horse'/'The Morning of the Mourning for Another Kennedy'. Stateside SS8054. Released July 1970.

'I Don't Have to Tell You'/'How I Spent My Summer'. Probe PRO581. Released March 1973.

Albums

Camelot. Original motion-picture soundtrack with Franco Nero and Vanessa Redgrave. Warner Bros. WS1712. Released August 1968.

A Tramp Shining. RCA SF 7947. Released August 1968.

The Yard Went On Forever. Stateside SSL 5001. Released December 1968.

Richard Harris Love Album. Stateside SSL 5025. Released September 1970.

Bloomfield. Original motion-picture soundtrack. Pye NSPL 18376. Released December 1970.

My Boy. Probe. SPBA 6263. Released February 1972.

Tommy. Orchestral version produced by Lou Reizner. Ode 9900. Released November 1971.

Slides. Probe. SPBA 6269. Released March 1973.

His Greatest Performances. Probe. SPB 1075. Released August 1973.

Jonathan Livingstone Seagull. Spoken Word. CBS 69047. Released August 1973.

I, in the Membership of My Days. Harris's poetry with musical interludes. ABC. ABCL 5056. Released August 1974.

The Prophet. Atlantic. Spoken Word. K50109. Released January 1975.

MacArthur Park. Compilation rerelease. Music for Pleasure. MFP50521. Released January 1976.

Camelot. London stage cast. That's Entertainment Records. TER 1030. Released April 1983.

The Webb Sessions 1968–69. Compiled by Glenn A. Baker. Notes from *Richard Harris: A Sporting Life* by Michael Feeney Callan. Raven Records. RVCD-52. Released January 1995.

Sources

In most instances, interviews were undertaken by the author, in Dublin, London and New York. The first phase interviews, most of which were excerpted in the original edition of this book, took place in the period 1989–90. Subsequent interviews were conducted in 1992–3 and 2002. Richard Harris was interviewed extensively by the author in 1975, 1985, 1988, 1989 and 1990. In the case of interviews conducted by a research associate, the interviewer credit is listed in brackets.

Chapter 1: Dermot Foley, Gerry Hannan, Len Dineen, Kevin Dineen, Donal Bagley, Willie Allen (G Hannan), Jim Roche, Betty Brennan, Charlie St George (G Hannan), Jack Donnelly, Manuel Di Lucia, Richard Harris. Geneaology: Anne Hayes, Francis Feighan, Michael Feeney Callan.

Chapter 2: Kevin Dineen, Deirdre Lloyd, Joe O Donovan, Cyril Cusack, J J Murphy, Manuel Di Lucia, Jack Donnelly, Betty Brennan, Dermot Foley, Richard Harris.

Chapter 3: Dermot Foley, Joe Lynch, James Booth, Cyril Cusack, Helen Fahy, Clifford Owen, Richard Harris.

Chapter 4: J Ringrose, Charlie St George, Dermot Foley, Joe Lynch, Ronald Fraser, James Booth, Cyril Cusack, Betty Brennan,Godfrey Quigley, Richard Harris.

Chapter 5: Godfrey Quigley, Jack Donnelly, Joe Lynch, Ronald Fraser, Leslie Phillips, Gordon Jackson, Noel Purcell, Lindsay

Anderson, Richard Harris.

Chapter 6: Frank Windsor, Lindsay Anderson, Joe Lynch, Jack Donnelly, Richard Harris.

Chapter 7: James Booth, Ronald Fraser, Tony Crawley, James Coburn, Richard Harris.

Chapter 8: Franco Nero, Jack Donnelly, Lindsay Anderson, Trevor Danker, Dermot Harris, Richard Harris.

Chapter 9: Gerry Hannan, George Roy Hill, Ronald Fraser, Franco Nero, Jack Donnelly, Richard Harris.

Chapter 10: Franco Nero, Jimmy Webb, Dermot Harris, Ronald Fraser, Joe Lynch, Jack Donnelly, Richard Harris.

Chapter 11: Ronald Fraser, Sandy Howard, Dermot Harris, Jimmy Webb, Richard Harris.

Chapter 12: Jack Donnelly, Ronald Fraser, Sandy Howard, Maurice Gibb, Deirdre Lloyd, Innes Lloyd, Patrick Garland, Trevor Danker, Richard Harris.

Chapter 13: Rod Taylor, Kevin McClory, Richard Lester, Don Taylor, Richard Harris.

Chapter 14: John Phillip Law, Sandy Howard, Jack Donnelly, Trevor Danker, Richard Harris.

Chapter 15: George Peppard, John Phillip Law, Cathy Fitzpatrick, Richard Harris.

Chapter 16: Godfrey Quigley, Len Dineen, Sandy Howard, Mick Doyle, Jim Sheridan, Kevan Barker, John B Keane (Francis Feighan) Aliki Michael, Sean Simon, Jack Donnelly, Peter Duffell, Richard Harris. Frank Sinatra and Jilly Rizzo's contributions are acknowledged.

Chapter 17: Lindsay Anderson, Sandy Howard, Terence Baker, Jack Donnelly, Richard Harris.

The further contributions of a large number of other generous participants, some of whom requested (and here receive) anonymity, are listed in the acknowledgments section of this book.

Bibliography

The following books and periodicals were consulted in the preparation of this work:

A Guide to American Film Directors, 2 vols. Scarecrow, 1981.

Anderson, Lindsay. *About John Ford.* London, Plexus, 1989.

Anderson, Lindsay. *Never Apologise.* London, Plexus, 2003.

Brando, Marlon. *Brando: Songs My Mother Taught Me.* London, Century, 1994.

Brandt, George (Ed). *British Television Drama.* London, Cambridge University Press, 1981.

Braun, Eric. *Doris Day.* London, Weidenfeld & Nicolson, 1991.

Coren, Michael. *Theatre Royal: 100 Years of Stratford East.* London, Quartet, 1984.

Cross, Brenda (Ed). *A Film Hamlet.* London, Saturn, 1948.

Douglas, Kirk. *The Ragman's Son.* US, Simon & Schuster, 1988.

Doyle, Mick. *Doyler.* Dublin, Gill & Macmillan, 1991.

Doyle, Mick. *Zero Point One Six.* London, Mainstream, 2001.

Elley, Derek (Ed). *Variety Movie Guide.* London, Hamlyn.

Griffiths, Trevor R and Woods, Carole. *Theatre Guide.* London, Bloomsbury, 1988.

Halliwell, Leslie. *Halliwell's Television Companion.* London, Granada, 1984.

Harris, Richard. *I, in the Membership of My Days.* US, Random House, 1973.

Harrison, Elizabeth. *Love, Honour and Dismay*. London, Weidenfeld & Nicolson, 1976.

Hillier, Jim. *The New Hollywood*. London, Studio Vista, 1993.

Horton, Andrews S. *The Films of George Roy Hill*. US, Columbia University Press, 1984.

Huston, John. *An Open Book*. US, Da Capo, 1994.

Keane, John B. *The Field*. Dublin, Mercier, 1975.

Knight, Vivienne. *Trevor Howard*: *A Gentleman and a Player*. London, Beaufort, 1987.

Lambert, Gavin. *Mainly About Lindsay Anderson*: *A Memoir*. London, Faber, 2000.

Lerner, Alan Jay. *The Street Where I Live*. US, Da Capo, 1994.

Littlewood, Joan. *Joan's Book*: *the Autobiography of Joan Littlewood*. London, Metheun, 2003.

Logan, Joshua. *Josh, My Up, Down, In and Out Life*. US, Bantam Doubleday, 1977.

Manso, Peter. *Brando*. US, Hyperion, 1992.

Manvell, Roger. *Shakespeare and the Film*. London, Dent, 1971.

Mast, Gerald. *Can't Help Singing*: *The American Musical on Stage and Screen*. US, Overlook, 1991.

Mates, Julian. *America's Musical Stage*. US, Greenwood, 1986.

McCrindle, Jospeh (Ed). *Behind the Scenes*: *Theatre and Film Interviews from the Trans-Atlantic Review*. London, Pitman, 1971.

Medved, Michael. *Hollywood vs America*. London, HarperCollins, 1993.

Monaco, James. *American Film Now*. US, New American Library, 1984.

Schickel, Richard. *Clint Eastwood*. US, Knopf, 1999.

Shipman, David. *The Great Movie Stars*. London, Angus & Robertson, 1973.

Smith, Sean. *J K Rowling*: *A Biography*. London, Arrow, 2002.

Speaight, Robert. *Shakespeare on Stage*. London, Collins, 1973.

Spoto, Donald. *Camerado*: *Hollywood and the American Man*. US, New American Library, 1978.

Storey, David. *This Sporting Life*. London, Vintage, 2000.

Variety Obituaries, 1905–86, 12 vols. New York, Garland, 1988–89.

Rosenfield, Paul. *The Club Rules*. US, Warner Books, 1992.

Webb, Jimmy. *Tunesmith: Inside the Art of Songwriting*. US, Hyperion, 1999.

Periodicals:

Irish Times, Hot Press, Los Angeles Times, New York Times, Washington Post, Irish Press archives, *Monthly Film Bulletin* (BFI), *Sight and Sound, Films and Filming, Photoplay, Life, Newsweek, Profile*, the *Guardian, Film Review, Daily Mirror, Daily Mail, Daily Express, Films Illustrated, London Evening News, US Magazine, Woman's Own, TV Guide* (US), *Indianapolis Independent News*, the *Hollywood Reporter, Variety* and *Record Collector*.

Filmographical information supplied by the British Film Institute, cross referenced and updated by IMDb on the internet. Theatre credits compiled by Michael Feeney Callan. Discography by Michael Feeney Callan and Peter Doggett.

INDEX

OCT   2005